BOLSHEVIK

SEXUAL

FORENSICS

BOLSHEVIK
SEXUAL FORENSICS

DIAGNOSING DISORDER

IN THE CLINIC AND COURTROOM,

1917–1939

DAN HEALEY

NORTHERN
ILLINOIS
UNIVERSITY
PRESS
DeKalb

© 2009 by Northern Illinois University Press

Published by the Northern Illinois University Press, DeKalb, Illinois 60115

Manufactured in the United States using postconsumer-recycled, acid-free paper.

All Rights Reserved

Design by Julia Fauci

Library of Congress Cataloging-in-Publication Data

Healey, Dan.

Bolshevik sexual forensics: diagnosing disorder in the clinic and courtroom, 1917–1939 / Dan Healey.

p. cm.

Includes bibliographical references and index.

ISBN 978-0-87580-405-7 (clothbound : alk. paper)

1. Sexual disorders—Soviet Union—History. 2. Sex crimes—Soviet Union—History. 3. Medical jurisprudence—Soviet Union—History. I. Title.

HQ72.S65H43 2009

614'.15—dc22

2009017369

CONTENTS

Figures and Tables vii

Acknowledgments ix

INTRODUCTION—Bolshevik Medicine and Russia's "Sexual Revolution" 3

1—Soviet Doctors and Bolshevik Justice 17

2—Sexual Maturity and the Threshold of Sexual Citizenship 37

3—Soviet Medicine and Rape as a Crime of Everyday Life 83

4—Doctors of the Mind and Sex Crime 104

5—Bodies in Search of a Sex 134

CONCLUSION—Reflections on the Fate of a Sexual Revolution 159

Notes 173

Bibliography 231

Index 249

FIGURES AND TABLES

FIGURES

Iakov L'vovich Leibovich (1889–?), Soviet Russia's first Chief Forensic Medical Expert   25

Lia Borisovna Leitman, 1920s staff gynecologist   54

A policeman's order and the physician's opinion   93

A collective act of expertise, signed by Professor N. I. Izhevskii   93

A patient diagnosed as a "false female hermaphrodite" in Kazan', 1936   143

Patient K.V., a 29-year-old Ukrainian villager, 1930   145

Patient K.G.E., 22-year-old brother of K.V., 1930   145

TABLES

2.1—Crimes against the Sexually Immature, Compared with Rape Offense Definitions, 1922 and 1926 RSFSR Criminal Codes   63

3.1—Rape Definitions, 1922 and 1926 RSFSR Criminal Codes   86

ACKNOWLEDGMENTS

Every Wednesday morning there was a corpse in the department's main hall.

It was April 2000, and I was visiting the Saratov Medical University's Department of Forensic Medicine. The corpse, invariably male and of a certain age, and procured from the city morgue down one flight of stairs, would be clothed and laid out in a tableau with a series of props: always among them was a vodka bottle (empty), a plate with rubberized food to simulate an unfinished meal, a knife, and perhaps some rubber imitation vomit. Around this improvised "crime scene," clustered white-coated students, male and female, busily taking notes and discussing "the case." The men were all destined for military medical service, the women, for the civilian healthcare system. Every week this morbid pedagogic exercise reminded me that the principal job of forensic medicine is normally the explanation of "cause of death." My own interest in the history of forensic medicine and its take on the Soviet "sexual revolution" seemed arcane in a Russia with a soaring vodka- and violence-fueled mortality rate, especially when that mortality rate confronted me every Wednesday in such concrete fashion.

There were plenty—in fact too many—reminders of the shrinking Russian population at the Saratov Forensic Medical Department. The city morgue downstairs was a busy enterprise, with buses, vans, and taxis arriving to carry the living and the dead to and from its dull portals. In the department itself, a constant stream of ancient combatants of the Great Patriotic War visited, seeking to have their status as invalids confirmed in writing. Their survival seemed endangered by changes to welfare provisions requiring this certification, and they keenly sought that piece of paper from forensic experts as a lifeline to minuscule pensions and benefits. Soon they too would be joining the queue of corpses downstairs.

In the face of such sobering daily thoughts, I was the beneficiary of the department's hospitality and great warmth. Professor Iurii Alekseevich Nekliudov, its director, received me like a foreign dignitary far beyond my mere post-doctoral status, and gave me unfettered access to the department's library. His colleagues were invariably indulgent of my improbable questions and free with their advice on how to live in Saratov. I am very grateful to Professor Nekliudov and the forensic department staff for their superb welcome. Also, at Saratov State University, I am indebted to Dmitrii Mikhel', whose assistance in obtaining photographs for this book was invaluable.

In writing this book I have incurred a long list of other debts too. The search for and collection of the many archival cases that populate the work was performed with imagination and zest by Natalia Ismailova (for Petrograd) and by Aleksei Kilin (for Sverdlovsk). Similarly energetic was Sergei Ivashkin, who gathered the hermaphrodite case histories in Moscow's main medical library. This book began life as a Wellcome Trust post-doctoral research project (no. 054869) at Glasgow University. It was supported there by Anne Crowther, Marguerite Dupree, and Evan Mawdsley, and the project also benefited from early encouragement by Susan Gross Solomon and the late John Hutchinson. My thanks to all of them for their faith in me, and to the Wellcome Trust for its generous support. My Swansea University colleagues and students, who endured my clumsy perorations on the Soviet hermaphrodite, deserve thanks. I benefited from support from the Arts and Humanities Research Council, which enabled research leave. In Amsterdam, Harry Oosterhuis provided the hospitality that enabled me to put the finishing touches on the manuscript. Audiences at various seminars heard early versions of these chapters on Soviet sexual maturity, rape, hermaphrodites, and the sexual revolution. Their responses alerted me to fresh viewpoints and saved me from some of my worst errors. I particularly want to thank the University of Michigan's graduate seminar on Russian history, which gave the chapter on rape a rigorous, and inspiring, reading, and also to thank Ann Arbor's Ron Suny, Val Kivelson and Doug Northrop for their collegial support.

Finally, I am incredibly fortunate to have Mark Cornwall in my life, and it is fair to say that without his influence, this book would not exist. Yet, however much he and all the others mentioned here have assisted me, as ever, the faults in this book are my responsibility alone.

BOLSHEVIK SEXUAL FORENSICS

INTRODUCTION

BOLSHEVIK MEDICINE AND RUSSIA'S "SEXUAL REVOLUTION"

That Russia experienced a "sexual revolution" in the wake of the Bolshevik political revolution of 1917 is considered axiomatic. Radical measures were adopted—some within weeks of the October seizure of power—to secularize marriage, to make divorce easy to obtain, to communalize childcare and housework, and later to legalize abortion on demand and to decriminalize male homosexuality. Vladimir Lenin and his radical socialists implemented a program that had roots not only in the European socialist tradition, but also in developments in Russia's liberal, professional, and intellectual circles, where impulses to increase the authority of law and medicine, at the expense of the tsarist autocracy, were strong.

"Modern" ideas about sexuality—the emancipation of women, the end or renovation of religious morality, the search for a new morality as part of a fairer social and political future, the application of apparently rational and scientific criteria to the sexual sphere—were hotly contested in tsarist debates about public values. In late Imperial Russia, doctors, lawyers, writers, social critics, and civic leaders who were engaged in these debates all agreed that a modern nation needed new forms of sexual regulation.[1] Whatever their differences, most commentators held science in particular esteem. The medical profession, including forensic experts, rapidly acquired cultural authority within and beyond the clinic, lecture hall, and courtroom, as purveyors of a fresh and convincing language of sexuality. Even elements in Russia's predominantly conservative Orthodox Church saw the value of "straightforward scientific talk rather than moral fables" in sex education.[2] The tsarist regime, marked by political paralysis, did little however to overhaul sexual regulation.

The short-lived liberal Provisional Government of February to October 1917 managed, in the realm of sexual regulations, to extend to women the franchise before collapsing in the face of war and political pressure. Coming to power on the heels of this collapse, the Bolsheviks acted as condensers for the widespread impulse to sexual modernity, when in their earliest declarations and later lawmaking, they implemented radical policies. These early declarations remained largely aspirational until the crisis of the Civil War (1918–1921) receded. The era of mixed-market economics, the New Economic Policy (NEP, 1921–1928), saw Bolsheviks and fellow-traveling professionals construct new medical and legal institutions that would give expression to sexual modernity. Forensic medicine, located at the conjunction of law and medicine, was uniquely placed to interpret the sexual revolution that was about to be promoted by the new regime.

What did "revolution" mean for sexuality? The Bolsheviks arrived in power with received ideas rather than a worked-out strategy for "sexual revolution." Russia's radicals had absorbed the European heritage of socialist thinking on sexuality, and certain works translated into Russian, such as August Bebel's *Women and Socialism* (1879) and *The Origin of the Family: Private Property and the State* (1884) by Friedrich Engels, were regarded as "catechisms" by party thinkers and activists. Critiques of the patriarchal family and the enslavement of women inside church- and state-sanctioned matrimony, an institution supposedly designed merely to protect private property, circulated widely in late nineteenth-century Russia. Russian socialists' major contribution to the "sex question" during the nineteenth century was Nikolai Chernyshevsky's canonical novel of ideas, *What Is to Be Done?* (1863).[3] The book depicted "new people" who subordinated their heterosexual but otherwise unconventional love lives to their social activism. Chernyshevsky laid out a scheme that celebrated women's self-determination through "fictional marriage," a device that liberated women of the intelligentsia from patriarchal oppression. His scheme emphasized the virtue of passionate, romantic love, wherever it might be found, over sterile devotion to matrimonial duty; it also trumpeted a radical rejection of jealousy as bourgeois and proprietorial. Yet this code of "free love" was itself subject to the needs of a movement for social and political change. These values were an integral feature of the radical socialist movement's critiques of middle-class morality by the time revolution came in 1917. An end to the strictures of patriarchy in marriage, a "free love" liberated from the exactions of property and religion, and a demanding cult of sublimation for the good of the coming revolution were commonplaces of socialist discourse, which sought a new morality based on collective principles.[4]

Of course, the ethos of deferral, sublimation, and subordination of personal pleasures and satisfactions to a "higher" purpose was neither originally nor exclusively socialist in Russian culture. Conventional morality, as propounded for centuries by the Orthodox Church, fostered deferral and sublimation as religious virtues. Taking this ethos to its extreme in 1891 in his controversial short story "The Kreutzer Sonata," Leo Tolstoy offered a bleak vision of sexual life as a destructive force, and proposed abstinence as the only moral alternative.[5] Silver Age novelists and poets celebrated Eros not as a goal in itself but as a path to transcendence, to the construction of a new spiritual life as secular utopia.[6] After the lifting of censorship in 1905, socialists were not alone in finding the commercialization of sex repugnant in boulevard literature and the new medium of the cinema.[7] By the last years of the imperial regime, Russians of many political and intellectual currents viewed sex as a powerful natural force that required channeling for civic and spiritual well-being. Sex, in the words of Eric Naiman, had become an "ideological signpost" for the Russian intelligentsia, a field of such significance that every thinker felt the need to incorporate judgments about it into his or her worldview.[8] Intellectuals and social critics deplored an apparent flourishing of "petty-bourgeois philistinism," in Russian summed up in the evocative word *meshchanstvo*. Where sex was under the microscope, the pathologies of *meshchanstvo* included patriarchy, jealousy, property ties, religious prejudice, ignorance about disease, prudery about the body, pleasure for its own sake, sexual "perversion" (an elastic classification), and the double standard. The flaying of the petty bourgeoisie for its sexual sins, real and ascribed, continued well into the Soviet period.[9]

Russian Marxists unhesitatingly accepted the authority of medical science to serve as a guide to the healthy direction of sexuality under socialism. Medicine offered a language of modernity that, for Bolsheviks, drained this controversial issue of "bourgeois philistinism" and satisfied the predominantly ascetic instincts of the party. For all their protests that they were not prudes, Soviet leaders of Lenin's generation—and many younger Bolshevik enthusiasts—were displeased by the lively popular interest in sexual matters. The prevailing view in the party, inherited from Russian radicalism, was that individual fulfillment must wait until the revolution was secured and socialism developed. Reasoning nevertheless that nature was not to be denied, the leadership adopted radical socialist laws on women and the family to channel sex rationally into what were presumed to be its natural grooves, undistorted by bourgeois values, including the distortions imposed by property considerations and religious morality.[10] Medicine would be the key to most sex questions previously framed as moral problems in tsarist regulation.

Medicalization crucially transferred authority in sexual matters from the individual to the collective, to be presided over by its agents, physicians, and specialists in sexology. This "rationalizing" current in

Bolshevik thinking essentialized sex as a force of nature that was meant to be mastered, that is, it saw sex as a natural, biological "essence" or resource to be harnessed, just as much as the coal of the Kuzbass mining region, or the hydroelectric potential in the Dnepr River. The revolution coincided with the rise in Europe of the new science of hormones, endocrinology, which at the time seemed to offer the key to understanding the origins of sexuality. During the NEP years Soviet science and its Communist patrons found the promise of sex-hormone research alluring, and its apparent revelations about the chemically determined sexual destinies of man and woman were congenial to the essentializing viewpoint. Soviet popular science and anti-religious propaganda reflected the Bolshevik essentialization of sex as a natural force by explaining the sex drive as a hormonal function, brashly refuting any transcendent moral underpinnings, and grossly underestimating the psychological dimension of sexuality.[11] Sexual enlightenment literature written by Soviet physicians drew on hormonal science to argue that sexual energy was, in the words of Frances Bernstein, "a natural elixir with wide-ranging benefits for the country's welfare."[12]

A dissenting trend inside early Soviet Bolshevism shared a reverence for science but expressed a diverging view of sexuality and sexual politics. Libertarians like Aleksandra Kollontai emphasized the psychology of self-realization, and understood sexuality as a component of that construction of a new self. To be sure, the new society and state had a role to play in the process: the socialist transformation of everyday life (through communal housework and childcare) would liberate women to express sexual desire on a level playing field with men. The libertarian view celebrated sexual autonomy and creative experimentation in personal relationships. Libertarians proposed an impatient timetable for sexual revolution when they argued that a new sexuality would emerge simultaneously with revolution. Kollontai insistently challenged the rationalizing call for sexual deferral and sublimation until socialism's final triumph. Her own exploration of the ideas of "winged eros" in her novels and short stories used these genres' ability to depict the interior lives of their heroines to highlight the role of psychology in sexual revolution. By showing the mentalities of women confronting the new sexual values, she suggested that new identities would emerge from the free exploration of sexuality. To be liberated, to join the historical project of socialism, desire required a voice, a history, and a future. Sex would be a force for transformation, a revolutionary force in everyday life.[13]

The early Soviet psychoanalytic movement developed some analogous ideas on the fringes of the new medical profession, where certain practitioners hoped that the Austrian psychiatrist Sigmund Freud's path-breaking mapping of the psyche offered the Soviet revolution a new understanding of the inner man. Its influence in officially sponsored sexology was sufficient to compel experts to acknowledge and explain for Soviet readers Freud's ideas on sexuality; Soviet experts in sexual medicine, however, largely evaded sustained engagement with psychoanalysis, and still less did they conduct research using its techniques. Although Soviet psychiatry was among the leading disciplines contributing to a new revolutionary sexology, it tended to prefer biosocial explanations that emphasized the material substrate of sexuality (often a hormonal, or more generally constitutional, basis) and assigned a supporting role to the influence of social environment. There was little room in this model for the complex workings of the individual psyche, and a profound Marxist discomfort with the potential irrationality of the unconscious mind.

Nowhere was the distinction between libertarian sexual "psychologism" and rationalizing "essentialism" clearer than in the ways in which sublimation was understood in the two camps. In discussing the rhetoric of wastage and conservation that permeated NEP-era Soviet medical literature on sexual enlightenment, Bernstein deftly sketches the distinctions:

> The [Soviet] sexual enlightenment approach to sublimation was the polar opposite of the better-known Freudian schema of sublimation and repression. If Freud's implicit model was the steam engine (trapped energy threatens to blow up the entire mechanism), the enlighteners posited a "bodily machine" whose primary problem was shortage rather than excess, always threatening to run out of steam just when its owners need it most.[14]

Having witnessed the dark and irrational forces unleashed by the whirlwind of revolution and civil war, Soviet sexologists and the ideologists who considered these questions recoiled from sexual sublimation figured as an irrational, destructive force. Instead they sought a sublimation of sexuality for positive purposes.[15] As Bernstein explains, the physicians active in Soviet sexual enlightenment recast the concept of sublimation by substituting the source of the energy to be displaced from the libidinous mind (the Freudian psyche) to the hormonally stimulated body. Thus, sex education, especially in prophylactic mode, recommended physical culture and social engagement as the formula to enable young people to channel their sexual energy. They did not need this energy to reproduce until marriage, once "sexual maturity" had been reached; in the meantime it could be diverted via abstinence, to physical exertion and public service.[16] By the late 1920s, the psychological understanding of sexuality shared by Soviet Freudians and sex radicals like Kollontai was judged too individualist, inward-looking, and insufficiently attentive to the problem of a newly intensifying class struggle. Both Kollontai and the nascent Soviet Freudians suffered politically as libertarian conceptions of the sexual revolution lost ground to a more collectivist and rationalizing approach favored by the party's dominant faction.[17]

Soviet rationalizers of sexuality considered that in the new society, healthy sex needed little or no explanation in psychological terms: the building of socialism was best served when desire was harnessed, and silenced. The suppression of discourse about sexual psychology proceeded at varying speeds through the 1920s. In ideology, the leadership quickly sought to assert a public reclamation of the private sphere for social purposes. This reclamation seems to have gathered strength soon after Lenin's death in January 1924, and it inaugurated a shift in party elite discourse away from the libertarian view of sex as personal fulfillment, as personal revolution. There can be no precise dating of the end of sexual libertarianism in early Soviet Russia; rather, one can see a consolidation of rationalizing rhetoric against sex radicalism beginning with the establishment of the NEP, and linked to Bolshevik anxieties about the return of capitalism and its alleged symptoms, including unbridled sex.[18] The posthumous publication of Clara Zetkin's 1920 interview with Lenin in which he expounded his attitudes toward sex and the woman question was probably a deliberate herald of this turn against sex radicalism. In that conversation, Lenin vented his mistrust of theories of sexual psychology, expressed the dominant "rationalizing" view of sex questions, and suggested that Bebel and Engels had written the last word on this subject.[19] Yet it was only the beginning of a decisive shift against sexually unorthodox views; until the Great Break of 1929–1930, avant-garde and second-rate fiction and drama published in the regime's own subsidized journals continued to revel in the exploration of the consequences of sexual revolution. Authors and dramatists sought ways of depicting a psychological view of sex as a means to define the new man and woman in socialist society. Censors grappled with these issues with an inefficiency, and uncertainty, that suggests to later observers the divergence of opinion inside the party on how to cope with sexual questions.[20]

Bolsheviks thus found that laying the foundations for a positive sexual ethos demanded vigilance on a surprisingly wide array of fronts, and they discovered medical authority was a key partner in this task. Similarly, they confronted the negative features of the new sexual life with the help of medicine. When considering sexual disorder—criminal acts such as rape or the abuse of youngsters, and troubling sexual questions like the hermaphrodite—Bolsheviks looked to forensic medicine to furnish "objective" facts upon which courts and administrators could base rational judgments. Institutions changed to reflect the new emphasis on science as a partner in sexual regulation. The early Soviet state satisfied long-standing calls to move forensic expertise from the jurisdiction of the police (in the prerevolutionary Ministry of Internal Affairs) to that of doctors (in the newly established People's Commissariat of Health). Medical expertise would at last be formally independent of police control. Soviet medical experts were given a host of new rights in criminal investigations to enhance the autonomy this move represented. Soviet Russia's chief forensic medical expert during the 1920s, Iakov L'vovich Leibovich, vigorously exploited this new dawn for the discipline. Sexual disorders figured prominently on his agenda because of their potential for making forensic medicine distinctly "Soviet." The radically rational, dispassionate, and "objective" approach to sex could be presented as a revolutionary departure both from tsarist and from capitalist views that relied on religious morality, prurience, and "philistinism." A network of forensic experts for each province was established, and the Soviet criminal codes of 1922 and 1926, and the criminal procedural code that underpinned them, incorporated a clear role for these "judges of the scientific facts."

In ways to be revealed in the coming chapters, Soviet forensic medicine institutionalized the party's technocratic, rationalizing understanding of sexuality, and contributed to the silencing of desire in the Soviet "sexual revolution." Ironically, few of the forensic experts who brought this vision to bear on sexual issues were in fact Bolsheviks; most had been trained under the tsarist regime and many were politically indifferent to radical socialism. Yet the Bolshevik desire to modernize criminal investigation and civil administration, and the experts' long-expressed desire to win greater authority for their discipline, dovetailed in the radical overhaul of legal medicine. Bolsheviks seeking to distinguish Soviet justice from its tsarist predecessor gave forensic doctors custody of the problem of sexual disorder and invited medical experts to participate as "judges of the scientific facts" in criminal and civil investigations.

Soviet forensic experts were now officially making pronouncements about sex in courtrooms and clinics. Path-breaking laws made their role vital across a range of sex-related dilemmas. Yet authoritative judgments about medical matters—the "scientific facts" of a case—carried with them assumptions about appropriate sexuality. Consciously and more often unconsciously, moral choices were embedded in the determinations made by "objective" forensic experts, and the repetitive, routine decisions taken by these experts laid down a sexual modernity with conservative features, an essentializing, rationalizing view of sexuality from the very outset of formal Soviet law enforcement.

Of all the new departures inaugurated in the Soviet view of sexuality, one of the most radical—and little noticed—was the abandonment of an age of consent in criminal law. (The tsarist age of consent had generally been 14.)[21] Bolshevik jurists instead adopted the concept of "sexual maturity" as the threshold of sexual citizenship: intercourse or sexual acts with a person "not having achieved sexual maturity" were designated crimes. To lawmakers this biological standard solved the problem of fixing an age of sexual majority that reflected all the social, ethnic, and geographic variation found within the Soviet republic. An elegant solution in theory, it proved extremely demanding to implement in practice. Leibovich and other leading forensic experts in research institutes addressed the challenge with anthropometric surveys of large samples of teenagers and with vigorous debate about the nature of sexual maturity. Meanwhile local medical experts applied the sexual maturity test in cases of alleged sexual abuse or rape of minors far less systematically. The forensic experts' focus on the female body's reproductive functions supplied a template for sexual maturity that ignored psychological development and imposed a grid of gender assumptions about maternity and about the absence of female sexual desire on the young Soviet woman's sexual citizenship. Tragically, the lack of a socially recognizable threshold for sexual self-determination, such as an age of consent, left Soviet girls and women vulnerable to aggression and contributed to popular confusion surrounding sexual values.

Although Soviet lawmakers tried to distinguish revolutionary from traditional tsarist and European law on rape by defining it more explicitly, and by acknowledging psychological pressure as an aggravating factor, Soviet forensic medical views of rape changed little from tsarist ones. The search for "objective" evidence focused on the physical body of the victim. Expert doctors regarded psychological evidence of violation with extreme suspicion and did not elaborate a methodology for obtaining data about mental trauma. The prerevolutionary textbook recommendation to treat rape claims by healthy adult women with skepticism would continue into the late twentieth century. A thirst for clarity in contentious sex crime investigations led forensic experts to avoid exploration of the victim's psychology or psychosexual development. Forensic experts rebuffed Freudian notions of the desiring female subject.[22] Instead, as in the tsarist era, the Soviet justice system, prompted by doctors, continued to fetishize women's physical virginity as the most authoritative of "objective" indicators of innocence. Society continued to associate physical virginity with the moral condition of innocence and few revolutionaries saw any contradiction in this linkage.

Despite this apparent reluctance to attend to psychological approaches in the interpretation of rape claims, psychiatry did play a role in the early Soviet sex crime investigation. Soviet legislation radically transformed the psychiatrist's place in the justice system, giving credence to the idea that sex crimes might be caused by mental disease.[23] In sex crime cases, psychiatrists were most commonly called upon to examine abusers of children and young people. Procedural codes required police and prosecutors to seek psychiatric expert opinions when the defendant in such cases appeared to be mentally ill. In contrast to the tsarist regime's reluctance to entertain the defense of nonresponsibility on the grounds of insanity, Soviet procedure allowed for it, and new institutions for legal psychiatric assessment and mandatory treatment were opened under health commissariat control. In reality the resources to provide compulsory therapy were limited. Psychiatrists were also hampered by the constraints of their science which was more adept at describing and diagnosing than at curing "sexual psychopathy." It was indicative that the primary explanation for sex-themed mental disturbance, degeneration, pointed backward to tainted heredity rather than forward to a plausible resolution.[24] Early Soviet, but still tsarist-educated, psychiatrists displayed little utopian enthusiasm for medicalizing the sex criminal; nevertheless, by participating in a system that elevated their expertise to a parity of esteem with other forensic sciences, they did much to embed in modern Soviet thinking a view of sexual disorder as caused by rare mental pathology.

The Soviet chief forensic medical expert, Leibovich, made the rare and seldom visible condition of the hermaphrodite a feature of his sexological agenda for medical experts. Tsarist law ignored the issue and administrators had improvised arbitrarily when dealing with individual hermaphrodites. A modern approach to the person with ambiguous or mixed male and female genitalia (and secondary sex characteristics) would be a vivid mark of the distinctive radicalism of Soviet medicine and law. Leibovich gathered statistics on "determinations of sex," and was successful in lobbying the Soviet government to give forensic experts in the localities a decisive role in pronouncing on the prevalent sex of persons of ambiguous sex: a 1926 directive to registry offices laid out procedures, innovative in international terms, for changing the passport sex of such hermaphrodites.[25] Meanwhile, around the country, ambitious doctors reported on cases of hermaphroditism they encountered in their clinics. These physicians, surgeons, and other specialists responded, often sympathetically, to requests by individual hermaphrodites for "clarification" of their sex. As techniques improved they usually proceeded by means of a surgical operation to restructure genitalia to conform to the social gender inhabited by the patient. As we shall see, Soviet medical treatment of hermaphrodites in the 1920s and 1930s anticipated western treatment regimes of the 1950s–1960s, demonstrating a "modern" grasp of the question. Simultaneously, in their aspirations and operations Soviet doctors treating hermaphrodites showed how a precociously modern medical approach could reinscribe and stabilize a two-sex gender order.[26]

By institutionalizing "objective" scientific investigation in the Soviet judicial and administrative system, Bolsheviks hoped for a modern, secular, and rational approach to sexual disorder. Medicine would replace religion and bourgeois moralizing as a source of authority in these often intractable cases. In this aspiration, Bolsheviks and their legal and medical fellow travelers adhered to a common trend toward secularization and medicalization in the treatment of sexual questions in the industrialized world. During and after the upheavals of the First World War, medical and public health officials bid for and acquired custody of many sex-related issues; in the nonsocialist world sex reformers and sexologists presented themselves as enemies of secretive Victorian morality, a prudish silence to be overcome by propounding sexual hygiene and enlightenment. Many sex reformers pointed to Soviet lawmaking and practices as leading the way to sexual modernity. The Bolsheviks did not single-handedly invent "sexual revolution" but tried to harness it to the requirements of a peculiarly Soviet, socialist regime.[27]

Looking for a Sexual Revolution

The history of the Soviet sexual revolution has primarily been told by examining what people said rather than what people did. Problems of access to sources tended to determine this focus; however taboos on the topic of sexuality during the Cold War also inhibited scholarship on both sides of the iron curtain. Historians of Russia's women began in the 1970s to explore the record of the sexual revolution through the lenses of women's liberation and later gender studies. The emphasis was on a recuperative project that revealed for a generation increasingly skeptical about the totalizing claims of Marxism what traditional historical and political narratives of revolution had trivialized: the role of women's emancipation and the women's question in Soviet history.[28] Scholars more recently have turned to literary and journalistic sources to illuminate, often with great insight, what commissars and critics thought and said about the Soviet sexual revolution. The NEP era was one of a plurality of views, demonstrable from debates in party journals, from literary works produced by non-Communist and Communist authors, from the sex-themed pamphlets and bestsellers of medical experts and the advice columns of newspapers. Censorship was inefficient, and commercial considerations in the market economy conditions encouraged editors to publish sex-themed material.[29] For the Communist regime it was, as Eric

Naiman and Frances Bernstein have argued, a time of considerable anxiety about authority that found vivid expression in literary, journalistic, and medical debates about sexuality.[30]

This book looks at the record of practices to enrich the narrative of sexual revolution. As Bernstein has shown in her study of early Bolshevik sex advice for the masses, the practices of medicine as documented in newly accessible archival holdings are a crucial source for understanding how the sexual revolution was to be disciplined immediately from its inception.[31] Her work shows how Soviet doctors imagined and encouraged positive sexual behavior that conformed to the dominant, essentializing understanding of revolutionary sexual values; in contrast, this book examines medical practices when negative behavior or conditions were encountered. Doctors' actions as forensic experts and clinicians were part of a wider range of "the repeated, routine practices of everyday life" that determined how the socialist revolution was made a reality.[32] The medical practices of these doctors were knitted into a larger, international process of transformation. Soviet sexology in its methodologies and outlook was part of a European-wide trend toward the state exploitation of "biopower," and in imposing an apparently "revolutionary," "rational" framework on human sexuality the Soviet version of sexual science did much to constrain it in new channels.[33] Work on homosexuality, prostitution, and infanticide has demonstrated the degree to which the Bolshevik interpretations of socialist sexual traditions, and policies of "sexual revolution," were formed by the science and medicine of the 1920s.[34] Few works have yet made a systematic examination of the grassroots practices of Bolshevik justice and administration when handling sexual disorder.[35]

In English-language scholarship, critical histories of forensic medicine are surprisingly underdeveloped (especially if one considers the current boom in forensics-based television dramas, which ought to stimulate a new wave of interest inside and beyond the academy).[36] Recent works explore the origins and struggle for professional recognition of forensic expertise in the United Kingdom and the United States. Much of this work focuses on the gradually increasing role of the psychiatrist in crime investigation and prosecution. Other significant areas of interest include the cultural transmission of modern forensic science from its origins in revolutionary France of the late eighteenth century to other nations, and the evolution of forensic laboratories and services to police investigators in various jurisdictions.[37] Continental historiography similarly focuses on issues of professionalization and institution-building.[38] Russian-language histories of tsarist and Soviet forensic medicine provide a fund of knowledge for the critical scholar but do not depart from an uncritical narrative of progress.[39] In English, imperial Russian forensic medicine has attracted attention for the light it sheds on doctors' demands for reform.[40] Ken Pinnow's work on Soviet forensic medicine and its studies of suicide during the 1920s underscores the sociological view of forensic problems taken by many of the same protagonists who inhabit this book.[41] This study, however, differs from the other works by putting forensic experts at the heart of the story in a major examination of their impact on the twentieth century's first and most notorious "sexual revolution."

To look for Russia's sexual revolution as seen by the forensic profession, I begin with sexual offenses as they were made visible in the Soviet courts of the 1920s, comparing archival sources in two localities with the records of discipline-shapers in the Soviet capital. The records of 194 criminal investigations and trials in two discrete samples are employed to show how Soviet doctors responded to their new role as interpreters of the sexual revolution. One sample of 66 sex crime cases is drawn from Petrograd (today's St. Petersburg) between the years 1922 and 1924; the second, consisting of 128 cases, is from Sverdlovsk (the Urals-region city today known as Ekaterinburg) at the end of the NEP era, between 1926 and 1928.[42] These temporal and regional variations furnish opportunities to analyze forensic medical practices comparatively. The episodic and fragmented nature of all surviving Soviet court records makes it impossible to find temporally coincident samples to compare these two regions, and no claim for the statistical representativeness of these cases is advanced. Their value lies in the patterns that emerge in the practices they record, and that is the focus of the analysis in this study.

Petrograd's extensive forensic-medical infrastructure, which often rallied collectives of experts to examine evidence in rape and sex abuse cases, contrasts vividly with the poorly resourced individual experts conducting investigations in Sverdlovsk. Indeed when considered in conjunction with the later date of the Sverdlovsk cases, the contrast in resourcing for forensic expertise illustrates the gulf between the regime's aspirations for these "judges of the scientific facts" and the economic and social realities that hampered the drive to modernize the regulation of sexuality.[43] The practices documented in these cases are set against the archival and published record of the aspirations expressed by leaders of the forensic discipline in the People's Commissariat of Public Health.[44] In addition to the archival record, extensive material is drawn from the Soviet medical journals and from forensic textbooks, manuals, and monographs published centrally and on the periphery during the 1920s and 1930s. The provincial capital of the mid-Volga region, Saratov, with its forensic medical facilities and medical school, furnishes a further source of contrasts with the two sample cities.[45]

To open a contrasting perspective on the medical profession's views of sexual disorder, and on the silencing of sexual desire, this book turns from criminal investigations to clinical encounters between early Soviet doctors and their hermaphrodite patients. Here the source base is a collection of case histories, consisting of twenty-six articles in regional and central Soviet medical periodicals describing thirty-six individual hermaphrodites, with the earliest case dating from 1919 and the latest from 1938. (The articles are listed under a separate heading in the bibliography.) By taking a longer historical perspective, and moving the story into the 1930s, presumed distinctions between custodial and civilian medicine, and between the "revolutionary" 1920s and "reactionary" 1930s, can be challenged. Despite the usual view that sex disappeared from the Soviet press during the period of cultural revolution (1929–1931), exactly half of the cases are described in publications appearing during the First Five-Year Plan (1928–1932), and a further third (12 cases) were published between 1933 and 1938.[46] That such material appeared—in increasing volume—in the Soviet medical press during the 1930s seems remarkable, given that so many of conventional Soviet sexology's voices did in fact fall silent as a result of the cultural revolution.[47] Censorship evidently did not forbid the publication of hermaphrodite case histories, despite the dangerous issues, including questions of sexual response, sexual pleasure, and disorderly intimate lives, that they raised.[48] These cases show that Soviet doctors probed the sexual experience of hermaphrodites in surprising detail: here were cases where the desiring subject was invited to speak. This sample's "representativeness," like claims for the sex crime cases, lies not in its statistical size or comprehensiveness, but rather in its revelations about how doctors searched for ambitiously modern solutions to the conundrum of sexual ambiguity. In the process, the case of the Soviet hermaphrodite reveals the ambitions and the limits of the "sexual revolution."[49]

This book begins by looking for reflections of the "sexual revolution" through an exploration of national and local forensic-medical institutions and then moves to an examination of particular themes in the case-book of sexual disorder. Chapter 1 offers an institutional history of Soviet forensic medicine, tracing tsarist legacies and controversies and demonstrating their impact on the institutions Bolsheviks put in place after 1917. It introduces the forensic investigators active in the two sample cities, Petrograd and Sverdlovsk, and the contexts within which they worked. The next two chapters examine the ways in which Soviet medicine imagined sexual desire—and especially female desire—as a physiological and not psychological question in the postrevolutionary courtroom. Chapter 2 explores Soviet Russia's experimental rejection of the age of consent in favor of a "sexual maturity" threshold of sexual citizenship, comparing the medical literature on definitions of the mature sexual subject with forensic expert practices in actual criminal cases of sexual assaults, mainly on young girls and women. Chapter 3 traces the ways in which medical understandings of rape evidence inherited from the tsarist regime were seldom questioned in the early Soviet era, leading to a recapitulation of gendered stereotypes about female sexual innocence and knowledge in rape investigations. The next two chapters look at two contrasting situations in which Soviet medical practitioners acknowledged and probed the psychology of sex. An examination of Soviet forensic psychiatry in chapter 4 discusses how the psychiatrist was given new credence by the Bolsheviks, who sought to elevate the medicine of the mind to a parity of esteem in the court with other types of scientific evidence. Chapter 5 shifts the focus from courtroom to clinic to explore an entirely unknown story: how hermaphrodites were understood and treated, formally under the guidance of Soviet forensic experts, but in fact in everyday encounters by local physicians and specialists, in clinics in the capital and provinces. The conclusion considers the ways in which the sexual revolution was transformed by the essentializing, technocratic approach to sexuality embraced by the Bolsheviks from the very outset of their regime, and reflects on the consequences for the subsequent evolution of Soviet, and post-Soviet, sexual politics.

Note on Conventions

Archival citations are given thus: GARF 482/2/30/6–77, where GARF indicates the archive acronym (explained in the bibliography) and the sequence of numbers indicate respectively the fond, inventory (*opis'*), file (*delo*), and page(s) (*list/listy*) cited. For ease of reference the crime case files will also be identified with a lead name of the perpetrator and year: LOGAV 2205/1/1969 (Lukomskii, 1922–1924). In the text I have used conventional English spellings for well-known Russian names (Tolstoy) rather than a modified version of the Library of Congress transliteration system; the latter is employed in the references. I have endeavored to use standard translations for legal and administrative terms: "prosecutor" for *prokuror*, "province" for *guberniia* and later *oblast'*, "police" for *militsiia*, "Criminal Investigation Department (CID)" for *ugolovnyi rozysk*. The names of the two sample cities varied during the decade that is the focus of this book, and I have tried to minimize any resulting confusion. St. Petersburg was named Petrograd, 1914–1924, and was thereafter Leningrad until 1991. The sample of crime cases from this city dates from 1922 to 1924, and the documents principally refer to Petrograd, as does this book when discussing these cases. Similarly, Ekaterinburg was designated Sverdlovsk from 1924 to 1991 and since the crime files date from 1926 to 1929, I refer to the city using its Soviet name, unless discussing earlier events.

ONE

SOVIET DOCTORS AND BOLSHEVIK JUSTICE

How did early Bolshevik law and institution building establish a new frame of reference—medicine—for understanding and ultimately shaping sexuality? A range of legislative measures enacted by the young socialist republic projected a radical vision of a modern, secular sexual order, and medicine was central to that vision. Implementing these measures was not as simple a task as making declarative statements in legislation. In the everyday surveillance and control of sexual disorder, the often poorly articulated ambitions of the socialist movement regarding sexuality contended with competing priorities in policing, justice, public health, and more general political struggles.

The Bolsheviks made forensic medicine a crucial prism through which they viewed sexual disorder. In theory this medical subfield was well positioned to fulfill the role at the intersection between medicine and law. Having developed rapidly in Russia since the Great Reforms of the 1860s, forensic medicine as inherited by the Bolsheviks in 1917 was an endeavor that had many ambitious leaders eager to assert and extend the authority of their specialist knowledge. The ways in which early Soviet policymakers attempted to reconfigure the forensic sciences shaped the context in which forensic thinking on sexuality emerged. Bureaucratic collapse and restructuring are part of this story, but the revolutionary era saw fresh attempts to establish new institutes and centers of learning for the discipline. Equally important for grasping the impact of forensic doctors on the shaping of Soviet sexuality are the laws that Bolshevik jurists enacted on sexual crime, and along with them, the laws governing the use of forensic expertise by police and courts. These legislative frameworks created a radically new environment that molded the everyday routines of medical experts in their interaction with the population and the Soviet police and justice system. Of course, early Soviet forensic experts conducted teaching and research, and provided expertise, in a much wider range of criminal and civil matters than sexuality alone. Nevertheless, their work on problems of sexual disorder was potentially a source of distinctiveness from the tsarist past, and from the approaches practiced in the capitalist West as well. Leaders of the discipline made use of such distinctiveness to trumpet the revolutionary character of their work, an appeal that might bring or sustain official patronage.

Making Russia's Forensic Medicine "Soviet"

Russians have a long history of turning to medical knowledge when crimes are investigated. Soviet-trained forensic experts, not only those writing in the most "patriotic" era of Stalinist science, but even those writing in the more liberal atmosphere of the 1960s, claim a tradition of forensic medicine stretching back at least to sixteenth-century Muscovy.[1] Their mandatory Marxist-Leninist viewpoint encouraged them to see the use of legal medicine before the nineteenth century as rare and confined to an elite in the tsar's court and governing circles. (Such expertise was mainly sought to explain mysterious deaths and in proving fitness for military service.) Additionally, their focus on the arrival in Russia of western, "scientific" medicine, which was initially limited to the elite, did not always encourage these doctors writing the history of their own discipline to consider the significance in jurisprudence of native forms of knowledge about bodies, harm, and healing. This seems especially true when indigenous expertise was practiced by women.[2] Such home-grown expertise could be used to prove that harm had come to a victim raising a complaint against an assailant, such as in rape cases. In sixteenth- and seventeenth-century Muscovite court records, Daniel Kaiser has found that the testimony of midwives about the condition of alleged victims of rape was a significant form of evidence in many routine trials.[3] In the disputes between ordinary members of Muscovy's town-dwelling population (including merchants, artisans, laborers, and peasants accused of rape, and women from similar social backgrounds as victims), Russian courts customarily referred victims to midwives to substantiate claims of sexual assault. Despite the arguments of Soviet historians of medicine that scientific forensic medicine did not have an impact on the population at large until the last decades of the tsarist regime, an indigenous tradition regarding medical expertise was well established even before the nineteenth century.

Recent scholarship contradicts the Soviet medical historians' contention that systematic use of forensic medicine, following western models, was not systematically applied in Russian criminal investigations until the

Great Reform era of the 1860s.[4] Developments in the eighteenth and first half of the nineteenth centuries laid the foundation for the expansion of Russian legal medicine. Peter the Great and his successors formalized the role of the state's physicians in criminal investigations. Moscow University professors of medicine began to include forensic matters among their lecture topics from the early nineteenth century, and the first Russian-authored textbooks of forensic medicine appeared in the 1820s and 1830s.[5] Most pre-reform pedagogy in this field concentrated on topics related to the examination of corpses in cases of suspicious death or suicide, rather than living individuals.[6] The government's first attempt to regulate the status of forensic medicine came in 1828; the Statute of Forensic Medicine decreed the outlines of a national structure of medical expertise that endured until 1917. At the local level, civil service district or town (*uezdnye* or *gorodskie*) doctors provided expertise on demand to police and courts. They were to be supplemented by a small proportion of doctors employed directly by the police, and when necessary by "other military, civilian and free practitioner doctors." The work of forensic experts was supervised in the provinces by provincial medical boards. These two lower tiers were subordinate to a central medical council, located in the Ministry of Internal Affairs.[7]

Russia's defeat in the Crimean War (1853–1856) spurred Tsar Alexander II to embark on the Great Reforms, which liberated the serfs and greatly modernized most aspects of central and local government, while attempting to retain the principle of autocratic rule. Public opinion, given freer expression in the reform era, looked forward to less arbitrary and more rational governance, including a fairer and more transparent legal system. Russia's criminal justice machinery was radically overhauled in 1864: inquisitorial adjudication in closed sessions based on written evidence was replaced chiefly by open, public trials structured on adversarial lines, with oral testimony. Prosecution and defense presented and questioned evidence orally, in contrast to the written submissions of the past. Those who gave testimony could be challenged in court by either side. Proceedings were generally open to the public, compelling all parties in the open courtroom to weigh the persuasive power of their arguments. Another significant innovation that distinguished Russia's new courts from other continental judicial systems was the introduction of jury trials for many serious crimes. Prosecutors and defenders had to appeal to popular notions of justice to influence a jury's decision, rather than persuade a judge with scholarly legal knowledge, which was the basis of European continental adjudication.[8]

The implications of the justice reforms for forensic medicine were profound. Doctors were now called upon more frequently to give opinions in all stages of a criminal case, and police and the courts operating in this new environment made much wider use of forensic medical expertise. (Much more use was reportedly made of specialists in obstetrics and gynecology in sex crime cases.)[9] The courtroom became a new platform from which medical knowledge was displayed. Previously, doctors' opinions were presented routinely only in the form of written statements bundled within a case file; these opinions had privileged status as a form of evidence immune from review. After the reforms, the doctor in the witness box was offered a new way to project and consolidate his cultural authority. The courtroom, however, also became a platform for confusion and embarrassment, for physician-experts were now subject to cross-examination by prosecution and defense, and medical opinions could be challenged by other protagonists in court.[10] The prospect of experts in open disagreement heightened the interest of the press and public in sensational cases; in the words of one early Soviet historian of the discipline, "society expected the resolution of questions that excited it from medical expertise."[11] Doctors stepping into the public eye now needed a higher level of theoretical and practical training in the specialized realm of forensic medicine, and this requirement tended to lead to improvements in the status and quality of forensic studies in Russia's medical schools in the second half of the nineteenth century. The reform process recognized this shift in status. A new university statute (1863) affirmed that universities should have faculties of forensic medicine; the Ministry of Internal Affairs launched a new journal in the field, *Archive of Forensic Medicine and Public Hygiene* (1865); and the reform of local government widened the powers of provincial medical boards (upgraded to "medical departments") within a revitalized provincial administration.[12]

Yet the discipline of forensic medicine still suffered, despite its elevation in late Imperial Russia. The recent scholarship of Elisa Marielle Becker has demonstrated in detail how legal reform "layered" new structures such as the open courtroom trial on top of often contradictory older regulations such as the 1828 Statute of Forensic Medicine and procedures, including the pretrial investigation stage in criminal cases, which remained secretive and inquisitorial.[13] (In the years 1865–1866, as the legal reform was being implemented, Fedor Dostoevsky vividly depicted the pretrial investigation and its bewildering atmosphere in *Crime and Punishment*.) Soviet-era chroniclers of the field are predictably quick to point out the flaws of the post-reform dispensation. Their primary complaint is that routine forensic expertise was still subordinated to the Ministry of Internal Affairs, and local state-employed doctors who served the police by examining corpses and victims of assaults were still creatures of the state's law-enforcement ministry, lacking full scientific independence and professional authority. In this critique Soviet observers tend to anticipate and justify the transfer of forensic medicine after the October Revolution of 1917 to the jurisdiction of Russia's first health ministry, the People's Commissariat of Health.[14] It is certainly significant that the lowliest operatives in the discipline were subordinated to the police; like many professionals under the autocracy, doctors had significant grievances against a regime that refused to grant them wide autonomy based on scientific and technical knowledge.[15] Yet perhaps the greatest defect of the field in prerevolutionary Russia was not its institutional setting, but its weakness in projecting authority and convincing the public and the government of its value.

Commenting in 1867 in the Ministry of Internal Affairs journal on the poor impression made by expert doctors in the post-reform courtroom, one observer wrote,

> Expertise has aroused a generally uncertain feeling of dissatisfaction. . . . To the public it seems that a science called upon to reveal the truth, in the form of the doctor-expert, should not be as it is. It sees the inconsistency, the contradiction and the confusion of forensic doctors. In the majority of their answers there is none of the solidity that characterizes knowledge, the restraint that sets the boundaries of the scientific, none of that self-confidence that easily convinces others.[16]

Assessing the position of expert doctors a generation later, the chief forensic medical specialist in Kharkov, colorful professor E. F. Bellin, argued that not much had changed for the expert in the courtroom since the 1860s. Doctors might have won some early procedural concessions that eased their jobs as scientists in the courtroom, but the medico-legal specialist was still ill-prepared for his role, and what is more, the science of forensic medicine was highly "imperfect" and required greater development. Doctors were still unfamiliar with the existing capabilities of legal medicine and unaware of its limitations as a science.[17] Like many other academic critics, Bellin saw the solution to these problems in further specialist education and training for the state's medical operatives conducting expertise for the police and courts. He nevertheless also argued for greater autonomy and professional respect for the individual expert. The procedural concessions won in the 1860s to allow doctors to attend the entire courtroom session (instead of being sequestered, like jurors, during the reading out of an often lengthy indictment, and during testimony by other experts), were not normalized in legislation, and could be withdrawn arbitrarily by judges.

Bellin himself had suffered the indignity of sequestration; it was not just applied to humble district doctors. The rights of the doctor to full participation in the court's activities (both during the trial, and before it in preliminary investigations) needed to be recognized in law. Bellin also argued—as did many other observers—that the state's refusal to pay honoraria for expertise actively discouraged the individual doctor, especially the intellectually accomplished free practitioner, from taking a professional interest in the field and its scientific development.[18]

In summary, the institutional locus of forensic medicine was not necessarily the discipline's principal defect. The low quality of expertise furnished by local state-employed doctors was the result of poor training and standards. Research into medico-legal matters needed development. The rights of doctors in the courtroom were weak and required enhancement and legislative guarantees. And doctors deserved to be paid for their services to the justice system. When forensic medicine was placed under the aegis of the People's Commissariat of Health in 1918, the intractability of these problems suggested that moving institutional homes would not be sufficient to resolve them.

Leading medical officials headed by monarchist academician G. E. Rein developed a plan to transfer all health matters to a free-standing "main administration" (with less standing than a full-blown ministry) in the final peacetime years of tsarist rule. It would have assumed responsibility for forensic medicine. The Rein plan for a conservative centralization of health provision was opposed by liberals and radicals in the medical profession, who anticipated that "decentralization and collegiality" would be the defining principles of radically reformed medicine. Eventually however the "cleansing hurricane" of the February 1917 Revolution so destabilized the state that it yielded a program of centralization from the left rather than the right.[19] After February 1917, war and political breakdown left the Provisional Government little time for entertaining new public health policies, although much discussion occurred in conferences that year.[20] In the chaos of 1917 the tsarist Ministry of Internal Affairs disintegrated, and with it potentially the remaining medical apparatus in the center and in the countryside. The arrival of Bolsheviks to power in October only accelerated the process. To counter this tendency, on 11 July 1918 the Bolshevik government established a People's Commissariat of Health, led by the charismatic Communist physician Nikolai A. Semashko. Its earliest structure included a department of "civilian medicine," within which a subsection on forensic medicine was immediately organized; the subsection was led by a pathologist, N. I. Loviagin, who left few traces in the archival record. After eighteen months, the subsection became a department of the commissariat in its own right, and it acquired the leader who would guide the discipline of forensic medicine through the 1920s, gynecologist Iakov L'vovich Leibovich (b. 1889).[21]

Detaching their health commissariat from the tutelage of the police (now organized in the new Commissariat of Internal Affairs), the Bolsheviks sent messages to supporters and to potential collaborators. To allies, Lenin and his party proclaimed the promise of a revolutionary socialist medical system, "accessible to all, free of charge and guaranteeing qualified therapeutic and medicinal care."[22] Here was a visionary dream of health care for everyone, a powerful message, easily understood, and with massive popular appeal. To potential collaborators, who like many technical specialists remained loyal to Russia but were wary of the new regime, the Communist program offered a sharp departure from the medical corporation's long-cherished liberal aspirations for "decentralization and collegiality." But Communists also appealed to doctors by ending the subordination of public health to police administration, the so-called "medical police" orientation of the old Interior Ministry view of medical affairs that had been an enduring source of frustration.[23] Henceforth medicine would be administered by medical professionals who understood the practices and science of health care.

For Semashko's new commissariat, the first years were dominated by emergencies imposed by the Bolsheviks' struggle against their many opponents in the Russian Civil War (1918–1921). Fighting epidemics and providing basic medical and sanitary aid to the Red Army and to workers supporting it in what was derisively called "Sovdepiia" (that is, the land of Soviet deputies—the Russian heartland concentrated around Moscow and Petrograd, to which Bolshevik territory shrank in the war years 1919 and 1920)—these were the priorities of the country's first health ministry in its formative months. It is characteristic of the revolutionary élan of the time that despite such a burden, and the paltry resources that were available to meet it, medical men collaborating with the new health commissariat devoted a remarkable amount of energy to planning a vision of a new, centralized and technocrat-led medical system. This was true of the forensic medical staff inside the commissariat as well. Even before Iakov Leibovich assumed control of the department of forensic expertise in early 1920, his predecessor Loviagin had convened a consultative commission that influenced early decrees on the discipline. Bringing together "Moscow professors: of forensic medicine, psychiatry, pathological anatomy, chemistry, a representative of forensic medical expertise, the chief prisons doctor, a legal consultant and others," the commission's work envisioned a forensic service relieved of tsarist-era bureaucratic and obscurantist constraint.[24]

A number of decrees ensued, not always in a logical sequence, but they demonstrated the Health Commissariat's support for a Soviet forensic expertise along new lines. Most significantly, from February 1919, doctors of forensic medicine in the provinces were to be employees of the medico-sanitary departments (by 1921 known as health departments, *zdravotdely*) of provincial soviet governments. The subordination of forensic doctors to the police was formally abolished. Symbolically another decree of that month proclaimed the severance in spatial terms by authorizing the provision of funds for "cabinets of examination" in local medical institutions. Police and court investigators (now known as "people's investigators") were required to use these spaces, rather than their own premises, when gathering medical evidence. The People's Commissariat of Justice underlined this transfer of authority by issuing guidelines to people's investigators requiring them to seek medical expertise in specific types of criminal cases and by setting guidelines on how medical evidence was to be obtained from living persons.[25]

On 28 February 1919, a "Decree on the rights and duties of state medical experts" set out the Health Commissariat's vision of the new regime's forensic service. The state medical expert was proclaimed "a scientific judge of the facts" in cases where his or her opinions were required; he should be permitted "spontaneous action and initiative at all stages of the judicial process, and be guaranteed full independence in his activity, opinions and conclusions." To this end, the expert's opinion was declared to be an "official" one with legal force when drawn up in the presence of two witnesses. His or her notebook *(zhurnal)* also became a state document with official status. Experts had the right to review police evidence, to visit crime scenes, and to question victims, accused persons, and witnesses. During all stages of the investigation, the expert was allowed to review the people's investigator's case file and to make notes from it, to be present in court during its sessions, and to question victims, the accused, and witnesses. Experts also had rights to protect the scientific integrity of their contributions. They could refuse to express an opinion where evidence was ambiguous or degraded (for example, when too much time had passed since the commission of a crime). They had the right to amend questions put to them by police and people's investigators. And they could confine their answers to matters they themselves deemed to be within the boundaries of their scientific competence. The intention to make medical experts "judges of the scientific facts" was confirmed and some of the experts' rights extended when the decree was reissued jointly by the commissariats of health and justice in December 1921.[26]

Iakov L'vovich Leibovich (1889– ?), Soviet Russia's first Chief Forensic Medical Expert.

Loviagin and after his death his successor Leibovich could point to the 1919 and 1921 decrees on forensic medical expertise as the heralds of "a new era in the history of forensic medicine" for Soviet Russia, apparently satisfying virtually the entire list of demands made by tsarist critics within the field. In 1923, now having been named the Health Commissariat's chief forensic-medical expert, Leibovich went further, and gave the elevation of expert doctors a socialist, ideological gloss.

> The forensic-medical expert is at the present time no longer a functionary [*chinovnik*] but a social worker, not an official person but a sociologist. And if there remain people who think otherwise, who disagree with the new position of the expert-doctor, then they live in the stifling atmosphere of the past, and do not understand the new social forms the revolution has created. But we forensic doctors no longer need heroes of the Chekhovian type.[27]

The passive, reactive stance of the tsarist-era medical expert (mocked as the sensitive but powerless hero of a Chekhov short story) would be replaced by the active thrust of the doctor-as-sociologist, whose task was nothing less than "the study and prevention of criminal acts so frequently coming hand in hand with somatic or mental disorders."[28] Here was a shrewd bid for the social relevance of medical expertise. One contemporary assessed Leibovich's career and contribution to the discipline in terms of this search for greater cultural and scientific authority:

> Leibovich's chief service consists of his striving to arouse interest in the broad masses in forensic medicine, to take it from behind the walls of the mortuary into the broad arena of social life, to encourage experts in their own form of propaganda for the right to citizenship of forensic medicine, as a social medicine.[29]

During the 1920s, Leibovich did invest prodigious energy in the dream of turning forensic medicine into a social science that would illuminate problems in the social body through its work in studying individual bodies. Through statistical investigations of questions such as the prevalence and character of suicide in the new society, he attempted to inspire a shift from the view of medical expertise as merely a routine function of the justice apparatus, toward a vision of proactive "diagnosticians of society" whose work would uncover social defects and suggest timely remedies.[30]

Since Iakov Leibovich's primary expertise was in the field of forensic gynecology, it was not surprising that he promoted Soviet legal medicine's role in defining and explaining problems of sexuality. It was characteristic of his interest in questions of sexual disorder, and his sociological methods, that he arranged for the gathering and compilation of statistics on the discipline's contributions to understanding in this area. Leibovich strenuously reported the number and purpose of examinations of living persons (including victims of sexual crimes) carried out by doctors for various authorities, using the internal forums of the Health Commissariat and the channels he set up to reach his medics in the field, and the police and court officials with whom they worked. He presented his statistics to the commissariat's governing board (*kollegiia*), and to its Expert Medical Council, a learned body with responsibility for tracking developments in the social and biological sciences affecting medicine. In 1925 Leibovich succeeded in launching a periodical, *Sudebno-meditsinskaia ekspertiza* (Forensic Medical Expertise), a clearing house of information for the network of legal doctors scattered around Russia. In its pages, the statistical evidence that doctors were dealing with an increasing number of cases of sex crime was noted and underlined.[31] As well, Leibovich's journal published transcripts of local and regional conferences bringing together forensic experts, local police, prosecutors, and judiciary to discuss matters of common interest, and sexual disorder routinely attracted a significant degree of attention. The peripatetic chief forensic medical expert was often present himself at these far-flung gatherings.[32] The sexual theme also appeared in many of Leibovich's other publishing projects during the 1920s. His editing and translation of textbooks of forensic medicine, handbooks for doctors in the field, and specialized foreign works, featuring sexual crime and disorder, supplemented his own publications dealing entirely with problems of sexuality for the legal doctor.[33]

As Soviet Russia's chief forensic medical expert, Iakov Leibovich made sexuality a significant part of the agenda of his department not simply because of his early training and research interests. Sex was an issue that had political clout in 1920s Soviet Russia. By emphasizing forensic medicine's potential to reforge understandings of wayward sexuality, Leibovich tapped a current of interest within the Health Commissariat and among many of its sponsors in the Communist Party. Purveyors of secular, dispassionate, and scientifically rational interpretations of human sexuality (especially when the sex in question was socially disturbing) were particularly in demand from a leadership dominated by the rationalizing perspective on the sexual revolution. It was a perspective that viewed sexuality with suspicion, best captured in the negative prescriptions against excess and debauchery that characterized much party and fellow-traveler writing on the issue.[34] Society's first defense against sexual disorder was a clear distinction between sexual health and sexual pathologies.[35] The rationalizing perspective also regretted and hoped to suppress loose, casual, and prurient talk about sex, whether in informal spaces or in the pages of party-sanctioned journals and newspapers. If the Health Commissariat's efforts to make sexual hygiene a feature of worker enlightenment was one side of the leadership's sexual politics, the opposite side was at least in part composed of social defenses against sexual disorders—excesses of sexual activity, misdirected sexual energy, inappropriate objects of sexual attention, sexual violence—and forensic medicine would reveal these pathologies to police and courts, to assist in their work of social defense. Sexual issues had the potential to make forensic medicine a "Soviet" enterprise, to distinguish the discipline from its tsarist predecessor by defining the sexually normal and abnormal in scientific, rational, dispassionate, and therefore revolutionary terms.

Forensic medicine in revolutionary Russia also had opportunities to distinguish itself as "Soviet" by asserting its progressive nature compared to its counterparts in capitalist countries, especially in Western Europe. The medicalization of sexual disorder was taking place in many modern states, at different rates and with differing emphases.[36] Russians engaged in research or clinical practices focused on sexual problems asserted that their work was more progressive because of its lack of bourgeois hypocrisy, its rejection of religion-based morality, and because of the revolutionary principle of the equality of the sexes. These scientists were perhaps poorly informed about the degree to which their counterparts in Europe and other industrialized countries attempted to bring sexuality into the secular and scientific realm. One of the signature characteristics of modern sexology wherever doctors and laymen promoted it was the assertion that science and rationality rather than prejudice and tradition should govern sexual matters. Yet the perception that Soviet sexological science was most thoroughly purged of "archaic" values and constraints circulated widely and served those protagonists in forensic medicine who were searching for expanded authority for their work.[37]

Bolshevik Frameworks for Legal Medicine

The basis for the new authority of forensic medicine was Bolshevik criminal law, which departed radically from tsarist and much western liberal legislation in many respects, including in its conceptualization of sexual crime.[38] The legal experts who drafted the first Criminal Code for the Russian Soviet Federated Socialist Republic (RSFSR), enacted in 1922, intended to make a clean break with a tsarist legal order that had actively rebuffed modern ideas of sexuality and gender equality.[39] Bolshevik sex-crime law was distinctive in its gender neutrality, its rejection of the language of traditional morality, and in its biomedical view of sexual life. It was also relatively terse. Its drafters brought the physician into the investigation of sexual crimes as a medical practitioner with a recognized expertise. Soviet criminal law also allowed judges to prescribe mandatory medical treatment, including compulsory psychiatric therapy, as an alternative "measure of social protection" (the Soviet euphemism for punishment), when medical grounds warranted it. The articles in the RSFSR Criminal Code that form the basis of the cases explored in this book were grouped under the heading "Crimes in the field of sexual relations," after articles against murder, bodily harm, and exposure to danger, but before those prohibiting insult and hooliganism, all in the same chapter on crimes against the person. Sex crime thus ranked in the minds of the drafters as a form of harm which, while seldom life-threatening, was injurious to the "health, freedom and dignity of the individual" in a specifically sexual way.[40] The sexual development of the youngster, the sexual inviolability of the individual (at risk because of physical, psychological, or economic weakness), and the sexual autonomy of the adult were counted as aspects of the human personality meriting protection in the new socialist state.

Three of these articles described sex crimes against young persons without distinctions based on gender. A key difference for the legislators was between penetrative and nonpenetrative acts. The first of the articles on sex with young persons, article 166, forbade sexual intercourse with individuals not having achieved sexual maturity, effectively, statutory rape.[41] Article 167 prohibited aggravated forms of such intercourse, in which defloration occurred, or "perverted forms" of sexual intercourse, which meant either oral or anal penetration.[42] The striking feature of these articles was the lack of an age of consent. Rather than state an age-tariff, Soviet law used the threshold of "sexual maturity" to describe the moment when sexual autonomy began, for reasons that are explored in chapter 2. It was an arcane biological standard, rather than one based on age with all its familiar markers. The opportunities for confusion, disagreement, and disputes resulting from this flexibility were a major source of irritation between doctors and law enforcers in the 1920s. Similarly, by making defloration an aggravating circumstance, article 167 compelled medical experts to examine victims for supposed physical "clues" to sexual innocence or experience, and here again, despite Russia's substantial heritage of medical writing on this subject, there was considerable scope for controversy.[43]

The third article, number 168, was vaguely formulated but meant to describe and prohibit nonpenetrative sexual acts with children and minors. Such acts were described as "corruption . . . by means of depraved acts" *(razvrashchenie . . . razvratnye deistviia)*, and in this particular article the phrase "children and minors" signaled that persons under the age of eighteen were intended by the legislators, regardless of their putative sexual maturity.[44] The concern for the protection of the young person's psychosexual development motivated the prohibition against adults engaging in sexual touching, display of genitals, or exposing youngsters to pornography or sexual play. Tsarist jurists, in the 1903 Draft Criminal Code had intended to criminalize these activities.[45] Bolsheviks, however imperfectly and implicitly, understood that such acts were regarded by sexologists as harmful for the child's developing sexual identity, and moved to punish them. Here the tasks for physicians and gynecologists were much less distinct than in cases of penetrative intercourse, since the acts in question rarely left any detectable signs on the victims' bodies. Forensic psychiatrists might however be consulted for expert opinions on the mental states of both perpetrators and victims.

Another group of articles protected the sexual inviolability of the adult. Rape was prohibited in the first part of article 169; legislators mentioned "physical or psychological force" and abuse of the helpless position of a victim as aggravating the offense and attracting higher sentences.[46]

Rape tended to fall firmly within the forensic gynecologist's remit when expertise was sought; rather rarer were such cases in which police and courts sought psychiatric expert opinions. In 1923, another section (169a) was added to this article to describe sexual harassment; this was a relatively precocious formulation and highlighted the Soviet claim to progressive sexual politics.[47] Compelling a person to go into prostitution, procuring and recruitment of women to prostitution, running "vice dens," and infecting a partner with a sexually transmitted disease were also punished in this penal code.[48]

In 1926, in conjunction with the formation of a federal Soviet Union and the provision for separate penal codes for each constituent republic, a revised version of the RSFSR Criminal Code was enacted. The most significant change introduced to the sex crime legislation was in sentencing provisions. Whereas the 1922 code was almost entirely characterized by minimum sentence limits, the 1926 revision set maximum prison terms. For example, in the 1922 code, rape not accompanied by aggravated circumstances was punished by a minimum of three years' deprivation of liberty, while in the 1926 version, a maximum five-year sentence was set. The new policy was intended to reflect concern over rising sexual crime while allowing judges more latitude to consider individual circumstances such as class, age, and education when pronouncing sentences.[49] From their inception, routine Soviet sentencing norms and practices were distinctively lenient, and judges were supposed to vary penalties according to the social profile of the criminal. Members of the "exploiting classes," viewed as enemies of Soviet power, merited harsher prison terms and penalties, while worker and peasant friends of the regime deserved lighter sentences, according to basic laws underpinning the criminal justice system.[50] Although the "class policy" in sentencing was relatively difficult to put into practice, since judges found most of their subjects were "toilers" of one sort or another and the leniency of penalties overall left modest room for discretion, class was still frequently referred to in sentencing documents. In the crime case sample used in this book, many examples of class-based favoritism in penalties for rape and sexual abuse will be discussed.

The 1919 and 1921 decrees on the rights and duties of medical experts, jointly issued by the People's Commissariats of Health and Justice, established the basic procedural frame within which Soviet forensic medicine worked. These decrees were supplemented, and to some extent contradicted, by the RSFSR Criminal Procedural Code (1922) that set out how crimes were to be analyzed and tried in Soviet Russia's courts. Experts complained that the Criminal Procedural Code failed to recognize many of the rights granted them under earlier decrees. In particular, the 1922 procedural code was ambiguous about where medical examinations were to be conducted, and also tended to restrict the expert's access to case files compiled by the investigators who commissioned their expertise.[51] Access to investigator materials was certainly an issue that arose in some of the forensic opinions this book explores. Just where examinations, especially intimate ones, were conducted, was undoubtedly a source of dispute and difficulty throughout the 1920s, when resources for furnishing most towns with forensic medical clinics were scarce.[52] It was also still possible, in procedural rules, for a judge to exclude an expert from observing an entire trial, although it is unclear how frequently such powers were used in the 1920s.[53]

In the early 1920s (according to at least one Health Commissariat survey), local experts felt that their new rights and functions were often ignored or violated by local police, prosecutors, and people's investigators.[54] Yet despite complaints about local shortcomings, the general direction of the new legislative framework, including the 1922 RSFSR Criminal Procedural Code, was toward greater authority for legal medicine in the courts. The procedural code institutionalized the responsibility of the Health Commissariat in directing the forensic medical service. It obliged investigators and courts to refer to health officials when doubts or dissatisfaction arose over expertise furnished by local doctors. If doctors' rights vis-à-vis the investigators who called on them were sometimes ambiguous, in the final analysis Soviet power installed the long-awaited separation of medical expertise from police functions, evincing an intention to accord doctors a significant degree of technocratic autonomy. As with the radical reform of justice during the Great Reforms, expert doctors, and the police and court investigators they worked with, felt challenged and revitalized by the impact of new Soviet arrangements. It is hardly likely that this fresh redistribution of responsibilities would have occurred without tensions on both sides of the functional divide.

Crimes in the Soviet policing and justice system were investigated in a two-stage process that was another inheritance of the Great Reforms. A pretrial investigation conducted in a secretive, inquisitorial fashion by police and justice officials continued to precede the usually open courtroom "investigation" or trial. In sex crime cases, Soviet procedural rules dictated that only victims themselves could raise complaints. Police and the more sophisticated criminal investigation department (*ugolovnyi rozysk*, hereafter CID) could only accept allegations of these crimes from third parties in narrowly defined circumstances.[55] Upon receipt of a rape complaint from a victim, the police *(militsiia)* were to collect basic information, not in theory including forensic medical evidence, and then pass on the details promptly to people's investigators in the CID. The "people's investigators," ostensibly better trained in the new Soviet penal law and procedure, were supposed to be the first agents to commission medical expertise in such cases, and in the sample cases they normally were.[56] This division of labor was logical: the laconic penal code imposed a surprisingly complex matrix of implicit questions about the nature of a sex crime on any given investigation, and the average policeman on the beat had little notion of the hidden complexity.

Forensic medical evidence would be sought as quickly as possible from the victim, although in outlying or poorly resourced areas the resort to a dedicated forensic specialist was unlikely. Often mothers brought their assaulted daughters first to a trusted midwife or local maternity hospital. As the police or CID investigated these cases, statements were gathered from the victim and any witnesses; a search would be conducted for the alleged perpetrator, who might be held in jail until the preliminary investigation was complete and prosecutors deemed the case ready to be passed to the courts. (Perpetrators were less often the objects of medical examination themselves, usually only if suspected of impotence or mentally infirmity.) Many cases were dropped or abandoned during the pretrial investigation for lack of evidence to support an indictment, or because facts emerged to undermine the victim's claim to sexual innocence.[57] When police and CID had completed their investigations they forwarded the case to prosecutors *(prokurory)*, who would determine if there was sufficient basis to try the suspect. The prosecution could initiate its own investigation, seek new forensic opinions, and decide to prosecute under a different article of the criminal code, if it was felt that the crime had been improperly qualified. In practice, people's investigators frequently opened a case file citing one criminal code article but found that circumstances such as the victim's "sexual maturity" or the question of defloration required requalification under another article. Satisfied that there was a case to answer, prosecutors would send the case file forward for trial in court.[58]

Sex crime cases routinely came before the lowest level of local ("people's"—*narodnyi*) court. These local courts were humble stages, far from the Soviet practices of Stalin's infamous political show trials, or the 1920s agitation-propaganda trials staged in places of entertainment to put across lessons about hygiene, political literacy, or women's emancipation.[59] In prerevolutionary practice, sex crimes were usually tried "behind closed doors," to safeguard public decency. In the decade after the revolution, most of these cases were tried in open sessions, reflecting the widespread revolutionary ethos that viewed secrecy about sex as a remnant of bourgeois, "philistine" morality, and favored instead blunt openness.[60] The adversarial system established during the Great Reforms was adapted to Soviet purposes, with defendants allowed to hire an advocate from an approved "college of advocates" for their defense. Very few accused sex criminals did, or could afford to, in the 1920s, although some cases to be discussed in later chapters show the important role that defense advocates assigned to expert medical opinion. Judges—nonspecialists whose chief qualification in this era was Communist Party membership or revolutionary sympathies—were accompanied by two lay assessors, members of the public, ideally proletarians, whose duty it was to monitor the administration of justice. They usually remained utterly silent. The trial records suggest a comparatively amorphous structure to these sessions. The judge could steer proceedings, call witnesses, and question all comers. Starting with the prosecutor's reading of an indictment, the court might then hear statements from both sides *(storony)*, usually testimony from the accused, the victim, and witnesses. Forensic experts could be questioned, and sometimes the trial adjourned while experts conducted examinations of victims. Medical expert opinions were evidently then delivered orally, in the open courtroom, and their technical language must often have lent the proceedings the air of "demonstrations" of patients so commonly used as a teaching technique in medical schools. Indeed, just as in the Great Reform ideal, these oral opinions were meant to educate the public. "The opinion of forensic-medical experts as judicial evidence must be accessible and comprehensible to all, for the court is educating the masses; the court is a living school, and in school everything should be comprehensible to the audience," said a Saratov prosecutor speaking at a 1925 forensic conference.[61] Concluding arguments from the prosecutor and, if there was one, the defense advocate, and then a final statement from the accused, normally ended the hearing. Judges and lay assessors often pronounced a sentence on the same day, and even in the same session. Appeals could only be launched on points of procedure and law (cassation), but where they appear in the records they nonetheless raised matters of substance and, frequently, issues relating to the forensic evidence applied in the case.

Forensic Medical Teaching and Research

Another token of Bolshevik promotion of forensic medical expertise was the degree to which the Soviet government invested in an infrastructure of research centers and specialist training for the profession. Here again the record for the 1920s was mixed, at least according to Leibovich and some colleagues within the discipline. The Health Commissariat's chief forensic medical expert was a weak politician when it came to securing resources for major showcases, particularly the dream of a national institute of forensic medicine. Calls for a centrally funded institute were discussed and approved by the Health Commissariat's Expert Medical Council as early as 1920.[62] Yet when the New Economic Policy forced budgetary economies on the commissariat the project was dropped. The initiative in developing specialized centers for the study of forensic questions slipped from Leibovich to other players and disciplines. Criminology, the study of the social and individual wellsprings of offending, attracted significant investment, and, from the medical sphere, psychiatrists benefited more than their physician colleagues. In the capital, Leibovich participated in a commission that eventually established the Moscow Bureau for the Study of the Personality of the Criminal and Criminality, which was dominated by psychiatrists.[63] The police established their own State Institute for the Study of Criminality and the Criminal in Moscow in 1925 with a brief that emphasized social over biological perspectives. Little concerned with strictly forensic matters, the institute, as a creature of the Commissariat of Internal Affairs, was steered by policing and penal priorities.[64] The Soviet capital also had a particularly well-resourced division of forensic medicine within the city government's health department.[65] Petrograd's provincial health department established its own specialized Forensic Medical Bureau (Otdelenie sudebno-meditsinskoi ekspertizy Petrogubzdravotdela) led by the nationally respected Professor N. I. Izhevskii[66] and a full-blown institute of forensic psychiatry (headed by Professor Lev Grigor'evich Orshanskii) that served the medico-legal needs of Soviet Russia's second city. As a provincial capital, the government of Ekaterinburg (renamed Sverdlovsk, 1924) had a health department with a tiny forensic medical bureau led by N. K. Bazhenov, the region's chief medical expert during the 1920s.[67] Authorities did not authorize a budget for a national institute devoted specifically to forensic medicine in Moscow until 1932. This vote of confidence in the discipline only came after Leibovich had been demoted for insufficient class-consciousness and was moved to a university post in Tomsk.[68] During the 1920s, the argument for a central institute in the capital could also be countered by the existence of a faculty of forensic medicine (in the Second Moscow State University, created from the tsarist-era Women's University Courses), led by the energetic professor Petr Andreevich Minakov, who also served the Health Commissariat on the Expert Medical Council.

During the 1920s, forensic medical research in the provinces remained similarly in the hands of regional university departments and medical schools. Some of these opened their own bureaus or centers for the study of the biosocial, anthropological, or psychiatric aspects of the criminal and crime detection, and their approaches reflected the interests and training of local experts. By the late 1920s, in addition to the Soviet capital, university towns including Leningrad, Saratov, and Rostov-on-Don—but significantly for this study not Sverdlovsk—had a forensic medical research facility of some type based in institutions of higher learning. Leningrad's prestigious Military-Medical Academy had its own long-established department of forensic medicine as well. The Health Commissariat, bowing to resource pressures in the 1920s, was largely compelled to devolve research into forensic sciences to a variety of interested agents. The result was an array of approaches to forensic issues, including sex crime, from the perspectives of criminologists, psychiatrists, and other experts.

Health officials had also treated the education of forensic medical practitioners as a priority when they deliberated infrastructure questions in the early years. Yet budgetary considerations constrained ambitions here too. One of the key functions of the central forensic medical institute envisioned by Leibovich, Minakov, and others in the early Soviet years was to be the education and qualification of practitioners in forensic techniques and legal requirements. With the ebbing of support for a national institute, its proposed teaching function also shifted, in Soviet Russia to be concentrated primarily in Petrograd/Leningrad. This choice testified to the inheritance of talent and organizations the former capital could call upon and, effectively, revive. The school founded in 1885 that eventually became the Leningrad State Institute for the Professional Development of Doctors was resuscitated after the Civil War as a post-diploma training academy for qualified physicians. In 1924 it began offering a course for doctors in forensic practice, and it opened a separate forensic medical department the following year. Medical experts around the republic were invited to attend, with financial support from their provincial health departments. A stellar collection of authorities educated under the old regime lectured here. Professor N. I. Izhevskii spoke on complex forensic investigation, psychiatrist Professor P. A. Ostankov on forensic psychopathology, and the celebrated radical jurist Anatolii F. Koni (1844–1927) on medical jurisprudence and forensic procedure. (Not above practicing what he preached, even at the age of 80, Koni appears in a 1924 case discussed in chapter 2 as a defense advocate.) By 1926, only 20 percent of Soviet Russia's forensic medical doctors had in fact journeyed to Leningrad for this course, yet between 1924 and 1931 the school's four-month course ran thirteen times and was taken by 355 doctors and 500 students with nonmedical qualifications.[69] The short course in Leningrad was not the only choice open to doctors seeking training in forensic techniques during the 1920s, because university departments of forensic medicine (in Moscow, Saratov, Rostov-on-Don, and elsewhere) also offered some level of instruction. Again, Ekaterinburg/Sverdlovsk lacked any forensic training in its university's medical school. As with research, teaching in the discipline was distributed unevenly around the country during this era.

The framework established by the Bolsheviks for bringing medical expertise into criminal investigations and courtroom trials was impressive in its modernizing ambitions, but its full realization was hampered by the chronic lack of resources and a significant degree of competition from other bureaucracies and stakeholders. Soviet forensic medical approaches to sexual disorder developed in this fragmented and heterogeneous environment. During the 1920s, forensic medicine continued to suffer from a lack of qualified specialists to fill the network of posts that the Health Commissariat's decrees established. The Bolsheviks' legislative and judicial framework implied that specialized knowledge of forensic medicine would be readily accessible to police, prosecutors, and judges, yet even at the end of the 1920s, many regions of Russia lacked the necessary institutes or bureaus to provide such expertise. The application of the new Soviet policies against sexual disorder would be haphazard where such expertise was difficult or impossible to obtain.

TWO

SEXUAL MATURITY AND THE THRESHOLD OF SEXUAL CITIZENSHIP

In this and the following chapter, two interlocking aspects of early Soviet sexual citizenship are examined through readings of forensic medical texts and practices dealing with sex crime. The first aspect is the threshold when sexual autonomy begins, and it is viewed through the lens of "sexual maturity"—the peculiar new standard the Bolsheviks set for protecting children and young persons from premature sexual activity. The second aspect is the problem of desire and its acceptable expression, examined through readings of rape cases concerning unambiguously adult victims. In both chapters, the focus is almost exclusively on men's sexual crimes against girls and women, often characterized by police and expert investigators as "rape," although it will become apparent that Bolshevik legislation made important if little-understood distinctions between crimes against younger victims and adults. The differences in how young people's sexuality and adult sexuality were conceived by police, doctors, and courts provide a framework for these two chapters.

If anxiety about the deviant might be expected to structure the authorities' concerns regarding sexual disorder in the new society, it might then be thought that men's sexual autonomy and the desire that such self-direction unleashed might be the object of study for experts. However, as these crimes were discussed, investigated, and described by forensic doctors, women's bodies remained the primary site where Soviet sexual citizenship took shape. Women's sexual autonomy, a promise of the Soviet "sexual revolution," was ignored by these crucially important scientists who conceived of female sexuality as a physiological function, with important consequences for how women were treated as victims in sex crime cases.

In all modern polities sexual citizenship comes with adulthood, usually marked by a specific age of majority. Minors are protected from the dangers of premature sexual activity, whether coerced or consensual. In modern states this protection has normally been based on an age of consent, or "age of protection" as it was generally known a century ago.[1] Most European states only began setting various ages of consent during the eighteenth and nineteenth centuries, and the age limits set were very low by twenty-first-century standards. These age thresholds were frequently set with female children in mind, as scientific ideas about the complexity and fragility of the female organism developed during the nineteenth century. Only later toward the end of that century, when new concepts of the sexual pervert and the homosexual entered medical vocabulary, did legislators begin to devote the same degree of attention to the sexual protection of male children. As late as the 1920s, many important European countries permitted sexual activity with persons as young as 12 or 13 years of age.[2]

In Russia during the course of the last century of tsarist rule, those responsible for drafting sexual regulation sought to move away from a religious and patriarchal conception of good and evil in intimate matters, and began to frame problems of wayward sexuality in terms of public health and order.[3] Prerevolutionary sex crime legislation dated from the early nineteenth century, and despite attempts to revise the law, remained very much focused on the protection of women's "honor" and on the enforcement of patriarchal norms. A woman was deemed able to consent to sexual intercourse and defloration at the age of fourteen; in the 1870s, Senate rulings created an intermediate age range when knowledgeable consent to defloration could be recognized in girls as young as eleven.[4] The 1903 Draft Criminal Code increased the protection afforded young persons of both sexes from the threat of sexual assault or abuse. This draft code reflected new social and medical ideas; it suggested the harm done to youngsters could be more than merely physical. It acknowledged that the psychological and even psychosexual development of the young person was a significant object to be protected. Modernizing tsarist legislators appreciated the international trend in medicine toward a conception of sexuality as an aspect of personality subject to a malleable trajectory of psychosexual development.[5] Youngsters abused by sexual offenders were endangered by the potential for long-term diversion from "normal" sexuality, that is, a heterosexuality conceived to be biologically based in nature. Thus a new offense of nonpenetrative sexual acts was proposed, protecting both sexes. Previously, only girls had been protected from such abuse.[6]

The draft code of 1903 was never fully implemented and yet the ideas that lay behind it surfaced in the legislation eventually adopted by the Bolsheviks when they inherited the problem of defining crime. The Bolshevik jurists who framed the first Soviet Russian criminal code in 1922 rejected much of the terminology describing sexual disorder in the tsarist penal law, while they continued to evince a fundamental concern for the equality of the sexes, the protection of the adult person's "sexual sphere," and in particular the protection of the "sexual sphere" of children and young persons. Yet there was also a radical departure from tsarist and most European legal practice. As explained in chapter 1, there was no age of consent or age of protection in the 1922 criminal code. Instead, articles 166 and 167 of the code (later consolidated in article 151 of the 1926 RSFSR Criminal Code) prohibited "sexual intercourse with persons not having attained sexual maturity [*polovaia zrelost'*]," with a penalty of not less than three years' imprisonment. Intercourse with sexually immature persons that resulted in defloration (*rastlenie,* in Russian a term with more figurative connotation than its English equivalent)[7] or was accomplished in "perverted forms" (*izvrashchennye formy)* was deemed especially harmful and was subject to a minimum five-year prison term. A person who had reached "sexual maturity" could agree to sexual intercourse and other penetrative sexual acts. Persons who had not reached sexual maturity were not free to give consent, and their partners were deemed criminals.

In these articles the Bolshevik jurists and the police who framed this legislation abandoned a specific "age-tariff" as the benchmark of the threshold of sexual citizenship, and invented a new standard, "sexual maturity." Unfortunately, the archival record of lawmakers' deliberations on sex crime is relatively scant, with little indication of the debate that accompanied this section of the criminal code. Nevertheless inference can suggest some rationales behind the startling decision.[8] Certainly, the path jurists chose was a radical one. They deliberately avoided defining the moment of sexual majority with a given birthday, that is, a moment recognizable to laypersons and low-level officials such as police. A "natural" biological transition took the place of a temporal threshold, and only experts with particular medical skills would be qualified to recognize its arrival.

The deliberate turn to medicine to define the threshold of sexual citizenship was a little-noticed but major investment in the authority of doctors to act as gatekeepers of the sexual revolution. In its sweeping radicalism it suggests a link to the vaunted separation of the health establishment from the police ministry affected by the Bolsheviks. Citing forensic medical authorities in the Health Commissariat rather than the Commissariat of Internal Affairs sent the message that technocratic expertise would assess the scientific facts of a case. In such a context, turning to doctors to define the arrival of sexual citizenship may have seemed to jurists to be a logical extension of this principle, especially if the jurists were reluctant to address the setting of an age tariff. Yet the law itself, with characteristic brevity, said nothing about how "sexual maturity" was to be defined or measured. Lawyers and police apparently presumed that setting this standard would be a straightforward matter. Soviet authorities did not provide an official definition until June 1934, when doctors, police, and prosecutors issued a set of guidelines ("Rules for out-patient forensic medical obstetric-gynecological examination") on handling sex crime. In the meantime, forensic medical experts filled the official silence with a range of definitions in their textbooks, in their debates, and most importantly, in their routine work for the police. For doctors, the scale of the problem was considerable: in 1925 in Soviet Russia there were 4,600 examinations of live persons to determine sexual maturity in criminal and civil investigations.[9]

Yet institutional developments could only be one factor contributing to the adoption of the new sexual maturity standard in 1922. Expert doctors themselves spoke ambivalently about the reasons for the standard. Only after a few years' experience of casework did high-level officials begin to explain to rank-and-file doctors why "sexual maturity" was adopted. As chief forensic expert of the nation, Iakov Leibovich gave contradictory accounts of the sexual maturity standard in his publications and in speeches to joint conferences of doctors, legal authorities, and police. In a 1928 textbook intended for wide distribution, he emphasized the distinctiveness of the policy by contrasting it with bourgeois law. If the laws of western European states and tsarist penal law set various ages of consent, he wrote, "our legislation observes an absolutely proper silence on the question of age" and recognizes the variability of sexual maturation in the Soviet Union.

> Recognizing that the sexual maturation of the peoples inhabiting the vast territory of our Union is in essence highly variable, and that aside from climatic and racial factors there are also sociocultural [*sotsial'no-bytovye*] and individual conditions that influence the development of the child, our legislation considers a biological determination of sexual maturity to be more correct, and accepts that each individual case of attempted violation requires a biological, i.e., a medical, expert opinion.[10]

The concept was thus the "absolutely proper" consequence of Soviet power's social vision of the nation as a pool of diverse "races" living in varied social and geographic circumstances.

Yet again in 1928, writing for the specialist readership of the journal *Issues of Public Health,* Leibovich adopted an ironic medical insider's tone that suggested greater irritation with jurists and their invention. In 1921, the drafters of the criminal code had shown Health Commissariat officials, including Leibovich, a version of the articles using the concept of sexual maturity. The chief forensic expert (speaking from hindsight) claimed to have recognized both the opportunity and danger: "As a doctor, I should have greeted [sexual maturity] with whole-hearted approval. But at the same time I warned that the term could cause confusion in practice, contradictory interpretations and so forth." The Health Commissariat accordingly recommended setting an age of protection at 15, but the Justice Commissariat pressed ahead with its "biological version." Leibovich tartly commented, "Now having in our dossiers several thousand cases of expert opinion (I speak collectively in the name of forensic doctors), armed with the results of numerous speeches and resolutions, we can confidently say that the term 'sexual maturity' is imprecise and unsuitable in legislation."[11] The majority of forensic medical experts Leibovich had canvassed during 1927 in professional conferences now wanted a clear age of consent, preferably 16.

Leibovich's comments suggest that jurists and police foresaw real problems in imposing a single age of protection across Soviet Russia. Lawmakers resisted a unified age of protection and ignored expert advice about the problems a medicalized threshold would bring. The jurists' vision of Soviet Russia as a pool of diverse climates and races prevailed, evidently because of the difficulties of governance a single age of consent conjured up. Jurists were well aware of these difficulties in another, related, context, where a different solution was in place: the minimum age for marriage. In 1918, Bolsheviks, in their first family code, adopted the tsarist minimum ages of 16 for women and 18 for men. According to Commissar of Justice D. I. Kurskii, the old regime's rules were retained to accommodate existing social conditions.[12] Yet these norms became the target of lively discontent within the Communist Party. Members from southern regions with Muslim populations to appease called for a lower marriage age, while those from European Russia demanded a higher age to protect women, and for eugenic reasons. The early Soviet politics of marriage age drew upon the same medical ideas about geography, class, and race that informed discussions on sexual maturation. Although nothing in the archival or published record links the adoption of the "sexual maturity" threshold in criminal law to later discussions about age of first marriage, the proximity of the issues and the passions they ignited suggest that in 1922 jurists resisted setting a unified age of consent with these tensions in mind. When considering the problem of sexual citizenship they sought to reconcile social phenomena—the diversity of customs and norms in a multiethnic polity—with reference to a material biological substrate, the individual's body, an object thought to bear evidence that could tie it to the collective.[13]

Despite doctors' protests, the sexual maturity standard remained in Soviet law, reappearing in the revised 1926 RSFSR criminal code. The tenacity of the biological standard was a signal that jurists, Communists, and some forensic experts continued to view setting an age threshold as a thorny social and political problem. Compelled to devise usable definitions of "sexual maturity," experts drew upon cultural assumptions embedded in Russia's sexological heritage. Wherever doctors looked they could see sharp deviations from any ideal standard of sexual coming of age. Such variations were normally ascribed to a small number of widely held axioms about "race," climate, and geography. These axioms in turn were modified and mixed with a social analysis of the role played in sexual maturation by environment and culture. Before and after the revolution, Russians perceived class as a significant determinant of when and how girls and boys arrived at sexual maturity. Finally, gender itself determined how sexual maturation was defined, measured, and interpreted, with eloquently varying approaches applied to the two sexes. Before examining how sexual maturity was applied in everyday sex crime cases from Petrograd and Sverdlovsk, a look at the ideas that Soviet doctors inherited and developed is in order.

Sexual Maturity in the Clinic

A sex education manual commissioned in 1882 by the Imperial Russian army for instructors of young men in military schools also served Russian medicine as a foundation text for the scientific conceptualization of puberty. Veniamin M. Tarnovskii's *Sexual Maturity: Its Evolution, Deviations, and Diseases* appeared in 1886 and was reprinted in 1891, becoming a standard reference work for educators, doctors, and lay members of the public concerned with the appropriate inculcation of "hygiene in the sexual sphere."[14] Laura Engelstein has indicated that Tarnovskii's manual focused entirely on male sexual development and the discipline needed by the young officer to avoid the evils of masturbation and an indulgence in the public brothel that might lead to sexually transmitted disease. Women appeared in the manual only as wives (endangered by disease) or prostitutes (who carried it).[15] In Tarnovskii's presentation, the gender of the pubescent human was implicitly male, and yet the factors that determined when puberty arrived and how long it took a boy to mature were universalized in his introductory chapter defining sexual maturity. Race and climate were key determinants of sexual maturation.

Race and climate mixed with assertions about geography in Tarnovskii's rules for predicting maturation. The farther south a particular country lay, the earlier sexual desire appeared in its inhabitants, the earlier puberty began, and the shorter the period of development to full sexual maturity. Southern "races" displayed heightened sexual feeling and experienced higher fertility rates than those who lived in cooler northern climates. In the Jews of Central Europe, sexual maturity "always arrives earlier" than in the "indigenous" population around them. Mixed-race combinations in which sexual intensity figured on both sides could produce hypersexual peoples given to pathological levels of desire; the "Metis of Mexico" furnished one example of such a people. Geographic conditions had a direct impact on sexual development: peoples living at higher elevations (like peoples living farther from the Equator) experienced later and longer puberty, and lower sexual desire and fertility. Coastal populations matured more rapidly than those inland.[16]

Tarnovskii's racialized geography of sexual maturation was widely repeated in Russian medical literature before and after the revolution. Certain "races" and regions were marked as extremes in this sexual geography, while the "Great Russians" of the central Russian heartland were figured as a "median" nation that displayed neither too excessive nor too premature sexual eruption.[17] Authorities presented the Jews as a favorite example of early and intense sexuality; the fact that Jews lived among the Russians and other nationalities allegedly demonstrated that differences of sexual maturation were grounded in "race," and were not merely a function of climate or latitude.[18] Another tsarist teachers' manual on sexual development asserted that "Polish Jewesses, the true offspring of their Palestinian mothers, have their first menses much earlier than the Catholic girls of Warsaw."[19] Here the difference was between first menstruation at the age of 15 years 6 months, and 16 years 10 months. Even those seeking to deny the primacy of race as a factor in the onset of puberty were forced to engage in a debate framed in racial terms. One diligent scholar using the techniques of anthropometry to measure schoolboy growth rates in 1890s Moscow was able to compare growth in Jewish pupils, who attended separate institutions, with that of "Great Russians." The Jewish boys' smaller chest development was accompanied by a shorter but more vigorous spurt of growth at puberty; yet in the view of this scientist, "the unfavorable conditions in which the vast majority of Russian Jews live" were responsible, not a racial substrate.[20]

If the Jews represented a national group "among the Russians" who illustrated one extreme of the racial determination of sexual maturation, Scandinavians and other northern peoples served an opposite function in this sexual mapping. Their sexuality was delayed by the cold climates and near polar latitudes they inhabited. Usually citing foreign studies, Russia's medical literature of sexual development commonly ascribed the late arrival of menstruation, or retarded sexual desire in young men, to Laplanders, Greenlanders, Swedes, and Norwegians. The onset of sexual maturity in these nationalities was said to be delayed until as late as 18 or 20 years of age.[21]

A significant axis in this sexual geography ran from north to south, and for many medical authorities a comparison between European Russians and the nationalities of the Caucasus was the most vivid indicator inside Imperial Russian, or Soviet, territory of the differences between national features of sexual maturity. The north-south axis was not solely racial but bore the weight of social and cultural perceptions too. In this matter, traditions of governance had a role to play in how the sexual life of the Caucasus was viewed. While in 1830 tsarist law had set the minimum age of marriage for Orthodox Russians at 16 for women and 18 for men, for subjects of the Russian Empire in the Caucasus who were "natives" of the region the minimum ages fixed by the same law were 13 and 15 respectively.[22] Russians increasingly began to view Caucasian early marriage practices, and the sexual life that accompanied them, as unfavorable for the health of both mother and offspring. Noting that the marriage minimum for the Caucasus was founded on the presumption "that inhabitants of southern countries develop earlier and therefore women become capable of producing offspring earlier," one St. Petersburg physician gathered evidence to prove that tragic social and cultural practices ordained dangerously "early marriages for child-women [*zhenshchin-maliutki*]."[23] His study, mandated in 1896 by the medical council of the Ministry of Internal Affairs, made an implicit comparison between the well-organized campaign to end child marriage in India, spearheaded there by European and Indian doctors, and the apparent silence about such practices in Russia's south. The Russian study yielded a mixed picture of the effects of early marriage: in this sample there was no greater risk of complicated births, nor was there a higher rate of infant mortality recorded among the babies born to "immature" mothers, although the mothers did experience more health difficulties themselves in later life.[24] The author of this study argued for further research to uncover the harmful impact of early marriage in the region. Significantly however, the north-south axis of comparison between European Russians and the nationalities of the Caucasus remained a standard reference point when doctors discussed sexual maturity during the twentieth century.[25]

Soviet specialists concerned with the question of sexual maturity replicated the north-south geography of puberty in their work. The moment of the onset of puberty depended, in a typical phrase used in 1923 by the director of a children's hospital in Baku, "on racial, climatic and socio-cultural . . . conditions." In the Caucasus, "girls of the European part of the population" matured at 12 to 13 years of age while "Moslem and Armenian girls" reached puberty at 10 to 11. Meanwhile, "European" and "native" boys were maturing at similarly differing rates. This doctor deplored early marriage in "the local especially Moslem part of the population" among which girls of 12, capable of conception, experienced their first pregnancies despite their still "childlike minds." Such child mothers preferred playing with dolls to caring for their far-from-robust offspring, who "rarely survived."[26] The north-south mapping of sexual maturity was accompanied by racial, social, and cultural stereotyping that blended biological assumption with cultural presumption. The timing of sexual maturation varied, the Baku hospital director wrote, noting that "in the dark races of the Caucasus it [puberty] begins earlier than in the light-haired Scandinavians, and in the North later than in the South."[27] Feckless Mediterranean nations contrasted with the games-loving northern Europeans in an account of the premature versus deferred sexual debuts of Russia's European neighbors:

> The peoples of the North have long recognized the utility of sport [in deflecting youth's attention from sex], and this largely explains the established statistical fact that among northern peoples (Swedes, Norwegians, English) a significantly large percentage of youths remain virgins until they enter into marriage. In contrast, southern peoples like Spaniards, Italians and so forth, among whom sport has recently not played an important role, even begin an active sexual life at the earliest possible age.[28]

Early sexual activity among the southerners, according to this self-appointed expert in human sexuality, a professor of the Leningrad Agricultural Institute, was the consequence of race and climate that triggered puberty at an early age, and a negligent upbringing that failed to organize youngsters' spare time and energy productively.

Leibovich domesticated these perceptions for the forensic medical specialist. "While in the south, for example, among Caucasian peoples, wives and mothers of 14 are frequently met, the 14-year-old inhabitants of the midlands and northern reaches of our republic are often still youthful teenagers." Tsarist and Soviet surveys of the age of first menstruation in St. Petersburg/Leningrad had demonstrated that at the northern end of the Russian axis of sexual maturity, the average age of first menstruation was relatively high (between 14¾ years and 16 years). "Undoubtedly the average age in Moscow or in the Ukraine is lower, and in the Caucasus and

Crimea, lower still."[29] Elsewhere, Leibovich sharpened his condemnation of the evils of Moslem patterns of early marriage and sexual life, condemning them for burdening "girls of our southern periphery."[30] The Soviet geography of sexual maturity, with its foreign and domestic permutations, was a commonplace of Soviet medical discussions.[31]

If race, climate, and geography produced one axis upon which to map the distinctive chronologies of puberty, class or social position furnished a competing grid for medical observers. The matrix of class presented an array of environmental influences on sexual maturation that delayed or hastened the arrival of a sexual life, often through instruction, the example of adults, or from aspects of lifestyle such as nutrition, sleeping arrangements, or occupation. Significantly, Russia's medical experts trained the class lens not on other races, countries, or societies, but almost exclusively on the "Great Russians" themselves. In contrast to expert views about race, climate, and geography, there was far less agreement over the influence of class on the timing and character of sexual maturation. The contradictions in views of the sexual debuts of peasants, workers, and the prosperous classes changed over time and, unsurprisingly, reflected political shifts in how each class and its lifestyle were seen by experts.

Russia's well-to-do classes were the first to feel the intrusion of expert prescriptions about the sexual coming of age, as the military commission for officer trainers of Tarnovskii's sex education manual exemplified. The military physician painted a broad canvas of the rich variety of dangers leading to premature and misdirected sexual maturation, and the influence of Tarnovskii's textbook left echoes in the warnings of later experts. The proximity of ignorant or lubricious servants, or older youths, was a constant danger preying on the children of the wealthy, leading to corruption via the spectacle of serving-class sexual relations or, worse still, deliberate and always inappropriately premature tuition in sexual activity. Such innocents were prime candidates for the vices of masturbation and early sexual intercourse whether with servants or prostitutes.[32] The cultural environment of the upper- and middle-class youngster needed constant monitoring: novels and theatrical performances with infamous content (Tarnovskii singled out ballet and magic shows) stimulated the sexual imagination too intensively and too soon. The school was a web of pitfalls. "At the present time youths in school spend more time sitting than adults ... especially in springtime while preparing for examinations" and the sedentary life led to anal and genital swellings, and wet dreams. To dampen students' ardor and toughen discipline, teachers should impose cold dormitories, cool classrooms, and cold baths. Exercise was vital to distract student minds from sexual themes: "gymnasts, acrobats, navvies and other unskilled workers easily endure sexual abstinence" because they are constantly on the move. For the young trainee officer, horseback riding could be valuable as long as he mounted a sturdy saddle and rode at a vigorous pace; riding bareback, or at a slower gait, could stimulate rather than obviate erections and emissions.[33]

Foods directly affected the timing, character, and intensity of sexual maturation, according to Tarnovskii and many subsequent authorities. Exotic ingredients and means of preparation signaled upper- and middle-class culinary tastes and triggered early sexual arousal and even puberty if regularly consumed in childhood. Young cadets should not be fed on "fried meat especially fowl . . . seafood, foods heavily spiced with onion, garlic, pepper, cinnamon, vanilla" nor given much "crab, squid, crayfish, shrimps, truffles, artichokes, celery, pineapples and so forth." Alcohol use in the teenage years was thoroughly condemned with the most stimulating drinks being "champagnes, old French wines, aromatic liqueurs"; Hungarian wines were said to be less arousing, while Tarnovskii brazenly ignored vodka or beer, the drinks most likely to fall into the hands of young recruits. If the exotic and foreign were dangerous, Tarnovskii likewise warned that "food that was not nourishing, or extremely monotonous food" might retard or pervert the sexual instinct. Cooks in boarding schools feeding middle-class children on the threshold of puberty should serve them "white meat, foods made of flour products, dairy products of all types, fried vegetables and water to drink" so as to reduce sexual arousal and yet stimulate physical development.[34] A simple but nourishing diet based on local products, avoiding the exotic and the foreign, was best suited to discipline and channel the youthful sexuality of Russia's prosperous classes.

Medical experts worried less about peasant sexual maturation. In the years before 1905, educated city-dwelling experts regarded Russia's rural inhabitants as innocent of sexual depravity, believing that excessively early sexual maturation was unlikely to affect the population in the countryside.[35] Indeed some authorities waxed lyrical about the delay to puberty that village life supposedly conferred, with its fresh air and its healthy lack of enervating stimulants and urban distractions.[36] Prerevolutionary large-scale anthropometric studies of women noted the later arrival of first menstruation in the peasant population (in contrast with their city counterparts in the working class), often ascribing this phenomenon to heavy workloads, poor diet, and a lower overall standard of living.[37] After 1905, as attitudes toward lower-class sexuality began to shift toward a more negative view of peasant sexual life, the previous view of vigor, innocence, and simplicity could occasionally be exchanged for one of corruption, poverty, and ignorance imposed by the patriarchal structure of village life. Nevertheless, in the work of forensic medical experts, the sexual maturity of peasants was a comparatively insignificant issue, since most victims of articles 166–167 (and later 151) were city girls, and the majority of experts were themselves based in the cities. Thus the application of the "sexual maturity" standard in criminal cases was confined primarily to the towns. The view that women in the countryside matured later persisted among forensic doctors throughout the 1920s and 1930s.[38]

In the Soviet Union of the 1920s, the well-fed middle-class youngster as candidate for premature sexual maturation appeared rarely in medical writing. Deprived of the virtuous experience of heavy labor and lacking the necessary "tempering" *(zakalka)* imposed by scarcity, "bourgeois" children, in the eyes of some NEP-era experts, arrived at puberty earlier than their "working-class" counterparts.[39] Yet the majority of medical authorities of the 1920s focused their attention more squarely on the working class when discussing the problem of sexual maturity. From their imperial predecessors they inherited a view of working-class pubescence as highly problematic.

For the prerevolutionary medical profession, the debut of sexual life in the working class was characterized by its misery and disorderliness. Tarnovskii wrote, "In factories and workshops where children and teenagers work the early and pathological development of sexual feeling is facilitated by extreme poverty, slovenliness, constant contact of the sexes in close quarters, [and] the lack of abstinence among parents and persons surrounding the youngster."[40] In the "working estate," sexual maturity arrived too early for reasons that were largely environmental, often with a biophysical tinge. Thus, "artificially high temperatures, a lack of pure air and the sedentary life" favored in workshops produced undesirable effects on the young organism, as did a lack of nutritious food.[41] At least as damaging in this regard was the "freedom of sexual relations" said by doctors to reign among the working classes.[42] After 1905, medical authorities expressed a predominant view that "disorderly, promiscuous family life, precocious childhood sex, and adult sexual indulgence" prevailed in the working class.[43] In this patriarchal urban environment the children of workers supposedly acquired awareness of sexuality far too early, from the wrong sorts of sources, and often in conjunction with damaging indulgence in alcohol and tobacco.

Soviet medical authorities speaking on working-class sexual maturation hoped, of course, to rectify these defects by applying disciplinary prescriptions previously promoted only for the well-to-do. In this hope they mirrored the aspirations of sexologists and psychiatrists who published on the sexual question during the 1920s.[44] The most significant trend in the work of forensic doctors was a sustained focus on the working class as the new scientific norm defining the onset and character of puberty. By contrast, NEP-era forensic medical research paid scarcely any attention to peasant sexual maturation.[45] As experience of the troublesome application of the sexual maturity concept accumulated, forensic authorities repeatedly expressed the concern that "the social position of the persons under study" needed to be at the heart of forensic thinking about the concept.[46] To Soviet crime analysts, the crime of intercourse with the sexually immature appeared to be an urban one, and the class most likely to be victimized, the working-class.[47]

This logic doubtless explains why forensic experts trained their attention on large samples of workers when seeking to establish benchmarks for "sexual maturity." A study of one thousand young women conducted at Saratov's Forensic Medical Institute by graduate student V. S. Piaternev in 1926 drew its sample population from factory workers and "members of social organizations" (likely the Komsomol and civil defense associations) composed of groups friendly to the revolution.[48] In her 1927 survey of the sexual debuts of 1,779 Saratov workers, Dr. L. B. Leitman, a relative rarity as a woman conducting research in the forensic discipline, expressed anxiety about the "low cultural level" of such respondents, some of whom were said to be recent migrants from the countryside. Yet the accounts of their sexual maturation she accepted as reliable because venereologists conducting "cultural-enlightenment work" in the clinic had elicited these accounts in structured interviews with their worker-clientele.[49] When both Leitman and Piaternev presented their findings to a December 1927 joint conference of forensic and judicial workers in Ivanovo-Voznesensk, it was assumed that sexual maturity would be calibrated using data from the working class, even if there were disagreements about how to characterize it. In a comment intended to defend his colleagues' work, Professor M. I. Raiskii of the same institute reminded the audience that Leitman and Piaternev had both chosen to study workers, "and therefore the social is accounted for."[50] It was a weak defense, as accounting for the social was not just accomplished by drawing on the right class for data, but on the ways in which data was analyzed. Often the analysis turned on a fundamental issue: gender.

Gender, not surprisingly, determined how researchers theorized sexual maturation in crucial ways. Women, as the predominant victims of sexual assault, were the chief focus of research, and for them doctors imagined sexual maturity as a biological and physiological condition. The bodies of girls and young women were subjected to the disciplines of the measuring tape and the card catalogue, recording their performance in the maternity ward. Authorities seldom problematized or discussed the sexual psychology of the maturing girl, except in terms that suggested an absence or lack of desire rather than the dawning of a sexual personality. In the rare cases when forensic medics looked for markers of boys' sexual maturity, they might examine anatomy, but they never failed to probe the psychological development of young men as a prime area of concern. Men's sexual maturity came to mean the mastery of an unruly but fundamentally uncomplicated sexual instinct, through distraction, willpower, and sublimation.

Simplistic and more complex physiological models of women's sexual maturity prevailed simultaneously. The onset of first menstruation alone was an unambiguous indicator that a girl had become a woman, in the view of many medical experts. Anthropometric scientists had gathered data on the ages of first monthly flows from samples of thousands of Russian women since the 1880s, establishing this event as the threshold of womanhood in the scientific mind with the persuasive power of statistics and questionnaires.[51] Medical manuals on puberty before and after 1917 held that first menstruation was the "external sign" of sexual maturity in girls.[52] Even Leibovich's first handbook for forensic medical experts published in 1923 explained sexual maturity cursorily, in terms of a girl's first menstruation, with only the briefest mention that other physical changes accompanied puberty.[53] The simple idea that the onset of first menses was identical to the arrival of sexual maturity influenced Soviet police, criminal investigators, and some prosecutors too, especially in the first years of the functioning of the "sexual maturity" standard, and when nonspecialist doctors gave evidence in rural districts.[54]

Forensic medical authorities only paid sustained attention to the definition of "sexual maturity" in women after the first Soviet Russian criminal code introduced the concept in law. Their publications on this issue appeared later in the 1920s, after experience of the application of the new biological threshold for sexual citizenship, in place of a conventional age of consent or protection, showed that the meaning of "sexual maturity" was less straightforward than Bolshevik lawmakers had anticipated. Forensic experts' definitions of female sexual maturity continued to emphasize physiological development over psychosexual considerations, but they tended to demote first menstruation to one among many signs of the onset of puberty. The influential Moscow gynecologist N. V. Popov supplied a much-repeated general definition. Sexual maturity was, he wrote, "the full capability of physiological fulfillment of all sexual functions of the given individual, without harmful consequences for his health, in the absence, of course, of abuse [*zloupotrebleniia*]."[55] Women's sexual maturity was burdened, however, by the array of functions it heralded:

> The sexual functions of women are much more complex and varied than the functions in men. The act of copulation and ejaculation completes men's sexual functioning, while for women this is just the beginning. The heaviest lies further ahead—pregnancy, birth, and nursing the child. All the physiological consequences of the sexual act fall on the woman, leaving men only pleasure. If a woman interrupts her pregnancy this does not ease her situation for abortion is rather harmful for her organism.[56]

The law punishing sexual intercourse with the sexually immature did not merely protect "public morality" in Popov's view, but safeguarded the individual woman from the consequences of premature sex, including the burdens on the young body of pregnancy. "[P]regnancy is not a joke but a complex and prolonged physiological process demanding the expenditure of much energy from the female organism." Thus Popov enumerated five distinct reproductive functions that demanded "physical strength and endurance" and that marked the achievement of sexual maturity. A young woman had to be capable of sexual intercourse, conception, sustaining a pregnancy, giving birth, and finally nursing her child.[57] To ascertain if a girl had reached sexual maturity, Popov recommended finding out if menstruation had taken place and measuring the pelvis to determine if it had developed sufficiently to permit a healthy birth. Finally, the subject's "general physical and mental development" should be considered in deciding if she was ready to perform all the functions of reproduction. Early Soviet forensic gynecologists generally held that women's sexual maturity was "a complex combination of symptoms" and not merely the arrival of menstruation.[58] When Saratov forensic gynecologist V. A. Riasentsev commented that "a woman is not a flower that blossoms overnight," he was taking aim at police, prosecutors, and nonspecialist doctors who saw in menstruation the sole herald of a girl's sexual debut.[59]

The Desiring Victim and the "Wrapper of Virginity"

Did Soviet forensic experts allow for any features of a psychological nature to enter their recipes defining sexual maturity in women? They inherited a medical and pedagogical outlook that denied the existence of natural female sexual desire, or placed it within very circumscribed spheres. The teenage girl suffered little if at all from the anxiety and stormy impulses that characterized the male youth's responses to his intensifying sexual feeling. One Baku pediatrician rhapsodizing on womanhood in 1923 said that woman's "eternal female psychology" and "feminine instincts" tied her forever to reproduction and domesticity.[60] Sexological experts of the 1920s of various stripes evaded discussions of the teenage girl's sexual appetite and psychology; if they did broach the subject, it was to warn that a Pandora's box of disorderly sexuality, premature, complicated pregnancy, and loss of the capacity to work or study awaited the youthful teenage girl whose instincts were not rationally educated toward the duty of reproduction.[61] Inside the forensic medical profession, Popov and others reflected this view by including in the "complex combination of symptoms" that they used to define sexual maturity a psychological criterion that required fully matured girls to be sufficiently "mentally developed" to be conscientious mothers.[62] It was a putative benchmark that measured preparedness for the burdens of parenting, not the appearance of a sexual personality. Only in 1934 would the natalist functionalism (and the social as opposed to individual significance) of this psychological criterion for sexual maturity be at last embedded in explicit rules that set common Soviet standards for determinations of sexual maturity.[63]

Of leading forensic experts, only Iakov Leibovich himself articulated a theory of sexual maturity that included an extended characterization of female sexual psychology in its developmental phase. The sexually maturing girl lost her unrestrained gaiety and grew more gloomy, capricious, and reserved as she displayed more interest in "erotic functions" without experiencing "sexual sensation" herself. Following a German model, Leibovich claimed that woman's psychosexual maturity was composed of three elements: an essential passiveness, a womanly reserve, and "pansexualism," the flooding of her entire organism with the sexual function.[64] Despite the onset of biological sexual maturity and the consolidation of this psychosexual complex of womanly essences, young women normally lacked experience of a "libido sexualis." The exception to this rule was implicitly one of class, in that living in cramped quarters allowed sexually innocent girls to observe the sex lives of adults, with the result that conscious sexual desire was aroused prematurely.

Leibovich's formula for the psychosexual maturation of young girls failed to command attention or favor in the forensic medical profession. He said little about it after first publishing these ideas in his major textbook on forensic gynecology in 1928. A clue to the inadmissibility of a psychosexual index to sexual maturation for practitioners of forensic expertise may be found in the 1927 Ivanovo-Vosnesensk joint conference of forensic experts and justice workers. In an extensive airing of the problem of "sexual maturity," legal doctors, police, and prosecutors discussed two papers from the Saratov Institute of Forensic Medicine. A paper by graduate student V. S. Piaternev, dealing with female development, used anthropometric measurements of one thousand Saratov factory workers and Komsomol members to arrive at a standard benchmark of sexual maturity applicable in forensic medical work.[65] Each of the subjects (females between 10 and 20 years of age) was measured in 27 different ways, with each measure taken three times and then averaged, a dizzying total of 81,000 measurements calibrated by hand. Piaternev and his team measured a range of factors including height, weight, circumference of head and shoulders, and breast development, but the most indicative measure of women's sexual maturity he discerned was the development of the pelvis. This criterion was key, he concluded, because so many complications arose from pregnancies in which young mothers lacked a fully developed pelvis. As a result, Piaternev concluded that the average girl "in our conditions" reached sexual maturity at 17 years of age, and full physical development at 19. His conclusion met with approval for its materialist, anthropometric methodology and, evidently, for the emphasis on reproductive efficiency it displayed.[66]

Dr. L. B. Leitman's paper at the same conference presented findings from a survey of 1,779 male clients of Saratov's sexually transmitted disease clinic, in an attempt to discern when sexual maturity arrived in young men.[67] Leitman conceived the question as one of sexual psychology as revealed through patient questionnaires. Her analysis of responses from these male factory workers to a sex survey conducted by the sexual diseases clinic turned entirely on questions about the men's first sexual experiences. Many men in her survey began their sex lives at an age that "significantly preceded the onset of sexual majority," with 29 percent claiming their first sexual experience between 9 and 17 years of age. Leitman found that 73.9 percent of the respondents reported as the motive for their first sexual activity "sexual desire," "marriage," or "love and attraction"—motives that she interpreted as stemming from the appearance of the "sexual instinct," and therefore indicative of the onset of sexual maturity. Men whose first experience was provoked by external forces, the result of "the influence of comrades," "drunkenness," or "a woman [who] seduced me" constituted a youthful minority, gulled into a premature sexual life. Leitman found that a worrying quarter of these young men "experienced insistent sexual desire before age 18," that is, they manifested signs of sexual maturity before the minimum marriage age.

Leitman's conception and analysis of sexual motives made her audience uncomfortable. (The fact that a woman doctor, one of the few present, was pronouncing before a primarily male audience on the sexuality of men, the gender almost never scrutinized in studies of sexual maturity, may well have contributed to this discomfort.) A lone Freudian, perhaps a psychiatrist, attacked Leitman's use of questionnaires

Lia Borisovna Leitman, staff gynecologist of the Saratov Institute of Forensic Medicine in the 1920s.

as ignorant of the "established laws" of psychoanalysis that showed sexual desire to be universally powerful in both women and men.[68] His invocation of Freud compounded Leitman's original offense in the eyes of the majority in the audience. The chief judge of Ivanovo-Vosnesensk Province, one comrade Nikonov, (almost certainly a party member) expressed great consternation that "[s]uch terminology as love, sexual desire, sexual curiosity" could be introduced into Leitman's "dilletantish" discussion without clear grounding in "the social characteristics of the person under study." Doctors attempting to mollify the judge said Leitman's use of the questionnaire methodology was perhaps "useful for preliminary work" but not sufficiently scientific to satisfy the needs of legal medicine: "anthropometric and functional investigation" would be more appropriate.[69]

The overwhelming majority of cases requiring doctors to make a determination of sexual maturity involved female victims. Leitman's quirky inquiry into men's sexual debuts, and the discomfort it inspired, demonstrate the problems involved in adding an index of psychosexual maturation to a comparatively well-established menu of physiological indicators of sexual maturity. Impressionistic, "loose" language about sexual emotions would not satisfy law enforcement authorities looking for greater clarity from scientific opinions furnished in criminal investigations. The danger that Freudianism (with its ideologically suspect basis in individualistic idealism) might be imported into the opinions of experts must have struck judge Nikonov as particularly unattractive; hence his comment that love and sexual life should only be discussed in their social dimensions.[70] In preferring definitions of women's sexual maturity that focused on reproductive capacity, doctors and the jurists who required their services relied on "materialist" criteria—bodies and their functions—that could be measured in unambiguous terms. Clarity added value to forensic doctors' determinations, especially when authorities investigated sexual crimes with their thin evidentiary bases.

By allowing for a degree of sexual desiring in the *victims* of sexual crime, the introduction of any psychosexual criterion for the sexual maturation of girls threatened to make the forensic expert's and criminal investigator's tasks more complex. As observers noted during the 1920s, uncovering the facts of a crime in cases of rape, sexual intercourse with the sexually immature, or other forms of sexual abuse, could be extremely difficult. Police investigations of this category of crime were incomplete, poorly conceived, and slow.[71] In most cases the main or sole evidence might be testimony by the victim and her family; if the victim had already begun "living a sexual life" (as the phrase went in medical and police reports), then there was likely to be little physical evidence of intercourse. Police and doctors worried that where there was no sign of physical violence, the victim might be making a false complaint against her alleged attacker for material gain, revenge, or to make good a promise of marriage, and there was little investigators and doctors could do to detect such illegitimate claims.[72] The notion that sexually mature girls had sexual "instincts" or responded to an awakening "libido sexualis" muddied already murky waters.

If a young woman could legally consent to defloration only once she had reached sexual maturity, how did revolutionary society recognize and acknowledge this moment? One path, the respectable one even in a radically socialist society, was through marriage, for which conventional age minimums were set in the Family Code. A girl had to be at least 16 years old, and from 1927, 18, to enter into a registered marriage. Yet these age limits appeared to contradict the criminal law that fixed a biological not chronological minimum for permitted sexual relations, and the contradiction exposed the reality that far from all sexual relations took place within the framework of registered marriage. It was of course criminal relations, presumed usually to be outside the marriage framework that concerned forensic experts most.

A significant aspect of the biological standard of sexual maturity was that laypersons did not easily recognize it. A man accused of intercourse with a sexually immature girl of 15, 16, or 17 years of age could argue that since he thought that she already menstruated he presumed she was sexually mature; or he might say she looked physically developed and therefore able to consent.[73] A girl of that age who had experienced her first menses, or who had acquired other adult secondary sexual characteristics, might well presume she had achieved sexual maturity. Forensic medical discourse was silent about the young girl's internal drama of self-recognition (as having achieved sexual majority and citizenship) that was an implicit backdrop to the biological minimum for sexual relations. Evidence of popular demand for expert confirmation of a girl's sexual reputation through medical examinations for virginity suggests that the revolutionary abandonment of an easily understood age of protection caused conflict over the social acknowledgement of a woman's sexual debut.

In another conference paper, this one analyzing examinations of living persons in investigations with a sexual element, Saratov's Dr. Leitman revealed that an important part of her work involved furnishing expertise to resolve family, marital, and social disputes over women's sexual reputations.[74] From 1923 to 1925, about eighty such examinations of women and girls had been conducted by the institute. These constituted just over 40 percent of the total number of examinations of living persons in sexual investigations undertaken during the period. (By way of comparison, 92 persons were examined at the institute in formal criminal investigations of rape charges.) Examinations of the sexual condition of women who were the objects of a family or social dispute about reputation were requested by these women themselves, or by police and social agencies. All of these women were under 30 and 27 percent were less than 16 years old. "A large percentage of [the entire sample were] girls who have been insulted by their neighbors, by co-workers, spurned by their husbands or suitors, who had used 'bad language' against them and accused them of having had secret pregnancies, abortions and sexual affairs." Husbands who doubted that their new wives were virgins, and wives who wanted to prove to their new husbands that they were sexually innocent, sought medical confirmation, in the form of a gynecological examination and expert opinion, from the forensic institute. Leitman approached the question of the sexual agency of these subjects cautiously, saying nothing about its relationship to their age or degree of sexual maturity. Indeed, in contrast to her later study of men and their sexual maturity, in dealing with women she preferred to direct her attention to the physical over the psychological. She disagreed with French forensic authorities who counseled a thorough observation of the "comportment, language and general appearance" of these women for signs of immorality, and claimed instead that the body of the applicant was the appropriate focus of inspection. Physical development, signs of degeneracy (that might fuel sexual appetite) or of a previous sexual and childbearing history were relevant, and the "most reliable indicator" of a sexual career was the damaged hymen. In spite of Leitman's insistence on the body as the source of the "truth" about these girls' and women's "sexual condition," it is striking that the examinations were being conducted for moral purposes: to prove a girl's innocence before an angry band of nosy neighbors or to reassure a husband who despite the "sexual revolution" still demanded that his wife be a virgin on her wedding night.[75] The intact hymen, no longer protected by the patriarchal mutual surveillance of the peasant village, was still a powerful symbol of innocence for these city-dwelling workers, who now looked to Soviet medicine to certify its integrity.

If medical experts complied with requests for such certification, some observers were appalled by the atavistic focus on physical female virginity, whether it originated in society's patriarchal values or in the phrasing of Soviet legislation. At the 1927 Ivanovo-Vosnesensk conference, chief judge Nikonov rounded on the prevailing interpretation of the word "defloration" *(rastlenie)* employed in article 167/151. The problem for Russians was that this word bore the ambivalent meaning of "corruption" as well as the gender-specific sense of the deprivation of virginity in women. The law as written and interpreted by police, doctors and courts appeared to suggest "that only a woman can be corrupted [*rastlit'*]."⁷⁶ Yet "for a boy as much as for a girl, the first sexual act carries an extraordinary and serious significance." To insist on a tsarist view that only "feminine honor" deserved protection was "incompatible with our socialist state." The hymen must not be fetishized:

> As we approach all questions scientifically, we should approach this issue scientifically as well, and say that there is no need for the privileged protection of women in this matter. Therefore there is no place for permitting such formal indications as the "wrapper" of virginity [*banderol' devstvennosti*] which at the end of the day does not decide all the questions, because for us what is important is the moral condition of the individual before and after the sexual act. We must not give a damn about this "wrapper" [*Nuzhno pliunut' na etu banderol'*], saying that all sexual intercourse with a minor is an offence and is treated as a serious crime.⁷⁷

Intriguingly this utopian position expressed the aspiration that men and women would enjoy absolutely equal sexual citizenship, purged of the patriarchal view of women's virginity as a mark of sexual reputation. For this Bolshevik, the "moral condition of the individual" was paramount, not the physical characteristics of the gendered body. Yet it was also this judge who then singled out Dr. Leitman's psychological definitions of "love" and "sexual curiosity" in youthful men as "dilletantish" and insufficiently class-conscious. Judging the "moral condition" of the individual victim of sexual crime was ultimately not the province of forensic experts.

Men's sexual maturity attracted far less attention from the forensic medical profession, chiefly because sexual assaults on young men were rarely reported or investigated.⁷⁸ Silence governed police and medical approaches to the issue. The law implied that sexually mature youths could consent to "sexual intercourse . . . accompanied by . . . the satisfaction of sexual passion in perverted forms." Experts and police appear to have preferred to ignore sexual relations between men and youths, except where violence or exploitation was alleged. In such cases, the forensic brief was to detect signs of violent harm on the body of the victim, and the question of the sexual maturity of the boy or youth was seldom raised. The question was also seen as irrelevant when men were accused as perpetrators of sexual assaults. To commit such crimes, they needed, by common assumption, to be sexually mature.⁷⁹

The rare expressions of Soviet forensic medical views of male sexual maturity consisted of both biological and psychological elements. By the 1920s, authorities in various disciplines had established that the onset of semen production constituted a universally recognized marker of the male sexual debut.[80] Although physicians and educators might link the appearance of seminal fluid to other physical changes such as emerging secondary sexual characteristics ("breaking" voice, facial and pubic hair growth), this holistic view of boyhood maturation as a somatic transformation was seldom found in the forensic genre of medical literature. The hydraulic rhetoric found in other disciplines of a mobilization of internal hormonal secretions that triggered the arrival of manhood, or worse, if the boy was a masturbator, the loss of "valuable albuminous substance" and hence the biological wherewithal to mature, did not appear in forensic medical writing.[81] Instead, legal medicine judged that in physiological terms, male sexual maturity was a relatively uncomplicated phenomenon when compared to the female. As Popov noted, in the sex act the man's burden was "only pleasure."[82] Dr. Leitman's justification for a questionnaire-led methodology in her study of male sexual maturity illuminates this common notion about men's sexual development:

> The sexual function of man is significantly simpler compared to the function of a woman and there are fewer characteristics for determining sexual majority in him, and therefore aside from anatomy-physiological examination, the question of the onset of sexual majority in man should be studied by other means, in part, there have been attempts to study it with the help of questionnaires.[83]

Forensic doctors conceived of men's sexual maturation as an unambiguous physical transition, but one with psychological significance.

Leitman's analysis of Saratov worker responses to the venereal clinic's sex survey revealed an implicit ideal pattern for sexual maturation, a pattern common in other sexological writing about male sexuality. The young man should defer sexual activity until he found himself impelled by the "sexual instinct" toward a loving relationship with a woman, preferably his wife. Sexual activity initiated under the influence of disorderly male comrades or casual female partners, or while drunk, was harmful implicitly because external factors were seen to be forcing a premature sexual life on the subject, with harmful consequences for his organism and social future. "[B]iology says the male organism achieves full development at 25," Leitman wrote, implying that men should wait until that age to begin a sexual life. Her ideal model of the male sexual debut was in fact well established in tsarist and Soviet writing about sex education and sexual enlightenment.[84] The significance of this ideal male debut, when considering the issue of sexual maturity as the benchmark of sexual citizenship, is in its distinctively psychological, internalized character. In contrast to the standards that forensic medicine devised for recognizing women's sexual maturity (and with it, sexual citizenship), the ideal path to adult manhood traveled via the psyche, not the reproductive organs. Forensic experts imagined men as bearing and expressing sexual desire; ideally, they had internalized the values of restraint, deferral, and self-mastery. Sex crime cases revealed to experts the moments when men failed to master that desire, and indeed when a criminal's acts struck observers as particularly savage or uncontrolled, it was most likely that psychiatric assessment would be sought.

Women were imagined as arriving at the threshold of sexual citizenship not as agents possessing sexual desire, but as baby-making machines. No forensic doctors interested in the problem of sexual maturity conducted surveys to discover when girls and young women first experienced sexual desire, nor did they ask what motives lay behind the first sexual experiences of females. They saw women's sexuality as passive and maternity-centered, and in the context of assessing sexual maturity there was no need to ask about women's emotional or social reasons for engaging in sex. In contrast, the sex lives of Dr. Leitman's male factory workers were historicized and endowed with a sociocultural and not physiological foundation. While the intention of Bolshevik sexual revolutionaries may have been to realize a gender-neutral vision of sexual citizenship, doctors responsible for defining the threshold of such citizenship recapitulated the trope of women's "biological tragedy" in their benchmarks.[85] The libertarian dream of sexual autonomy for women in a socialist society, Kollontai's aspiration that in the new society women would become desiring sexual agents in their own right (just as men were), was undone by biomedical experts whose science was permeated with cultural fears of feminine sexuality.

Sexual Maturity in the Criminal Investigation

The number of complaints in the 1920s to the Soviet authorities of sex crime involving a sexually immature victim was comparatively modest, and the number of these that were eventually tried in a Soviet courtroom formed a smaller proportion still. From this study's total sample of 194 sex crime cases, 44 involve some application of the sexual maturity standard, with most of these 44 trying charges under the relevant "sexual maturity" articles of the criminal code.[86] Officially the public was supposed to report sex offenses to the criminal investigations department, the CID *(Ugolovnyi rozysk)* of the police, but many cases originated in complaints to other officials, especially police on the beat *(militsiia)*. The "people's investigators" operating in the CID in theory possessed more technical and practical expertise with complex sex crimes. Yet in the early years of the Soviet regime, the quality of investigation was poor. One jurist assessing sex crime investigations in 1927 ruefully noted that cases initiated at the police level moved slowly because operatives did not understand the relevant criminal code articles, had a poor grasp of the concept of "sexual maturity," and filled case files with "completely superfluous and unnecessary" materials before passing them to the CID.[87] Poor quality forensic medical expertise figured prominently in jurists' complaints about these cases: careless determinations that defied logic or ignored the terms of Soviet legislation were evidence that local police failed to instruct examining doctors correctly, and that local doctors lacked appropriate training.[88] In prosecutions under the sexual maturity standard found in the Petrograd and Sverdlovsk samples, police and medical application and understanding of the standard varies considerably. The Petrograd cases, dating from 1922 to 1924 reflect the first years of operation of the Soviet Russian Criminal Code and unsurprisingly the novelty and concealed complexities of the concept produced confusion that was probably unanticipated. In the Sverdlovsk sample of similar prosecutions conducted between 1926 and 1929, wide variations in the degree of sophistication of interpretations of the sexual maturity standard appear. In remote Urals settlements lacking trained jurists and forensic medical experts, local district doctors *(uchastkovye vrachi)* were often given minimal direction from unschooled police investigators. Meanwhile, in the city of Sverdlovsk experts and investigators displayed greater familiarity with the concept of sexual maturity, even if they could not always agree on how to recognize it.

Procedures dictated that police and CID respond primarily to complaints when raised by victims and their families or guardians.[89] As discussed in chapter 1, the preliminary investigation yielded a dossier with evidence, including forensic medical opinions, witness testimony, and statements by victim and defendant. Many cases were dropped or abandoned during the preliminary stage for lack of evidence to support an indictment, or because facts emerged to undermine the victim's claim to sexual innocence.[90]

When police and CID had completed their investigations, they forwarded the dossier to prosecutors, who would decide if there was sufficient basis to try the alleged perpetrator. The prosecution could decide to pursue the case under a different article of the criminal code, if it was felt that the crime had been improperly qualified. A case of "sexual intercourse with a person not having achieved sexual maturity" could be transformed into a rape inquiry, if the victim was found to be fully mature by doctors.

Police and CID operatives displayed confusion when investigating sex crimes with older children and teenagers as victims. The wording of the relevant sex crime articles in the law set out a range of distinctions between acts, between victims, and between penalties that led authorities to requalify cases as they moved from denunciation to investigation to trial. Sexual intercourse with obviously prepubescent children caused the authorities little misapprehension; such crimes could be unambiguously qualified under article 167 (or 151 after 1926) condemning intercourse with a person not yet sexually mature.[91] More confusing for investigators were cases in which pubescent or teenage youngsters figured as victims of sexual assaults, and these cases reveal most about forensic medical and police notions of gender, innocence, and sexual agency.[92] It is this category of cases that is investigated in the section below. If scant evidence of coercion was detected, police investigating a 16-year-old girl's claim of rape by her employer might ask questions about her sexual maturity, and thus her right to consent to intercourse (under article 166) or defloration (article 167). The alleged crime in police sights shifted from ordinary rape (article 169) to the statutory rape of someone not yet sexually mature, with consequences for how the victim's testimony was judged and how her sexual citizenship was conceived.[93] Girls as young as 13, who had a sexual history or who had engaged in continuous relations with their assailant, also found their sexual maturity under scrutiny as police, criminal investigators, and prosecutors struggled to determine if a crime in Soviet law had occurred in these ambiguous cases.[94] By requalifying a crime, prosecutors could dramatically shift the terms by which a sexual relationship was understood, and with it, the penalties (if any) for the men and youths accused of sexual crime.[95]

As police and forensic experts investigated these offenses they produced narratives in the form of complaints, witness testimony, and records of interrogations of the accused. These records present in repetitive and often contradictory fashion the basic social and personal circumstances of the given sexual crime. Police records of these investigations suggest that criminal investigators started by trying to establish the social locus of the sexual assault. When teenage girls brought complaints of rape or attempted rape to the authorities, they were closely questioned about their relationship with the assailant (or assailants). Such questioning made sense to police and to some medical experts, for many, perhaps most, rape victims who made complaints accused men and youths whom they knew well. Often there was an economic relationship between the parties that could color the moral perception of the police. Girls working as nannies seem to have been particularly vulnerable to abuse by fathers of the babies they minded. Lodgers renting a room or a corner in a

TABLE 2.1

Crimes against the Sexually Immature, Compared with Rape Offense Definitions, 1922 and 1926 RSFSR Criminal Codes

1922 Article	1922 Description	1922 Penalty	1926 Article	1926 Description	1926 Penalty
166	Sexual intercourse with person not having achieved sexual maturity	Minimum of 3 years imprisonment, strict isolation	151(2)	Sexual intercourse with person not having achieved sexual maturity	Maximum of 3 years imprisonment
167	As above, accompanied by "defloration or using perverted forms"	Minimum of 5 years imprisonment	151(1)	As above, accompanied by "defloration or using perverted forms"	Maximum of 8 years imprisonment
169(2)	Rape, resulting in suicide of the victim	Minimum of 5 years imprisonment	153(2)*	Rape of a person not having achieved sexual maturity, rape resulting in suicide of victim, rape of a person by several persons	Maximum of 8 years imprisonment
169(1)	Rape, i.e., sexual intercourse using physical or psychological force, or abusing the helpless condition of the victim	Minimum of 3 years imprisonment	153(1)	Sexual intercourse using physical force, threats, or intimidation, or with deception to abuse the helpless condition of the victim (rape)	Maximum of 5 years imprisonment

* The 1922 RSFSR Criminal Code's article 169 on rape did not include the rape of non-sexually mature persons as an aggravating circumstance. Such a crime could be punished under articles 166, 167 (if defloration or "perverse forms" occurred), or 169. Evidently legislators sought to clarify the situation by specifying the crime in 1926, in article 153(2).

household with a teenage daughter took advantage of their proximity to the object of the crime. Employers in town and countryside exploited their young employees, and teachers could be accused of abusing the pedagogic relationship with secondary school pupils.[96] Fathers were not immune from violating their own daughters; while incest had no status as a crime in Soviet law, the rare cases when it was reported attracted zeal on the part of investigators, betraying an anxiety over the "perversion" of family relations.[97] Rapes by persons unknown to the victim are rare in this sample, perhaps reflecting reluctance in this age group to report a rape without corroboration by neighbors or work comrades, and thus risk the prospect of damage to reputation that could ensue.[98] Group rapes, more frequent in rural areas according to commentators in the 1920s, do not figure prominently in this sample, although one particularly savage and extended case of the sexual exploitation of a Komsomol member received newspaper coverage in Sverdlovsk in 1929, drawing parallels with the infamous 1926 Chubarov Alley trial in Leningrad.[99] Police investigators sought to illuminate the social context of the sexual assault so that they could establish the credibility of the complaint. Experts familiar with rape cases pointed out that victims sometimes reported the offense for dubious motives, with disputes over alleged promises of marriage being a primary source of rape claims that masked a history of previously consenting relations with a partner.[100] One of the key tasks of police investigators was to unravel the relationships between rapists and their victims to reveal what jurists called "the truth" *(istina)* of the crime—if one had been committed.

Soviet criminal legislation imposed on police investigators a matrix of implicit questions about the degrees of physical and psychological harm resulting from a sexual assault. (See Table 2.1.) The answers to these questions often determined the classification of the crime and the punishments that could follow. They also determined the kinds of medical expertise that were sought from examining doctors. While the governing legislation was comparatively brief, the relationships between the articles of the criminal code in fact allowed for many interpretations of a given case, as Table 2.1 illustrates. It was not uncommon for investigators and prosecutors to requalify a crime as they gathered and digested information. Multiple medical examinations of the same victim were often required to prove the newly classified offense. In ambiguous cases where teenage girls were the victims, the question of whether the girls had reached sexual maturity was normally a fundamental one, yet inexperienced or untrained police frequently neglected the issue. Other questions, focusing on the degree of harm inflicted, loomed largest in the minds of the authorities. Was the act accompanied by defloration, or had the victim previously "lived a sexual life?" Was the violation fully accomplished or had only an attempt been made? Apart from damage to the hymen, which was privileged in law by the status of "defloration" as an aggravating circumstance, did the assault or assaults leave any trace of physical harm on the victim's body? Was there evidence that the victim had offered resistance to her assailant? Had the victim attempted or committed suicide in the aftermath of the violation?[101] Questions about harm accompanying a sexual encounter enabled police to establish whether a crime had been committed, but the sexual maturity standard, the distinction between "sexual intercourse" and "rape," and the emphasis on "defloration" as the greatest harm inflicted on the person, implied varying penalties and potential confusion in defining the crime.

The Ambiguities of Female Innocence

On 8 December 1923, Minna Fidel', a 16-year-old Petrograd shop assistant, complained of attempted rape at the hands of her employer, Aleksei Tunenin. While working in his repair shop in the city's Central Market, she said that Tunenin came up to her from behind, and managing to lift her blouse and tear her underwear, "he began touching [her] sex organs, trying to insert his penis in them."[102] On feeling a "sharp pain," Minna ran out of the shop bearing her ripped underwear in her hands. She complained about Tunenin to a group of market stall-holders, all women, who reacted in a concerted fashion. One sent for Minna's mother and examined the panties for blood (none was found); another made the girl sit down and put a shirt between her legs. The women gathered a crowd of passers-by, called Tunenin out of his shop, and escorted him to the nearby police station, where the complaint of rape was made. The progress of this case from the day charges were made to the resulting courtroom trial five-and-a-half months later illustrates how even police and prosecutors in one of Russia's capitals found the application of the law so problematic.

From the outset, the investigating officers qualified the crime as an attempted rape under article 169(1).[103] The police immediately arranged for a medical examination of Minna, which took place that day. Professor S. F. Proskuriakov, a specialist in venereology in a nearby hospital (not on the staff of the city's forensic medical bureau) examined her for evidence of rape. He found "a fresh, bleeding tear on the hymen, thighs smeared with fresh blood, no bruises or marks or other harm on the body." The hymen was still intact, and the cut was superficial. In his conclusion on 8 December he said that sexual intercourse had not taken place, and that there was no objective evidence of the girl having offered any resistance to Tunenin.[104] On 12 December, the criminal investigator working on the case commissioned a second examination of Minna, this time conducted by a forensic medical expert, Dr. A. A. Matushak, who pronounced her hymen intact and undamaged, and her body free of any abrasions or bruises that might indicate a struggle had taken place. A chemical examination of liquid found near the hymen (four days after the event) revealed no trace of sperm. His conclusion was even more unequivocal: "copulation (a sexual act) as such did not occur."[105]

Concerned that this official expert opinion obscured evidence found by the first examination, the criminal investigator interviewed professor Proskuriakov on 31 December. Proskuriakov confirmed his original account of Minna's condition on the day of the alleged crime. Satisfied that the case was strong enough to go forward, on 25 January 1924 the investigator forwarded an indictment to the procuracy for a decision to take it to trial. Only in mid-February did a prosecutor examine the case and realize that the criminal investigator had ignored the issue of sexual maturity. At no point had doctors been instructed to determine whether Minna had reached this threshold. The prosecutor sent the case back to the investigator with a lesson in the new Soviet penal code:

> Our legislation in the Criminal code of the RSFSR in the section "Crimes in the field of sexual relations" introduces, aside from the concept of majority, the concept of "sexual maturity" as well. From the materials presented in this case file this concept is not apparent, yet the qualification of the criminal action depends on its application. Thus if it is established that citizen FIDEL' Minna has not achieved sexual maturity, then it follows that citizen TUNINEN [sic] should be charged under articles 13 and 166 [of the Criminal Code]; in the opposite case, the charges you have made under articles 13 and 169 remain in force.[106]

The criminal investigator duly ordered a new forensic examination of Minna Fidel' "to establish the sexual maturity of the victim" on the date of the incident. Minna's third appearance before doctors took place on 27 February 1924 at the Petrograd forensic medical bureau under the guidance of Dr. Vera A. Degtiarova, a forensic gynecologist on the bureau's staff, in the presence of the criminal investigator and a woman acting as a witness.[107] Degtiarova concluded that "it is possible to consider that by 8 December 1923, citizen Fidel' had achieved sexual maturity," and as a result, the qualification of the crime as the attempted rape of an adult person (under article 169[1]) stood.

Degtiarova's medical opinion significantly ascribed sexual majority to the 16-year-old shop girl Minna, who was deprived of the protection afforded by articles 166 and 167 by the gynecologist's determination. Rather than proving attempted sexual intercourse, the criminal investigator now had to demonstrate that a violent act of intercourse had been attempted, and evidence from the first two medical examinations offered only the slimmest suggestion of a struggle: the blood and minor cut that Professor Proskuriakov observed on the day of the incident. When the case finally came to trial on 22 and 23 May 1924, Proskuriakov was present to confirm his observation, qualifying it by remarking, "I cannot consider myself an expert on questions of rape and I have never studied this question."[108] His expertise was thrown into question by courtroom testimony from Professor L. Okinchits, a gynecologist from the city's State Institute of Medicine.[109] The slight tear seen by Proskuriakov was difficult to credit since the forensic examination of the girl four days after the incident showed no evidence of an abrasion or mark on the hymen; it could not have healed (as Proskuriakov suggested) in such a brief period. If it had existed it could have been the result of "masturbation [or] by wiping with a rough shirt [referring to the shirt given by market women to Minna] or some kind of hard object." The most plausible explanation for the blood observed on 8 December 1923 was the onset of menstruation; Okinchits argued that "great intervals" between periods could occur when a girl began to menstruate, and the court found this explanation convincing. Noting that Degtiarova's report quoted Minna as saying that she had begun menstruating in February 1924, the court arrived at its own chronology of Minna's irregular first periods, the first on the day of the alleged rape, and then a second, two months later. It used this inference and "the integrity of the hymen that does not display any signs characteristic of rape or attempted rape" as the basis for its acquittal of Tunenin.[110]

Before examining how various medical experts conceived of sexual maturity, it is worthwhile considering in this example the manner in which the concept was ignored, resurrected, and deployed by the actors in Minna Fidel's case. Typically, even when the sexual maturity of a given victim should plausibly have been investigated (if, for example, the girl was under 18 but over 12 or 13 years of age), the first examination she normally endured was to establish evidence of rape or defloration, and to detect signs of violent struggle. Cases from Petrograd show that low-level criminal investigators, and the doctors and midwives who furnished medical opinions, did not spontaneously ask if victims of this age group were sexually immature and thus protected from any sexual interference whatsoever. Knowledge of the new Soviet penal code was patchy and partial. Like the criminal investigator of Minna Fidel's claim, officials on the ground needed to be prompted by better-trained prosecutors to seek medical expertise about the possibility that the victim of the crime under investigation was in a sexual sense a "minor."[111]

These jurists intervened not solely to ensure that girls and young women were afforded the full protection of Soviet penal justice, although the intent of the sexual maturity standard was to save youngsters from any contacts during a formative period of their lives. Particularly in ambiguous cases with little evidence of a violent struggle, legal officials also called for determinations of sexual maturity to settle whether the victim was entitled to consent to sexual initiation. In doing so they called the victim's moral character into question, implying or directly arguing that the victim's claim against the accused rapist was in bad faith. In 1923, in one Petrograd case of intercourse and defloration with a sexually immature person (article 167), the complainant Valentina Sokolova, 17 years old, was herself finally charged with making a false accusation for gain when prosecutors evidently reinterpreted her story and the medical evidence gathered to support it. A lodger had initiated a sexual relationship with Sokolova at the age of 13 in 1919, and only when her parents became aware of the liaison four years later was a complaint made to police.[112] Typically, the first medical opinion (furnished on 26 June 1923 by the central Forensic Medical Bureau) followed police directions to report on "the condition of her sex organs and the time when she lost her virginity"; the police assumed Sokolova was or had been a "minor" and did not raise the issue of sexual maturity. Commenting in passing on her physical condition, the two examining doctors mentioned her labia majora were "not fully developed" but later said her breasts were of "conical form, very well developed." They concluded that Sokolova had lost her virginity "long ago and it is even possible that this was four years ago," and that she had frequently had intercourse since then; they made no declaration about her sexual maturation, evidently because they had not been asked to do so.[113] Perhaps a month later, a second forensic examination of Sokolova was sought, this time specifically to determine the timing of her sexual maturation. The opinion, furnished by Dr. A. A. Ogievich, a forensic expert nearing retirement (he qualified in Warsaw in 1884), failed to state precisely when Sokolova had reached maturity.[114] When suspicion turned against her, prosecutors argued that she had indeed been sexually adult by 13, when she had first consented legally to defloration and intercourse. Now it was argued that she had tried to extort "a significant quantity of goods" from the lodger in exchange for dropping the complaint.[115]

Police, medical experts, and prosecutors displayed a range of conceptions about what should constitute sexual maturity. As the legal lesson from the Petrograd prosecutor in the case of Minna Fidel' suggests, many officials at lower levels took little notice of the new, biological threshold for sexual citizenship and continued instead to think in terms of an age of majority.[116] There is more evidence of an enduring focus on age in the Sverdlovsk sample of cases from 1926 to 1929, surprising since by then the demanding biological standard of sexual maturity had been in force for several years. Yet the isolation of many settlements and the ignorance of the law on the part of local midwives and doctors who examined victims as well as on the part of police investigators who commissioned these medical opinions contributed even in the late 1920s to the on-going significance of the age of the victim. In 1928 in the remote settlement of Saraninskii Zavod, a criminal investigator, district physician, and a trade union representative, all men, examined a deaf-mute victim of rape and agreed that "according to physical and spiritual [*dukhovnoe*] development" she was over 15 years old.[117] On this basis the court accepted that she had reached "sexual maturity," confusing chronological and biological criteria. Effective witness testimony and medical evidence of her very recent loss of virginity convicted the young man who raped her and a teenage girl accomplice who led the deaf-mute victim into this danger. In rural Russia the idea of "sexual maturity" had evidently made little impact. Other Sverdlovsk-region cases show that outlying police or courts eventually did request a determination of sexual maturity, and medical experts furnished extremely brief opinions that appear to have been founded almost entirely on the age of the subject. In such cases the tsarist age of majority, 14, was the threshold usually upheld by these officials and doctors.[118]

Many more cases illustrate officials' focus on biological criteria to determine when sexual maturity began, and reliance solely on menstruation might still have occurred even in the late 1920s. As Minna Fidel's Petrograd case demonstrated, the onset of first menstruation could be a key factor used by prosecutors and courts to define whether a girl was free to consent to intercourse. Yet when forensic gynecologist Degtiarova examined Fidel', menstruation was just one of a range of signs of maturation applied by this expert.[119] In Sverdlovsk region, with its relatively isolated and deprived settlements, some district physicians and officials thought only of menstruation when checking for sexual maturity in teenaged victims. Mariia Tiagunova, a 13-year-old raped repeatedly by her peasant father, was examined at least twice in April 1928 by district physicians in Verkhne-Ufaleiskii Zavod, over one hundred kilometers from the provincial centers of Sverdlovsk and Cheliabinsk. The first examination confirmed the girl's lost virginity; her sexual maturity only became an issue sometime later in a second examination. A doctor at that time wrote that Mariia "had achieved sexual maturity (first periods [*kraski*] started about ½ a year ago)."[120] Here the appearance of Mariia's periods and the onset of sexual maturity were identical in the blunt formula presented by this physician.

Yet higher-level officials and doctors in the Sverdlovsk region were unlikely to agree that the onset of menstruation was a sufficient criterion on its own to define sexual maturity. The complaint of Serafima Zhukova against a well-off peasant in equally distant Rezhevskii district eventually attracted the attention of Sverdlovsk city justice officials, a smart defense advocate, and a leading gynecologist for this reason.[121] In 1925, Zhukova, an illiterate 13-year-old from a poor peasant household went to live with 20-year-old Mikhail Golubtsov as a nanny to his children and an extra pair of hands in his large and comparatively well-off peasant household. In July 1926, Golubtsov took Serafima haymaking in the forest, and while resting he exploited their isolation to rape the girl, depriving her of her virginity. The next day Serafima complained to village police and was examined for evidence of rape at the local hospital. She returned there for a second examination two months later. Doctors could not agree about Serafima's sexual condition; the first gave the opinion that she was "a minor" on the basis that she had only begun menstruating a week ago, while the second pair of doctors concluded rather vaguely that she "is in the period of [sexual] maturity," saying that Serafima's own account of her periods confirmed this. They wrote, "sexual maturity is determined by the moment of appearance of menstruation."[122]

It took three months, but in December 1926 a senior prosecutor in Sverdlovsk wrote to the Rezhevskii district prosecutor to complain about this limited definition of sexual maturity. The accused peasant Golubtsov had petitioned that he had witnesses to the fact that Serafima had menstruated before "the sexual act," implying that she was legally entitled to consent to intercourse and defloration. The Sverdlovsk prosecutor advised that further investigation of the indicators of maturity in Serafima's case, and the timing of her menstruation, were necessary to close a file now stalled in the investigation stage.[123] In January 1927, the Rezhevskii people's investigator obtained a "supplement" to the second medical opinion from the same hospital doctors, who argued that while menstruation "is not the sole indication of sexual maturity in woman, yet from the medical viewpoint it is a highly characteristic indication determining this." They restated their conclusion about Serafima's sexual condition at the time of their September examination, but now in more precise terms that suggested a wider range of criteria: "On the basis of an examination of the external and internal sex organs and other correlating indicators (breasts, general configuration [of the body]) we conclude that citizen Zhukova has not yet achieved sexual maturity."[124]

Progress toward a resolution of this case was slow. In March 1927, the

Sverdlovsk division of the Urals Provincial Court assumed control and summoned a forensic gynecologist for advice.[125] The record of his or her recommendations was not retained in the case file, but the transcript of the trial of Mikhail Golubtsov, held in an open session in Sverdlovsk district court on 1 June 1927, shows that one of the leading gynecological specialists of the region, V. G. Peretts, attended as an expert witness and answered questions from both the prosecution and defense.[126] The impartial performance of Peretts in the court illustrated in miniature Chief Forensic Expert Leibovich's ambitions for the forensic doctor as a social diagnostician.

When Serafima Zhukova testified, Peretts was invited to question her, and he asked if she had menstruated before and after the event. "Before that time, once before in the spring [of 1926] I bled (menstruation)," the transcript reports her saying with a clarification perhaps supplied by the court secretary. Serafima then said that after the event "bleeding [*kraski*] appeared in the autumn." Peretts then asked the girl if at that time she had any hair on her body; she responded saying there was not much hair "on my stomach" and also only a little under her arms. Proceedings were adjourned so that Peretts could examine Serafima privately "to determine her sexual condition at the present time, and about her possible sexual condition at the moment of the rape, i.e., had she achieved sexual maturity."[127]

Peretts also received a series of written questions from Golubtsov's defense advocate about sexual maturity and in particular the relevance of two witness statements confirming that Serafima Zhukova had already been menstruating before the sexual act occurred.[128] Peretts evidently examined the girl and wrote his response to the advocate questions during the brief recess in the trial. The gynecologist's written answers were also included in the trial transcript and offer a revealing backdrop to his careful pronouncement that "[a]t the very least she was already at the onset of sexual maturation" when the crime took place.

Peretts began with the assessment that Serafima was presently mature "in a sexual sense," and he listed a range of secondary and primary sex characteristics to support this judgment. He mentioned her "well-developed breasts, hair covering her pubis and underarms," and he noted that her external and internal sex organs were "partially developed." In response to one of the advocate's questions, Peretts supplied his own composite definition of sexual maturity: "Appearance of menstruation, often viewed as a sign that ovulation is taking place at the same time (the process of maturation of eggs), the appearance of hair growth on pubis and under arms, accumulation of fatty layers on the thighs and a general rounding out of the form, growth in the breasts."[129]

It was a definition that was similar to those appearing in forensic medical textbooks and manuals by this time. Peretts was also aware of the geographic and class dimensions of sexual maturation. Again in response to questions put by Golubtsov's defender, Peretts stated that sexual maturation began "in the girls of our region" at ages 11–13 years in city-dwellers and 13–15 among peasant girls. Maturity could and did sometimes occur before age 14. Peretts concluded that the appearance of menstruation in Zhukova some months before July 1926 (at age 14) was an indication of the onset of sexual maturity. Evidently Serafima Zhukova had matured at about the correct moment for a peasant girl of the region, and while menstruation figured prominently in this well-informed assessment of her condition, it was by no means the only factor.[130]

The opinion of Peretts persuaded the court to accept defense arguments for requalification of the crime, from the violation and defloration of a sexually immature person (article 151[1]) to the rape of a sexually mature person (article 153[1]), with a corresponding reduction in the potential sentence, from eight to five years' maximum in prison. The court still issued a relatively severe sentence of three years six months deprivation of liberty, pointing out that Golubtsov had used physical force to commit the crime and implying too that his position as Zhukova's employer enabled him to put her in a defenseless position.[131] The court resisted any suggestion that her biological maturity necessarily implied a right of sexual access, emphasizing how Golubtsov had physically subdued the girl who refused consent but in the forest had no means at her disposal to offer effective resistance.[132] Significantly, Sverdlovsk city prosecutors and experts imposed their understanding of sexual maturity, as more than merely a matter of first menstruation, on this case from an outlying district.

A composite definition of female sexual maturity was well established in Petrograd by 1924, with forensic bureau staff experts such as the gynecologist Degtiarova furnishing "textbook" opinions covering a subject's physical development, state of nourishment, breast growth, hair coverage, genital size and pigmentation, and reported onset of menstruation.[133] By the end of the 1920s in the Sverdlovsk region, it was primarily urban doctors like Peretts who were most likely to apply similar standards when quizzed about the sexual maturation of teen victims of sexual assault. Yet even as late as 1927, Sverdlovsk city's chief forensic medical expert, N. K. Bazhenov, could resist the application of such a composite physiological definition of sexual maturity when the subject was under the old tsarist age of protection of 14. In that year he issued a determination in one case that acknowledged a range of physiological indicators of maturity but dismissed them since the girl in question had not yet turned 14.[134] Bazhenov's 1929 forensic-medical manual for police and investigators laid out a similarly age-centered understanding of sexual maturity even if his own expert opinions showed, on occasion, more sophistication.[135] In this manual he perhaps was attempting to square the circle, making a difficult biological standard simple for nonphysicians to implement in their criminal investigations. In one opinion based on a trial-recess examination of Klavdiia Gileva, Bazhenov used anthropometric calibrations to assess the rape victim's physical development, and a typical composite of physiological indicators, to establish that the 15½-year-old had reached sexual maturity. In this case, Sverdlovsk region judicial authorities took over responsibility for the proceedings from rural investigators and summoned the forensic expert to attend the trial and provide on-the-spot expertise where outlying officials had failed to apply the sexual maturity standard.[136] Even in the late 1920s, isolated and ill-trained police investigators and medical practitioners in Sverdlovsk region did not approach these crimes asking whether the victim had achieved sexual maturity as the law required.[137] In such circumstances the dissemination of a more sophisticated, composite model of sexual maturity beyond the offices of a handful of well-informed Sverdlovsk city gynecologists and forensic experts seemed a distant prospect.

Since Soviet legislation substituted the biological standard for an age of sexual protection for young persons, the physical development of teenage victims complaining of sexual assault could be closely associated in prosecutors' and some doctors' minds with the moral condition of these victims. Youngsters with well-developed bodies attracted more scrutiny of their behavior for evidence of having "lived a sexual life." In their opinions, doctors seldom made statements referring to the morality of the subjects they examined, confining themselves to ostensibly "objective" information. Doctors in Nizhnii Tagil Hospital in December 1926 wrote of one 13-year-old victim they examined:

> the subject citizen Mazurina Anna at the present time has fully achieved sexual maturity; there are no indications that her defloration is recent, for the reason that citizen Mazurina with regard to her sexual condition has already been living a sexual life for several months. It is not possible to establish the ages of the persons with whom she lives a sexual life.[138]

Such dispassionate language relieved medical experts of responsibility for passing moral judgment on their subjects but inevitably led people's investigators and courts to decisions with unambiguous moral intent.

It was clear to prosecutors in the case of Anna Mazurina that her sexual behavior provoked doubts about previous medical opinions that deemed her merely "in the period of sexual maturation, but that has not yet been achieved" as a doctor opined just a month before the Nizhnii Tagil doctors' verdict. Mazurina's spontaneous appetite for sexual play with boys of eleven, and full sexual intercourse with at least one man of eighteen, was "an abnormality for her age in the sexual sphere" that was impossible to ignore.[139] Mazurina complained that she had been raped by 18-year-old Nikolai Vorob'ev in June 1926, losing her virginity on that occasion, but because she was found to have had intercourse since that time voluntarily with a "series" of sexually mature partners including Vorob'ev, it proved impossible to establish who was responsible for taking her virginity. The people's investigator sent the case to be quashed after four months of inquiries and four medical examinations of Mazurina.[140] The prosecutor's ascription of "abnormality" in the "sexual sphere" may have hinted at his intuition of an inborn defect, perhaps the amplification of libido thought by sexologists of the era to be typical of degeneration. Prosecutors viewed her apparently self-directed sexual career as a function of her sexual maturity.[141]

In a similar case, however, the sexual immaturity of 13-year-old Iuliia Rybakova in the Urals town of Pervoural'sk indicated to people's investigators and jurists that Rybakova's extreme sexual behavior was the result of external influences.[142] Having been sexually initiated by visitors to her crowded communal flat, Iuliia was repeatedly forced by her alcoholic mother to have relations with strange men, probably for payment. Ultimately four men and two women (Iuliia's mother and the landlady who facilitated these visits—again, probably for cash) were charged with various offenses relating to the "corruption of her morality." The severest penalties were reserved for the landlady who had profited from Iuliia's exploitation and the man who had taken her virginity; all others eventually were released on amnesty five months after their trial. The "utterly corrupted" Iuliia's later trysts with two younger men were not regarded as "socially dangerous" since the damage (defloration and with it, moral corruption) had already been done; these men received suspended sentences.[143]

Iuliia Rybakova's sexual behavior appears to have come to police attention because of a neighbor's testimony about the girl's "having become greatly corrupted" at the hands of the adults in her life.[144] These cases reveal a significant degree of social monitoring of maturing girls' sexuality. Concern for reputation was a significant motive when parents or guardians launched complaints of sexual assault, as well as a motive for seeking medical confirmation of the "sexual condition" of teenage daughters, as Dr. Leitman of Saratov had pointed out in 1925.[145] In sex crime cases from Petrograd and Sverdlovsk, disputes over the facts of the case often turned on the reputation of the victim. Medical evidence saved or destroyed reputations. Procedural rules required that an investigation of a sexual crime go forward even if the victim withdrew her complaint. In June 1922, 15-year-old Aleksandra Popova became embroiled in a contested claim of group rape, naming three youths between 17 and 19 years old as her assailants during wedding festivities in Storozhilovka village near Petrograd. Popova said the youths threatened to tell her aunt unless she agreed to sexual intercourse with them, but the young men said she willingly had relations with them. A week after the incident, Popova obtained a certificate from a village midwife that attested to the girl's loss of virginity and her "not entirely developed" body, while expressing sympathy for her "misfortune."[146] Seven weeks later the people's investigator conducting the inquiry sent Popova to the gynecological clinic of Petrograd's premier medical institution, the Military-Medical Academy, asking about her condition in greater detail. The clinic's director, Dr. Stefanovskii, was rather less sympathetic, contradicting on the basis of unstated "objective data" Popova's testimony that she had never menstruated, while observing that "the peculiarity of the form of her hymen" suggested she might not have been penetrated at all. This authoritative medical opinion encouraged the court to acquit the three youths on all counts; articulate but equivocal medical evidence undermined the complaint, and the midwife's declaration of loss of virginity. In Storozhilovka, rumors had circulated about Popova's sexual encounter with the youths, and Popova's aunt was likely responsible for launching this investigation and the consultation with the local midwife, evidently fearing her niece's loss of reputation. The outcome showed how biomedical science might prove a double-edged sword for protecting a girl's reputation.[147]

In two Sverdlovsk city cases, parent or guardian initiative launched rape investigations, apparently egging on people's investigators to pursue a case despite its weaknesses. In each example, the individuals bringing the case to the attention of the authorities evidently sought to save the teenage girl's reputation, yet in both cases medical expertise combined with poor police work led to results unsatisfactory to the accusers. In April 1927, Anastasiia Maslykova, a 14-year-old nanny, told a friend (after an interval of 24 hours) of having suffered attempted rape at the hands of her employer, the father of the children she cared for. A week later her guardian denounced the man to police, and a senior investigator advised lower-level officials to first ascertain Maslykova's sexual maturity.[148] Yet after a month this had still not been done, earning the investigator on the case a sharp reprimand about the delay and about accepting a denunciation of rape from individuals other than the victim herself. If a girl had achieved sexual maturity she was effectively supposed to complain for herself in the view of the police official who reprimanded the investigator; biological development determined moral responsibility.[149] In any event, Maslykova was not sexually mature, at least according to Dr. Bazhenov, whose forensic examination took place more than five weeks after the alleged assault. She was also presumably physically unharmed.[150] The fact of her sexual immaturity might have worked to Maslykova's benefit had it been established rapidly after the complaint, especially if corroborating evidence emerged. Yet after an interval of three months and having questioned Maslykova himself, the senior investigator sent the case to be quashed for lack of proof. Without medical evidence of harm, or witness testimony, the claim made on her behalf was worthless. Poor police direction of the investigation, including late and incomplete instruction of the forensic medical expert, allowed it to collapse.[151]

In the second Sverdlovsk case involving a contested reputation, the victim was just a year older, and Dr. Bazhenov deemed her to be sexually mature. In May 1928, Anfisa Arzhannikova went walking in a park with a girlfriend, and the pair accepted the offer of a paddle across the river Iset from three youths in a rowboat. Later they came ashore and strolled in the park's forest. What ensued is unclear given the variety of versions reported, but four days after the walk in the park, Anfisa's mother complained to police that one of the men had attempted to rape her daughter. Anfisa had disappeared that day and was not found until the afternoon of the next day, in the company of another strange man, having purchased a vial of vinegar essence, a drug popularly used for both douching and suicide.[152] Bazhenov examined the teenage girl very promptly after the claim of attempted rape, finding her hymen intact and her physical development and history of menstruation commensurate with a diagnosis of sexual maturity.[153]

Officials were divided about how to proceed with the case; evidently junior-level police and justice workers believed that the man, Katugin, 19 years old and a worker, should answer for a crime, and in the face of some dissent from the district prosecutor, these officials managed to obtain a conviction for attempted rape. The prosecutor protested that Bazhenov's medical evidence revealed no trace of force used against Arzhannikova and argued that the girl's conduct was dubious enough to mitigate the offense.[154] In August 1928, the worker Katugin received a significant three-year prison term for the attempted rape. One of his boating companions was then immediately charged with being an accessory to the crime and was punished in December 1928 with a year's suspended sentence.[155] In the summer of 1929, a successful protest against these sentences by another prosecutor before the plenum of the Urals Provincial Court was based in large part on the lack of medical evidence of assault. The rest of

Katugin's sentence was annulled and he was released. Although not stated, Arzhannikova's sexual maturity evidently had an impact on prosecutors who protested against her case: she was viewed as morally responsible for her sexual conduct. The biological sexual maturity standard conferred moral obligations, and perceptions of a girl's reputation were influenced by her physical development.

It is difficult to gauge the extent to which laypersons understood the sexual maturity threshold, but one source for such perceptions emerges from these cases in the form of defendants' comments about their victims and their ability to consent, and also from official responses to the comments. Occasionally, well-informed defendants reveal their perceptions when questioned or in appeal documents. Naturally these narratives were told by men accused of a serious crime and do not necessarily reveal the "truth" about their motives, but they can be read as guides to beliefs about sexual permission and about the new biomedical standard. The Sverdlovsk lodger who engaged in a long-term sexual liaison with his landlady's goddaughter, 13-year-old Aleksandra Chernoskutova, described to a people's investigator (in interrogation in 1926) how medical evidence might have been used to staunch the flow of rumors about the affair:

> I advised [Kosykh, the landlady] to take Chernoskutova for a medical examination, but Kosykh delayed all the time, and only when the rumors really began to spread and Kosykh already had begun to believe that they clearly and supposedly plausibly described my relations with Chernoskutova, did she begin to try to find out about it from her, saying that she would take her for an examination. I did not know anything about this and only heard about it from Kosykh's nephew, Tagil'tsev, who told me that Chernoskutova told him in the flat that she "had been used" [*ispol'zovana*] and that she had supposedly been raped by citizen Popovtsev, [a neighbor] living in our building in the summer of 1925, when Chernoskutova was living with him as a nanny. Then I heard that Chernoskutova went for the examination to a doctor and complained to the police.[156]

Evidently this defendant had in mind a request for medical expertise "from below" described by Dr. Leitman of Saratov. The lodger asserted when prompted by the investigator that sexual relations with Chernoskutova would be a crime, not giving a reason but evidently referring to her young age and supposed physical immaturity.[157] (It was in Chernoskutova's case that Bazhenov had resisted declaring her sexually mature because she was less than 14 years of age.) For other defendants, the inability of many girls to declare or reveal their exact age (in a society with few accessible written records and a high illiteracy rate) and the inability of investigators and courts to confirm their ages with documents was a grievance. One convicted rapist in Petrograd complained in 1923 that his "'victim'" had been believed by police and investigators to be just 12, but then admitted in court to being in fact 16, one of a series of facts that might have been interpreted "in my favor."[158] Two youths charged with sexual intercourse with the sexually immature but "utterly depraved" Iuliia Rybakova in 1927 in Pervoural'sk were given suspended sentences because this court acknowledged that they were unable to recognize that Rybakova "was still in a state of not having achieved sexual maturity."[159] They were the exception to a general rule in these cases of rape and sexual intercourse with teenage girls; police investigators and prosecutors demonstrated virtually no anxiety about whether defendants could recognize the sexual maturity standard. Yet defendants appealed to alternative views of appropriate sexual access to teenage girls when they argued that social factors such as perceptions of age and physical development, awareness of menstruation, or evidence of sexual experience were justifications to sexual access.

The Simplicity of Male Sexuality

These cases contain very little explicit reflection of concern about the sexual maturity of young men, despite the fact that many defendants were in their teens and thus well below the definitions of ideal masculine sexual maturity presented in Soviet medical literature. Virtually no one dealing with cases of teenage male sexual aggression asked if these youths had achieved sexual maturity. The notorious "simplicity" of the male sexual function and its primitive pleasure imperative were unquestioned axioms when cases of intercourse with persons not having achieved sexual maturity were investigated. Only infrequently were sexual criminals examined by doctors to prove that they were physically capable of committing the crime. These examinations focused on somatic factors such as overall constitution, sex organ development and size, and reflex functions.[160] In the entire sample of sexual crime cases for Petrograd and Sverdlovsk, only five cases of assaults on boys (all by older youths or adult men) are found, and these reveal a particular view of sexual agency that ignored the physical development of the "victims" but focused instead on the problem of male socialization and, occasionally, male prostitution. In none of the same-sex cases were questions asked about whether a young victim was sexually mature and free to consent to sex "in perverted forms."[161]

In the few cases of heterosexual intercourse or rape that resulted in examinations to determine the sexual maturity of younger male defendants, exceptional circumstances led to this application of forensic medical expertise. In an unusual Petrograd investigation of 1924, two young men, a 17-year-old Komsomol student and a 20-year-old metalworker, had the famous defense advocate A. F. Koni pleading their case, which may account for the decision to bring the youths before a full forensic-medical commission for examination.[162] The commission, including the gynecologist Degtiarova, applied a range of physical criteria to establish the young men's sexual "development" (the word maturity was not used), focusing on their build and constitution, the development of their sex organs, and the cremaster reflex. Following a list of questions presented by the people's investigator, the forensic experts declared that these youths were "sufficiently physically and sexually developed to have intercourse and to commit defloration."[163] The young men were convicted in part because this examination established their ability to commit the crime; traces of the force they used on their 18-year-old victim were also detected by this same forensic team. Their social origins and excellent advocate were responsible for the court's leniency, as their rape yielded a one-year prison sentence for the older worker and an even lighter suspended sentence for his 17-year-old accomplice.[164]

The case of Anna Mazurina, the 13-year-old rape claimant investigated in the years 1926–1927 for "abnormality for her age in the sexual sphere," also involved the medical examination of four of her male partners to establish their sexual maturity. Two boys were 11, and two were 18 years of age. A junior people's investigator, Riabov, commissioned expert opinions on the boys and youths, apparently confused by how to qualify the crime. When a senior prosecutor reviewed Riabov's work on the case, he slated it for qualifying the offense under the wrong criminal code article; a new people's investigator took over the inquiry.[165] This prosecutor said nothing about the expertise conducted on the four males, but the new investigator clearly had little regard for the expertise on the 11-year-old boys. Dr. Aleksandr Nikolaev, forensic medical expert in Nizhnii Tagil and chief physician of the town's First Soviet Hospital had issued an opinion that might have been medically plausible but was ambiguous in moral and practical terms: "they have not achieved sexual maturity because it is not possible for them to have sexual intercourse. Arousal of the sex organ may have occurred."[166] The previous day he had conducted examinations of the boys and wrote that "no signs of sexual maturity were observed. In sexual terms they are undeveloped."[167] Although Dr. Nikolaev said nothing on the tiny scraps of paper certifying his expertise about how he arrived at these opinions, what stands out in his statements is the contradictory tension between mechanistic functionality ("arousal of the sex organ") and biological undevelopment. How was it "not possible for them to have sexual intercourse" yet possible to achieve an erection? Nikolaev was trapped between a medical view of sexual maturity as a composite physiological process (in these boys, an incomplete one) and the policeman's understanding of ability to commit a specific type of crime.[168] The doctor's contradictory phrases slipped from a biological innocence to a moral one, and this view was rejected by the new people's investigator on the case. In February 1927, the new investigator argued for the case to be dropped, commenting on Nikolaev's judgment that "a person having a sexual connection at the age of 12 years [sic] has sexual arousal and may have sexual intercourse." It was thus not possible to establish who had taken Anna Mazurina's virginity, because any of the four protagonists might have been capable of it, and no other evidence linked the crime of defloration to a specific youth.[169]

Junior investigator Riabov's clumsy handling of this case, with its redundant expert opinions about male sexual maturity, stands in stark contrast to the overwhelming majority of sex crime cases in this survey. Police routinely presumed that teenage boys and young men were entirely capable of committing sexual acts and assaults. (It was perhaps only under pressure from defense advocate Koni that Petrograd authorities considered sexual maturity in the 1924 case against two worker-rapists.) The perceived simplicity of the male sexual function found its reflection in a systematic presumption of sexual potency and even arousal. Boys, teenage youths, and young men were sexually alert beings possessed of supposedly uncomplicated physiology. The silence on male sexual maturity in these cases is a resonant one, throwing the sexual development of boys and youths back into the sphere of culture, morality, and social control.

Conclusion

When considering the misery and confusion that the sexual maturity standard generated for teenage victims of sexual crime, and the authorities who investigated it, Leibovich's tart comment that "the term `sexual maturity' is imprecise and unsuitable in legislation" seems bitterly apt. Parents discovered that pleas for the restoration of a daughter's reputation rested upon the successful passing of obscure medical tests. Victims were frequently subjected to repeated medical examinations, some of them extremely intrusive and often performed with policemen and male witnesses present. Doctors lacking the necessary training were often required to conduct these inspections without adequate guidance from people's investigators, and physicians themselves seldom had training appropriate to this specialized role. Failing to take the initiative in these cases by educating people's investigators about the sexual maturity standard, local forensic experts seldom rose to Leibovich's challenge to become diagnosticians of society. Police investigators were remarkably ignorant of the sexual majority standard in Soviet criminal law, and lacked a basic understanding of how forensic experts defined and recognized it. The criminal codes with their brevity on sexual crimes were surprisingly difficult to apply in practice.

Doctors on the ground generally had to arrive at quick determinations of sexual maturity without the luxury of forensic gynecological training or the leisure to survey medical literature on this issue. In Petrograd and Sverdlovsk, their expert opinions did nevertheless broadly follow the assumptions about gender and class that permeated the professional literature. Fundamentally their work translated the sexual maturity standard into a biological template against which girls and women were measured. District physicians and local forensic experts did not indulge in elaborate anthropometric inspections of individual sex-crime victims, in contrast to the researchers who espoused such materialist approaches to the issue. Yet the focus on a girl's physical development, on the presence of a modest range of primary and secondary sexual characteristics, on the moment of first menstruation, and on the question of defloration, fetishized the female body as the source of "truth" about sexual maturity and thus sexual citizenship. Female sexual maturity was a productivist concept that classified girls and women according to their reproductive functionality. Still, at this important conjunction of medicine and law, female sexual maturity also operated as a moral concept that defined who was entitled to protection from sexual abuse, who was entitled to make decisions about "living a sexual life," and who suffered from "an abnormality for her age in the sexual sphere."

The biomedical threshold for sexual citizenship deprived individuals of easily accessible knowledge about their own transition to adulthood. It imposed a collectivist standard on the individual that could only be assessed by specialist expertise—hence the resort to medical examinations even in marital disputes or rows about a girl's bad reputation. By elevating defloration to an aggravating circumstance in these crimes, the sexual maturity standard assisted in the sorting of girls into the innocent and the ruined. Instead of consigning the "wrapper of virginity" to the dustbin of history, Soviet criminal law and the forensic expertise that served it had the effect of sustaining patriarchal surveillance over the hymen. Virginity acquired a modern, Soviet, "wrapper."

Perhaps the most tragic impact of the biomedical threshold for sexual citizenship was the popular ignorance that accompanied it. Nowhere in Soviet legal or medical literature of the 1920s was the question of explaining the meaning of the sexual maturity standard to the population ever addressed. In the popular press (so far as I can judge) sexual maturity was seldom mentioned as such; when crimes under the relevant criminal code articles were reported, the victims were described as "minors" and age was the implicit criterion that justified the protection afforded them by Soviet law.[170] Yet there was no age of consent or age of protection, and so there was no universal, socially recognizable boundary between what might be permitted and what was forbidden. Soviet girls and women would appear to have paid a heavy price for the absence of this clear boundary.

THREE

SOVIET MEDICINE AND RAPE AS A CRIME OF EVERYDAY LIFE

Did Russia's revolutionaries actually believe that rape would disappear as a crime under socialism? Despite the claims of some historians, such utopian sentiments are difficult to find in the writing of jurists and experts confronting the daily effects of this crime.[1] Leading ideologists did not consider rape a problem worthy of extended consideration. The Marxist tradition linked the rape of women to conflict between men over property. Early party ideology implied that rape was somehow a "relic of the past" or a "depravity" reflecting bourgeois man's proprietorial view of women. Amid the violence of revolution and civil war, rape acquired a rich penumbra of metaphorical political meanings, but the physical violation of actual women attracted far less ink.[2] As the emergency subsided, Bolshevik jurists writing the Soviet Russian criminal codes of 1922 and 1926 described rape in blunt terms that gave no clues to its ideological significance. The very first drafters of Soviet criminal law appeared to believe that men's sexual violence against women would be a constant feature of social life.[3] Observers commenting on the Soviet understanding of this crime agree that the authorities did little to investigate the gendered foundations of sexual violence in Russia.[4]

The Bolsheviks' lack of interest was mirrored by historians who have not extensively investigated Soviet views about rape. Eric Naiman's study of the Chubarov Alley gang rape in 1926 Leningrad is the only sustained exploration of revolutionary and early Soviet ideas about rape in recent historiography.[5] For Soviet officialdom, Chubarov Alley became a landmark; Naiman dubs Chubarov "the year's—indeed, the decade's—representative sexual crime." Sensational newspaper reports resembling prerevolutionary feuilletons, hand-wringing commentaries from Communist luminaries, and show-trial staging were features of the prosecution of the Chubarov rapists. This was no routine trial, but a political test of strength between Politburo factions, with Stalin and Bukharin condemning Zinov'ev and the Leningrad leadership for poor stewardship of the city's Komsomol and workers. In party thinking, the Chubarov episode also represented a disturbance of the tenets of the New Economic Policy. Demoralized worker-youth, confused by the ambiguous messages of this "transitional" period, sought to recapture the heroic violence and masculine bravado of the civil war era, or were lured away from Communist values (however they might be defined) by the attraction of petty-bourgeois pleasures such as drinking, gambling, and indiscriminate sex. The exemplary sentences handed down in December 1926, including five death penalties implemented in January 1927, greatly exceeded the penalties normally attached to gang rapes. Prosecutors justified this by requalifying the crime not merely as rape but as a form of banditry dangerous to Soviet law and order. In the Chubarov case the collective aspect of the crime was its most sinister element in the official view.[6]

The Chubarov gang rape was an exceptional one for the publicity it received and the political significance the party assigned it. Soviet authorities did not normally give rape this degree of attention. In the day-to-day administration of justice during the 1920s, rape was investigated without Chubarov-style press publicity and politicization. As with assaults against the sexually immature, rape investigations were often poorly conducted by police, investigators and the courts. The character of the crime, and the gender prejudices of the authorities, gave rape investigations specific features that distinguished them from other types of sex crime casework. Forensic medical experts participated in this work and brought with them a long heritage of medical views of rape that underwent surprisingly little revision despite the sexual revolution. Medical expertise in rape investigations reinscribed gender norms in powerful new ways. By examining Soviet legal and medical views of the rape of adult women, the role of the medical expert in its ideal form can be sketched. It is then possible to look at some actual investigations of unambiguously "sexually mature" victims, to trace the patterns of practice that expert doctors adopted in the postrevolutionary era. A significant determinant of medical practice was the distinction between a victim claiming loss of virginity and one who had been "living a sexual life." As in the vexed question of sexual maturity, the forensic medical contribution in rape investigations often concentrated attention on victims' bodies, and the moral conclusions to be drawn from a reading of the "objective signs" found there. In their interpretations of rape cases, medical experts displayed mistrust and even disbelief in female sexual autonomy.

Legal and Medical Routines

The penal codes of 1922 and 1926 were comparatively clear about the meaning and significance of rape as a crime "in the field of sexual relations" (see Table 3.1). In contrast to French law, which evaded an explicit definition of "rape" until 1978, revolutionary Soviet legislation offered an explanation of the crime (as sexual intercourse using force) accompanied by a broad definition of the kinds of coercion that rapists might use.[7] The absence of consent to intercourse was "the essence of the crime," two Ukrainian lawyers said. Soviet jurists emphasized the novelty of recognizing "psychological force" as being of equal gravity to physical assault when considering the crime.[8] Psychological violence was "no less dangerous" than physical force and demonstrated the advanced thinking of Bolshevik legislators, who were said to appreciate the "social helplessness" of modern women seeking a foothold in waged work and public life.[9] The difficulty for Soviet authorities investigating rape was, as in other jurisdictions, in distinguishing from the often scant evidence whether consent had been given or denied, and whether force had been used against the woman making a claim of rape.

It is probably not possible, given the fragmented and disaggregated condition of the sources, to provide an accurate statistical account of the prevalence of rape in 1920s Soviet Russia. The social history of rape in Soviet Russia still needs to be written.[10] As will become apparent in this chapter, it is difficult to say what compelled women to report a rape to the police, and to pursue an accusation through the Soviet justice system. For women with party connections or in unionized employment, making a complaint to the women's department of the Communist Party (Zhenotdel) or to their trade union could be alternative routes to a form of justice.[11] What does seem clear is that sexual violence against women had increased alarmingly since the beginning of the century. Statistics focused on reported cases and primarily on convictions, the last stage in the long and often interrupted process of criminal investigation. In Moscow province from the second quarter of 1924 to the third quarter of 1926, convictions for rape constituted the "overwhelming majority" of convictions in sex crime cases at 65.4 percent.[12] The total of reported "sexual crimes" in Sverdlovsk province in 1927 and 1928 exceeded 1,750 each year. If as in Moscow province, the proportion of rapes to other sex crimes in these figures was about two-thirds, reported rapes in Sverdlovsk province alone for these years were running at about 1,150 per annum.[13] Criminologists reported that the number of sex crimes recorded nationally was on the increase in mid-decade. Data assembled from the police and the central statistical directorate reportedly showed a total of 9,521 recorded sex crimes in 1925, and 8,198 in just the first three

TABLE 3.1

Rape Definitions, 1922 and 1926 RSFSR Criminal Codes

1922 Article	1922 Description	1922 Penalty	1926 Article	1926 Description	1926 Penalty
169(1)	Rape, i.e., sexual intercourse using physical or psychological force, or abusing the helpless condition of the victim	Minimum of 3 years imprisonment	153(1)	Sexual intercourse using physical force, threats or intimidation, or with deception to abuse the helpless condition of the victim (rape)	Maximum of 5 years imprisonment
169(2)	Rape, resulting in suicide of the victim	Minimum of 5 years imprisonment	153(2)*	Rape of a person not having achieved sexual maturity, rape resulting in suicide of victim, rape of a person by several persons	Maximum of 8 years imprisonment

* The 1922 RSFSR Criminal Code's article 169 on rape did not include the rape of non-sexually mature persons as an aggravating circumstance. Such a crime could be punished under articles 166, 167 (if defloration or "perverse forms" occurred), or 169. Evidently legislators sought to clarify the situation by specifying the crime in 1926, in article 153(2).

quarters of 1926.[14] Although the source is unclear, this figure would seem to reflect the total for actual convictions. As such, it represented a huge increase, perhaps as much as tenfold, in the number of convictions for sex crimes compared to the last peacetime tsarist years.[15] This huge increase in convictions for sex crime may be explained partly by the relatively low rate of full convictions secured by tsarist courts, and by the disorder and brutalization of the 1914–1921 period. Undoubtedly, low rates of *reports* of rape characterized tsarist society until the very last years of imperial rule. The huge increase in reports during the 1920s may also reflect an increased willingness on the part of "emancipated" Soviet women to launch, and pursue, rape claims, and a belief that justice might be available from the revolutionary legal system.

Local people's courts heard all rape trials in the first instance, and only thereafter did some defendants appeal their sentences to the Supreme Court. The RSFSR Supreme Court reviewed the rape convictions (specifically under article 169) of approximately 1,000 men in 1925 and

2,000 in 1926. These figures for appeals alone suggest that convictions for rape, at the primary judicial stage, were already running into the several thousands in 1926.[16] Nationally, the average sentence for rapists was two years six months' imprisonment; as with other crimes, judges were directed to inspect the class credentials of the convicted rapist before fixing the sentence, and the low average tariff for rape suggests they did so indulgently. Nevertheless, only some 10 percent of rapists who appealed obtained a reduction or annulment of their sentence, while the Supreme Court confirmed the vast majority of original sentences.[17]

These statistics can only give an impression of the scale of the most persistently pursued instances of sexual violence. Advice to police, criminal investigators, and lower courts regarding rape trials, and archival records of investigations, show that these figures were the tip of an iceberg concealing an unknown but sizeable quantity of rape claims that failed or went unrecognized. Cases were dropped because of a lack of evidence or because (as in cases of sexual assaults on minors) information emerged that compromised the victim's claim that she had refused consent to intercourse. The Sverdlovsk provincial procuracy, reviewing the work of local courts for 1925, condemned prosecutors in Cheliabinsk for allowing a rape complaint by one Zabolotina against a citizen Pereskokov to come to trial. By the time the judge heard the case, the parties had married and were reconciled; the bemused court gave the new husband a three-year suspended sentence. The Sverdlovsk procuracy deemed that "inasmuch as Zabolotina had become the wife of the accused" the case should have been abandoned during the pretrial investigation, or when prosecutors ran a final check before sending cases to court.[18] Of 868 cases of "sexual crime" handled by the Sverdlovsk province's police force during the first half of 1928, 184 cases were quashed at the preliminary investigation stage: 142 for lack of evidence of a crime and 42 for other reasons, such as reconciliation of the parties.[19]

"Did Copulation Really Occur in This Instance?"

What particular expertise did forensic doctors bring to the Soviet rape investigation? Textbooks and manuals written by leaders in the discipline of forensic medicine focused almost exclusively on the search for physiological, not psychological, evidence of violation. In this they differed very little from tsarist manuals.[20] A Sverdlovsk medical manual for police investigators put it bluntly: "Did copulation really occur in this instance? Was violence employed? Did defloration occur[?]"[21] The emphasis was on what the Saratov forensic gynecologist, L. B. Leitman, described as "objective data": physical injury, bruising and scars, damage to the hymen, and similar clues on the bodies of victim and perpetrator that a violent assault had taken place. By contrast, the testimony of victims was to be approached with extreme skepticism.[22] Whatever the "revolutionary" value of including rape using "psychological force" in the penal code, forensic experts were reluctant to lay claim to specialist knowledge about the psyche of the rape victim.

In this matter, early Soviet forensic specialists followed a long-standing caution in tsarist textbooks and manuals that women's claims of rape were often motivated by malice or greed. The psychological aspect was beyond the competence of the physician and fraught with ambiguities best left to police and courts to judge. The earliest forensic medical textbook by a native Russian dealing with sexual crimes and conditions, Sergei A. Gromov's *Brief Exposition of Forensic Medicine* (St. Petersburg, 1832), noted that many women complained of rape to seek compensation for loss of honor *(beschestie)*, and to force the accused into marriage.[23] Vladislav Merzheevskii's imposing and influential manual of forensic gynecology (1878) editorialized at length about the unreliability of many claims of rape:

> the rape victim often relates how the accused 'lured' her into the hayloft, or that the criminal was only 'playing' with her at first, and then suddenly raped her, covering her mouth with his hands. With such testimony (and it occurs quite often) the question arises: surely an adult woman, belonging, as is often the case in such matters, to the lowest estate, understands why she is being lured into the hayloft, what the `game' with the young lad leads to, and finally could the criminal in attempting to rape the victim cover her mouth with both hands, or even one?[24]

Typically in Soviet forensic manuals, a similar attitude was transmitted via the catechistical device of the "controversial question" handed down across the revolutionary divide from earlier generations, with little or no attempt to supply a "Soviet" gloss. "Can one man rape a completely healthy, conscious and struggling young woman?" asked the nation's chief forensic medical expert Iakov Leibovich in a 1923 forensics manual. The answer cast doubt on all but the most violent encounters; only "if the man is very strong or in particularly favorable circumstances" (the use of a pillow to stifle the victim for example), might such a scenario be given credence.[25] Leibovich's more elaborate 1928 manual of forensic gynecology continued to uphold this line despite some concessions that "nowadays" the physical differences between assailant and victim must be considered. "Generally complaints of rape from adult women capable of resisting [an attack] require great caution and objectivity and very often are groundless."[26] As a token of how exotic a genuine rape of a healthy, conscious, and alert adult woman might be, Leibovich offered the example of a rapist "who trained himself using some of the holds of French wrestling, until he was able to hold down any strong adult woman in a position, convenient for coitus, that she would be incapable of escaping."[27]

As in cases involving questions about the sexual maturity of sex crime victims, police procedural reasons also influenced doctors to avoid the psychological aspects of the victim's claim. Any probing of the psyche of the victim risked straying into an analytical quagmire: female desire. Discipline-leading specialists in forensic gynecology evaded extended exploration of the desiring victim, rejecting psychoanalytic explanations of female sexuality. Psychological accounts of women's sexual behavior, by allowing for desire in the *victims* of sexual crime, threatened to make the forensic expert's and criminal investigator's tasks vastly more complex. The medical expert claimed he was leaving moral judgments to the police and the courts. In preferring indicators of physical harm in rape cases, doctors and the investigators who required their services relied on "materialist" evidence—bodies and their functions—that seemed to reduce the prospect of ambiguity, and lent an air of solid credibility to forensic opinions.

The activities and influence of forensic doctors in the "everyday" or unpoliticized 1920s rape investigation can be examined from court records of Petrograd (1922–1924) and Sverdlovsk province (1926–1929). Petrograd had a significant cadre of specialists, and the dedicated Forensic Medical Bureau of the city health department headed by Professor N. I. Izhevskii. Police resorted routinely to the services of these individuals in rape cases. In outlying districts of Sverdlovsk province, by contrast, local doctors were often given minimal direction from unschooled police investigators. Meanwhile in the city of Sverdlovsk, experts and investigators displayed greater familiarity with the importance and capabilities of forensic medicine in rape cases.

The chief difference between the two locales and periods in procedure is the activity of commissions of forensic medical experts in many of the Petrograd files. Here the ambition to bring a range of views to bear on the medical evidence and to produce a collective scientific opinion was realized. It also allowed senior experts in the province's Forensic Medical Bureau to direct and instruct junior colleagues. Any off-stage management of the process by, for example, criminal investigators in discussion with Professor Izhevskii, is not evident in the written record. However, it seems likely that heavy-handed guidance would not be necessary; an experienced forensic expert would quickly observe from the investigation file and circumstances any interpretations that police were already applying to the case. Professor Izhevskii frequently chaired the forensic commissions, and the bureau's staff gynecologist, Vera A. Degtiareva, usually attended as well.[28] By contrast, in Sverdlovsk province, even later in the 1920s, investigators rarely obtained medical expertise from collectives of specialists. The lone expert was the rule. Sverdlovsk by this time did have a bureau of forensic medical expertise (led by N. K. Bazhenov), but it evidently had few dedicated staff members; instead, expertise was obtained by drafting in specialists as required from local hospitals, maternity clinics, and psychiatric facilities. As in cases of "sexual maturity," the quality of that expertise varied considerably.

"Now I am a Lost Person"

In 1927, chief judge Nikonov of Ivanovo-Vosnesensk province had expressed a socialist's dissatisfaction with the penal code's emphasis on defloration, and what he dubbed the "wrapper of virginity," as the primary locus of damage in sex crime cases. Innocence was for socialists a moral, not a physical, quality, he argued before one of Leibovich's joint conferences of jurists and forensic medical experts.[29] Although Nikonov was referring to the sexual violation of minors, his point resonates with the way that police, forensic experts, and the courts dealt with the rape of adult women. The "wrapper of virginity" was the point of departure for any official person confronting a rape claim, whether the investigator was a humble midwife *(akusherka)* in a village medical station, a militia duty officer taking down the details of a claim of violation from a victim, or a commission of forensic experts composing a typewritten "act of expertise." Paradoxically, the focus on physical virginity was not mandated by the law on rape. In contrast to statutes on sex with minors, the criminal code articles dealing with rape said nothing about defloration as an aggravating factor. Yet the question of whether a woman had lost her virginity was a key one in rape investigations, showing that cultural and social considerations motivated individuals in these dramas as much as legal ones might.

Indeed, women who lost their virginity as a result of rape in the Soviet 1920s spoke bitterly about their loss and they (and often their families) pursued their claims vigorously. Avant-garde notions that physical "innocence" was a mere primitive fetish, an atavism on the verge of dissolving in the face of a "sexual revolution," had limited currency even inside party structures. A Komsomol member wrote to police in the following terms about her experience of rape:

> and at the moment he threw himself on me like a beast, I asked him what are you doing, he did not spare my virginity [and] raped me, I ask the court to investigate my case and bring Zuev to responsibility, now I am a lost person [and] I ask that this burden be taken from me; I attach to this complaint a certificate from the doctor; [signed] N. Oshchepkova.[30]

Oshchepkova was not alone in feeling herself to be a "lost person"; her girlfriends in the Komsomol cell, to whom she immediately revealed her misfortune after it happened during a party near Sverdlovsk, understood instantly that she had lost something of value and they acted to help her in her claim (in this case, against a fellow Young Communist of a cynical cast). The women advised her first to seek a medical certificate and then to report the assault to police. Oshchepkova appeared four days later in a small town hospital with a letter from a Komsomol leader commissioning a medical examination for evidence of rape. Her loss of virginity confirmed, the next day, doctor's certificate in hand, she formally denounced Zuev to the police. The conviction that physical virginity mattered was shared up and down the country by parents who sent their daughters to forensic experts for "certificates" *(spravki)* confirming intactness or documenting damage to the hymen—not only in formal rape claims but often to pressure a young man into keeping a promise of marriage or to restore a young woman's reputation among neighbors and co-workers. Saratov's Leitman denounced what she called a "primitiveness of mind" that fetishized the hymen and drove women to debase themselves once they had "perished."[31] Women who "lost" their "innocence" after rape sometimes attempted suicide, so deep was their sense of annihilation. So indelibly written in the script of rape in Russia was the tragic turn to self-destruction that Soviet law mentioned the suicide of the victim as a particularly grievous outcome with harsher consequences for the rapist.[32] Despite the extraordinary freedom of the Soviet "sexual revolution," a woman's physical virginity continued to matter intensely to ordinary Russians.

It also mattered to police investigators trying to reconstruct the events surrounding claims of sexual assault. Soviet jurisprudence did not accept a woman's rape claim on its own merits, but demanded substantiation in material evidence and witness testimony, when available. If the putative rape victim was young and unmarried, even the humblest militiaman understood dimly that a medical examination was part of the evidence-gathering routine. Yet police and even more senior criminal investigators in the provinces seldom knew what questions they ought to ask of the expert. They gave raped women chits bearing laconic instructions telling the expert to provide an opinion on "sexual intercourse" or to conduct an "examination for clues" without any further elaboration; it was not unusual in Sverdlovsk province for the victim to be sent to a doctor or midwife without an official, written request at all. The response from the doctor could be equally terse. On one side of a slip of paper addressed to the "Sovhospital duty doctor," a policeman in Nizhnii Tagil requested the conduct of "an examination of the bearer Citizen Nikonova Mariia Ivanovna . . . of her for sexual intercourse, give an opinion [*sic*]." The barely legible response was scrawled on the reverse of the same scrap: "During examination of citizen Nikonova Mariia Ivanovna a broken hymen, traces of blood in region of sex organs, on thighs and on blouse were observed."[33] CID investigators frequently found such evidence failed to answer basic questions such as when the victim had lost her virginity or whether other injuries or traces of a struggle were observed. Many rape claimants were sent to doctors for second and even third examinations as a result of poor instruction from police; doctors unschooled in forensic science did not always appreciate what data was required of them.

On the opposite end of the spectrum, Petrograd's forensic medical service produced exemplary "acts of expertise." Responding in 1924 to a request from the Petrograd police, a commission of three experts in the city's forensic medical bureau including Professor Izhevskii and the gynecologist Degtiareva examined 19-year-old Elizaveta Voskova and produced a typed report, extracted from the commission's hearings of a series of cases. It efficiently described the victim's account of the assault, and gave details of her general health and development (effectively indicating that the subject was sexually mature and therefore able to give consent to sexual acts). The examination turned directly to the condition of the hymen, describing its tears and bleeding in unambiguous terms, and noted, "A finger enters the vagina with difficulty and is surrounded smoothly by it. No traces of a struggle on the body." These details, combined with testimony from the accused furnished the key evidence to sentence Voskova's two assailants to four-year prison terms.[34] Whether the forensic expert was a country doctor furnishing the briefest of opinions, or part of a sophisticated city team of dedicated experts, in rape cases the "wrapper of virginity" was one of the principal factors in their deliberations.

This case also illustrates one of the techniques used by forensic medical specialists to arrive at a judgment about a subject's claim to have been a virgin prior to rape: the digital examination of the vagina. A woman's relative sexual experience was commonly said in the forensic literature to be evident by application of this digital standard, with no apparent concern for physiological or psychological circumstances that might lead to variations.[35] In an investigation against five Petrograd workers accused of raping 20-year-old Ol'ga Rubina in 1923, a forensic medical commission (with Izhevskii and Degtiareva) met just one week after the crime, examined Rubina, and determined that she had lost her virginity within the previous ten days in a struggle that left bruising and other physical indications.[36] Police doubted Rubina's claim to physical and moral innocence because the young woman had placed herself in an ambivalent situation. Rubina and a girlfriend went boating with the five workers and they were attacked on an isolated island in the Neva River.

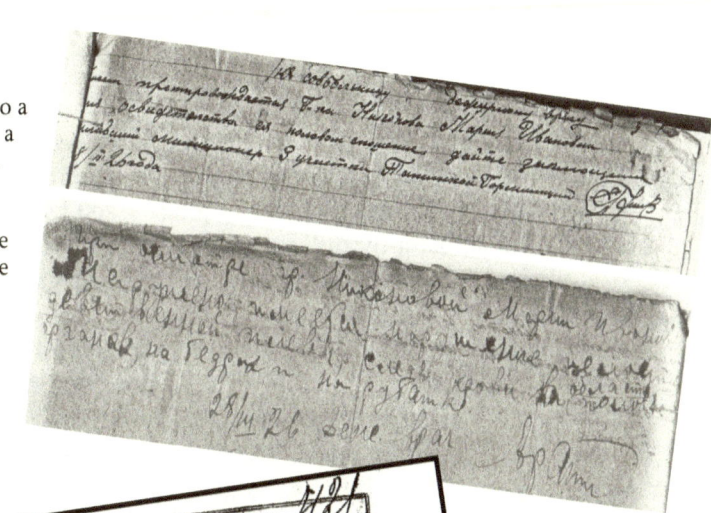

A policeman's order to a physician to conduct a medical examination of Mariia Nikonova, and the physician's expert opinion on the other side of the same slip; Nizhnii Tagil, Sverdlovsk Province, 1926. *Source: GASO 340/1/149/3–3ob*

A collective act of expertise regarding Elizaveta Voskova, signed by Professor N. I. Izhevskii, issued by Petrograd's forensic medical bureau, 1924. *Source: LOGAV 2205/1/1670/12*

The girlfriend put up sustained resistance and escaped on a barge, but Rubina's failure to escape was regarded with suspicion. Even with the forensic medical commission's conclusion confirming Rubina's recent loss of virginity, during the trial the judge asked gynecologist Degtiareva why Rubina apparently did not defend herself, and about the scientific grounds for stating that Rubina had in fact been a virgin before the crime. Typically uncomfortable with the psychological question, Degtiareva merely confirmed that trauma could account for Rubina's failure to resist, but she went into graphic detail based on textbook lore about the digital examination that demonstrated to the doctor's satisfaction the young woman's innocence.[37] Digital inspections of victims to confirm virginity were routine in the Petrograd sample of rape cases, and the use of specialized instruments to probe women's sex organs was probably common as well.[38]

Exemplary, "textbook" examinations for virginity could be conducted by well-trained experts in the Urals too. Sverdlovsk city's chief forensic medical expert, N. K. Bazhenov, taught in the region's School of NKVD Administrative-Police Workers and eventually wrote a forensic handbook in basic language aimed at the "lower administrative-police worker."[39] The rape case files in which he appears as lone expert in NEP-era Sverdlovsk show a degree of comparability with the deliberations of Petrograd's commissions of experts earlier in the decade. In a case of a naïve country girl duped by her new "friends" in the city, Bazhenov's extensive (but handwritten) "act of expertise" carefully notes the victim's physical development and describes the freshly damaged hymen and the condition of the vagina, which permitted entry of one index finger. He concluded that the rupture of the hymen had taken place within the past four days and that the digital examination indicated only one or two episodes of intercourse had occurred.[40] Yet such exemplary "textbook" inspections appear to be rare in the rape cases preserved in Sverdlovsk's archives. Small-town "sovhospital" doctors and midwives said nothing in their "certificates" about the techniques used to examine rape victims, giving laconic comments on the sex organs and implying that inspection was brisk and blunt, an interruption in a busy day.[41]

Whether in Petrograd or Sverdlovsk, poorly framed questions to doctors from the police often resulted in repeated examinations of victims or interrogation-style querying of the experts and their opinions. That criminal investigators so often had to return to the medical evidence even in confirmation of virginity cases indicates how casually the evidence was regarded and understood at the lower levels of the justice system. It also shows how complex the gathering of clues in rape cases could be, and how little such intricacy was anticipated by Soviet jurists when they framed a new legal order. In 1923, an apparently recent recruit to Petrograd's forensic medical services failed to say anything in his written conclusion about the timing of a victim's loss of virginity; police investigators sent the victim back for a second examination that would refer to the time factor in unambiguous terms. As a result, this 22-year-old's first experience of sexual intercourse was deemed to have happened "during the time period" under investigation. On the basis of the second expert report, a trial would have proceeded, but the victim and her "rapist" agreed to marry and the bride-to-be successfully petitioned to drop the case.[42]

Contradictory expert opinions in unusual circumstances also compelled investigators to commission more than one medical examination. In Petrograd with its rich network of experts, it was possible to recognize and diagnose rare sexual conditions, but more than one examination was necessary. In 1924, a Putilov Factory metalworker—in revolutionary myth metalworkers from this vast plant were the aristocracy of the proletariat—was convicted of raping a young woman who apparently retained her physical virginity after a first, consensual, encounter with him. An initial examination the day after the reported assault showed fresh scratches and abrasions to the victim's face and sex organs, yet her hymen was only grazed. Counterclaims by the accused that he had previously had sexual intercourse voluntarily with the victim were not entirely deflected in her ambiguous testimony. Three weeks later a CID investigator convened a forensic medical commission consisting of Professor D. I. Shirshov, a gynecologist at the city's prestigious Military-Medical Academy, Degtiareva for the city's forensic medical bureau, and a venereologist. The investigator put four questions to the commission, which examined both the worker accused of rape and the victim.[43] Doctors examined the worker Abramov to confirm that he was "sufficiently developed physically and in a sexual sense for the commission of sexual intercourse with defloration." Such inspections of the perpetrators of rape were comparatively rare; it seems likely that an element of class-based indulgence motivated the CID investigator's question. Turning to Abramov's victim, the forensic experts stated that based on the evidence of injury found initially, she had been subjected to "sexual intercourse with use of force on 31 July 1924." They confirmed that she had reached sexual maturity by this date—implying that she was capable of giving or refusing consent. Asked if it were possible that she had intercourse before this date without damage to the hymen, the doctors responded, "The anatomical structure of citizen Mariia Levitskaia's hymen permits the suggestion that she may have had sexual intercourse before 31 July 1924 (the opening of the hymen permits entry of a finger which is well enveloped)." In court the worker received a one-year prison term for the rape.[44] Rare cases of women who had experienced intercourse yet remained "virgins" were frequently discussed in pre- and postrevolutionary medical lore, and this learned group of experts was well aware of the phenomenon.[45]

Another source of repeated forensic examination was the discovery that specialist expertise was required. Petrograd's forensic expert commissions also deployed experienced specialists in psychiatry and venereology when circumstances called for a collective opinion that took advantage of recent scientific advances available to doctors. The rape of Pavla Pershina, a 19-year-old living with her aunt in a communal flat in June 1924, was investigated by a commission composed of two gynecologists, two psychiatrists, and an unspecified forensic expert. Taunted by Kulikov, a 19-year-old electrician living in the same flat, Pershina's aunt suspected that he had violated Pershina and she compelled her niece to raise a complaint. Investigators evidently suspected that Pershina had consented to intercourse (as Kulikov claimed) and for this reason requested psychiatric expertise about her mental as well as physical state. Any imputation of sexual immorality flowing from physical signs of degeneration was denied by the psychiatric team.[46] Signs of syphilis however were detected on Pershina's genitals, and both parties were subjected to a further commission of medical examination, this time including two venereologists. The second commission concluded that Kulikov's infection "is older in relation to the syphilis of citizen Pershina"; it declared that she caught syphilis from Kulikov "and not the reverse."[47] He was convicted of both rape and infection with a venereal disease, and sentenced to three years' imprisonment.

Even when loss of virginity was confirmed, police investigators were not automatically persuaded that rape had taken place. In Soviet legal thinking the crucial, moral, element of the crime was the refusal of consent to intercourse.[48] In successful rape prosecutions, police and courts had to be satisfied that the victim had demonstrated her refusal—either by virtue of getting witnesses to the crime (by crying for help, for example) or through resisting the rapist and leaving evidence of a struggle that could be detected on the bodies of the assailant or victim. In many cases, especially when the victim was in a remote setting or was silenced by force or threats, she might be unable to raise the alarm and attract witnesses. Doctors and CID investigators sought traces of a fight—bruises, scratches, blood blisters—and read these as evidence of the moral character of the victim, despite prospects that ambiguous or innocent explanations might be found for such marks.

Such light injuries healed within a few days and timely medical examination was necessary to gather the often crucial evidence. In the case from Nizhnii Tagil mentioned at the start of this section (and illustrated at the top of p. 93), an alert investigator sent Nikonova, a rape claimant, whose recent loss of virginity had just been medically confirmed, back to the doctor for a second examination on the day of the assault. In a note to the doctor, the investigator wrote, "the above-mentioned expert opinion [i.e., the first] raises doubt by not mentioning forcible external signs such as bruises, blood blisters on the body of the victim." The same hospital doctor noted minor bruises on Nikonova's upper, inner thighs and these allayed "doubt" about her sufficiently to produce an indictment mentioning the forensic evidence and leading to a trial.[49] By the time the case came to trial, just two months after the alleged rape, accused and victim had registered a marriage and the case was quashed after cross-examination of both parties by the judge. Nikonova explained in court that intercourse had been voluntary and that her mother had compelled her to raise a complaint.

In these new circumstances, it was accepted by all parties that the bruises and blood observed by the doctor in his two examinations the day of the "rape" were no more than typical traces of voluntary relations. Forensic medical literature before and well after the revolution observed the difficulties in distinguishing between evidence of a vigorous but consensual sexual encounter and rape. There was a long heritage, not challenged by the "sexual revolution," of viewing women's resistance to intercourse, and of the absence of female desire, as a natural feature of conjugal relations.[50] Nondesiring, "uncorrupted" women did not submit to intercourse without the application of some degree of necessary force, whether from a husband or a rapist, according to this logic.

"Citizen Repkina Has Been Living a Sexual Life for a Long Time"

It is therefore not surprising to observe that when a sexually experienced woman (who had "been living a sexual life" in the typical Russian phrase) made an accusation of rape, police investigators and forensic experts relied heavily on indicative bodily injuries as a key means of substantiating the claim. Successful rape prosecutions in these circumstances would usually also be founded on evidence provided by witnesses; as with the virgin rape-claimant's testimony, a sexually active woman's word about the rape she had endured was not sufficient to satisfy police, prosecutors, or courts. Yet in the case of the sexually experienced woman, injuries normally had to be relatively substantial to convince the authorities. Doctors, if consulted in a timely manner, furnished expert opinion that could be crucial in deciding a case.

A spring 1922 rape case considered in Petrograd province illustrates how difficult it was for an experienced victim to persuade investigators of her claim if there was no physical injury to confirm an assault. Mariia

Khorina, 18, a peasant in Zaluzhaia village, raised a complaint of rape against two young peasants after an incident occurred while a brigade of farmers was sorting potatoes. She had been dragged to a trench and assaulted; no one had apparently heard her cries for help, although one witness did notice her tears after Mariia returned to the potato store. Khorina's mother took her that day to a village medical station where she was examined by a paramedic, whose vague observations mentioned bloodied clothing and inflamed sex organs but nothing specifically about serious injury. It took two weeks for investigators to order a formal forensic examination, which was conducted in a hospital; again, it said nothing about serious injury but confirmed that the hymen had long been broken. "Thus even by means of the medical examination the fact of rape is not confirmed," wrote a senior provincial prosecutor, quashing the case as unsubstantiated.[51]

A similar story from Sverdlovsk province in 1927 shows that it remained difficult later in the decade to secure sufficient evidence to convict the rapist of an adult, sexually experienced woman. Mariia Repkina, 22 years old, a poor peasant, was abducted and raped on a road just outside her home village by an 18-year-old peasant, classified as moderately prosperous. The young man rough-handled her and used threats of violence to quell her resistance; when she eventually complained to police she was sent to the nearest medical station where she was examined "to establish rape." The doctor tersely reported "no indications of rape" were found. A month later an investigator sent questions to the doctor about details that were overlooked in his first certificate. The doctor replied that "no traces of injury in the region of the external sexual organs were present, and also there were no other indications of rape; citizen Repkina has been living a sexual life for a long time."[52] Only a confession by the attacker, secured in a face-to-face confrontation between victim and perpetrator (*ochnaia stavka*, a typical device of Soviet police investigations), satisfied a prosecutor that there was a case to answer, and the rapist was tried and sentenced to two years' imprisonment. In similar cases, forensic expertise, however elaborate, revealed no evidence of injury and offered little "substance" (in terms recognized by investigators and courts) to the claims of the sexually experienced woman.[53]

Vicious assaults accompanied by cruelty and indiscriminate violence could move doctors to depart from the dispassionate and laconic prose they usually cultivated in the expert report. Recognition of exceptional violence yielded convictions. The rape of 52-year-old Pelegeia Dmitreva by three hooligans in the village of Pinevka, near the town of Irbit, two hundred kilometers east of Sverdlovsk, was confirmed by one "forensic doctor" Pashintsev who described her injuries and "nervous mental depression" in a two-page opinion, just a day after the attack. Dmitreva's thighs, shoulders, and sex organs were bruised and scratches marred her face; the dimensions of these injuries were measured and catalogued. She had been choked to prevent her from crying out, as evidenced by the marks on her throat. Pashintsev concluded, "a rape has taken place here, accompanied by the use of crude force and insults."[54] The doctor's sympathy for the victim, and disgust for the primitive cruelty of her assailants, found expression in the extended data he amassed in a prompt and systematic fashion; its effect was to give scientific and moral weight to the relatively stiff four-year sentences each rapist received.[55]

Doctors did not need to resort to emotive language to suggest which rape claims they regarded as more worthy. Their training, as reflected in the forensic medical literature, informed them that victims who reported rape promptly and whose stories were straightforward, were more likely to be telling the truth. Claimants who made allegations long after the event, or whose stories were complicated by the murkiness of internal family disputes or quarrels over proposed marriage to the offender were to be approached with great skepticism. In their professional writing, doctors stressed the credibility of "objective" physical indicators of rape, which of course, were easier for them to document.[56] In this aspect doctors were conforming to the preferences of police investigators, who sought clarity of narrative and unambiguous motives from supposed rape victims, especially when there was no loss of virginity to offer as proof of violation. To be vindicated a woman had to act decisively and with exceptional presence of mind. Victims of rape in these circumstances were wisest to report the crime immediately and to enlist quickly the help of bystanders who could be used later as witnesses; there were few cases of this type, suggesting that victims, like doctors and police, understood that without "objective" evidence their rape claims would not be followed up by authorities.[57]

Although the concept of "psychological force" in rape was highlighted in Soviet jurisprudence, in the everyday rape investigation police and courts did not regard medical experts as the appropriate judges of whether such force had been used. In cases where the rape victim was sexually experienced and showed no evidence of beatings or injury, doctors might well recognize the victim's psychological trauma, but they seldom mentioned it in their acts of expertise. Aleksandra Morozova, the wife of a Petrograd policeman, who claimed she had been raped by another policeman while her husband was himself under arrest for theft, had not been physically injured but subjected to "mental violence" in the words of the prosecutor summing up the case.[58] She was examined by staff experts Degtiareva and P. P. Aksakov of the Petrograd forensic service in January 1924. Neither the relative novice Degtiareva nor the more seasoned

Aksakov were ignorant of the trauma suffered by rape victims, or the circumstances of this case, yet their act of expertise concentrated on the physiological "condition of her sex organs" alone. The assessment that "mental violence" had compelled Morozova into a sexual relationship with her husband's colleague was in the hands of the prosecutor and, ultimately, the judge, who disallowed the claim.[59]

Medical experts were part of a system of investigation that did sort people, often arbitrarily, into worthy and unworthy victims, and rape claims were a lightning rod for this systemic moral triage. An attempted gang rape in the town of Krasnoufimsk (Sverdlovsk province) of Agrafena Novak, wife of a railway worker, in 1928, illustrates how even a tersely worded medical "certificate" *(spravka)* could become a linchpin when the victim of rape became embroiled in a wider social conflict over her reputation. On 18 August 1928, Agrafena, returning home from a party and reportedly swaying from drink, was set upon by three men (all metal workers at the same depot as her husband, and all three of them Communists). They attempted to rape her but were disturbed by passersby. Agrafena told her brother and husband about the attack within twenty-four hours, and was referred to a district clinic for examination on 20 August. A certain Dr. Iakovlev confirmed her bruises "on right and left upper extremities," on her inner thigh, and under the right eye; he indicated that these marks should be considered for presentation to the court as "light injury" *(povrezhdenie legkoe)*. He said nothing in his "certificate" about Agrafena's sex organs or her claim of rape (although Agrafena later said she told him about the rape). Evidently, a childless 27-year-old married woman was presumed to have long been "living a sexual life," and Dr. Iakovlev regarded her sexual condition as self-evident. Her claim of sexual assault was not an "objective" sign of rape, and thus not worth recording in his assessment.[60]

Agrafena's husband seized the certificate and kept it so that he could apply for a divorce. According to the court's sentencing document, "She only turned to the Zhenotdel for help on 6 September, because the most incredible rumors and jokes were circulating about her and her husband Frants Novak." With considerable energy she tracked down the rumormongers and gathered evidence against her attackers; when Frants Novak divorced her and threw her out of the house, he gave her back the medical certificate. Only then, a month after the assault, convinced she needed the certificate before a charge would be considered, did she go to the police and lodge an official complaint. By this time her reputation was in shreds and it may be that the Zhenotdel refused further assistance, for there is no more evidence of their involvement in this case.[61] Agrafena's attackers were convicted of rape, and given relatively stiff sentences, on the basis of the medical certificate of "light injury" and the testimony of witnesses. On appeal, however, their crime was requalified to attempted rape, and their sentences were considerably reduced. The decision of the appeals court rested on the witness testimony indicating that the gang had been interrupted before rape could be carried out. The initial prosecution had incorrectly qualified the crime.[62] The prosecutor's apparent oversight was compounded by this typically circumspect medical opinion that failed to record any examination of the sex organs and said nothing about the subject's own claims and motives. Novak's drunkenness and lack of an escort in a public place after dark made her a morally ambiguous victim.

The arbitrary moral filtering of rape victims with a sexual past could work to protect them as well, and medicine could be mobilized to serve the cause. In another gang rape investigation conducted just months earlier in the environs of Krasnoufimsk, medical expertise about an adult woman who had been "living a sexual life" contributed to a case that was eventually heard in an exemplary hearing on International Women's Day (8 March 1928).[63] The protagonists were all peasants from an outlying village, Potashki, and the crime followed a harvest-party in September 1927, with home-brew and dancing. The victim, Aleksandra El'kina, had been scolded for dancing by a man with whom she had been "close (even sexually close)" according to the indictment; he beat her and she left for home. She accepted the offer of an escort from Nikolai Ponomarev who in fact organized the crime. When they set off "a gang of lads fell upon her." They covered her mouth to prevent her from screaming and took her to an isolated bath hut. On the way they beat her, slapped her about the head with turnip leaves *(vkatali v golovu travy repaia)*, apparently hoping this would terrify her without leaving marks. The men took turns raping her, remaining silent to disguise their identities; then "they left her there on the spot unconscious." El'kina reported the rape when she regained consciousness the next morning.[64]

The following day she underwent the first of three forensic medical examinations; in a single sentence the Potashki village doctor confirmed the extent of facial bruises and a light injury to her right cheek. A second doctor, this one in a district hospital, examined El'kina "for bodily injuries" two days later and took more time to describe her condition. While in general it was satisfactory, he confirmed her facial bruises, noted that El'kina reported pain "in the lower part of the stomach," and assessed her as displaying a "slightly reduced . . . work capacity" as a result of her injuries. At least a week later, the Potashki village doctor saw El'kina again, this time to examine her "in relation to the sex organs." It was impossible to detect evidence of violence to her sex organs, he wrote, as her hymen had been broken for a long time; there was no bruising caused by hands holding open the thighs or choking the neck, signs characteristic in rape.[65] The case file does not record the thinking of police investigators as they commissioned these successive forensic opinions, yet the sequence indicates a typical pattern. The initial concern in rape cases where virginity was not an issue was to document physical injuries as evidence of a struggle. In this sequence the second, more elaborate opinion from a hospital doctor mentioning work capacity *(trudosposobnost')* was designed to underscore the serious nature of the damage done to this victim and the loss to society of her economic contribution. The final opinion, apparently in response to specific questions, demonstrated an investigator's awareness of the more arcane signs of rape and suggests that at this time CID workers were running the investigation.[66] By the time of the trial a narrative appropriate to the Women's Day holiday had been composed. A woman's right to "live a sexual life" without fear of patriarchal violence was made clear in the indictment and affirmed in the stiff exemplary sentences handed down in court.[67]

Conclusion

However revolutionary a woman's right to "live a sexual life" seemed in the 1920s, the ways in which everyday rapes were investigated by police and medical experts did much to reconstitute patriarchal relations and constrict women's sexual autonomy. As in more "conservative" countries, early Soviet routines of gathering evidence trained attention on the female victim and her moral character. Soviet forensic experts, following the policeman's cues, seldom turned to examine the perpetrators of rape, nor did they normally imagine that such examinations would yield relevant "objective" data. A systemic presumption of male sexual potency dictated that the average perpetrator of rape need not be examined on this account; only in extraordinary instances of somatic or mental illness were men the subjects of expertise. The focus on the victim as the repository of signs was not merely commonsensical or pragmatic. The focus on the sexually receptive partner was also a symptom of the enduring view of this sexual posture as "feminine," as nondesiring when behaving respectably, and as subject to a necessary measure of force in order to make intercourse possible. The receptive partner was the object of social control and scrutiny across a gamut of social relations. As in the construction of "sexual maturity," the feminine was held to be problematic and the masculine, uncomplicated.

Physical virginity, not mentioned in Soviet law on rape, remained at the heart of forensic medical attention in rape cases for a cluster of social and cultural reasons. Sexual innocence was a social construction, and physical virginity remained its primary signifier, conveyed through village and urban society by reputation and rumor. It was symptomatic of the limits to sexual revolution that only a tiny handful of Soviet authorities who were engaged in the routines of rape investigation could see and denounce the "primitiveness of mind" that dealt in such signifiers. Effectively, doctors who proposed to replace the flawed knowledge about a woman's innocence or experience based on hearsay with the incontrovertible "objective data" of medical examinations of sex organs, dealt in the same signifiers, giving an ancient taboo a new gloss of scientific authority.

The "refusal of the psychological," a reluctance to explore the interior world of the rape victim, showed the forensic profession's unwillingness to challenge the discourses of sexual innocence and corruption associated with this crime. Bigger forces beyond the forensic discipline contributed to the refusal too: the widespread discomfort with Freudian psychoanalysis in the Soviet medical profession, and the instantly ideologized controversies that were ignited when individual sexual desire was explored in NEP literature and party debate. Even the positive Soviet sexology of enlightenment for sexual health displayed professional nervousness about extended discussions of sexual psychology. Moreover, police investigators and courts demanded clarity of expertise, and they viewed excursions into the desiring subjectivity of the rape victim as dangerous detours from such clarity. In both investigations of "sexual maturity" and of the adult victims of rape, Soviet forensic practice was a significant contributor to the silencing of desire even during the "sexual revolution."

In the quest for scientific authority, forensic experts sought to purge their practices of moralizing language and indeed deferred to police and courts as the proper judges of the moral facts of a case. Dispassionate medical certificates and extracts from "acts of expertise" grounded experts' claims to be "judges of the scientific facts." In document after document, doctors carefully reiterated their acceptance of a boundary between medicine and justice. Professionally, the performance of objectivity was a logical strategy for establishing and consolidating the revolutionary gains for the status of the medical expert. In a real sense, the dry language of medical certificates and acts of expertise was a performance. Forensic experts communicated to each other in different registers. When doctors spoke to their colleagues in forensic manuals, conference papers, and journal articles about the everyday rape investigation, they did not eschew moral judgments but warned each other instead about the dilemmas they confronted. Could a healthy adult woman be believed if she claimed to have been raped by a man acting alone? Where did the boundary between "normal, vigorous" and "coerced" sexual intercourse lie, and was it discernable? What kinds of rape narrative are most likely to be false? How can a doctor know if a woman is telling the truth? In posing such questions to each other, forensic experts implicitly recognized that they were embedded in a regime of moral distinctions, and that their "scientific judgments" were implicated in that regime.

FOUR

DOCTORS OF THE MIND AND SEX CRIME

At the beginning of the twentieth century, Russia was not perhaps a country with a normal psychiatric profession, if by "normal" we mean something similar to what was then found in Germany, France, or Austria. In these lands, a significant proportion of doctors of the mind practiced privately and served a middle- and upperclass clientele. To be sure, during the nineteenth century the psychiatric profession in central and western Europe had established itself by caring for the insane of all classes in asylums erected by the state. Optimism about psychiatric medicine prevailed after revolutionary France's Philippe Pinel "liberated" the madman from his chains, and the English John Conolly proclaimed the therapeutic value of "nonrestraint" for the asylum patient. Asylums grew in number, and size, across the continent. They acquired a very real role as places of confinement for the awkward and maladapted that was not, however, balanced by a genuine ability to cure the insane. A century of clinical experience and research in psychiatry yielded no equivalent to the rapid advances in sanitation and bacteriology that, by 1900, had conferred such power over disease on other branches of medicine.[1]

By 1900 many leading European psychiatrists had abandoned the disappointments of asylum medicine for the more alluring prospect of private practice. These trendsetters turned their attention from those affected by extreme mental illness (schizophrenia, psychosis, and major nerve disorders) to patients whose problems were of a lesser order. In the private clinic and consulting room, individuals suffering from neuroses, neurasthenia, and from various kinds of "borderline" psychopathic disturbances were now examined and treated using the new tools of psychological medicine. Sigmund Freud, his couch, and his bourgeois patients became the iconic symbols of this new approach. Freud's psychoanalysis was partially constructed upon three decades' development of a new science, sexology.[2] In the last quarter of the nineteenth century, another Austrian, Richard von Krafft-Ebing, laid the foundations of sexology, the modern medical understanding of sexuality and sexual disorders. Krafft-Ebing's greatest work, *Psychopathia sexualis* (first edition, 1886; final, twelfth edition, 1902), was the first major scientific catalog of the varieties of "sexual psychopathy." Historians have pointed out how Krafft-Ebing made the transition from asylum manager to director of a private clinic, and how the clientele furnishing the raw material for his construction of sexual psychopathy correspondingly changed from indigent and criminal subjects to more affluent individuals, including people of higher social standing than the psychiatrist himself.[3] Krafft-Ebing's catalog of sufferers, from those who exhibited the "contrary sexual instinct" (homosexuality), to fetishists, sadists, masochists, and others, expanded from edition to edition as literate patients recognized themselves in the pages of this first sexological manual, and sent their life stories to the author for interpretation and publication. The modern medical taxonomy of sexual disorder was the product of a dialog between articulate patients and an enterprising psychiatrist.

In late tsarist Russia, psychiatrists were attuned to these developments, but the institutional environment and its discontents focused attention on weightier questions than the cataloging of fetishists and the soothing of neuroses. Russian psychiatrists were few in number (only 350 practiced in the entire Russian Empire in 1916), and they drew their principal sources of income from employment in asylums, hospitals, and university clinics; only just before 1914 did a significant proportion begin to turn to private practice.[4] The tiny size of Russia's middle class accounted for the limited extent of psychiatrists' nonstate income. Most psychiatrists labored in provincial government *(zemstvo)* asylums, and a very large proportion of their patients were the seriously mentally ill, often, the criminally insane brought to the asylum by police or confined there by courts. The leading Stalin-era historian of psychiatry goes so far as to claim that Imperial Russia's first doctors of the mind learned their craft primarily through such police work.[5] His assertion is exaggerated, but it points to the most painful question that the Russian psychiatric profession of this era faced. The profession, a creation of government health and education reform policies of the mid-nineteenth century, generally had by the end of the tsarist regime an embittered relationship with authority. Conflicts over the committal of patients, over the presence of police and jailers in asylums, and thus over the profession's claim to autonomy based on medical expertise were at the center of this antagonism. The defining question for psychiatrists was, "Who runs the asylum?" The state's answer was equivocal, but its administrative and judicial orders forced zemstvo psychiatrists to admit "dangerously insane" offenders, sometimes accompanied by armed guards, to their premises. The use of manacles to restrain these "patients" persisted and apparently even expanded after the 1905 Revolution. In the aftermath of 1905, political prisoners were sometimes confined to asylums for the insane as a form of preventive custody; psychiatrists lacked the political traction to do more than protest in their conferences at such abuses. (Even those conferences were the subject of heavy-handed police surveillance.) Psychiatrists' conception of their expertise as a form of medicine was severely tried by a regime that seemed determined to utilize psychiatric facilities as an extension of the prison system.[6] Imperial Russian psychiatrists, especially those working closest with the justice system, looked forward to the day when state arbitrariness would be replaced by a rational law-based legal system, one that would accord psychiatry a larger share of authority in the treatment of the criminally insane.[7]

In Russia's specific social and political conditions, the peripheral question of psychotherapy to treat the disorders of "minor psychiatry" (neuroses and the maladjustments of everyday life, including sexual disorders) gained the attention of doctors of the mind later, and less securely, than in central and western Europe. The rise of various strands of psychotherapy in late Imperial Russia has been described by historians of Russian psychoanalysis, and by cultural historians who look beyond Freudian approaches to other forms of the talking cure. The latter point out that in a political system in which literature necessarily served as the most significant public space for the exchange of ideas, novelists Leo Tolstoy and Fedor Dostoevsky did as much to herald the prospects for psychotherapy as the psychiatrists who analyzed their literary work. Indeed, as Irina Sirotkina has demonstrated, the "psychographic" genre—the medical analysis of an author and his work—became a characteristic way for Russian psychiatrists to establish their credentials as psychotherapists.[8] By such means the psychiatrist reached the literate public, displayed his diagnostic skills, hinted at therapeutic solutions, and additionally, commented on the moral and mental health of the nation.[9]

Russia's endangered sexual health became an important part of the psychiatric agenda in the late tsarist era, under the influence of the reception of sexology and psychotherapy. Krafft-Ebing's *Psychopathia sexualis* was first translated into Russian in 1887, and Russia's own Krafft-Ebings imported its diagnostic nomenclature into the Russian language during the 1890s. New translations of the twelfth edition appeared as censorship relaxed and the pace of developments in psychotherapy took off after 1905.[10] Sexological knowledge and the techniques for acquiring and disciplining it began to circulate beyond the psychiatric profession. In the wake of 1905, officers and army chaplains anxiously considered the benefits of the new sexual science for bringing unruly cadets' masturbatory and homoerotic impulses under control. Educators contemplated an apparent surge in youthful sexual disorder, and looked to medical experts for guidance.[11] The language of sexual psychopathy rapidly moved into politics, and as Evgenii Bershtein notes, "The Krafft-Ebing concept of `sexual psychopathy' became a convenient rhetorical and conceptual weapon in the arsenal of leftist radical and revolutionary journalism."[12] The diseases of sexual excess, of misdirected desire, and of sexual violence took on an immediate political taint in the hands of radicals: homosexuality, sadism, fetishism, and masochism were the province of a degenerate exploiting class, an aristocracy declining into physical irrelevance, along with its helpmate, a gendarmerie addicted to sadism. "Politicized with extraordinary swiftness" in the last years of tsarism, the idea of sexual psychopathy in Russian hands was, in Bershtein's view, an instrument "not so much for the deployment of a new regime of power, as for the destruction of the old social and political regime."[13]

The psychiatric profession was nevertheless the source of the new language of sexual disorders, a new language that it hoped to apply to concrete examples of the problem.[14] The profession's ability to propound this language in tsarist courts was always limited by the reluctance of authorities to accept mitigating psychiatric testimony. It is likely that before the 1917 Revolution, few criminal trials were held with supporting expert psychiatric evidence using the new model of sexual psychopathy.[15] Psychiatrists based the model, as propounded before and after 1917, on a fluid combination of biological and social factors that shaped the human personality. Degeneration was a fundamental root cause of sexual psychopathy in Krafft-Ebing's account. For Russian mind doctors, who were normally predisposed to assign more weight to the influence of environment, hereditary degeneration was still often the soil upon which disorders of sexuality were said to grow.[16] Degenerate subjects experienced an early and intense onset of sexual feeling and often as a result, they prematurely initiated a sex life. From this physiological beginning, behavioral anomalies reached pathological proportions. Impulsiveness, an unbalanced moral sense, deviousness and malign desires, and emotional instability could be combined with an apparent ability to function normally in society. Such subjects, like all psychopaths (the sexual variety was just one of many types psychiatrists identified), often passed as normal, but they episodically gave way to desires that healthy people rejected.[17] In 1912, V. P. Serbskii (1858–1917) described typical sexual psychopaths as "people who [may be] married, with families, who are mentally developed, but who from time to time commit pederasty or experience an unusually strong urge to bestiality, intercourse with small children, necrophilia or some other manner of deformed activity."[18] Another form of degenerate psychopathy was age-related: old age brought a weakening of the moral sense combined with a late flare-up of sexual urges, often corrupted by a lifetime's accumulated cynicism. Exhibitionism and sexual abuse of children and youth of both sexes were frequently perpetrated by degenerate middle-aged and elderly men. Psychiatrists contended that such individuals might be sick, not bad, and ought to be closely examined by experts before courts decided whether they should answer for their crimes.[19]

Bringing the Psychiatrist Inside

Virtually from its inception the new Soviet regime worked assiduously to cultivate good relations with doctors willing to work with it, and psychiatrists were among those most determined to do so. Within the framework of its new policies on health and medicine (discussed in chapter 1), the Soviet government created new institutions to foster psychiatry, a major indication that the Bolsheviks wanted to bring psychiatrists "inside" after years of oppositional struggle with tsarism. Senior and younger psychiatrists grasped these new opportunities with enthusiasm, regardless of whether their political affiliations were sympathetic.[20] As part of the general restructuring of forensic medicine, psychiatry's relationship with the police was clarified by the creation of the Health Commissariat, which separated scientific expertise from police and courts in its own institutional home.

In the capital and some major cities, health officials rapidly established special organs of forensic psychiatry with a remit to furnish expertise to revolutionary courts. In Petrograd in November 1918, the Diagnostic Institute of Forensic Neurology and Psychiatry (with Lenin's name later added) was founded under the direction of Lev Grigor'evich Orshanskii, a long-serving St. Petersburg psychiatrist. Another psychiatrist from Petersburg, P. A. Ostankov (1868–1949), also served on the institute's expert panels. Before the revolution, Ostankov had flatly rejected the offer of a professorial chair to replace Serbskii, who had resigned his chair in the celebrated Kasso affair when Moscow professors left their posts in protest against repression of student protesters.[21] A. K. Lents (1882–1952), an enthusiast for psychiatric applications of physiologist I. P. Pavlov's theory of conditioned reflexes, and later the leading psychiatrist in Minsk, served on many expert panels in the institute's early days. The Diagnostic Institute examined as in-patients just under three hundred subjects annually in its first three years of operation, despite the extreme privations of the Civil War.[22] In Moscow in 1919, a young prison psychiatrist, E. K. Krasnushkin (1885–1951), established the Soviet capital's first penal psychiatric team running a fifty-bed department in a prison hospital. In the spring of 1921 (on the premises of the Prechistenskii Mental Hospital), Moscow's Institute of Forensic Psychiatry, having appointed E. N. Dovbnia (1880–1947) director and Krasnushkin chief scientific researcher, opened as a separate medical institution to house suspects and prisoners under psychiatric observation in a secure environment.[23] The institute was soon renamed after Serbskii, whose role in the Kasso affair conferred hero status.[24] These two centers of forensic-psychiatric research, teaching, and expertise became the leading Soviet institutions of their discipline. In other major cities (Saratov, Rostov-on-Don, and Odessa in Soviet Ukraine), smaller bureaus devoted to the study of the "personality of the criminal" and furnishing expertise to local police and courts were founded by university psychiatric departments or prison mental hospitals. These local facilities brought psychiatrists and justice workers together and made significant contributions to the development of Soviet criminology.[25]

Ekaterinburg (renamed Sverdlovsk, 1924) lacked any such facility, despite its status as capital of the vast Urals province and the presence of the Urals State University with its medical faculty. It was not until 1922 that the medical faculty managed to find one Dr. Fishman to lecture in psychiatry. Although Fishman supplied virtually all the psychiatric expert opinions in the Sverdlovsk sample of sex crime cases examined later in this chapter, almost none of his personal details have survived. The case files do indicate that Fishman practiced as a psychiatrist in the city's hospital for nerve and psychiatric patients, very likely his main salaried position. The region's medical press shows that while Fishman was not the only psychiatrist in the Urals, the province did not boast a particularly lively culture of psychiatric research and clinical practice. Sverdlovsk's best-known Soviet psychiatrist, the maverick G. V. Segalin, during the eclectic 1920s propounded utopian theories of genius as a pathology and, to judge from court records, took little interest in forensic matters.[26]

Whether working as individuals or in a collective, forensic psychiatrists were chiefly concerned with the question of a suspect's mental capacity to answer for his actions, or imputability *(vmeniaemost')*. Tsarist legal procedures had assigned a role to the psychiatrist as forensic expert, and this approach was based on criminal law enacted in 1845 and still in force in 1917. Police investigators who thought a suspect "does not have a healthy mind [*zdravago razsudka*] or suffers from a mental illness," were to consult a doctor, or verify their suspicions "via interviews with the accused himself and with those who are most likely to know about his actions and thoughts." In 1888, the Ministry of Justice supplied police with a list of questions they should bear in mind, covering the suspect's parentage and heredity, childhood, past illnesses, sex life, family and occupational circumstances, and recent changes of behavior. If after this preliminary investigation a prosecutor agreed that the suspect's mental capacity was in doubt, the suspect would be examined by doctors in a preliminary hearing of the district court, and a ruling given about his imputability, his mental capacity to understand the nature of, and to answer for, the crime under investigation. The penal code provided for those accused of violent crimes who suffered mental illness to be held indefinitely in asylums, with release dependent on a two-year observation period. (Caring for these disruptive patients was a particularly sore point for psychiatrists.) In most investigations involving nonimputable suspects, the case did not reach the trial stage in an open court; the preliminary hearing would hear medical evidence, dispose of the criminal charge, and transfer the suspect to doctors' care.[27]

Soviet regulation in these matters followed a very similar pattern, but significant differences upgraded psychiatry's authority in the justice system. With their new position under the Health Commissariat, psychiatrists like all expert doctors now had the right to operate as "judges of the scientific facts," to participate in criminal investigations and in court hearings as expert witnesses with nominal independence from police interference. The founding of special institutes further elevated the status of forensic psychiatry. In the Soviet procedural code that underpinned criminal statutes, much resembled prerevolutionary forms, but there were signs of greater esteem too. Investigators were enjoined to seek medical expertise when they suspected mental illness on the part of a perpetrator, and a 1924 circular from the People's Commissariat of Justice set out a list of questions—virtually identical to the 1888 justice ministry instructions—that police should ask of doctors when confronting these cases.[28] Courts would then review the evidence, in pretrial *(rasporiaditel'nye)* sessions in complex cases, and rule on whether the case should proceed or be quashed, and whether the suspect should be sent for compulsory medical treatment. The Soviet rules, unlike tsarist ones, let police and courts seek second expert opinions and reject expert testimony in the judge's sentence; nevertheless it was a mark of the respect accorded to technical expertise that new opinions could only be sought from experts nominated by Health Commissariat officials, and that a court's departure from expert opinion had to be recorded and justified in court and in the sentence document. Moreover, Soviet rules said that determinations of nonimputability should be announced in full trial sessions, even if previously adopted in a preliminary session. This appeared to institutionalize the oral, public review of psychiatric evidence regarding the suspect, and given the complexity of such cases, the attendance of the psychiatric expert in open court was now increasingly likely.[29]

Through regulations like these, the Bolsheviks brought psychiatrists inside the system to serve the needs of criminal justice in ways that answered some of the prerevolutionary critiques of the relationship between the tsarist regime and doctors of the mind. Psychiatrists engaged in forensic duties received a parity of esteem with those who had other forms of medical expertise. This parity was possibly the most radical innovation of the Soviet revolution for psychiatry. Mind doctors' principal claim to this esteem was as secular, scientific experts capable of explaining the deviant individual's motivation and behavior. Soviet Russia's leading forensic psychiatrists of the 1920s were closely involved in the establishment of criminological laboratories for research into the personality of lawbreakers. Sharon A. Kowalsky shows that psychiatrists played an important role as founders of Soviet criminology. They did not see a contradiction between their "biological" focus on the individual criminal and the socioeconomic outlook of Communist ideology. Early Soviet psychiatrists believed that their explanations would contribute practical solutions to problems of crime, and they secured patronage by holding out the prospect of new, "Soviet," answers. At the 1926 Second All-Russian Congress of Forensic-Medical Experts, A. K. Lents, already a professor in Minsk, noted that psychiatry looked not only backward to the motive factors of crime, but ahead to reintegration: "The new attitude toward the criminal consists in the detailed study of his peculiarities, with the goal of re-equipping him for social life and labor."[30] Psychiatrists in their public statements accepted the primacy of the economic and social determinants to the formation of the human personality, and when speaking to the justice system they eschewed the language of "classical" Enlightenment criminology that posited a subject with the free will to commit evil or good. In Kowalsky's words, they claimed that "only by understanding the relationship between the individual criminal personality and socioeconomic conditions could crime be eliminated."[31]

What was the significance of bringing the psychiatrist "inside" in Soviet investigations of sex crimes? In their explanation of criminal motives in cases of sexual assault, abuse, and rape, early Soviet psychiatrists offered themselves as "judges of the scientific facts." Bewildering forms of sexual disorder and deviance, under tsarist legislation conceived as offenses against "honor" and "chastity," and in tsarist journalism subjected to lurid, politicized, and moralizing scrutiny, were now to be explained using the language of sexual psychopathy and of sexological science. Dispassionate, rational, and "objective" diagnosis had moral and juridical consequences. Some offenders were clearly mentally ill and nonimputable; others belonged to the category of "borderline" personalities, the psychopaths and neurotics, whose actions could be explained with the new language of sexual psychopathology (and whose legal status was the source of much debate). Still others would be deemed mentally fit, genuinely malign persons in whom "the mechanisms of criminality themselves come from the old structure of life with its exploitation of female, especially child, vulnerability."[32]

The psychiatrist in the sex crime investigation was thus enabling authorities to distinguish between the mad and the bad, using a medical lens that, in its cool rationality, set Soviet justice apart from prerevolutionary "bourgeois" morality. Scientific expert opinions that could explain the motives for inexplicable crimes would also have the benefit of enlightening a populace steeped in "religious and petty-bourgeois prejudice" in matters of sexuality. The open Soviet courtroom trial in sex crime cases, a contrast with the prerevolutionary preference for closed trials of rapists and abusers, was a feature of the revolutionary era's faith that sexual frankness led to enlightenment. In theory at least, sex crime cases would lose their sensational, mystifying character, and the psychiatrist in the courtroom would use modern science to explain sexual disorder to the masses. The sex crime trial could thus play its part in instructing the Soviet population in the regime's novel sexual values. Psychiatrists performed another duty as diagnosticians by helping the authorities to specify appropriate "measures of social protection" (the Soviet euphemism for punishments—a word disallowed in early Soviet jurisprudence). Having identified the source and nature of some offenders' crimes in pathology, psychiatrists would offer their expert opinions about the type of social protection best suited to the person. For the nonimputable, this would normally be compulsory medical treatment, while for "borderline" personalities and those judged capable of answering for their crimes, ordinary prison or special corrective-labor confinement might be prescribed.

Who Commissioned Psychiatric Expertise—and Why?

The number of cases with some form of psychiatric expertise appearing in the sample of 194 sex crime cases gathered for this book is 28, with 19 in the Petrograd sample and the rest in the Sverdlovsk group. Thus in these investigations, psychiatrists were called upon in just under 15 percent of the cases. While claims for representativeness of the crime case sample must be treated with caution, this low proportion does serve as a reminder that men who were thought to be mentally healthy perpetrated the great majority of sex crimes. It also suggests that early Soviet authorities and doctors applied psychiatry's construction of the sexual psychopath, and indeed any other psychiatric diagnoses, quite sparingly. This limited resort to psychiatry must be borne in mind when examining the evidence from these crime cases, for recent historical work, and the 1920s sexological and psychiatric material upon which it is based, emphasizes the influence of psychiatry in early Soviet approaches to sexual disorder. Psychiatrists wrote vividly, and at some length, about sexual crime in 1920s Soviet Russia, but their monographs often relied upon studies of already convicted sex criminals held in prisons; psychiatrists' input in the police and court investigation stages, before conviction and imprisonment, was far from universal. Evidently, with such studies, the psychiatrist-as-criminologist was attempting to attract further sponsorship for his expertise in these earlier stages of crime investigation.[33] In cases of rape and sexual assault, as noted in previous chapters, the female victim was the most urgent subject of medical expertise in the search for evidence of physical, not mental, damage. The male perpetrators of rape and sexual abuse were far less often the subjects of expert assessment, whether physical or mental. Yet it is symptomatic of the gendering of medical attention that male perpetrators were most often the object of psychiatric assessment. Men's deviant desire (for specific kinds of sexual gratification) could be imagined as a psychological pathology explicable by psychiatric reasoning.

It is also noteworthy that the smaller, earlier sample of Petrograd sex crimes yields the larger proportion of cases with some form of psychiatric expertise.[34] Apart from the arbitrary nature of the sample, the lack of psychiatric facilities and personnel in the Urals region must also account for this discrepancy. As seen, Petrograd was one of the country's leading centers of psychiatric medicine and forensic expertise, while Sverdlovsk, despite its status as a provincial capital and a university town, had only a very basic forensic medical and psychiatric network.

Police and people's investigators turned to psychiatrists for a variety of reasons, usually to examine suspects (for their motives, or imputability), and less frequently, victims (to assess damage, and occasionally, moral character).[35] Investigators were most likely to call for psychiatric expertise in cases of sexual abuse of or assaults on children and young persons. These crimes puzzled the police for their apparent lack of motive. Unlike rape, which authorities explained as a relic of patriarchal attitudes, and which male police investigators might unconsciously understand (and perhaps even empathize with) as a failure of masculine self-control, abuse of the young was a matter the police could not explain.[36]

Questions to experts show the desire to understand motive. A thorough Petrograd investigator, one Bogdanov, wrote the following rationale for commissioning psychiatric opinions in the case of a man who confessed (it turned out, falsely) to anal intercourse with pubescent girls and boys: "there is doubt about his individual physical and mental health, because the actions committed by the citizen, being criminal, at the same time somehow suggest an unhealthy condition in the accused in the form of pederasty, sadism and the mind [*v forme pederastii, sadizma i psikhiki*]."[37] Petrograd social workers who uncovered the abuse of a 12-year-old boy by his guardian, a 30-year-old musician and party member, reported the case to the local authorities as one of "sexual perversion," and eventually a people's investigator commissioned opinions from psychiatrists on "the state of health of Tyrin . . . who is suspected of crimes under art. 168" (nonpenetrative sexual acts). A panel of two psychiatrists supplied an extensive description of the man's sexual psychology and deviations, yet he was deemed fit to answer to a court.[38] Same-sex relations with minors were sufficiently disturbing to merit psychiatric explanation, as were assaults on very young children.[39] Some referrals show that police linked expert confirmation of "sexual perversion" to the question of imputability. Another Petrograd male offender with young boys was sent to Orshanskii's Diagnostic Institute for assessment; his admission of his crimes "without embarrassment" and his reportedly limited mental development led to suspicions that he might not be capable of answering for his crimes.[40]

As this case also suggests, the abnormal behavior of suspects after arrest was a significant factor compelling police and investigators to seek expertise, to ensure that a subject was fit for trial. One Petrograd people's investigator, a comrade Shtrikher, figures as a punctilious gatherer of expert opinions on all aspects of the cases he dealt with. In a well-publicized 1924 case of rape, abuse of authority, and fraud by Mikhail I. Miats, a party member and ex-metalworker who now managed the city's syndicate of alcohol shops, investigator Shtrikher summoned Professor Ostankov and another psychiatrist, Tarle, to examine Miats in prison. They were to assess "the condition of the mental faculties of the prisoner and his imputability for the crimes ascribed to him and at the present time." To judge from the conclusions of these two expert psychiatrists, Miats's explosive "outbursts and swearing" and his "inclinations to hysterical confabulation" (and likely his symptoms of chronic alcoholism) led Shtrikher to call in the experts, yet Miats was still judged capable of standing trial.[41] In May 1927 a gang rape in Sverdlovsk resulted in the arrest of four youths ages 16 to 18; police immediately noted that a gang member, Dmitrii Zvedeninov, a working class 17-year-old, acted oddly and sent him "for examination to establish his abnormality," to the city's chief forensic medical expert, physician N. K. Bazhenov. Bazhenov directed that his psychiatrist colleague, Fishman, see the suspect, and the same police directed Fishman "to establish his [Zvedeninov's] nervous condition and give an opinion, because he is accused under art. 153 part II" (aggravated rape). On the back of the police order-sheet, really, just a scrap of paper, Fishman hastily wrote that the youth "suffers from congenital mental underdevelopment." As a result of these few lines, the youth was later acquitted.[42]

After people's investigators conducted the preliminary investigation, prosecutors occasionally intervened to commission psychiatric evaluations of suspects. A Petrograd prosecutor argued before a preliminary session of the city's criminal court in January 1923 that a suspected rapist should be sent to the Diagnostic Institute on grounds "that the behavior of the accused raises doubts about his will [*voli*] that must be investigated." The court agreed, and the suspect spent perhaps a month in the institute before Orshanskii and a staff psychiatrist, V. Liustitskii, deemed him mentally ill, at which point his case was abandoned.[43]

In the 1920s, political direction of the day-to-day work of the Soviet justice system was sufficiently sporadic or light of touch to allow the accused, their advocates, and their families to request and occasionally receive expert psychiatric opinions that might mitigate guilt or even exculpate a defendant. Later in the 1930s, under Stalinist policing and justice practices, authorities appear to have routinely denied the accused access to mitigating psychiatric expertise.[44] One of the fiercest criticisms made about early Soviet forensic psychiatry by the Stalinist cohort that assumed control of the discipline in the 1930s was that criminals knew enough about psychiatric medicine (including aspects of the borderline condition of psychopathy) and the laws on compulsory medical treatment to demand a diagnosis on that basis. In 1936, a Moscow expert observed that during the early years of Soviet penal psychiatry, "one came up against psychopaths who already held a belief in their reduced responsibility or non-responsibility [for crimes], aggressively insisting on their right to lawless, antisocial behavior in connection with their illness." Even worse, such criminals knew that they were classified as "patients" and used the language of medicine to demand "cures" and to protest against the length of "treatment" they had to submit to compulsorily.[45] The hope of securing such a determination inspired defendants to claim they suffered from a mental infirmity or even a history of full-blown madness. Individuals did this with varying degrees of sophistication and understanding of psychiatric discourse. Their bids for exculpation on these grounds are excellent examples of Michel Foucault's "reverse discourses," in which patients (or would-be patients) absorb and read back medical discourse to doctors to promote their own interests.[46]

Among this study's sample, several instances of psychiatric expertise requested by the accused and his supporters appear, and the record of success—from the defendants' perspective—was mixed. Access to psychiatrists' assessments did not automatically lead to reduced sentences or therapy in an asylum rather than confinement to a prison. Transparently opportunistic bids for medical mitigation were not honored by the supposedly soft-hearted idealist doctors of Stalinist imagination.

Yet Mikhail Miats, the director of Petrograd's network of alcohol shops, and accused of rape, was notably successful in securing a "second opinion" about his mental condition. Miats, a Communist, was adept at pulling strings. After people's investigator Shtrikher obtained a declaration of his fitness to stand trial from state psychiatrists Ostankov and Tarle in July 1924, Miats sought and underwent a second examination, evidently commissioned at his own initiative with the help of a defense lawyer and, perhaps, connections in the provincial health department. This "second opinion" was likely paid for privately. Miats's new assessment took place during the course of a voluntary stay at the Forel Hospital, where he checked in for treatment of "traumatic neurosis" after his release on remand from prison in the weeks before trial in early September 1924. On 4 August, a commission of doctors led by psychiatrist V. V. Sreznevskii confirmed the diagnosis of traumatic neurosis, based on "contusion . . . at the [Civil War] front, after which there were episodes of paralysis and aphasia and convulsive fits." Sreznevskii's team prescribed "therapy in a special psychiatric hospital in conditions of good nutrition and care, to be followed by a period of treatment in a countryside or sanatorium setting." The party member's defense advocate then wrote on the eve of the trial to the court, demanding that Sreznevskii be summoned to testify, effectively, against the state's expert psychiatrists Ostankov and Tarle. The advocate hoped to stage a confrontation between rival experts reminiscent of the old regime's judicial contests. The Soviet court however rejected this stratagem and called only the state's experts, sending them copies of Sreznevskii's psychiatric assessment for refutation.[47] Miats stood trial and was sentenced, in circumstances discussed later in this chapter.

Very few defendants in sex crime cases had defense advocates working for them, or Communist Party connections that might be used to gain access to medical opinions. Occasionally, however, defendants without supporters might obtain concessions involving psychiatric expertise. The case of convicted rapist Egor Shestakov, 30, a peasant from Monastyrskoe village near Nizhnii Tagil in Sverdlovsk province, shows how central legal officials might intervene where local police, prosecutors, and judges failed to recognize the need for specialized medical opinions. In this case, the mental capacity of the victim, Kleopatra Kosykh, was put in doubt by the paramedic and the midwife who examined her twice during the long initial investigation. They confirmed her loss of virginity but both times noted mental abnormalities, concluding on the second occasion that she could not appear in court. Nevertheless, on 31 January 1925 the trial of Shestakov took place in the town of Tagil and he was sentenced, on the basis of her testimony, to two years' imprisonment for rape.[48] Shestakov appealed this decision, apparently without the assistance of lawyers.[49] The RSFSR Supreme Court found that prosecutors mishandled the qualification of the crime and dealt with Kosykh's mental deficiencies carelessly. A mentally abnormal person was forbidden by law from being interrogated as a witness and yet the indictment based the crime entirely on her testimony. The higher court ordered a new trial with "the mandatory conducting of medical expertise on the victim Kosykh."[50] At a retrial in Sverdlovsk, Shestakov was convicted of rape, but he received a suspended sentence as a person not constituting a danger to society, in part, because Fishman's psychiatric assessment of Kosykh raised doubt (perhaps, inadvertently) about her ability to report events faithfully. In this case, central legal officials, prompted by an illiterate but articulate peasant who understood the value of medical evidence, spotted a defect in justice procedure involving the use of forensic psychiatric expertise, and moved to correct it.

Families acted as informal advocates and demanded psychiatric intervention when they were aware of histories of mental illness on the part of defendants who were relatives. Another Petrograd case, pursued by the meticulous investigator Shtrikher, involved the rape and subsequent suicide in July 1923 of a 20-year-old worker, victimized by a 25-year-old shop clerk, Dmitrii Ivanov, who conducted a string of concurrent liaisons. Shtrikher commissioned an autopsy and forensic gynecological report on the victim's corpse, a chemical analysis of her clothing, and also a handwriting analysis of the suicide note to authenticate its authorship. After Ivanov had spent four months in remand prison awaiting trial, his brother Pavel appealed to the court to recognize his chronic mental illness. On the day of this application, Pavel discovered his brother had been confined to a "pacification" *(smiritel'naia)* chamber for five days without a doctor's visit:

> I decided to wait to see the doctor and tell him what was happening. Dr. Zeks said that he has gone out of his mind, then in order to have him sent for an expert examination [*ekspertizu*] I should get a court decree. . . . I tried to explain that cit[izen] Ivanov D. D. is afflicted by mental illness [*on*

oderzhim dushevnoi bolezn'iu] and showed him the papers, but cit[izen] Zeks did not care to look at them.

   Cit. Ivanov D. D. has been afflicted by mental illness for a long time. *I request that you take the appropriate measures.*[51]

Pavel Ivanov attached certificates confirming that Dmitrii had spent two weeks in the Petrograd St. Nicholas the Miracleworker Hospital in 1919, suffering from paranoia and hallucinations, and two military certificates from 1920 and 1921 exempting him permanently from service on the grounds of "a severe form of mental illness with hallucinations." The Petrograd court responded by commissioning A. K. Lents to examine Ivanov in prison; the accused was judged mentally unwell and in need of further examination at the Diagnostic Institute, and within a month the court decided to acquit him.[52] In cases where families were aware of a history of mental illness, their petitions and appeals could secure favorable psychiatric expert opinions.[53]

Authorities, including experts, gave opportunistic appeals for expertise short shrift—but they can be read as an indication that the discourses of psychiatric illness and the expert opinion in criminal cases was well enough known at the lowest levels of society by the 1920s. Magnus Iakovlevich Kivi, a Petrograd pimp accused in 1924 of sexual intercourse with girls between the ages of 10 and 13, claimed in interrogation that he was impotent and even proffered a medical certificate purporting to confirm the condition from a private physician, who made a living curing sexually transmitted diseases. Kivi perhaps did not anticipate that he would be sent to a psychiatrist (Sreznevskii) for assessment of his sexual capacity, but the Petrograd forensic medicine bureau made this enlightened decision after receiving the commission "to establish the sexual impotence of the accused" from a people's investigator. Sreznevskii found no indications of impotence, providing an extended survey of the suspect's physiology, reflexes, and mental character. Police established that the private doctor's certificate was fraudulent, and Kivi's claim to impotence was contradicted by the detailed psychosexual profile the psychiatrist presented.[54]

In another, more harrowing, case of systematic abuse by a father, stretching over sixteen years, the criminal used medical discourse to frame an appeal to the Supreme Court.[55] From the testimony of relatives, the police established that Ivan Mikhailov, a conductor on the October Railway and a widower, had coerced sex with a niece and two daughters repeatedly since 1907 in his own home. Mikhailov's relentless sexual demands finally drained the forbearance of his children when Mikhailov forced his 16-year-old son Nikolai to rape his half-sister Lidiia in his presence. (Lidiia reported the rape, and charges raised against Nikolai were eventually dropped.) Ivan Mikhailov had tattoos of "figures with erotic content" on his body; he was alleged by his children to have engaged in sex with dogs and cats as well as his immediate family. Three psychiatrists acting as a panel, Professor V. P. Osipov (1872–1947) of the Military-Medical Academy and Ostankov and Sreznevskii, noted Mikhailov's chronic alcoholism but deemed him mentally fit and responsible for his actions. In sentencing him, the court cited expertise that diagnosed Mikhailov as suffering from "reduced mental capabilities and a pronounced sexual psychopathy, but not to a degree excluding imputability." The court further found that because his "sexual anomalies bore such a sustained and prolonged character and continued to threaten society, and were impossible to eradicate by methods of medical treatment, that Mikhailov is an exceptionally socially dangerous element." He was sentenced to a comparatively severe ten years' imprisonment.[56]

Within three days, Mikhailov submitted a plea for his sentence to be transformed into a term of compulsory psychiatric treatment, a plea that was laced with medical metaphors and arguments.[57] He acknowledged his designation by the court as a socially dangerous element, comparing himself in relation to society to an "infectious disease for the human organism." His "sexual passion," he said, "had infected his blood many years ago" and drove him to seek outlets for his sexual energy when his wife refused him. Aware of the "shameful passion" that he inflicted on his family, he said this passion came upon him in "mad, irresponsible fits." The medical opinion that he was "*vmeniaemyi* but suffering from sexual psychopathy, was like saying a man has healthy limbs, heart, liver and stomach, but that he is crazy." Mikhailov argued that he was responsible for his actions at work and in his day-to-day affairs, but that in sexual matters over the past few years, "I completely lose . . . control of my will and reason." In the presence of a sexual object he forgot everything, "I satisfy my lust like a savage animal." Mikhailov insisted that he was sick, but he questioned the specialists who designated him as "incurable." Many such "incurable sexual psychopaths" had been successfully treated by "modern science," he insisted. What was the point of imprisoning him if he was sick and "incurable"—would it not be more sensible to subject him to the "supreme measure" (i.e., to execute him) as a socially dangerous element, if that was the case? Corrective detention was unlikely to rehabilitate him if he was incurably ill. Mikhailov concluded by asking the Supreme Court to amend his sentence "to give me the opportunity to correct myself through intensive medical therapy for my mental infirmity."

The Mikhailov file does not record the reaction of the Supreme Court, but the appeal was probably denied, as he remained in prison, according to a medical certificate issued less than a year later. On the edge of death from tuberculosis, Mikhailov was seen by a team of medical specialists who recommended his early release. Ironically, they invoke the incurable nature of this life-threatening illness as the justification for lifting his sentence.[58]

Sexual offenders like Mikhailov were surprisingly aware of the medicalization of sexuality, and of its potential linkages to exculpatory madness, as their bids for transfer from prison to the medical system demonstrate.[59] Soviet legislation on such matters was only a matter of months old when these cases came to trial, so popular awareness of the discourse of sexual psychopathy probably originated in prerevolutionary journalism, boulevard literature, and entertainment.[60] Any anticipated softening of the criminal's position in psychiatric institutions for compulsory therapy was a misplaced hope. The few institutions that existed in urban Russia in the 1920s quickly filled up, and the dream of providing inmates with individualized medical attention and stimulating routines of exercise and education was never genuinely realized.[61] Psychiatrists in this era were nevertheless scarcely the soft-hearted "liberals" that Stalin-era leaders of the forensic psychiatric discipline would complain about in the 1930s and 1940s. If the so-called psychopaths of the 1920s presented articulate challenges to the authority of the specialists who assessed them, their pleas stood little chance of success.

Police and prosecutors also commissioned psychiatric opinions about the victims of sex crime, although they did so less often than for perpetrators. The reasons for having the objects of sexual assaults assessed by doctors of the mind fall into two general categories that present a marked difference between the Petrograd and Sverdlovsk samples. Psychiatric assessments of victims of sex crime in Sverdlovsk and district took place when the victim was known to be, or perceived to be, mentally deficient or underdeveloped. (Chronic or inborn deficiencies of learning and perception were denoted in Russian in these files by the term *slaboumie* [imbecility, idiocy].) Here the legal authorities were concerned that particularly vulnerable girls and women should be protected, and they also sought to deflect objections that such victims were unreliable reporters of criminal acts committed against them. In Petrograd, the cases in the sample show that investigators feared that some youthful victims were corrupted, and they sought psychiatric evaluations of their moral and sexual innocence or experience. The distinctive difference between the two samples may likely be, in part, a mere chance occurrence related to the survival of cases in the archives. Nevertheless, the character and resources of each locale suggest additional factors. Petrograd's urban corruption had long been a focus of concern, and the theme of the big city as source of degeneration was well established in Russian thinking. People's investigators were well aware of the potential of the city to deprave its young inhabitants, and psychiatrists in Petrograd reflected these concerns in their frequent diagnoses of degeneration. By contrast, Sverdlovsk, and the vast outlying Urals province, was a setting of modest towns and villages, with poorly trained police and medical personnel, and the problems of peasant poverty and hygiene, including the exploitation or outright assault of mentally vulnerable girls, surfaced repeatedly.

In Sverdlovsk, rural police and medical staff could be slow to recognize a victim's mental incapacity, as the case of Shestakov's rape of Kleopatra Kosykh, mentioned previously, indicates. In that case it took an appeal to the Supreme Court to compel local officials to commission psychiatric assessment of Kosykh's ability to account for the events of the crime. In another Sverdlovsk investigation that ran from 1925 to 1927 before being quashed, the mother of pregnant Tais'ia Alikina initiated a paternity suit on her "imbecilic" *(slaboumnaia)* daughter's behalf, against a 19-year-old man from her settlement.[62] A Sverdlovsk court threw out the claim and stated that the case should have been treated as a possible rape investigation, since the daughter's mental incapacity, only confirmed by a rural medical station and a Sverdlovsk city doctor six months after the event, rendered the circumstances dubious. Later, the same court ruled there was no rape case to answer. A senior prosecutor, one Bernshtam, objected vigorously to this ruling and argued from the medical opinions that Alikina "is mentally impaired and therefore not only physical but also psychological methods of force could have been used against her—in the form of persuasion or threats."[63] Despite a retrial in early 1927, the rape charge again failed. The case had foundered on the failure of officials at the lowest level to recognize a crime and engage medical expertise promptly.[64]

The questions that Petrograd investigators put to medical experts about the victims of sex crime, in this sample, focused on the "moral constitution" of the child-victim. People's investigator Bogdanov (a knowledgeable detective) commissioned expertise by sending the experts a list of thirteen questions about the accused and his victim in a case of sexual abuse of a 14-year-old girl. A neighbor observed Mariia Dubova counting five rubles as she left the flat of Vladimir Mutovozov, a 32-year-old church deacon. It was alleged that she had suffered abuse at the hands of the deacon, but another possible explanation for what the neighbor saw was that a corrupted minor was counting the earnings of an illicit sexual transaction.[65] Seven questions concerned Dubova's physical and mental condition, including a question asking about "her moral constitution: perversity, etc." and any evidence of degeneration she displayed. Bogdanov, mirroring contemporary presumptions, reasoned that the girl's deafness might also be a source of sexual disorder.[66] A panel of experts including psychiatrists Tarle and Shumkov deemed Dubova without mental deviations and continued, "there are no signs of perversity or any indicators of physical degeneration."[67] In this way her sexual innocence and, consequently, her status as a victim was confirmed by psychiatric experts. In a similar fashion, another Petrograd rape case resulted in a conviction after the 19-year-old complainant, Pavla Pershina, was examined to establish "the state of her health" by a panel including Orshanskii and Ostankov. Despite the fact that "there are signs of physical degeneration (high forehead, third eyelid etc.)," these experts said that "in Pershina's mental sphere no deviations from the norm are observed." This expert opinion went some way to allowing the prosecutor to construct Pershina as a victim rather than a party complicit in a concealed sexual liaison.[68]

Medical and Moral Diagnosis

In the majority of sex crime investigations in the sample, psychiatrists were called on to address the explicit or implicit question of a suspect's *vmeniaemost'*—imputability, or responsibility for criminal acts. The sample shows that only a very few of the individuals subjected to psychiatric assessment were judged *nevmeniaemyi*–nonimputable, or not capable of accounting for their criminal acts, because of mental illness. The diagnoses that psychiatrists made in these cases, and the way they presented their findings in their written and oral statements, demonstrate the lines that they drew between the criminally responsible perpetrator and the individual incapable of answering for his actions. The power of the psychiatrist to remove persons from the justice system was used extremely sparingly. Other individuals were judged responsible, and later guilty, but escaped extended sentences by virtue of apparent mental defects. The majority of sex criminals in this sample involving psychiatric assessment were deemed sane, and the particular functions of the doctor in the criminal investigation and in court as the "judge of the scientific facts" illustrate how these psychiatrists understood and deployed the language of sexual psychopathy, as a medical metaphor for moral judgment.

In the sample, just three persons (one woman and two men) in the Petrograd cases and just one young man in Sverdlovsk were effectively deemed nonimputable. The similar criteria for these medical judgments show that psychiatrists shared a relatively rigorous understanding of the concept of nonimputability. No casual use of the psychopathy diagnosis to exculpate the sex criminal appears in the sample.

The case of the rapist Zvedeninov in 1927 in Sverdlovsk, mentioned previously, shows prosecutors applying psychiatric expertise to construct a morally neutral "bystander" from a criminal participant. The city's overburdened expert psychiatrist responded to a police request for an assessment with four hastily scrawled lines on the reverse of the policeman's note, concluding that Zvedeninov "suffers from congenital mental underdevelopment. Fishman." The 17-year-old, one of a gang of four youths of worker background who assaulted factory-worker Irina Dudina, a woman "of casual behavior," became the prosecution's key witness. Questioned as a "bystander," he confirmed Dudina's testimony about the circumstances of the assault. It was on this basis that Zvedeninov's three accomplices were convicted. Fishman was not summoned to explain his assessment of the key witness in court. In its sentence the court noted Fishman's opinion of this key witness as "mentally underdeveloped" and the judge agreed that "he committed [his crime] under the influence of his comrades. As a result, measures of social defense of a criminal-corrective character [i.e., imprisonment] need not be applied." Zvedeninov was immediately acquitted, and indeed the other three convicted gang-rapists were soon released on the basis of their youth and worker status.[69] The file illustrates minimal participation of the psychiatrist (typical in many of the Sverdlovsk cases) in a process directed by prosecutors. Legal personnel, and not forensic experts, were willing to read the diagnosis of "congenital mental underdevelopment" flexibly, to transform an accomplice into a "bystander" with credible testimony.[70] Fishman's diagnosis of an inborn mental defect, or feeblemindedness, which prevented development toward full adulthood, was nevertheless typical of the kind of profound, long-term mental disorder that merited exculpation, in the eyes of forensic psychiatrists.

A similar case of "severe feeblemindedness," in Mariia Komarova, a 20-year-old Petrograd woman accused of procuring girls from an orphanage (in league with the pimp Magnus Kivi), resulted in apparent exculpation on these grounds.[71] Psychiatrist Sreznevskii, acting for the state, examined Komarova during the trial on the premises of the court, noting her "physical and mental degeneration with functional disorders of the glands of internal secretion" and her "notably severe feeblemindedness." Unfavorable heredity, a thyroid disorder, and her "cretinism" rendered the subject incapable of orienting herself in her environment, of recalling the past, or of resisting malign influences. Such an individual was not capable of accounting for or understanding her past actions, and as Sreznevskii hinted in his expert statement, she could not be counted a conscious member of the working class: "Even the most significant events of the recent past have left little trace on her memory. She cannot tell with certainty in what year the October Revolution occurred, when Lenin died, what sort of war happened, etc." This dramatic demonstration of a subject in the courtroom had a significant impact on the judge's decision. The court deferred judgment on her role in the abuse of the orphanage girls and sent her to the Diagnostic Institute "for investigation of the question of her full non-imputability." There, Orshanskii and Liustitskii needed only a week of observation to confirm Sreznevskii's findings, although they evaded an explicit conclusion about her imputability. The file ends here so its outcome cannot be known, yet, the severity of Komarova's condition is indicative of the degree of mental underdevelopment that jurists and doctors agreed was liable for diversion from the legal to the medical channel.

The mental incapacity necessary to send a criminal to the medical system could also be the result of severe trauma or chronic mental illness. A pretrial investigation of Vasilii Petrov, accused of raping two nannies who worked for him, heard from a prosecutor and a defense advocate that Petrov's doubtful behavior raised questions about his "will," and he was sent to the Diagnostic Institute, where he appears to have remained for an extended period. Orshanskii and Liustritskii established that Petrov had met with a blow to the head from falling planks; he suffered "from mental illness in the form of traumatic mental deficiency [*slaboumie*] (*Dementia post traumatica*); he was in the same condition at the time of the crimes ascribed to him."[72] In the case of accused rapist Dmitrii Ivanov, whose brother intervened to demand that "appropriate measures" be taken to recognize his sibling's mental incapacity, the cause of the accused's debilitating hallucinations and paranoia was never revealed. Yet the brother produced documents showing that the severity of Ivanov's illness had excluded him from military service. Lents, acting for the court, agreed he must therefore be examined in the Diagnostic Institute, and he was evidently acquitted on this basis.[73]

These cases of deferral of judgment, of diversion from the legal to the medical system, and of acquittal on the basis of mental incapacity show that the defendants accused of sex crime who received forms of medical mitigation were the victims of profound conditions that manifested themselves in dramatic ways, evident to laymen. Thus police investigators and prosecutors as well as family members sought psychiatric assessment or treatment in place of courtroom trials and imprisonment. Strikingly, in these cases the language of psychiatric diagnosis and assessment avoided all mention of sexual psychopathy. The sexual persona of the accused was scarcely mentioned at all in these expert opinions; instead degeneration, unfavorable heredity, trauma, and inborn defects were cited and probed.

Psychological factors that psychiatrists deemed relevant here included memory (for example, Komarova's inability to recall the date of the October Revolution) and consciousness (for example, Petrov's chaotic emotional states, fits, and "reduced . . . imagination"). Psychiatrists characterized none of these subjects who received medical mitigation in sexualized language, and such language formed no part of the discourse of judicial investigation.

In the Petrograd sample, two cases fall between the categories of these nonimputable individuals and the conclusively imputable. These two intermediate cases show a relative avoidance of the language of sexual psychopathy. Both defendants were formally judged imputable for their crimes, yet both obtained forms of quasi-medical mitigation after serving a symbolic portion of their sentences. The Communist director of Petrograd's alcohol shops, Mikhail Miats, convicted of rape, was tried over four days in September 1924, sentenced to four years' imprisonment, and at the same time ordered "to submit to compulsory medical treatment."[74] In court the psychiatrist Ostankov explained how aspects of Miats's erratic behavior were attempts "to simulate insanity"; a report in the Petrograd evening newspaper does not mention psychiatric comment on his sexual appetites. In one line only of the pretrial assessment (with Tarle), Ostankov had noted Miats's understanding of his sexual life: "He does not deny that he gave a great significance to sexual liaisons with women and does not deny that he had liaisons with two of his employees, but with the remaining three he did not have sexual intercourse."[75] Having decreed Miats to be mentally sound and imputable, the state's experts Ostankov and Tarle paved the way for prosecutors to refute the privately commissioned "second opinion" by Sreznevskii about Miats's mental capacity. That opinion, as mentioned earlier, found evidence of "traumatic neurosis" and prescribed rest and good food in a sanatorium. It was completely devoid of discussion of the subject's sexuality. Ultimately, Miats successfully asserted his credentials as a friend of the regime in his last words to the court, and the sentence to both imprisonment and compulsory medical treatment, which the court insisted was for "a nerve (not mental) illness," may be seen as a token of the residual esteem in which he was held.[76] A little over six months later, Miats was examined by a team of unnamed doctors, and the court ruled that he met the requirements of regulations for early release on the grounds of an "organic disease of the central nervous system."[77] A friend of the regime, with a nose for working the system worthy of Ilf and Petrov, Miats was freed from prison for his sexual crimes not on the basis of a diagnosis of sexual psychopathy, but on the grounds of an underlying somatic illness.

The other intermediate case involved Nikolai Potapov, an 18-year-old ship's stoker, accused of nonpenetrative abuse of two girls, one 12, the other just 2½ years of age.[78] This literate, nonparty worker with no previous convictions was sent by a Shlisselburg people's investigator to the Diagnostic Institute for assessment of his mental capacity; evidently, the bizarreness of his sexual touching of the younger child mystified the police, and his actions plus his admission of guilt put his sanity in doubt. In their expert statement, Orshanskii and Liustitskii said nothing about Potapov's psychosexual character. They concluded he was only mildly nervous but otherwise in full mental health during and after the time of the crimes ascribed to him. Thus certified imputable, Potapov was sentenced to three years' imprisonment. Yet, ten months later the court released him, citing "his demonstration of love of hard physical work," "his proletarian background," and his young age. This was not mitigation on medical grounds, but it had a medical basis in the psychiatrists' determination that the young man was essentially mentally healthy and capable of rehabilitation, and the court relied upon this opinion to declare that this work-loving proletarian "did not constitute a danger to society." Untainted by the discourse of sexual psychopathy, another friend of the regime, this time a young worker in whose name the Communist Party ruled, was exculpated in a textbook example of class-based Soviet jurisprudence.

The Taint of Sexualized Language

Paradoxically, psychiatrists made most reference to sexual psychology and the psychopathology of the sex criminal in cases in which they affirmed the criminal's imputability, and the court decreed him guilty. A medicalized language of sexual impulses might appear to early twenty-first-century readers as a form of psychiatry-led sympathy, but in the context of these cases from Petrograd, it is striking how elaborations of sexual psychology appear to be concentrated in cases where perpetrators were pronounced mentally sound and guilty of their crimes. The discourse of sexual psychopathology adhered—whether consciously or unconsciously—most often to those condemned morally for sexual deviations.

The boundary between moral and medical health was an ambiguous one that could yield ambivalent outcomes in the justice system. Psychiatrist Aleksandr V. Triumfov, in his expert opinion confirming the imputability of an abuser of two girls of 10 and 12, explained in a Petrograd court "how it was possible in general for such acts to be committed with children . . . in conditions of absolute health." He wrote, a desire to satisfy his sexual desire with children may be facilitated by either 1) mental illness, or 2) a peculiar perversion [*svoeobraznym izvrashcheniem*] of the sexual feeling, s[o] c[alled] sexual psychopathy, or 3) impossibility of satisfying the sexual urge in the normal fashion because of weak potency, a physical defect, a pathological fear of normal copulation, etc., but in conditions of a lowering of the moral level and habitual retardation [*zaderzhkakh*], e.g., in the elderly, without however the presence of mental illness.[79]

Here sexual psychopathy sat ambiguously somewhere between full-blown mental illness and willful sexual deviance caused by a "lowering of the moral level." Principally, Triumfov was keen in his courtroom expertise to clarify the boundary between conscious awareness of society's "moral level" and a total lack of conscious morality ("mental illness"). He reported an apparent absence of sexual desire in his subject: "In questioning the accused it was not possible to establish the presence of any sexual psychopathy, for he categorically denies not only the fact of his desire (sexual) for the girls, but in general [he rejects the concept that anyone might] satisfy his sexual desire with children." Triumfov also dismissed the defendant's pleas of alcoholism, reminding the court that alcoholism was no mental illness in itself but only "an indication of an unstable nervous system [that] may bring with it other disorders and a lowering of moral boundaries." The court cited the expert testimony when it sentenced this worker-defendant to two years and six months. Yet the abuser eventually served only eight months, successfully petitioning for amnesty. It is not clear why release was granted, but the prisoner's worker status and possible links to the Communist Party may explain the leniency he was eventually shown.[80] By denying all sexual desire in his interview with the forensic psychiatrist, the subject frustrated Triumfov's attempt to deploy the diagnosis of sexual psychopathy, and perhaps neutralized its taint.

The language of the sexual psychology of perpetrator and victim, used by the psychiatrist in court, could be a powerful tool justifying a guilty verdict. In the case of a 38-year-old Finnish sawmill worker, Leontii Eshoi, accused of nonpenetrative sexual abuse of a 12-year-old neighbor, the psychiatrist Shumkov attended the trial and examined both victim and accused. He concluded that the girl had grown up without physical or mental disorders, but that she now suffered from a "nervous disorder in the form of severe hysteria . . . continually . . . following the sexual act." Damage to the victim here did include sexual traumatization in a child. Shumkov deemed Eshoi mentally sound and imputable, and if he did not note any severe "sexual perversions" in his assessment of the perpetrator, he had nonetheless to comment on the possibility. The court cited Shumkov's conclusions in its relatively firm three-year sentence (with strict isolation and deprivation of rights), and Eshoi did not launch an appeal or apparently enjoy early release.[81]

The case of church deacon Vladimir Mutovozov shows psychiatrists discussing the abuser's sexual psychopathy in even more extensive detail. A preliminary examination by a multidisciplinary forensic medical panel (including Tarle and Shumkov), while confirming Mutovozov's imputability, described his masturbatory habits, his means of achieving erection and orgasm, and his exhibitionistic desires and acts. In court, Tarle repeated this descriptive exploration of Mutovozov's sexual world while insisting on the man's mental health and responsibility for his actions. The deacon, described as a member of the intelligentsia and because of his church post regarded as an enemy of Soviet power, received a stiff four-year sentence with strict isolation.[82] Two psychiatrists from the Diagnostic Institute examined his victim Mariia Dubova and found her "without mental deviations, lacking any signs of [sexual] perversity or any indicators of physical degeneration." This diagnosis enabled the police and courts to ascribe innocent motives to the 14-year-old girl. Mutovozov's violent threats were cited as the reason why Dubova did not put up a struggle. In the prosecutor's indictment, her moral character was further embellished with a note of class-based sentimentality and a nod to her healthy hereditary background. Her father, a worker at the Arsenal Factory, was "a man burdened with a large family . . . in good health, does not abuse alcohol, who has raised his daughter with absolute morality." Responsible, sober, and unproblematically virile, this worker was a living exemplar of the conscious proletariat. Psychiatrists did not employ such moralistic language, but their scientific discourse was a convincing foundation from which prosecutors could represent Dubova as socially and hereditarily pure.[83] The expert contribution made the contrast with a sexual predator suffused with a psychology of deviant desires vividly evident.

Same-sex abuse of boys attracted a similar insistence on the imputability of the perpetrator, combined with an extended description of the perpetrator's deviant desires. Shumkov and another psychiatrist (whose signature defies decryption) explained the psychosexual world of the declassed gentry musician Aleksandr Tyrin, 30, who despite his class origins had been a member of the Communist Party prior to arrest. Police investigation revealed that Tyrin had two years before adopted 12-year-old Ivan Niskevich, whom he first encountered among a group of orphanage boys loitering in the Tauride Gardens, a notorious haunt for rent boys. Tyrin knew these boys not only because they frequented the gardens, but also because he played piano at the orphanage. After living briefly with Tyrin, Niskevich ran away and police found him among a group of boys sheltering in the October Railway Station.[84] In their expert assessment, Shumkov and his colleague wrote,

> On the sexual sphere and desire side, the following observations: persistent masturbation, weak attraction to the opposite sex, love for beautiful boys of 12–14 years old; he likes their eyes, cheeks and white teeth. Denies sexual intercourse. From youth experienced [sexual] satisfaction in games with children. During the hungry time [the civil war era] invited children in from the street, caressed them and let them stay the night. With regard to Niskevich, Ivan, 14 years old, experiences an especially loving feeling, pointing to the boy's attractive physical qualities. Not denying that he slept with the boy in the same bed, [he however] denies indecent acts. From the anamnesis it is evident that the subject suffers from bed-wetting. Secondary education unfinished, having left the fifth class of secondary school [*real'noe uchilishche*] of his own will. On the basis of the above and the circumstances of the case one comes to the conclusion that at the present time Tyrin suffers from a nervous illness in the form of neurasthenia, with episodes of bed-wetting and masturbation; in sexual relations normal desire for women is weakened. It is possible that a perversion of desire for his own sex for objects aged 12–14 is present.[85]

The court paid tribute to the expert psychiatric elaboration of this psychological world in the sentencing document. Condemning the ex-Communist to two years' imprisonment (without loss of rights), it repeated in voyeuristic fashion the key features of his sexual persona: "According to the experts' opinion, Tyrin is distinguished by persistent masturbation, reduced desire for the other sex, at the age of 30 has not known a woman [*v tridtsatiletnem vozraste ne znaet zhenshin*], [displays] love for beautiful boys aged 12 to 14 years; is attracted to their eyes, lips and the whiteness of their teeth." These desires, in the absence of a profound mental illness, were criminal, not pathological, in the eyes of the court. Psychiatrists in other same-sex cases made similar determinations, employing the language of sexual psychopathy in their expertise.[86]

Conclusion

From their vanguard status among the leaders of the "medical opposition" to tsarism before 1917, psychiatrists rapidly adapted to the Bolshevik regime and its vision of a modern and centralized medical system serving the new state and society. The activities of forensic psychiatrists hint at a revolutionary optimism about the relationship that doctors of the mind would enjoy with the new "owners of the cherry orchard." Now the technical and diagnostic skill of psychiatrists was given parity of esteem with other forms of medicine, and they were brought inside to work with police, courts, and prisons, ostensibly as partners under the aegis of a physician-directed commissariat of health. The new partnership with the criminal justice system gave psychiatry fresh opportunities to expand its influence via the nascent discipline of Soviet criminology. Sharon Kowalsky points out that psychiatrists as diagnosticians of the criminal mind received a measure of respect—and the resources that flowed from that respect—as they examined and diagnosed *convicted* offenders in the Soviet penal system.[87] Revealing the motive for criminality long after the fact, when the murderer or rapist was already behind bars, appears to have favored these psychiatrists' advance into criminology. The study and interpretation of a "captive population" with a well-documented history and incentives to speak to the doctor (the prospect of medical mitigation of the punishment) made the penal psychiatrist's task, in methodological terms, a simple one. For each potential case history the narrative trail was already there in the court's dossier, and in front of the psychiatrist sat a subject with genuine reasons to be talkative. It is not surprising that future historians would be captivated by the richly textured case histories written up by these doctors in their 1920s treatises exposing sexual assault, castration, defloration, and homosexual abuse.[88]

What the Petrograd and Sverdlovsk records show however is the relative absence of the psychiatrist in the preliminary and courtroom stages of the sex crime investigation. The modest proportion of cases featuring forensic psychiatric expertise of any kind indicates that whatever the interest in pathologies of sexuality expressed by Orshanskii and his Moscow colleague Krasnushkin and others in print, the diagnoses these psychiatrists provided were rather exquisite rarities, especially if they were delivered as part of the pretrial investigation rather than as a result of visits to penal facilities after the subject was convicted.[89] With such *convict*-focused research and publications, these leading Soviet psychiatrists sought to prove their value to criminologists from other disciplines, and justify their bid for greater control over the sex offender.[90] Fishman, run off his feet in Sverdlovsk's psychiatric hospital, was in no position to plot such advances, and the region's best-known psychiatrist, Segalin, was engrossed in the study of genius, not criminality.

In practice, even the well-resourced Petrograd or Moscow forensic psychiatrist was competing for control with other forces. Police investigators deemed the vast majority of sex offenders to be sane and therefore beyond the reach of psychiatry (at least, until incarceration). In the sampled Petrograd cases, psychiatrists, when called upon, often worked in forensic medical commissions or panels that positioned their expertise alongside that of somatic specialists: physicians, gynecologists, venereologists, specialists in disability, and so on. Frequently these panels were led by the chief forensic medical officer of Petrograd, N. I. Izhevskii (a senior forensic generalist), and their multidisciplinary and collective character could dilute psychiatric influence. The formal assessments the collectives produced left no trace of disputes in the examination room or conference hall: a smooth, univocal discourse of harmonious forensic science was apparently the ideal that Izhevskii and his teams sought. The prospect of conflicting scientific opinions in the courtroom was apparently evaded by Soviet prosecutors and judges through this mechanism, and the attempt to bury rapist Mikhail Miats's self-commissioned "second opinion" also hints at official striving for clarity and a lack of ambiguity. Where the sampled cases do present a significant psychiatric input, the opportunities to seize the limelight and extend the influence of the doctor of the mind as leading investigator were circumscribed by collective practices. Perhaps this collective supervision, and its frustrations, led Orshanskii and his Moscow colleagues to turn to the convicted sex offender in prison as a subject they could make use of to construct a uniquely psychiatric interpretation of sexual pathologies.

The issue of imputability—contentious in print—was apparently much less so in forensic psychiatric practice. Doctors in these cases consistently restricted the diagnosis of nonimputability to the most severely mentally ill or disordered. The sexual psychopath was regularly pronounced answerable for his actions, showing that both medical and legal authorities resisted Russian psychiatry's move into borderline conditions of neurosis and maladjustment when the question of the sex offender arose. The claim that soft-hearted psychiatrists of the 1920s exculpated the psychopath in excessive numbers is not borne out by the cases examined in this sample. If there was medical indulgence in these cases, it was not for the sexual psychopath, but for the regime's class friends, who might gain access to a reduced sentence or early release by virtue of ascribed proletarian status, or ties with the Communist Party. Such indulgence was exclusively in the power of judges, police, and prosecutors to grant, exposing another limitation to the autonomy of the psychiatrist as "judge of the scientific facts" in these cases.

The limited scope for medical mitigation available in practice did not prevent bids for exculpation launched by perpetrators of sex crimes, and their lawyer-advocates and relatives. Strikingly sophisticated in their access to the language of psychopathy, or their search for authoritative medical expertise, these bids hint at a society already versed in the extensive claims made for psychiatry by its prerevolutionary proponents.[91] The bids also suggest that perpetrators and their families and advocates were alert to the opportunities that were apparently presented by the parity of esteem conferred upon psychiatry by the Bolsheviks. These actors in their own microhistorical dramas could see the authority placed in the hands of psychiatrists when suspects were sent to Petrograd's Diagnostic Institute for assessment or when a psychiatrist was summoned to court to conduct an on-the-spot evaluation of a defendant. The new Soviet mechanisms of forensic psychiatry produced incentives for individuals to "speak psychiatrically" in Bolshevik terms.[92] In this sense the new mechanisms produced modern psychiatric subjects—and their simulators—teaching individuals to present themselves in terms set by the medico-moral language of psychiatry. It was the psychiatrists' parity of esteem with other forensic scientists, not their soft-hearted indulgence, that yielded the "psychopaths who already held a belief in their reduced- or non-responsibility" that so exercised Stalin-era critics of 1920s forensic psychiatry.

Yet the claim that forensic psychiatrists casually deployed the sexual psychopathy diagnosis in their expert opinions is also impossible to substantiate from the cases examined in the Petrograd sample. The scientific language of sexual desires, motives, and acts was for the most part reserved for the bad, not the mad. In expert assessments and courtroom testimony, psychiatrists explained the sex criminal's motives and demystified the perverse by using extended descriptions of the sexual psychology of the offender. They might point to a biological flaw in the sex offender's constitution—degeneration, a weakened nervous system, neurasthenia—but they routinely pronounced the same individuals answerable for their crimes, handing them back to the legal system to deal with. Few if any claimed that sexual psychopathy could be cured using medical means. Distinguishing the nonimputable from the imputable and demystifying the sex criminal's motives: these were the chief functions the forensic psychiatrist performed for the authorities. The extent to which doctors of the mind might believe that they could effect a change for the better in these subjects is not apparent from the individual crime cases. The pattern of use suggests rather a pessimistic prognosis. Evidently, psychiatrists used the language of a disease category (psychopathy) to describe and explain immoral behavior, and drain it of sensational or voyeuristic content. There was a subterranean connection here with the prerevolutionary politicization of the language of sexual psychopathy noted by Bershtein.[93] If before 1917, such language was a weapon in the hands of radical leftists looking to condemn their class enemies, after 1917 its sober, scientific variant issued from psychiatrists working within a radically leftist regime, seeking to explain sexual disorder, and to designate moral deviants from the new order.

These early Soviet psychiatrists used sexualized and sexualizing language to describe criminals who would as a rule receive exemplary punishments. When sex offenders obtained mitigation on medical grounds, psychiatrists made little if any mention of sexual motives, desires, and actions: desire did not speak in these cases. Even in the "humane" 1920s, in the Soviet court the language of sexual psychology could evidently only be a negating, dangerous discourse, a means of classifying new social enemies.[94] Yet, as the next chapter explores, the language of sexual psychology had other uses, beyond the courtroom. Inside the Soviet clinic, "living a sexual life" and the psychological problems this presented for hermaphrodites were actively explored by physicians. Their practices offer a contrasting perspective on the ways in which Soviet medicine conceived of the sexual psyche.

FIVE

BODIES IN SEARCH OF A SEX

Through recorded history, the person of mixed male and female sex organs and sexual characteristics has been a figure of fascination and dread. Described in poetry and myth, exploited by bards, scandalmongers, and freak-show hucksters, the hermaphrodite[1] has occupied a small but significant space in the cultural order. In the Greek myth of the lovely child of Hermes and Aphrodite, as a model of sublime beauty and exquisite sexual dualism, the hermaphrodite inspired awe. Jewish and Roman law and Christian traditions deriving from them highlighted society's fear of the individual with two sexes. Jewish prescriptions dictated when hermaphrodites could be treated like men (they were forbidden to shave, for example) and when like women (they were disqualified from paternal inheritance and from serving as witnesses or priests). Roman legal tradition, revived and adapted from the sixteenth century in western Europe, established a framework for coping with the two-sexed individual. Parents assigned a sex to such infants at birth and raised them in that sex; at the threshold of sexual maturity the child was permitted a once-in-a-lifetime chance to select "the warmest sex" (the prevailing sex conceived in terms of sexual desire for an "opposite" sex). This attractively tidy framework required that the hermaphrodite remain in the adopted sex ever after. Hermaphrodites nevertheless experienced a more complex reality. It is not surprising that most of the surviving stories of lives lived by people of ambiguous sex are narratives dominated by confusion, doubt, reversals, and public scandal.[2]

The social integration of the two-sexed individual was never an easy process in Western culture, with its emphatic division of humanity into two distinct sexes.[3] In early modern Europe disputes over inheritance, property, and civil rights and duties arose when hermaphrodites were uncovered. Integration became even more urgent, historians have argued, in the modern era as democratic ideals posited the fundamental equality of all. Political equality could not be allowed to dissolve the hierarchy of the two sexes. The same liberalism that promoted democracy also held up science as the final arbiter of the truth about sex. Biologists of the nineteenth century sought "reliable criteria of sexual classification" not simply to establish sex-specific characters but also to establish "a 'natural' order of the sexes in relation to each other."[4] The reconsideration of sex roles along scientific principles was an urgent project for a democratic order that undermined older forms of political status.

Beginning with Michel Foucault, historians have turned to modern stories of the hermaphrodite to learn more about the contemporary gender order. In his introduction to the autobiography of Herculine Barbin (a French hermaphrodite whose public discovery in 1860 and change of legal sex aroused intense popular, juridical, and scientific curiosity), Foucault asserted that modernity insists on a single clear sex in every citizen. The ambiguities and confusions characteristic of earlier regimes were intolerable as science and the politics of population management advanced. He also noted that from the eighteenth century, biological medicine delved deeper into the body of the hermaphrodite to reveal the "truth" about sex: internal organs gradually became the conclusive sign of the "authentic" sex of the hermaphrodite. Foucault noted too the coincidence in the rise of biomedical interest in the hermaphrodite, with the increasing medicalization of the homosexual, another process underway in the final third of the nineteenth century. Ambiguities of sex, whether physical or psychological, now came under sustained scientific scrutiny.[5]

Applying these hypotheses in a detailed study of French and British medical case histories of hermaphrodites, Alice Domurat Dreger has argued that modernity required the erasure of the person of ambiguous sex. Dreger does not deny that such persons, in search of "badly desired identities," themselves demanded solutions to their sexual ambiguity from medicine. Yet she emphasizes the paternalism and ambition of doctors who used the extraordinary opportunities furnished by the appearance of hermaphrodites in clinics to advance their own professional medical and cultural authority. In the late nineteenth and early twentieth centuries, the "age of the gonads," medical experts applied new biological knowledge to assess the "truth" about sex from internal sex glands (testes and ovaries). The diagnostic practice of the age was to disregard the hermaphrodite's external anatomy and psychological profile when sexing the patient. The sex glands trumped all else, frequently justifying many French and some British doctors' prescriptions that patients exchange their lifelong gender, described as an "error of sex," for the "true sex" of their internal organs.

Errors of sex were particularly abhorred for the "same-sex" marriages inadvertently contracted by undetected "pseudohermaphrodites" (i.e., individuals having one sex's external genitalia—or an approximation thereof—and the internal sex glands of the opposite sex) with unwitting spouses.[6] Patients however found it wrenching to comply with doctors' prescriptions of a change of social sex.[7]

During and after the First World War, improved techniques in exploratory and cosmetic surgery, and breakthroughs in understanding the functions of the sex hormones, emboldened doctors to explore procedures to "clarify" the sex of hermaphrodites. In Britain and in the United States, pioneering experts began to question the emphasis on the "true sex" of the gonads in determining therapy for hermaphrodite patients.[8] These pioneers, influenced by specific clinical encounters, argued that secondary sex characteristics, upbringing, and psychology mattered when treating the hermaphrodite. Commentators on U.S. medical history note that a period of "idiosyncratic" approaches dawned in the decades after 1918, arguing that despite the apparent flexibility of these new diagnoses and treatments, their purpose was yet again to fix the hermaphrodite in the two-sex social system.[9] By the 1950s, U.S. doctors "won out over the threat of the hermaphrodite," erasing ambiguous bodies with surgical "reconstruction" and hormonal "therapy." Patients were thus enabled to "pass" in the role of a single, unambiguous sex—as clearly female or male.[10] Concern for the impact on American patients of these "modern" therapies for intersex conditions generated much of the study of the medical history of the hermaphrodite. As a group, North American intersex patients now vocally challenge the nature of their diagnoses and the terms by which they are treated.[11]

The transatlantic migration of this narrative—from British and French cases at the end of the nineteenth century to U.S. intersex activism at the end of the twentieth century—shows up a significant gap in our understanding of this medical history. Historians have overlooked European variations on these themes, especially the continuities and ruptures produced by the rise and fall of fascism and communism. The recent histories of the hermaphrodite have tended to focus attention on liberal democratic regimes. Following Foucault, historians of hermaphroditism see the combination of liberal democracy and scientific modernity as a key determinant, facilitating a colonization of gender by hubristic doctors eager to project their authority. Yet scientific modernity was not confined to the democratic West, and the power conferred by medicine as a discipline was wielded in other social and political regimes too. The experience of Soviet Russian hermaphrodites, and the history of their encounters with medicine, offer new perspectives on this narrative.

Beginning with an exploration of Russia's traditions of responding to the hermaphrodite before 1917, this chapter examines the ways in which Soviet medicine, interpreting the values of the Bolshevik sexual revolution, came to develop its own "solutions" to the problems posed by this obscure form of sexual disorder. Soviet doctors' responses to the hermaphrodite reveal explorations of the sexual personality of the individual patient—explorations that ran counter to the usual refusal of "psychologism" in Soviet approaches to sex.

Russian Perspectives on the Hermaphrodite

Scholars of Russia have had very little to say about the social history of hermaphrodites and how the Russian state and society viewed them.[12] In part this is the result of silence: Russian legislation, for example, said nothing (from its origins in the tenth century until 1926) about how individuals of ambiguous sex were to be treated. Subordinated to the cultural orbit of Byzantium and Orthodox Christianity, Muscovy did not inherit the Roman legal tradition that influenced lawmakers and philosophers after the Renaissance in western Europe.[13] The ambitions of one physician of the Great Reform era, that Russian law should acquire predictable standards for dealing with the person of ambiguous sex, went unrealized. Summarizing his findings after reviewing the case of a peasant-hermaphrodite examined in 1865 in St. Petersburg, he wrote:

> Taking into account such cases and the examples discussed of pseudo-hermaphroditism, the consequences of which in our enlightened time are even marriages between men [braki . . . mezhdu muzhchinami], not to mention other curious misunderstandings that could possibly be encountered in life as a result of this, it goes without saying, that it is desirable for our legislation to pay the necessary attention to this public and juridical question which in our opinion is of no small importance.[14]

Evidence from late nineteenth- and early twentieth-century case histories suggests that secular Russian authorities, when confronted with cases of hermaphroditism, responded with administrative improvisation. A native of Tver' province, living in St. Petersburg in 1897, was dispatched to her native village for a medical examination and to have her birth records altered.[15] Other individuals, who came to the notice of authorities after committing a crime or causing a disturbance, might be sent for a doctor's opinion as to their sex, but a change of their officially registered ("passport") gender was denied, perhaps because they were viewed as maliciously deceptive.[16]

Doctors in late tsarist Russia, in comparison to their European colleagues, approached the hermaphrodite more tentatively, less confident in their ability to reveal a "true sex" in their patients. Numerous provincial reports of the hermaphrodite as biological curiosity, without always insisting on gonadal sex, were published in Russian medical journals from the 1860s to 1890s.[17] The power to prescribe sex had not only a scientific dimension, but a legal one that generated anxiety, not confidence. In 1898, the prominent legal physician Professor E. F. Bellin diagnosed a peasant factory worker as a "male internal pseudohermaphrodite" on the basis of two undeveloped testes detected on either side of her shallow vaginal opening. Nevertheless, he would not reclassify as a man this person who had lived for twenty-four years as a woman. He declared that she was "sexless" *(bespolyi)* because of her inability to reproduce.[18] Bellin's reluctance to pronounce on his patient's "civil rights" (as he referred to the official designation of her sex) reflected the discomfort of doctors under the autocracy. Like their counterparts further west, Russian doctors based their professional claims on technocratic expertise, yet the conservative tsarist regime refused to confer full authority on these men of science. In addition, doctors, like the peasants and workers they treated, were disenfranchised politically. Laura Engelstein has argued that in the case of the female prostitute and the male homosexual, Russia's doctors were slow to adopt western medical models of sexual anomaly and pathology when they themselves were powerless subjects of a patriarchal tsar.[19] The hermaphrodite fell under the same shadow that retarded the pathologization of the prostitute and homosexual in late Imperial Russia.

Yet the empire could also harbor pockets of exceptional modernity. The leading European specialist on the hermaphrodite was a Polish subject of the tsar, the director of the gynecological department of Warsaw's Evangelical Hospital, Franz Neugebauer.[20] His landmark tome published in 1908, a collection of two thousand cases of ambiguous sex gathered from historical and contemporary sources, had the effect of transforming the hermaphrodite case from isolated clinical story into a recurring, apparently frequent, human phenomenon.[21] Only about fifty of the cases originated on Russian territory. The overwhelming majority were drawn from reports in the German-language medical press of central Europe, as well as from publications in France and Britain. Neugebauer's professional energies also focused westward. His training was finished in Germany, Austria, and England; he traveled extensively to conferences in the United States and western Europe, and the British Gynecological Society and the Academy of Medicine in Paris counted him as a member. Neugebauer's limited analytical gifts did not prevent him from having a large influence on European medical understanding of the hermaphrodite. He was a tireless promoter of the gonadal diagnosis of "true sex," and following from this, insistently warned against the social dangers of "errors of sex." "Accidental" marriages between persons who (in terms of their gonads) were of the "same sex," and the inadvertent homosexuality this threatened, justified the intervention of medical authority in Neugebauer's moralizing view.

To the end of the old regime, Russian officialdom nevertheless viewed the scattered hermaphrodite individuals it encountered as a problem for medical police.[22] Bureaucratic considerations closely circumscribed the role of doctors in managing persons of ambiguous sex.[23] The Russian Orthodox Church could dissolve marriages on grounds of infertility, which might incidentally include medical confirmation of a spouse's dubious sex.[24] The annual recruitment of conscripts, accompanied by medical screening for defective physiques, threw up a small number of young hermaphrodites living as men, who were quickly rejected as unsuitable for military service.[25] Occasionally, the state-mandated medical examination of prostitutes turned up cases of hermaphroditism.[26] On the eve of the First World War, the government knew about the latest medical views but continued to refuse doctors custody of the hermaphrodite. In 1913, an anonymous observer from the Ministry of Internal Affairs rejected medical claims to be able to recognize a "true sex" in most hermaphrodites, and criticized the latest proposals in Prussia to permit medical expertise a decisive role in adjudicating such cases. In the opinion of the police ministry, no such concessions to Russian doctors were desirable.[27]

The Revolution and the Hermaphrodite

The World War, the 1917 revolutions, and the Civil War transformed the political, institutional, and scientific context for Russian medicine, and the interpretation of the hermaphrodite changed with it. The police ministry's jurisdiction over health matters was formally broken, in 1918, when the Bolsheviks launched the People's Commissariat of Health, discussed in chapter 1. The consequences for the medicalization of the hermaphrodite flowing from this change would be very significant. Also profoundly important for the medical appropriation of the hermaphrodite was the commissariat's sponsorship of research in endocrinology, and particularly the study of the sex hormones. Advances in the field, especially in central Europe, spurred early Soviet enthusiasm for research in sex-hormone function in animals, in "rejuvenation" therapy for humans, and crucially, in attempts to control human gender and sexual anomaly using gonad implants.[28]

Soviet science normally observed a division of labor on the murky question of gender and sexual anomaly. Forensic medicine enthusiastically appropriated hermaphroditism, under the aegis of the Soviet chief forensic medical expert, Iakov L. Leibovich, as a physiological problem with social significance. Homosexuality, sometimes referred to in medical literature as "psychical hermaphroditism," was generally left for psychiatrists to deal with. Such a division of labor differed little from research agendas in Europe; what was unusual was the ambiguous political status of same-sex love in the early Soviet regime. In the new Soviet Union's European republics, "sodomy" had been removed from the statute book, and some psychiatrists counseled toleration and sympathy for the "congenital" homosexual.[29] Soviet medical and legal authorities generally interpreted this new disposition as a politically progressive stance, part of the sexual revolution, which contrasted with the continued criminalization of male homosexuality in Britain, Germany, and virtually all of central Europe. Even in France, where sodomy had been decriminalized during the French Revolution, a demographic crisis worried doctors, and heightened suspicions of homosexuality, including putative same-sex love between "pseudohermaphrodites."[30] With Soviet revolutionary sexual legislation to point to, Russian doctors could afford to be more sanguine than French or British counterparts about supposed "same-sex" relations uncovered between the hermaphrodite and his/her partner. The "specter of homosexuality" would not be an early driver of Soviet medical concern for the hermaphrodite.[31]

Leibovich set out to produce the hermaphrodite as a feature of the social body through statistics. Like the rape victim and the suicide, persons of ambiguous sex were counted and established in the forensic medical agenda.[32] Among the various "examinations of living persons" that forensic doctors recorded, "determinations of sex" were routinely included. In 1921 in Petrograd and Saratov, local experts were already anticipating sex-determinations in their statistical reports.[33] By 1925, fifty-four such examinations out of a total of 60,000 "examinations of living persons" were conducted for all of Soviet Russia.[34] In 1931, Moscow reported three examinations for sex-determination, Leningrad just one, while Saratov reported ten.[35] These were hardly large numbers, but to chart them systematically was a departure from the medical police practices of the old regime, and a token of the modernity of Soviet medicine. With more consistency than before 1914, Russia's doctors now embraced the gonadal test for the determination of "true sex." Leibovich's 1928 forensic gynecological textbook devoted an entire chapter to the techniques of palpation, stimulation of the sex organs, rectal examination, and exploratory surgery (laparotomy, an early, invasive surgical method, and later more modest biopsies) that could be used to detect the presence of ovaries or testes in hermaphrodites.[36]

The high-water mark of the chief forensic medical expert's influence over the question of the hermaphrodite came in 1926, when the Commissariat of Internal Affairs (which oversaw registry-office functions) issued a circular on hermaphrodites. "Citizens with characteristics of hermaphroditism (two-sexed), who wish to change name and surname to correspond to the revealed sex" received the right to apply to alter their passport sex. Their local health authority was required to form a medical panel with the compulsory participation of a forensic medical expert to confirm the citizen's "hermaphroditism, while indicating the predominance of a particular sex (male or female)." The circular laid out a procedure "for the correction of all the applicant's documents" for registry offices (ZAGS, where births, marriages, divorces, and deaths were recorded) to follow upon receipt of the medical panel's decision.

Reconstructing how the 1926 regulations on changes of passport sex for hermaphrodites actually worked would necessitate a laborious trawl through municipal-level registry archives. One clue to their use comes from a 1926 newspaper report on "incomplete people" who sought out Professor I. A. Golianitskii at the Dostoevskii Hospital, apparently attracted by his claims to be able to "reconstruct" such persons into one clear sex.[37] Golianitskii, a surgeon whose wartime experience included transplant experimentation, invited the newspaper's reporter to meet one of his patients, formerly Vera, who now lived as Vladimir after a successful series of operations to "clarify" his male sex. Three other patients, all originally women, were also now considered men after undergoing as many as nine surgical operations. Two of the patients had re-named themselves, officially changing their identity documents. The third (born Praskov'ia) had evidently lived sometime informally as a man, using the male name Pavel at work and even "marrying" a woman who did not suspect there was anything unusual about her "husband". The report implies that Praskov'ia had long ago falsified her identity documents to become Pavel, and it is silent on whether an official change of passport sex was attempted. Such ambiguity suggests that the 1926 regulations for changing passport sex, designed to enable medical experts to assist the hermaphrodite citizen, might still embroil doctors in cases of counterfeit documentation and "fraudulent" marriages.

Despite Leibovich's efforts to publicize the circular, few doctors describing individual cases of dubious sex mentioned it in the case histories discussed later in this chapter. The approach generally adopted by these Soviet doctors seldom required a life-shattering change of passport sex.[38] In the post-Stalin USSR, legal reform to enhance "socialist legality" meant that citizens of ambiguous sex were required to apply to the courts for a change of recorded sex. A court would review the medical evidence provided by forensic specialists.[39] The proliferation of paperwork typical of late-Soviet daily life rendered the alteration of passport sex extremely burdensome for intersexual patients. A 1974 decree of the Council of Ministers of the USSR made it the function of each issuing organ to alter the passport sex of these citizens' papers. Doctors however complained that it was "absolutely inappropriate" for mentally unstable patients to apply to a series of agencies where they were known with such an unexpected request.[40]

Encounters in the Clinic

Having established the understandings of and procedures relating to hermaphrodites that were available to early Soviet doctors, an examination of clinical encounters between medical professionals and their patients of ambiguous sex can offer insights into uniquely Soviet approaches to the problem.[41] The demands and questions put by hermaphrodites to their doctors can illuminate their expectations of the medical profession and popular ideas of gender and sexuality. The ways in which Soviet doctors responded to these questions display or imply a range of ethical concerns. Soviet clinical practice in encounters with the hermaphrodite can be read to assess how physicians interpreted the values of "sexual revolution" when pressed to make major decisions about the gender and sexuality of an individual patient.

This discussion of clinical encounters between early Soviet doctors and their hermaphrodite patients is based on case histories published in the Soviet medical press between 1919 and 1938. To train attention on the sexual lives and psyches of these cases, the sample has been filtered to focus on the articulate adult patient.[42] While in no way a "comprehensive" survey of Soviet hermaphrodite cases, the sample of patient-doctor encounters is sufficient to trace the key characteristics of this medical literature. These stories of medical practices can be explored for their keys to the "sexual revolution."[43]

Soviet medical periodicals experienced varying degrees of ideological and party supervision; the sharpest peak of party interference in science was during the First Five-Year Plan of 1928–1932, when toleration of specialists inherited from the tsarist regime was at its lowest. During a "cultural revolution" at the outset of the plan, Marxists were imposed by the party as institutional leaders in most disciplines, and the rituals and rhetoric of academic disciplines were "sovietized."[44] From this time, institutes were required to set plans for scientific research, with health priorities focused narrowly on the most productive sectors of the workforce.[45] Isolated and extraordinary cases, randomly encountered in a clinic reception room, were not meant to be a priority for research, or presumably, for articles about them in these periodicals. Paradoxically, as noted in the introduction, exactly half of the cases are described in publications appearing during the First Five-Year Plan, and a further third (12 cases) were published between 1933 and 1938, the years when Soviet sexology otherwise disappeared from view, not reappearing until the 1950s.[46] Examining cases from both the 1920s and 1930s offers opportunities to compare medical approaches and techniques across the 1930 divide between the sexually "revolutionary" and "silent" eras. Perhaps this rare deviation from Stalinism's desexualized medical discourse was "licensed" by the censors' perceptions that it was primarily the patients' bodies that were "defective," and developments in surgery seemed to present a triumph over anomaly. Scrutiny of "damaged" sexual functionality was therefore admissible, following the materialist terms of Soviet science. The endocrinological basis of the sex drive (in hormones produced by ovaries and testes) supplied an irreproachable foundation for this logic. The degree to which censors had scientific training for the surveillance of articles like these remains an open question.

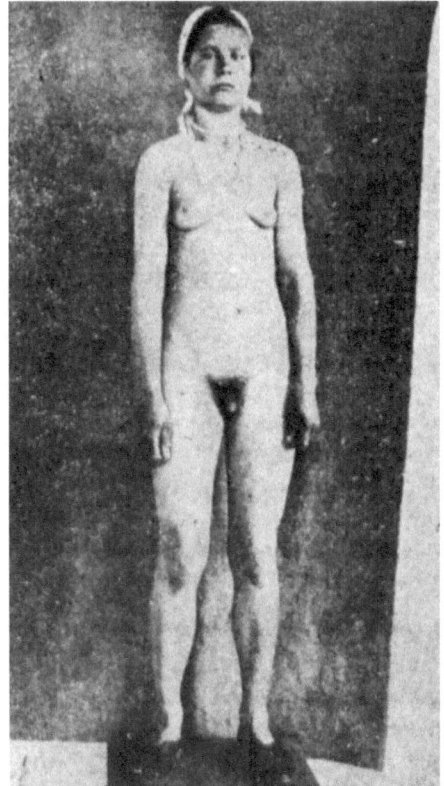

A patient diagnosed as a "false female hermaphrodite" in Kazan', 1936. Source: Iu. M. Irger, "K kazuistike lozhnogo zhenskogo germafroditizma." *Kazanskii meditsinskii zhurnal,* no. 10 (1936): 1262–64.

These narratives follow conventions that by this time were well established in western biomedical case histories of the hermaphrodite. The typical hermaphrodite case history opened with an introduction discussing the problem of physical sexual ambiguity according to the author's understanding of the current state of scientific knowledge. Occasionally, the author might embellish this with learned references to the hermaphrodite in classical Greek or Roman mythology, but such comments were relatively rare in Soviet medical cases.[47] A description of the patient encountered by the author follows, often distinguished from the interpretive text surrounding it by a smaller typeface to indicate that this was empirical data. The passage invariably included a physical description of the patient, sometimes in extensive anthropometric detail. Almost all the narratives include some discussion of the patient's psychological development, character, and experience of social adaptation. Photographs of the subject frequently appear, in several cases without any attempt to conceal the patient's identity (although only in one case is the full name of a hermaphrodite recorded; usually initials were used). Making visible the bodily anomalies of these patients was a long-standing practice in publications of hermaphrodite case histories. Via photographs anomalous organs were more easily described, while the patient's gender persona and social position might also be presented or suggested, depending on the style of image employed. The empirical section of the case history usually concluded with a diagnosis and reflections on therapeutic interventions. Where attempted, these interventions, usually surgical in nature, were described along with their outcomes. For many doctors, this was the end of their article, but some intellectually ambitious practitioners returned to the state of the question of hermaphroditism to draw conclusions based on their clinical experience.

The language of these case histories lacked political rhetoric, as did the overwhelming majority of texts describing specific patient cases in Soviet medical periodicals. (From the 1930s, these journals often opened with highly politicized editorial articles, and certain genres such as discussions of health provision could be heavily imbued with Five-Year Plan rhetoric.) Even in forensic medical textbooks, where a more militant tone might be adopted when discussing, for example, homosexuality after the 1934 Stalinist sodomy ban, the treatment of hermaphroditism was essentially free of party discourse.[48] When the patient's social experiences and concerns were mentioned, doctors framed them in the language of *"byt"* (everyday life) and thereby bracketed them in an ideologically acceptable fashion, even if they failed to drain these narratives completely of their extraordinary and even entertaining character.[49]

What motivated the early Soviet hermaphrodites described in these texts to seek medical assistance? What complaints about their bodies did they make? What desires did they express to the doctors they consulted? Of the 36 individuals in this sample, the overwhelming majority (27) chose to go to the doctors themselves. Only a small proportion—4 persons—were "discovered" involuntarily by the authorities (e.g., during military recruitment health checkups), and 3 were referred by family members. In the remaining 2 cases the motivation for referral is unknown. The high degree of self-selection in the sample suggests that patients had an expectation that scientific medicine had solutions to the problem of indeterminate sex. It is striking too that 15 of the 27 self-referring patients were peasants by social class, since Bolsheviks and the educated intelligentsia more widely agonized over the peasants' mistrust of biomedical medicine. Peasant reliance on nonscientific medical help ("wise women," herbalists) was just one of the many obstacles to the modernization of the countryside.[50] Another index of reliance on biomedicine in this matter is the fact that for 11 individuals, the medical encounter described in the sample article was not the first they had sought regarding their hermaphroditism. These patients had "shopped around" for medical opinions and therapies, some of them intensively and insistently, and their histories could include information received from earlier consultations.

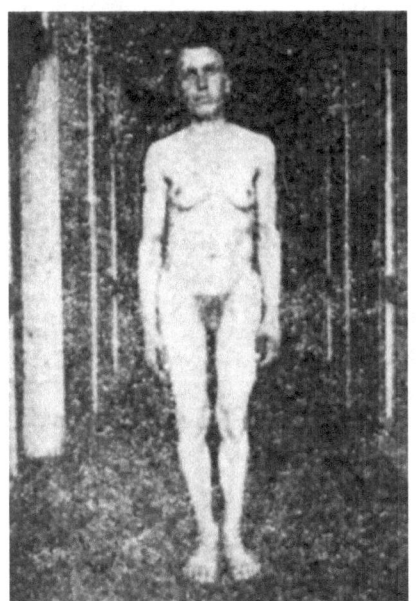

Patient K.V., a 29-year-old
Ukrainian villager, 1930

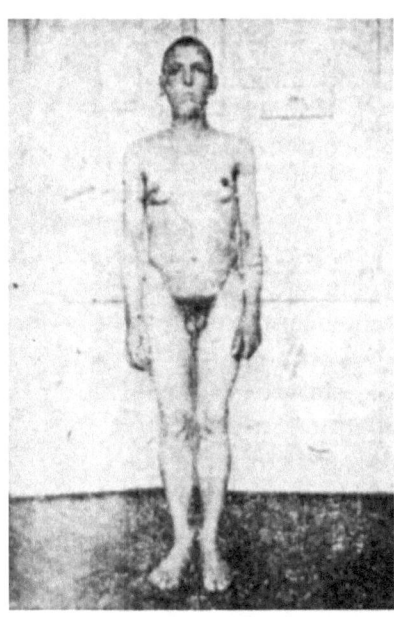

Patient K.G.E., 22-year-old brother
of K.V., 1930

The motivations expressed by patients for seeking the doctor's help were diverse. Most complained about the evident difference between their own external genitalia and that of the people around them. All the individuals in this sample received at birth a specific gender designation, and were raised as male or female. Yet their bodies did not conform convincingly to the gender they inhabited. In 1930, Kiev doctor V. L. Beder typically introduced a patient in the following manner: "Patient K.V., 29 years old, a villager, Ukrainian, entered the clinic on 14 December 1930 with complaints about the faulty development of his sexual apparatus."[51] The doctor continues:

> He first noticed this at age 12, realizing that he urinated from somewhere near the perineum, and not like other boys, which he was able to confirm by observing his friends of the same age. He first turned to a doctor in 1917 at the age of 16 to complain about his abnormalities, asking if an operation would help him. At age 18 he first noticed the development of mammary glands, which continued to grow until his twentieth year when development stopped. He has never noticed emissions of any kind of liquid from the mammary glands.

Like many hermaphrodites in these texts and those produced by doctors elsewhere, K.V. experienced alienation not only because of sexual dysfunction.[52] Urination, something one is accustomed to thinking of as a private act, for this group of individuals carried and carries a social significance, especially in childhood as a confirmation of gender. This significance must have been amplified in the Ukrainian countryside where public/private distinctions were weakly observed. A further challenge to K.V.'s "masculinity" appeared with the development of his breasts. While these appendages did not prevent him from marrying, or even from having a relatively frequent (if unsatisfying) sexual life with his wife of five years, according to the doctor they caused "collisions in family life." K.V., and his 22-year-old brother K.G.E., also found to be a hermaphrodite, asked the doctor to remove their mammary glands. In describing their psychology, the doctor conveyed their acute sense of damaged manhood. Of the younger brother he noted, "he feels he is entirely a man, although he is conscious of his sexual inadequacy." "Male" hermaphrodites came to doctors in the hope that their unstable claims to masculinity might be buttressed.

In a similar way, hermaphrodites living as women sought clarification of their gender identities, often with similar notes of desperation and insistence. In autumn 1935 a young Saratov woman turned to that city's Medical Academy, complaining about the abnormal structure of her sexual organs, and her failure to menstruate. She had facial hair that she was forced to shave periodically, and she was evidently bemused by the size of her clitoris. "The patient asked that we make of her something definite in a sexual sense, saying at the same time that she only feels desire for men."[53] In 1928, a 30-year-old patient entered a clinic in the southern port of Odessa; despite enjoying a relatively unproblematic childhood, her adult life was fraught with confusion caused by sexual desire and "fear that her abnormal sexual structure would become well-known in the village."[54] Her doctors noted:

> She has visited many doctors but never received a direct answer. In the past four years she has not discussed this with anyone. She is very anxious, frequently ready to lay hands on herself, feels "anger at the whole world." In the past two years she has devoted herself to social work in the village (zhenotdel [i.e., the Communist Party's women's department]) in order to forget her unbearably difficult position. Now she has come to our clinic with an insistent request to give her a decision about whether she is a man or a woman. . . . She is prepared to undergo any form of intervention so that she can join the ranks of those with one sex.

For some hermaphrodites socialized as women, the demand that doctors reforge the individual by making some kind of physical intervention to clarify sex was linked to a desire to have a child. The Zhenotdel activist from Odessa said she envied her girlfriends who got married and had babies. Others, like 20-year-old N. who in 1930 presented herself at the university gynecological clinic in Baku, suffered rejection from spouses because of their infertility.[55]

Marital harmony was another insistent worry. Even if their infertility could not be alleviated, hermaphrodites with spouses (or hoping to obtain one) frequently sought medical assistance to facilitate a more enjoyable conjugal life. In 1927 in a Siberian industrial town's gynecological clinic, a peasant girl of 17, with plans for her future, was found to be more male than female, with a four-centimeter penis and a shallow vaginal opening. "In turning to us for help," the director of the clinic wrote, "from his [*ego*] side there was one request—to get rid of everything reminiscent of a man, and create the possibility of having a woman's sexual life, because she already has a fiancé [*zhenikh*]."[56] Hermaphrodites' aspirations for what they regarded as normal conjugal pleasure, and doctors' reporting of them, are unusual features of Soviet medical discourse. Normally, Soviet sexologists in their prescriptions for a healthy sexual life carefully evaded the whole question of pleasure in sexual relations, not wishing to provoke excessive interest in sex and inadvertently debauch Soviet youth. In their counseling, they reasoned that so long as fundamental rules of physical and mental hygiene were observed, nature would take its course in an unproblematic fashion.[57] When hermaphrodites entered the clinic, however, they brought with them a confused set of messages from nature. Soviet doctors found themselves compelled to speak rather more explicitly about the mechanics of pleasure when dealing with hermaphrodites.

These patients were painfully aware of the physical differences between themselves and those around them, but a few in the sample lacked any awareness of their own hermaphroditism. They turned to medicine to resolve other health issues; hernias, swellings, or tumors caused them pain but did not induce any doubt in their minds about their supposed sex. Still others complained of infertility, but again without doubting their sex. Doctors did not necessarily reveal the full "truth" of their diagnoses to such individuals, and their actions and rationales reveal variations in the practice of medical secrecy.

In one typical case, a 62-year-old unskilled factory laborer, Evdokiia K., complained of a tumor in the groin, and her doctor, Professor L. A. Krivskii of Petrograd's prestigious Military-Medical Academy, operated in 1919. She was found to have partially developed testes and seminal vesicles, which were removed. After further examination of the patient, the professor concluded Evdokiia K. was in fact male, but he decided not to tell her. "[W]e did not consider it necessary to disappoint a person who had lived 62 years in the role of a woman by telling her that she was of the other sex."[58] Indeed, this professor used Evdokiia in a "demonstration of the patient" to his students prior to the operation, switching into Latin to describe her sexually ambiguous condition, and also when informing students that the only way to determine the sex of her internal organs would be after her death, in autopsy. In two cases described by a pair of Baku doctors in 1930, women complaining of infertility, who turned out to be hermaphrodites, were subjected to surgery that was largely exploratory (rather than therapeutic) and were not told about their "true" diagnoses.[59] The Baku doctors complained that little psychological data could be gleaned from their patients, describing both as "women of little culture" (they were peasants, one Turkish, the other, Russian). Between the Petrograd professor and the Baku physicians one can see the contrasting ethics of disclosure and patient care. The professor went to great lengths to avoid "disappointing" his patient with a shocking disclosure, and the operation he conducted was entirely therapeutic, solely to relieve suffering. Despite the fact that he was in a sense "using" the patient in a teaching capacity, he spoke in Latin to conceal his diagnosis from her. In the process he was also giving his students a clear lesson in the principle of *"lozh' v spasenie,"* the "lie for the patient's own good," an aspect of Soviet and post-Soviet medical treatment in especially difficult circumstances like cancer.⁶⁰ The professor evidently felt that his patient's age was another factor arguing against disclosure. Like many Soviet physicians confronting younger examples of "errors of sex," he might perhaps have adopted a different course with a hermaphrodite on the threshold of living a sexual life.

By contrast, the Baku doctors operated on their hermaphrodites primarily to satisfy their curiosity about the nature of their gonads (were they testes or ovaries?). They dismissed these patients as backward and uneducated, and therefore unreliable narrators of their own histories. The substantial interpretive conclusion in their article is an unusually wide-ranging critique of the scientific literature on hermaphroditism, suggesting that the nontherapeutic, exploratory operations they conducted were primarily intended to further their research and establish themselves as authorities in this area. Their lack of empathy with peasant patients was probably compounded in the case of the Turkish "woman," whose gender and cultural background prevented her from speaking openly about her sexual discomfort.⁶¹ The Russian medical profession's view of the subject peoples of the south and east of the old empire and new Soviet Union was steeped in orientalist prejudices even as it proclaimed its liberal civilizing mission.⁶² The Baku doctors displayed the darker side of Soviet medical paternalism, in which exploratory surgery to satisfy scientific curiosity could be imposed on "women of little culture." The boundaries between therapy and experimentation were poorly delineated in Soviet medical practice, as they were internationally in the interwar period.⁶³

"More Modern" Soviet Therapy

In the majority of cases (28 out of 36 in this sample), Soviet doctors made offers of medical assistance to the hermaphrodites they confronted. Patients applying to doctors in the 1930s were slightly more likely to be offered therapies, and this may simply reflect the increasing availability and safety of surgical interventions that doctors in most big cities could by this time provide. In earlier years, both medical infrastructure and scientific knowledge appeared to lag behind an existing aspiration to "correct the sex" of these patients. In 1922, the chief forensic medical expert, Leibovich, counseled against surgical operations to assist the individual with ambiguous genitalia, saying that clinicians must await further technical developments.⁶⁴ Occasionally cases appear to reflect this stance by revealing nothing in print about any assistance offered to patients, stopping abruptly with a diagnosis.⁶⁵ Surgery was however the therapy of choice for the medical experts in this sample, with 23 out of 28 cases featuring some form of operation, usually as the centerpiece of treatment. Less frequently, doctors also attempted hormonal therapy (implants of sex hormone-producing tissues, in 3 cases) and psychiatric assessment and possibly counseling (in 4 definite and 3 possible cases).

Attitudes toward surgical help for hermaphroditism were in transition in the first half of the twentieth century. As early as 1900, the European authority Neugebauer had, in characteristically moralizing fashion, distinguished three types of surgical assistance for such patients. He called *"opérations d'urgence"* the surgery given to patients in acute physical distress resulting from their deformities (such as that received for her tumor by 62-year-old Evdokiia in 1919). Such "emergency operations" were ethically necessary because they conformed to the Hippocratic oath's injunction to relieve suffering. *"Opérations de complaisance"* (of obligingness, of kindness) assisted the hermaphrodite-victim of an "error of sex" to live according to the sex of his or her gonads. For example, if ovaries were identified, the patient's external genitalia should be rendered as feminine as possible, and s/he should live as a woman. Again, such operations, and the identity transformations they might impose, were ethically sound in Neugebauer's view. However, he condemned *"opérations de complicité,"* surgical interventions that made physicians complicit with the unnatural desires of their patients. By furnishing cosmetic changes to the sex organs that pandered to the wishes of hermaphrodites without reference to the "true" sex of the gonads, doctors performing "complicitous operations" allegedly facilitated debauchery. In the early decades of the twentieth century, a substantial proportion of medical opinion in Europe followed Neugebauer's lead on this question.[66]

Soviet doctors, under the influence of the revolution's sexual values, paid little attention to these distinctions. Just as their case histories expressed no anxiety about the "specter of homosexuality" looming over the hermaphrodite, their attitude toward patient-pleasing cosmetic surgery was comparatively relaxed. They seldom mentioned Neugebauer's moral classification of surgical operations. In fact, in the leading Soviet textbook on forensic gynecology of the 1930s, experts E. E. Rozenblium and M. G. Serdiukov, reflecting on their experience of resolving hermaphrodite cases, contrasted such "conservative" attitudes with a "more modern direction":

> The question of the necessity of conducting such operations in cases of hermaphroditism has not been settled conclusively by science. There is a conservative viewpoint that considers it superfluous to use any such surgery on hermaphrodites. The more modern direction founded on the basis of endocrinological data, by which it is entirely possible to exert influence on the endocrine status, freely permits the full expediency of surgical intervention. The creation of specific organs or the removal of superfluous ones (the

creation of an artificial vagina, the removal of a hypertrophied clitoris, etc.), and also transplants of sex glands corresponding to the sex, undoubtedly makes a definite foundation and a differentiation of the endocrine status [as male or female] possible by the surgical method. The successful outcome of such operations yields satisfaction in social, moral and everyday terms [*moral'no-bytovoe i sotsial'noe udovletvorenie*] for both patient and surgeon, and the individual results of such operations speak to their full expediency.[67]

This optimistic conclusion to a chapter on hermaphroditism overstated the ability of doctors to regulate the "endocrine status" of these patients through "transplants of sex glands." It is significant however that such materialist fundamentals underlay approval for what was in effect cosmetic surgery on the sex organs. Doctors said they were simply clarifying "a definite foundation and a differentiation of the endocrine status," repairing, if you will, the physiological "base" of sex rather than overtly pandering to its "superstructure" in the psychology of desire. They could then move from the hormonal adjustment of the sex gland to the corresponding genital modifications ("creation" and "removal"), believing that they were completing a process of restoration—helping nature reassert itself. If this implicit ideology of the hormonal base and the desiring superstructure found its way into a textbook treatment of hermaphroditism, the actual practice of physicians offering therapeutic assistance was in fact seldom tied to a marriage between gland implants and cosmetic surgery. Implants were infrequently employed, but surgery was often offered and attempted.

Yet this surgery, even when intended to relieve suffering, could kill. Stefan Ivanovich Sh., just 21 years old, died after an operation in 1924 in a Krasnodar clinic. Tormented by the tiny size of his penis, and the fact that it did not contain a urethra, which necessitated his crouching like a woman to urinate, he insisted on having surgery to fit an artificial urethra. The doctors reporting the case did not discuss the complexities of this experimental procedure, nor did they say anything about the ethical considerations, if any, that preceded the decision to operate.[68] This early case was only published in 1935, and the doctors may have felt that the dangers of this operation were self-evident to readers with a memory of conditions for surgery in the early 1920s. By the 1930s, an awareness of the possibilities for surgical intervention was more widespread. One doctor encountering a very strong-willed collective farmer in his Tashkent clinic in 1938 gave up trying to convince her that she was in constitutional terms more male than female (he even argued that her shoe size—41— was somehow masculine). Her conviction that she was a woman derived from her upbringing and way of life. He agreed to use plastic surgery to enhance her life as a woman by expanding the vagina but he warned her that the procedure was very demanding and possibly fatal. He sent her home to rest and recover from previous treatments before any attempt to construct the artificial organ was made.[69]

Many Soviet doctors found the requests of hermaphrodites for cosmetic alterations to their genitalia wholly unproblematic regardless of the "true sex" of the petitioner. While they did not use ideological language, their actions and statements suggest that for these Soviet practitioners, Neugebauer's ethical scruples against surgical pandering to patients who had suffered "errors of sex" were seen as retrograde bourgeois moralizing. When confronted with insistent demands for procedures within their abilities, Soviet doctors often complied. The "clarification of sex" or the "completion [*dodelka*] of sex" justified the interventions.[70] In any event, they described the reasons for their actions in print to their colleagues in this way, which suggests that to them the idea that such interventions constituted appropriate therapy was self-evident. The alacrity with which Dr. V. L. Beder ordered that the two hermaphrodite brothers in his Kiev clinic should have their mammary glands removed is one example. In the case of the Siberian 17-year-old with a fiancé waiting in the wings, who was considered by her doctor to be a man, not a woman, a similarly accommodating attitude emerges. The physician makes no mention of the dangers of a homosexual marriage resulting from an "error of sex." Instead, the doctor apparently felt little compunction about elaborate surgery to expand the vagina, and perhaps only a slight worry that the removal of her penis-like clitoris would be ill advised (although he was reluctant to state why):

> With an undeveloped penis and a very narrow entrance to the vagina, our subject was not entirely able to have a sex life; it was decided therefore to adapt to this purpose the existing female features, beginning with plastic surgery . . . . During the removal of the stitches seven days later, the patient noticed that the penis remained in place, and began insistently demanding that it be removed. Amputation was performed. On the eighteenth day the patient signed out of hospital in a good frame of mind.[71]

The patient's determination to be rid of this appendage and to join one unequivocal sex was ethical justification enough for this doctor.

"We Must First Decide If These Persons Can Be Men"

Soviet doctors, influenced by the sexual revolution and convinced of the potential of surgical and hormonal science, widely adopted therapeutic approaches to hermaphroditism that anticipated work in the West by a decade or more. What is even more surprising, except perhaps to students of the Russian provinces, is that some of the most visionary work was taking place beyond the big scientific centers of Moscow and Leningrad. One gynecologist, Z. A. Andreeva at the Ob-gyn Clinic of Perm' University in the Urals region of western Siberia, stands out as an innovative practitioner. In 1928 she published a study of three hermaphrodites whom she had been able to treat simultaneously.[72] Her approaches and conclusions are useful to compare with the methods adopted by U.S. urologist Hugh Hampton Young in the 1920s and 1930s, methods that would shape the protocols on treating hermaphrodites in the United States and western Europe after standardization in the 1950s.[73] Young's evolving criteria for assigning a "true" sex, and embarking on a surgical "correction," in cases of adolescent and adult hermaphroditism increasingly relied on consideration of libido and "psychological sex."[74] These criteria were evidently influenced by the turn in Western societies, heavily marked by Freudian ideas, toward interiorized views of sex as a psychological drive. By contrast, and as might be expected considering the tenor of the Soviet sexual revolution, Andreeva's approach minimized the significance of sex psychology, but emphasized the social role each patient inhabited. This view was illustrated in the way she framed her patients' dilemma in the opening lines of her article, explaining that their physical defects "robbed them of the possibility of a definite place in life, placed them somehow beyond society."[75]

Two of her patients, despite their sometimes very masculine social characteristics, identified as women, who wanted children. During the Civil War, B., a 24-year-old lathe-operator, had even led a Cheka (secret police) detachment on food-requisitioning raids while dressed as a man.[76] Yet in peacetime she lived as a woman, albeit with "a stubborn, hard [*tverdyi*] character." She was married, but neither she nor her husband was satisfied with their limited sex life. The second patient, N., 29 years old and in a troubled marriage, had according to her own account read what scientific literature about sexuality she could find, and as a result, feared that she would become homosexual. N. had consulted a doctor about her shallow vagina, and he had used a probe to attempt to stretch it to accommodate sexual intercourse; these efforts proved unsuccessful, and N. "offered her husband his freedom" after four years of life together. They were apparently still a couple at the time of Andreeva's report. A third patient, 19-year-old K., a peasant with above-average education, was far less certain of her sex. Raised as a girl in spite of doubts about her sex at birth, she felt desire for both sexes and had experienced erections and ejaculation in intercourse with women.

Dr. Andreeva discussed the origins of hermaphroditism in humans via hormonal, chromosomal, and embryological theories with an assured command of the German-language scientific literature.[77] According to these theories, her subjects, with their masculine sex glands, were constitutionally male. Removing the glands and/or supplementing them seemed to offer one resolution, through some combination of "castration" and transplants. Yet as she surveyed unfavorable reports by a range of European doctors, she concluded that hormonal therapies "had yet to enter more or less widespread clinical practice." She dismissed these as of no clinical value, a fair assessment in 1928; it would not be until the production of artificial hormones in the 1930s and 1940s in western countries that doctors would embrace hormone treatments for intersex patients.[78] Andreeva turned to the question of "operations enabling a sex life for the deformed sex organs of hermaphrodites." In her summary of the German literature, she found authorities rejecting as "impermissible" surgical adaptation that contradicted the revealed sex of the gonads, in other words, Neugebauer's *operations de complicité*. Meanwhile she noted that European gynecologists, willing to operate when the changes conformed to the gonadal sex revealed by the physician, had accumulated considerable positive clinical experience in plastic surgery to alter the sex organs.

Andreeva argued forcefully that such a moral distinction was itself impermissible, and primarily for social reasons:

> Life is more complex than these principles. Hermaphrodites who count themselves among a sex that does not correspond to the character of their sex glands, usually seek medical advice and assistance when they have already reached maturity, when their social position has been well established in accordance with one or the other sex, and they categorically refuse correction of their sex in conformity with the character of their sex glands. Many clinicians confronting this question are inclined when determining the sex of the hermaphrodite, to see it as necessary to take into account the social position of the patient and his personal [*lichnye*] interests.[79]

How should a physician assess that "social position"? Andreeva saw that the patient's social adaptation to his or her existing physical attributes was at least as significant in determining effective therapy. Embodiment, as read by the community, linked the individual to society. She evaluated the prospects for her three cases in the following manner:

> What should be our approach to such subjects of the male sex, who consider themselves female and occupy the social position of women in society? To resolve the question we must first decide if these persons can be men [*byt'*

muzhchinami] or can they be made into such. Fertilization in our cases, obviously is out of the question; as far as the ability to live a sex life in the role of a man, then only the third of our patients has realized this possibility, evidently the two others from the size and weakness of their erections cannot be men [*ne mogut byt' muzhchinami*]; they both live a sex life as women and in this regard some adaptation has obviously occurred.[80]

Andreeva believed that to "be men" her patients needed phalluses of a credible size and functionality; only K. possessed this organ, and only she might be encouraged to consider assuming a male gender role. Just as in other hermaphrodite case histories, where the method of urinating had gender significance for patients and physicians, so the size and behavior of the phallus was not a personal matter but one with social consequences. (The possession of a "credible" phallus would become the key factor in U.S. medical protocols determining which sex to assign to newborn intersex infants in the 1950s, and remains so to the present time.)[81] Switching to the masculine pronoun to refer to K., Andreeva reported that the 19-year-old was "already aware himself of the falseness of his position as a woman" and was "on the verge of identifying himself as his true sex, and trying to adjust to a transformation of his social position." K. had asked for time to consider the doctor's offer of surgery to make the genitalia appear completely masculine.[82]

Andreeva's other two patients, B. and N., "despite their undoubted male sex glands, cannot conduct their sex lives as men; they have long adapted to a woman's role in that regard; their social position as women is long established, both are married and have reasonably capably organized their family lives. To speak of a change of sex to correspond to the genuine character of their sex glands would make no sense for them; it would put them in an even more difficult social situation." Andreeva therefore offered them cosmetic operations "to adapt their sex organs to the women's role in their sex lives." They consented to the removal of their testes, located in their labia, which made intercourse painful. B. also requested that the "sex organ" (meaning the penislike structure she possessed) be removed. Candidly for a Soviet doctor, Andreeva explained to the patient that amputation would probably result in loss of sexual sensation, and informed of this outcome, B. decided not to proceed.[83] Adaptation to "pass" as women had its limits for this doctor, and for her patients. "Doubtless these palliative operations do not completely satisfy either the patient or the doctor," Andreeva concluded; she looked forward to the moment when hormonal treatments would move from experimental to clinical use. Here again was the Soviet faith, typical of the 1920s, that hormones held the key to sex and might transform what the surgeon's knife could not.

Conclusion

The impact of the world's first socialist "sexual revolution" on the treatment of hermaphrodites was profound. Institutionally, the question was radically overhauled to give medicine custody of the hermaphrodite. The newly established forensic medical leadership eagerly seized upon the dilemma of the intersex patient and concretized it in statistics. These numbers did not "create" an epidemic of sexual ambiguity, but did display the persistence and geographic distribution of a minor but disturbing biological and social phenomenon. Doctors won the state's recognition as the appropriate authorities to pronounce on the "true" sex of intersex citizens, with the 1926 decree on changes to "passport" sex. The leap between 1913, when the tsarist police ministry rejected medical authority in these cases, and the 1926 decree embedding that authority in administrative procedures, was radical, and its medicalizing trajectory aligned it with the general direction of the Soviet sexual revolution.

Intriguingly, however, experts and patients may have invoked the 1926 decree rather less often than this revolutionary leap might have suggested. The much vaunted "errors of sex" that the decree was designed to address found new solutions—solutions that had their own scientific and "Soviet" value. The "age of the gonads" when physicians decided how to treat the intersex patients based on the "truth" of their internal organs (ovaries or testes) was already slipping away in 1926. However much Soviet gynecologists and other medical experts continued to view these organs as indicators of "true sex," they no longer accepted that a rigid adherence to gonadal sex should dictate the terms of therapy. In part this was because by the late 1920s, European science was becoming discouraged about the prospects for dramatic therapies based solely on glandular treatments; endocrinologists had conclusively demonstrated that a straightforward substitution of one set of glands for another was insufficient to generate a change of sex, or sexuality, in humans. Science was pointing toward a more complex model for the origins of sex difference, even if faith in the transformative value of the hormones would remain high for many years to come.[84]

Yet science alone did not determine how Soviet doctors worked. Values of the "sexual revolution" also informed the decisions of these clinicians. With their relaxed view of homosexual relations, and their rejection of Neugebauer's moralizing therapeutics, Soviet doctors saw the problem as a social one, in which the reintegration of the distressed individual into a collective was the foremost priority. Stabilizing the patients' claims to their existing social sex—their gender role as they performed it in the community—by use of cosmetic surgery made ideological and practical sense. "Doubtless these palliative operations do not completely satisfy either the patient or the doctor," Andreeva observed, hinting at unstated difficulties with the full resolution of the surgery involved. Yet palliative operations resulted—or were intended to result—in citizens whose outward performance of their sex roles conformed to an existing history, and an existing passport. Thus, by enthusiastically embracing as "palliative" Neugebauer's reviled *opérations de complicité,* Soviet physicians rendered the 1926 decree virtually redundant, especially as surgical techniques and resources improved in the 1930s. No startling, life-transforming identity change was necessary if patients could be settled into the gender they had inhabited from birth.

Naturally there were cases that do not conform to this model, in which the treatment failed, in which the temptation to experiment overshadowed the duty of care, or in which the expert's resources and abilities were not up to the task.[85] Yet these extraordinary encounters between early Soviet doctors and their intersex patients seem to reveal a unity of purpose between expert and lay person. Various patients showed an eagerness to "speak medically" and to become medical subjects, if that would grant them what we could call a settled gender identity. Doctors responded energetically. They were made vividly aware that their knowledge of apparently "objective" anatomy and physiology, its interpretation in diagnoses, and its manipulation in therapeutic practices, all had major social and moral consequences. The stakes were high, but so too might be the rewards. In an era when the sex hormones still occupied the glamorous frontier of scientific knowledge, the urge to engage in experimentation could be irresistible, even if it meant indulging in a "lie for the patient's own good." It is striking that both Andreeva in 1928, and authorities Rozenblium and Serdiukov in 1935, spoke of the "satisfaction" not only of the patient, but also of the doctor who successfully "corrected" the sex of the distressed hermaphrodite. The "more modern direction" of palliative surgery, unencumbered by bourgeois philistinism, was something to inspire a degree of pride, especially in the 1930s, as surgery became a more realistic option for Soviet clinicians confronting this obscure but dramatic challenge.

In some ways, the Soviet approach to the hermaphrodite in the 1920s and 1930s resembled the willingness of the American urologist Hugh Hampton Young to grant "complicitous operations" when the lived sex of the patient prevailed over the gonadal sex detected by the doctor. The rationale for Soviet operations might be expressed in rather different language from that employed by the American, emphasizing the "social" and the "collective" over the "individual." Individual satisfaction on the part of the Soviet patient was sometimes represented as a fortuitous by-product; it was not always the self-evident primary goal of therapy. Yet as in Young's U.S. cases, therapeutic choices could be the result of a close and careful study of the patient's life-history, psychosexual development, family situation, and existing personality. Andreeva's strikingly sympathetic and sensitive probing of the sexual psychology of her patients was the foundation of her therapeutic decision making. Psychological factors evidently counted for Soviet doctors, even in the 1930s: in the case of the Soviet hermaphrodite, it was necessary to invite desire to speak. In stark contrast to the negative value of sexual psychology adhered to by the forensic psychiatrist as early as the 1920s, here was a rare positive reading of sexual psychology, well into the Stalin era, as vital to the integration of the "damaged" but loyally Soviet individual into the collective.

CONCLUSION

REFLECTIONS ON THE FATE OF A SEXUAL REVOLUTION

The Bolshevik regime assigned medicine a very significant role in interpreting sexuality in its negative as well as positive guises. A closer look at those negative phenomena and how medical experts surveyed, diagnosed, and interpreted them offers a fresh perspective on the "sexual revolution" of the Soviet 1920s. The roots of the Stalinist ideology of sex grew from the "revolutionary" and "modernizing" soils of the first years of the Bolshevik regime. Day-to-day medical practices, closely tied to policing and justice systems, became a means by which the essentializing, technocratic, and collectivist vision of sexuality so prevalent in the Communist Party was mapped on society. With the authority of science, and despite its practitioners' protestations of "objectivity," medicine participated in setting new moral boundaries. The outcomes produced a form of "sexual citizenship" (perhaps a terminological anachronism in this context) that was peculiarly Soviet, and quite distinct from the visions propounded by fellow-traveling international sex reformers.

Soviet medicine with its dedicated health commissariat acquired a degree of technocratic authority, at first glance apparently free of police oversight characteristic of the old regime. For the forensic medical expert the new arrangements seemed especially promising, because the revolution put a clear distance between the police and courts on one hand and the "judges of the scientific facts" on the other. The distance appeared greater in theory than it turned out to be in practice. And sometimes experts showed little anxiety about their proximity to the new regime's organs of authority.

From the very beginning, the mechanisms of Soviet justice subtly tied the forensic expert to a range of duties binding the physician to police and prosecutors. The new criminal and procedural codes created a web of obligations for medical experts, obligations that they had not always had the opportunity to discuss and shape in dialog with lawmakers. The enactment of the sexual maturity standard, instead of an age of consent, over the objections of Iakov Leibovich before the launch of the 1922 criminal code, and over the sustained objections of the forensic medical profession during the 1920s, was a key imposition from outside the discipline. The unanticipated complexities of the sex crime legislation, requiring consideration of biological maturity, physical virginity, and implicitly, assessment of social factors, even in "simple" and "clear" cases of rape, added to the medical expert's caseload and often necessitated repeated examinations of victims and perpetrators. That rural physicians and city experts had to respond to these demanding duties, often without adequate training and resources, only emphasizes the burden the new legislation imposed. It also underlines the limitations of these doctors as autonomous agents of a disciplinary power.

Moreover, certain psychiatrists embraced the new regime with particular enthusiasm, and it is striking that penal psychiatric facilities were among the first new *forensic* institutions of any type created by Soviet power, within months of the October Revolution. Parity of esteem with other forms of forensic knowledge was an unprecedented opportunity for the psychiatrist as recognized expert. Yet parity naturally brought the doctor of the mind "inside," nearer to the police and prosecutors, and assigned the psychiatrist a role that almost immediately appears to have been subordinate to these authorities.

Another mark of the equivocal autonomy of the forensic medical expert, from the very outset in the early 1920s, was the apparent aversion that the new justice system displayed for contests, in open courtrooms, over contradictory scientific evidence. The 1924 case of Petrograd rapist Mikhail Miats, the Communist Party member who commissioned a private psychiatric assessment that contrasted with the state's own report (discussed in chapter 4), is a rare instance in this sample of such a contest over the "scientific facts." Soviet justice apparently preferred that scientific evidence arrive in the courtroom issuing from a single mouthpiece. The first stage of crime cases, the lengthy preliminary investigation process, enabled police and prosecutors to sift and challenge expert evidence long before it came to a public airing in court. Prosecutors often selected and invited particular experts to give evidence at a trial. The forensic medical expert's autonomy meant little if his expertise was not used or heard. Strikingly, the well-resourced Petrograd forensic medical bureau frequently convened panels or commissions of experts, who issued a collective "act of expertise" signed by all the presiding specialists. The collective opinion was supported in court by one of the named specialists, such as the gynecologist Vera Degtiarova, or Petrograd's leading penal psychiatrist,

Lev Orshanskii. None of the collective expert assessments observed in this sample contains a dissenting opinion. The practice of collective forensic expertise reduced the likelihood of scientific disagreement, first in the forensic clinic and then later in court.

The authority of science in the new Soviet courtroom relied on a curious paradox: the contested nature of scientific knowledge, the questioning and weighing of evidence, was a key source of its claim to disciplinary power, and yet expertise was encouraged and shaped into a univocal discourse by police, prosecutorial, and courtroom practices. This paradox was not exclusively Soviet; by their nature all justice systems strive for clarity of evidence. Yet early Soviet justice, radicalizing the tsarist judicial notion of the essential truth *(istina)* of a case, operated in such a way as to conceal expert disagreement during the preliminary investigation, and to reduce or eliminate expert disagreement at the trial stage. This homogenization of scientific expertise was implemented not only by hard-nosed Bolsheviks but also by a range of agents including liberals like the jurist A. F. Koni, the Petrograd forensic generalist Professor N. I. Izhevskii, and many medical experts with no political affiliations. Their ambition to project technocratic authority in the courtroom dovetailed with Bolshevik schemes to radicalize justice in the name of a modernizing socialist society. In its institutional, cultural, and practical arrangements, early Soviet forensic medicine was still closely bound to the police and courts, despite the formal relocation of the discipline in the health commissariat. Its autonomy had fuzzy, but tangible, limits.

In their performances as experts, forensic doctors adapted familiar practices from the world of clinical medicine to the new stages of the forensic medical bureau clinic, penal psychiatric hospital, police cells, and the courtroom itself. The act of providing expertise was inherently something different from a private doctor-patient encounter. Petrograd's commissions of forensic experts, and courtroom inspections of victims and perpetrators there and in Sverdlovsk, resembled "patient demonstrations" typical of the medical-school lecture hall. Even one-to-one inspections of rape victims deep in the Soviet countryside normally took place in the presence of witnesses, who were supposed to sign the physician's statement in confirmation. Forensic expertise was a public, not private act. In common with the educative function of the patient demonstration in lecture hall or hospital ward, expert opinions were staged events in which the subject's bodies and minds, characteristics and injuries, were uncovered, shown, and explained for lay audiences. Such demonstrations had moral implications that doctor-experts could seldom escape, however much they might protest their "objectivity" as "judges of the scientific facts." In the nonforensic patient demonstration moral problems arose frequently enough. Professor L. A. Krivskii's 1919 hospital ward demonstration to his students of the "male" hermaphrodite Evdokiia K., in which he refused to "disappoint" the elderly patient by revealing her "true" sex to her, describing it instead to his students in Latin, serves as an example. The public and educative nature of the forensic expert's practice as revealer of deeper truths was well suited to delivering implicit moral messages: of damage done, of innocence lost, or of disturbed passions and drives.

The Bolshevik terms by which sex crime was measured further compelled forensic experts to venture into moral territory. This was most vividly evident when experts passed judgment on the sexual lives of girls and women. In medical assessments of sexual maturity, the subject's biological condition became in effect her moral passport. Either she was immature and by law an innocent "victim," or she had reached sexual maturity, and emerged from inspection as a figure of ambiguity because she legally might consent to sexual relations. Similarly, the high penalty for intercourse accompanied by defloration with an immature person forced forensic experts to regard the hymen as the principal indicator of young women's sexual condition. Given that Soviet legislation continued to privilege the physical "wrapper of virginity"—so prized in wider Russian society—it is unsurprising that forensic specialists also persisted in viewing it through lenses inherited from the past. Reporting on the sexual development and condition of the object of sex crime could scarcely be an act stripped of values and prejudices.

Another eloquent arena for medical moralizing developed when early Soviet sex crime trials resorted to forensic psychiatric expertise. With their attention focused on the perpetrators of sex offenses, Petrograd psychiatrists reserved the language of sexual psychopathy for those men in the dock who were seen to be answerable for their crimes. In the practice of early Soviet forensic psychiatry, the psychopath in the sexual sense was not mentally ill, or at least was rarely so mentally incapacitated as to be worthy of exculpation or medical mitigation. A sexualized diagnostic language—the exploration of sex fantasies, histories, desires, impulses—was, at least in this sample of cases, only deployed to explain an individual's criminal motives. Offenders who were diverted to psychiatric treatment were not stained with sexualized language; their mental illnesses were in origin somatic, not psychic. Sexual psychology with its language of desire was a highly tainted discourse in this particular arena, from a very early moment in the history of Soviet sexuality.

The study of sexual crime as seen through the eyes of early Soviet medical practitioners shows that as a professional group these physicians were deeply unwilling to engage in extensive exploration of sexual psychology. In this they mirrored their colleagues occupied with sexual enlightenment for the Soviet masses, for these experts offering advice on how to live a positive sex life in the socialist society avoided mapping the normal psyche's sexual development. Whatever modishness Sigmund Freud's theories held for NEP-era Soviet pedagogy and cultural studies, the relative failure of these theories to find support in the medical disciplines, which were crucial to the shaping of Soviet sexuality, is undeniable. Forensic experts evaded discussion of the internal sexual dramas of the maturing girl and boy, said remarkably little about the trauma caused by rape and sexual abuse, and only reached for a language of sexual psychopathy when explaining the motives of criminals, who would not become patients these doctors wished to claim. (The Soviet model of sexual psychopathy owed little to Freud in any case.) Positive Soviet sublimation was founded not on the damming and diversion of libidinous psychic energy, but rather on a physiological model that imagined male and female sex hormones furnishing the power to fuel physical culture and social activism. In a similar fashion, Soviet doctors considering negative sexual phenomena rarely attributed them to intense psychological pressures or unconscious blockages. Instead, the question of origins was set aside, left for other disciplines to identify (perhaps as the result of bad upbringing or environment). If doctors discussed these origins at all, degeneration, hormonal disorders, or ailments of the nervous system were seen as the cause: sexual disorders originated in the body, not the mind.

The desiring subject was such an unwelcome figure in Soviet sexological thinking that perhaps only the hermaphrodite could present problems insurmountable enough to compel doctors to invite the patient to speak about desire, even into the "reactionary" 1930s. In the clinic, "desire" might be explored privately, between doctor and patient; such a medical encounter contrasts sharply with the forensic expert's task of "demonstrating" a subject before a courtroom as part of a moral lesson. The Soviet clinician confronting the dilemma of the hermaphrodite claimed a "modern" and objective approach. Doctors rejected the conservative moralizing of some western medical experts who were authorities on this obscure question. Fear of homosexuality did not mark the Soviet medical view of the hermaphrodite's social adjustment. Physicians, gynecologists, and surgeons offering therapy to intersex patients were motivated by a determination to help the patient achieve a functioning sexual life. In this goal they usually saw little value in determining a "true" (gonadal) sex to which the patient should conform. Instead they sought to stabilize the gender performance of the patient by "completing" or "clarifying" the physical sex of the patient's body. To arrive at an assessment of the social gender of the patient, physicians were forced to probe the sexual psychology of the hermaphrodite, and many doctors recorded the developmental sexuality of their patients in case histories. To doctors who offered treatment to hermaphrodites, the path to a "modern" approach was via the social and psychological, and from there, back to the body. The body should conform to the psychological and social sex inhabited by the individual, since that would cause the fewest "collisions" in personal or public life.

The sum total of these medical and legal views, applied to the "sexual revolution," was a very peculiar Soviet form of "sexual citizenship." Naturally, few Bolsheviks beyond the libertarian camp would have recognized the concept of "sexual citizenship." It is a late twentieth-century construct, although its roots date from the modernizing sexual regulation adopted in many industrialized countries, and the international sex reform movement of the late nineteenth and early twentieth centuries.[1] The idea of sexual citizenship is familiar to contemporary readers as the intersection between the citizen's public rights and duties on the one hand, and the private sphere of the body, gender, and sexual life on the other. Contemporary sexual citizenship is forged as individuals, expressing their sexuality or indeed adopting sexual identities, negotiate their relationship with the communities in which they live.[2] A liberal democratic view of citizenship as negotiated by individuals in an open society did not apply in Russia, of course. Before the revolution, citizenship was a matter of estate *(soslovie)* and of a complex mixture of communal, ethnic, and religious affiliations. After 1917, collectivist ideology swept away tsarist complexities but also introduced a new grid of identity based explicitly on class and less explicitly, but no less significantly, on nationality, identifying the "socially friendly" and "socially alien" and allocating rights and obligations accordingly.[3]

Soviet lawmakers and ideologists distributed sexual rights and duties along lines determined by the ideology of class and ascribed social character. Understanding their ideas of "sexual revolution" and its peculiar sexual citizenship requires an appreciation of this structuring principle. To be clear: the freely desiring individual citizen was not an intended endpoint of the Bolshevik sexual revolution. The collective, desexualized, gendered, and biologized model of sexual citizenship promoted in Soviet sexual enlightenment discourse, and in the visions of medical experts confronting sexual disorder, was a product of political principles that distributed obligations and "rights" (in a circumscribed, Soviet sense) to classes and national groups according to the Bolshevik assessment of the group's "political consciousness" and historical modernity.

The imposition of the sexual maturity standard instead of an age of consent in sex crime law illustrates this primacy of the Bolshevik sociopolitical hierarchy, with its trajectories from "primitive" to "modern" and "backwardness" to "consciousness." The sexual maturity standard, reading physiques in medical terms, sought to protect the developing body as a resource for the collective, regardless of that body's social location in a "primitive and backward" or "modern and conscious" community. The different customs regarding sexual debut within Russia (earlier marriage in the peasant countryside than in the town) made fixing a single age of consent contentious enough. "Conscious workers" in the Russian city ideally waited until mature adulthood to begin a sex life, while "backward" peasants, lacking access to modern medical advice and the prophylaxis of physical culture and organized political work, would continue to engage in sex earlier than their city cousins. The early marriages of child brides and Russian perceptions of early sexual debut in some non-Russian, and especially Muslim, ethnic and national communities within the RSFSR, made the transition from "backwardness" to "consciousness" seem even further off. The law's biological sexual maturity threshold for sexual citizenship took the possibility of earlier maturation in Russia's southern regions into account, while simultaneously protecting the young organism from premature exploitation in communities that practiced child marriage.[4] Soviet sexual citizenship bound the individual body to a collective ideal expressing a social and historical mission, a "civilizing mission" that encompassed colonized and colonizer in a dialectic of modernization.

How deeply did popular understanding of the Bolshevik messages about "sexual revolution" penetrate? That would be the subject of a fascinating, and difficult, study; yet certain features of this book indicate an apparent inclination on the part of some people to "speak medically" in Bolshevik terms when dealing with sexual disorder. Parents' and families' turn to forensic medical experts to tell the "truth" about a girl's disputed innocence or corruption, witnessed by Dr. Leitman in Saratov in 1925, and sometimes evident in the crime case files of Petrograd and Sverdlovsk, hints at a population responding to the medicalization of what was once a moral issue. The degree to which ordinary people realized that sexual maturity had replaced an age of consent is impossible to gauge in these sources. Certainly these actors in microdramas about sexual innocence and experience perceived medicine as offering a form of proof, or at the very least a weapon, in these disputes. Similarly the rape victim's turn to the local midwife or Soviet hospital for a certificate *(spravka)* to confirm her injuries was showing awareness of the mechanisms by which a claim was lodged. The precocious attempts by sex offenders to have themselves diagnosed "sexual psychopaths," and occasional bids by perpetrators of sex crimes to have their charges mitigated by claiming impotence or a sexual dysfunction, also display a crude medical consciousness. The complaints lodged by family members when a mentally ill relative was charged are another example. Finally, the articulate hermaphrodite's persistent search for a medical solution to intractable dilemmas of sexual indeterminacy suggests a lively awareness—or even over-estimation—of the possibilities of sexual science that were publicized in the popular press. All actors in these microdramas about sexual disorder realized, or quickly learned, that medicine had a major role to play in shaping their stories, and they responded by seeking to engage with medical forms of evidence, advice, and treatment.[5]

What impact on Soviet sexuality did the early medicalization of the "sexual revolution" have? The roots of the perceived "conservative turn" in sexual regulation of the Stalinist 1930s look much more pervasive from this exploration of the day-to-day medical management of sexual disorder in the 1920s. With David Hoffmann, one is tempted to ask how much of a turn away from a "revolutionary" Eros toward "Stalinist family values" really occurred.[6] The Soviet medical profession's "highly normative approach" to problems of sexuality, its view of excessive and disorderly sex as wasteful and damaging, and its essentialist view of the two genders and their natural roles, were prerevolutionary inheritances that the Bolshevik revolution institutionalized.[7] By giving medicine custody of the management of sexual order and disorder in the 1920s, Lenin's Communists laid down an essentializing, desexualizing, reproduction-focused, and collectivist sexual framework that would mark Soviet sexual regulation to the end of the Soviet regime and beyond.

A turn in the regime's *methods* for managing that collectivist sexual framework there certainly was. It is undeniable that sexual glasnost all but evaporated under the pressures of Stalin's Great Break and the First Five-Year Plan (1928–1932). In ideological terms, as Eric Naiman has shown, the terrors for Communists exposed during the 1920s by the various literary and prosaic discourses on sexuality had to be extinguished if a new utopia free of such fears was to be built.[8] Any taint of sexual pathology in Soviet society had to be expunged. Frances Bernstein charts the end of Soviet sexual enlightenment as the Health Commissariat came under new leadership in 1930. The party's ideological thrust with its focus on ramping up socialist production allowed no quarter for "[e]pidemics of nervousness and venereal disease" that doctors proffering sexual enlightenment had set out to cure.[9] As Bernstein explains, the enlighteners themselves became the victims of their own success. First, the "heady pace of the Five-Year Plan was just what the doctor ordered"—the endless prescriptions of Soviet-style sublimation of sexual energy in physical exertion and socially valuable work now had an unimpeachable outlet of world-historical significance: the construction of socialism. Second, by gradually securing a publishing monopoly on sexual advice literature, the Health Commissariat was in a better position to strangle the genre silently in 1931.[10] The Soviet Union's links with international sex reformers were also quietly severed at this time, with the abrupt cancellation of the World League for Sex Reform's planned Moscow conference in 1931, and the end of Soviet participation in its deliberations.[11] The decline in the birthrate accompanying the forced-pace industrialization and urbanization of the 1930s worried a leadership constantly considering the prospect of war with Europe's great powers, and this fear lay behind the changes in legislation on homosexuality, abortion, and divorce that the government imposed in mid-decade.[12]

Against this backdrop, the fate of forensic medicine under full-throttle Stalinism highlights the tensions between continuity and change in the fate of the "sexual revolution." In contrast to other outposts of Soviet sexology, legal medicine was not shut down, but instead its operations were quietly drawn closer to police requirements. Its practitioners in the center and periphery continued to serve as a key instrument to measure and define sexual disorder, but they did so in radically changed conditions. Gone were the noisy joint conferences of medical experts and legal personnel. The journal *Forensic Medical Expertise* also disappeared. Its editor, the "revolutionary" forensic gynecologist Leibovich, was denounced for insufficient class-consciousness and sent to a university post in Tomsk in Siberia. He was replaced as the chief forensic medical expert by toxicologist Vladimir Mikhailovich Smol'ianinov, a far more politically compliant official.[13] Under Smol'ianinov, the long-hoped-for Central Institute of Forensic Medicine opened in 1933 in Moscow. The training of experts and the commissioning of expertise became more systematic and centralized. As the secret police absorbed the regular police into a single People's Commissariat of Internal Affairs (NKVD) in 1934, forensic experts drew closer to the investigatory authorities. There was even discussion behind the scenes of bringing forensic medicine under direct police control. For an interval in the mid-1930s, the leading institution of forensic psychiatry, the Serbskii Institute, was transferred from the control of the Health Commissariat to the Justice Commissariat; it returned to the formal jurisdiction of health officials in 1940. Ultimately, the price of ostensible autonomy, that is of keeping forensic experts within the Health Commissariat, evolved in practice into a tighter degree of day-to-day subordination to police requirements.[14]

Those stronger police ties found expression in the regulation of sexual expertise. In June 1934 the new Institute of Forensic Medicine's gynecologists, led by N. V. Popov, sat down with the NKVD and the

Justice Commissariat to write directives to physicians supplying expert opinions in sex crime cases. These "Rules for ambulatory forensic medical obstetric-gynecological examination" clarified some of the ambiguities that had plagued early Soviet experts.[15] They also confirmed the collectivist imperative for sexuality, the silencing of desire, and the essentialist understanding of gender that had characterized forensic medical practice even in the "revolutionary" years of the 1920s.

The vision of female sexuality as nothing but a means to reproduction, absent of desire and, implicitly, of self-direction, permeated these instructions. The 1934 "Rules" explicitly and emphatically distinguished a juridical definition of sexual maturity from its biological derivative: doctors should "not confuse the concept of 'sexual maturity' in the biological sense with 'sexual maturity' from the point of view of forensic medical practice." New social criteria distinguished juridical "sexual maturity" from the common medical definition. Three factors, to be sought in combination, defined forensic medical sexual maturity: the ability to give birth and nurse a baby, the "necessary mental development" required to raise a child, and "readiness to live an independent existence." In addition, ambivalent expert opinions were expressly forbidden: a girl was either sexually mature or not, in this forensic medical sense.[16] N. V. Popov's complex definition of sexual maturity of the 1920s now included new "social criteria," evidently intended to lengthen the period of a young woman's sexual minority. A girl of 16 or 17 could be physically an adult but according to the legal definition of sexual maturity propounded in these rules the law did not regard her as prepared for a sexual life. This biosocial vision of women's maturity that deferred sexual life until a complete physical development was accompanied by education and an ability to support mother and child resembled in some ways the NEP-era calls from some Communists to raise the legal marriage age. The ideologized discourse of sexual life and sex education of the Stalin era supports a reading of the 1934 "Rules" as imposing a longer sexual minority too.[17]

The new forensic medical rules perpetuated the focus on the hymen and women's physical virginity as the most credible evidence in rape and sexual abuse cases. Experts received explicit and extensive guidance on every conceivable variation this piece of flesh could exhibit: its size, shape, consistency, thickness, elasticity were all to be cataloged. The exceptional possibility that a hymen might be flexible enough to permit some degree of intercourse raised particular anxiety, with the indications listed. The definition of virginity was not spelled out in these rules, but examinations for it were to include not merely a study of the hymen but of the external sex organs too: "the totality of all objective data in the examination, [including] the sex organs as a whole" had to be considered in determinations of virginity and opinions about defloration.[18] In contrast with judge Nikonov's utopian determination to send the "wrapper of virginity" to the dustbin of history, legal officials, police, and forensic medical experts elevated the everyday practices of low-level medical experts into a state-mandated standard of sexual innocence predicated on the intact hymen. The rarified vision of men and women enjoying equal sexual citizenship, purged of patriarchal obsessions with atavistic physical markers of sexual reputation, evaporated with these rules.

Further commentary on gathering evidence in rape cases showed that the men who wrote these rules continued to regard women as unlikely to tell the truth about the crime. "Objective" evidence trumped mere claims from the assaulted woman in these rules. If a sexually experienced woman claimed rape, the directives implied that she was not to be taken seriously. "In all cases of examination of the `rape' [sic] of those who have lived a sex life EARLIER," a bimanual internal examination of the vagina was suggested, "following the general rules for obstetric-gynecological examinations." Such invasive examinations were not permitted if a girl claimed defloration, although the digital test of the vagina (routine in early 1920s Petrograd cases of rape) might be employed to verify the claim. Experts were advised to examine the rape-claimant's body for bruises, blood blisters, and scratches. In their conclusions the experts should not merely catalog these injuries but supply an opinion "about what these injuries signify." Were they relevant to the crime under investigation, that is were they the result of a struggle against an attacker, evidence of "self-defense"?[19] In the Soviet legal system, the most credible rape claims were those that were supported by physical injuries and thus told expert physicians more reliable stories than did the woman who suffered them. As we have seen, such attitudes were not handed down from newly triumphant Stalinist Thermidoreans determined to roll back the "sexual revolution," but were present and prevalent in Soviet policing and forensic medical and judicial practices from the very beginnings of the Soviet project.

Despite the "obstetric-gynecological" title these 1934 "Rules" carried, implying a focus on women alone, the male body and psyche did appear in them in minor, but eloquent, asides.[20] In rape cases the rules instructed experts not to forget "the guilty party," and if little time had elapsed since the crime, to examine him for "traces of injuries on the body, sustained in process of struggle," and to check for stains on undergarments. Such clues to recent, violent sexual activity were again "objective" signs that might give substance to a woman's claim. It was symptomatic of the "simplicity" of male sexuality as seen in the expert opinions of the 1920s, that these rules remained silent about male sexual maturity; likewise, no guidance appeared on how to examine men for claims of impotence. The psyche of the male sex offender was however mentioned. The expert was reminded, where sexual violation of children occurred, to seek a "specialist psychiatrist" to examine the perpetrator, because these perpetrators were often "imbeciles, idiots, epileptics, schizophrenics, alcoholics, etc."[21] This aside confirmed the tendency, seen in the sex crime cases of the 1920s, to confine the application of psychiatric expertise to men who abused younger children, and to narrow the range of mitigating diagnoses primarily to the extremes of developmental and biological defects. (The alcoholics mentioned here would soon be reclassified by jurists as wholly responsible for their crimes.)[22] Nowhere did the category of the "sexual psychopath" appear in these rules, although occasionally in the 1930s, that label and its terminology might appear in psychiatric assessments of sex criminals.[23] For the experts, prosecutors, and police who standardized the provision of expertise in sex crimes in 1934, male sex-offenders were unproblematic creatures who, when they attacked adult women, were presumed to be rational and answerable for their deeds.[24]

The 1934 "Rules" said nothing about diagnosing or "correcting" the intersex patient, although in asides hinting at lesbian sexual assault, the prospect of the "masculinized" woman was mentioned.[25] In part this oversight reminds us that the encounter between society and the hermaphrodite was a rare and extraordinary event. The failure to draw attention to the 1926 "passport" sex-change regulations in these rules suggests their redundancy: by the 1930s, with "complicitous surgery," the hermaphrodite could often be erased, and a confirmed man or woman put in the place of the ambiguous citizen. This was a function of clinical medicine behind closed doors, not a job for forensic experts or bureaucrats. There was no role for authorities in charge of identity documents when "sex changes" in the registry office were no longer necessary. Advances in surgery in the 1930s had made the erasure of the hermaphrodite possible, but medical dreams of the erasure of the intersex citizen had already been part of the "revolutionary" sexual project of the 1920s.

These 1934 "Rules" consolidated a foundation of basic premises about sexuality, premises that had existed from the very origins of the Bolshevik project, and premises that would inform official views on sex to the end of the Soviet system. By cloaking the debut of sexual citizenship in an obscure biomedical standard, the rules robbed the individual of self-determination in the most private sphere of the young adult's life. The "sexual maturity" threshold confused those who "lived a sexual life," and enabled men to evade responsibility for exploiting girls and young women. It multiplied the intrusive and doubtless traumatizing examinations the youthful victim of sex crime had to endure. Even more brutally, by investing so much in women's physical virginity, these rules divided the state's view of women into the "innocent" and the "corrupted." In practical terms, the rules effectively said that only "innocents" could present credible evidence of rape. The rules also implied a very bleak outlook for the victims of rape who had "previously lived a sexual life"—virtually denying them the possibility of a successful prosecution against their attacker unless they bore physical evidence of a violent assault. All Soviet citizens, particularly girls and women, paid a bitter price for this botched experiment in the engineering of socialist sexuality.

The Soviet "sexual revolution" was a complex event, one without a single starting point, and despite the emphasis on the Great Break of the years 1929–1930, one without a particular end as well. Bolsheviks discovered that the engineering of socialist sexuality was a complicated business and could not be handed over to any single discipline or stakeholder for custodianship. As my frequent references to recent scholarly works on this "revolution" indicate, many disciplines contributed to the impression of a Bolshevik revolution in sexuality in the 1920s. The activities within these disciplines promoting positive sexualities, or diagnosing negative ones, directed their attention at very different spheres of the "revolution." Medical practice confronting sexual disorder was one such engagement with the "sexual revolution," and its actions were built upon an unexamined heritage of patriarchal and paternalistic attitudes toward sex, citizens, and patients. The medicalization of sexuality was a distinctly modern project, but one freighted with assumptions that contributed to the obscuring and undermining of libertarian sexual utopianism. The end of the libertarian dreams of revolutionary sexuality as a transformative political force came not only from prudish Bolsheviks or ruthless Stalinists, but from communities of experts who shared a common scientific vision of gender, sex, and modernity.

NOTES

Introduction—Bolshevik Medicine and Russia's "Sexual Revolution"

1. Laura Engelstein, *The Keys to Happiness: Sex and the Search for Modernity in Fin-de-Siècle Russia* (Ithaca, NY: Cornell University Press, 1992).
2. Engelstein, *The Keys to Happiness*, 245.
3. N. G. Chernyshevsky, *What Is to Be Done?* trans. Michael Katz (Ithaca, NY: Cornell University Press, 1989).
4. Richard Stites, *The Women's Liberation Movement in Russia: Feminism, Nihilism, and Bolshevism, 1860–1930* (Princeton, NJ: Princeton University Press, 1978); Engelstein, *The Keys to Happiness*, 377–81. For a discussion of the "creation of the collective body" in this discourse, see Eric Naiman, *Sex in Public: The Incarnation of Early Soviet Ideology* (Princeton, NJ: Princeton University Press, 1997), 26–78.
5. Lev Nikolaevich Tolstoi, "Kreitserova sonata," in L. N. Tolstoi, *Povesti i rasskazy* (Moscow: Sovremennik, 1987), 273–336. On the debates this story sparked, see Peter Ulf Møller, *Postlude to the Kreutzer Sonata: Tolstoi and the Debate on Sexual Morality in Russian Literature in the 1890s* (Leiden and New York: E.J. Brill, 1988). For the early Orthodox view of sex, see Eve Levin, *Sex and Society in the World of the Orthodox Slavs, 900–1700* (Ithaca, NY: Cornell University Press, 1989).
6. See for example Olga Matich, *Erotic Utopia: The Decadent Imagination in Russia's Fin-de-Siècle* (Madison: University of Wisconsin Press, 2005).
7. Engelstein, *The Keys to Happiness*, 359–420.
8. Naiman, *Sex in Public*, 45.
9. Naiman, *Sex in Public*. For an introduction to *meshchanstvo*, see Nataliia Lebina, *Entsiklopediia banal'nostei. Sovetskaia posvednevnost'. Kontury, simvoly, znaki* (St. Petersburg: Dmitrii Bulavin, 2006), 231–34. On perversion, see Evgenii Bershtein, "'Psychopathia sexualis' v Rossii nachala veka. Politika i zhanr," in *Eros i pornografiia v russkoi kul'ture/Eros and Pornography in Russian Culture*, ed. M. Levitt and A. Toporkov (Moscow: Ladomir, 1999), 414–41.
10. For Bolsheviks on asceticism, see Naiman, *Sex in Public*, 37; for rationalizing values, see Stites, *The Women's Liberation Movement in Russia*, 317–45; and Wendy Z. Goldman, *Women, the State, and Revolution: Soviet Family Policy and Social Life* (Cambridge: Cambridge University Press, 1993).
11. On Soviet exploitation of hormone science to undermine religious faith, see Frances L. Bernstein, "'The Dictatorship of Sex': Science, Glands, and the Medical Construction of Gender Difference in Revolutionary Russia," in

Russian Modernity: Politics, Knowledge, Practices, ed. David L. Hoffmann and Yanni Kotsonis (Basingstoke, UK, and New York: Macmillan Press, 2000), 138–60; Naiman, *Sex in Public,* 143; and Dan Healey, *Homosexual Desire in Revolutionary Russia: The Regulation of Sexual and Gender Dissent* (Chicago, IL: University of Chicago Press, 2001), 154–58.

12. Frances Lee Bernstein, *The Dictatorship of Sex: Lifestyle Advice for the Soviet Masses* (DeKalb, IL: Northern Illinois University Press, 2007), 132.

13. See essays in Alexandra Kollontai, *Selected Writings of Alexandra Kollontai,* trans. Alix Holt (London: Allison & Busby, 1977). Kollontai published a collection of stories under the title *Liubov' pchel trudovykh (The Love of Worker Bees)* in Moscow in 1923; see Naiman, *Sex in Public,* 208–9.

14. Bernstein, *The Dictatorship of Sex,* 134.

15. Naiman catalogs the sexual violence present in the revolutionary discourses of the years 1917–1921 in *Sex in Public,* 57–78.

16. Bernstein, *The Dictatorship of Sex,* 151–58.

17. On Freudians, see Aleksandr Etkind, *Eros nevozmozhnogo. Istoriia psikhoanaliza v Rossii* (St. Petersburg: Meduza, 1993); Martin Miller, *Freud and the Bolsheviks: Psychoanalysis in Imperial Russia and the Soviet Union* (New Haven, CT: Yale University Press, 1998). Acknowledgement of Freud without engagement was a commonplace of early Soviet discussions of homosexuality; see Healey, *Homosexual Desire in Revolutionary Russia,* 140–42. On Kollontai, see Barbara E. Clements, *Bolshevik Feminist: The Life of Aleksandra Kollontai* (Bloomington: Indiana University Press, 1979). In literature, the psychological depiction of sex issues fell afoul of party critics by the late 1920s as well; see Gregory Carleton, *Sexual Revolution in Bolshevik Russia* (Pittsburgh, PA: University of Pittsburgh Press, 2005), 197–224.

18. Attacks on Kollontai's fiction and its sex radicalism began in 1923, and were tied to her oppositional activity; see Clements, *Bolshevik Feminist,* 227–36. Naiman points to a discursive turn in literature and ideological language, away from sexuality as unbridled force, as part of the revolution's whirlwind, during 1924 and 1925. In its place came a determination to assert the primacy of public claims on the private sphere; he cites Lenin's widow, Nadezhda Krupskaia, who in 1924 said, "Perhaps earlier it was not clear that a division between private life and public life sooner or later leads to the betrayal of communism." Naiman, *Sex in Public,* 92.

19. Stites, *The Women's Liberation Movement in Russia,* 89–99, 258–69. Zetkin's interview was first published in Russian in 1925 and later translated in Klara Zetkin, *Reminiscences of Lenin* (New York: International Publishers, 1934), 44, 49.

20. See, e.g., Christina Kiaer, "Delivered from Capitalism: Nostalgia, Alienation, and the Future of Reproduction in Tret'iakov's 'I Want a Child!'" in *Everyday Life in Early Soviet Russia: Taking the Revolution Inside,* ed. Christina Kiaer and Eric Naiman (Bloomington: Indiana University Press, 2006), 183–216; and Carleton, *Sexual Revolution in Bolshevik Russia,* 141–43, 171.

21. Engelstein, *The Keys to Happiness,* 78.

22. By contrast, American forensic medical authorities began to admit the psychological dimension of rape, and many had abandoned the insistence that a healthy adult woman capable of resistance could not be raped; these authorities apparently expressed less anxiety about false rape claims. See Stephen Robertson, "Signs, Marks, and Private Parts: Doctors, Legal Discourses, and Evidence of Rape in the United States, 1823–1930," *Journal of the History of Sexuality* 8, no. 3 (1998): 345–88.

23. In the United States, the role of the psychiatrist in furnishing expertise to courts in sex crime cases was not widely recognized until after the Second World War, with New York City adopting some measure of recognition in the late 1930s; see Stephen Robertson, *Crimes against Children: Sexual Violence and Legal Culture in New York City, 1880–1960* (Chapel Hill: University of North Carolina Press, 2005), 206. In interwar Britain, medical experts argued for sex criminals to be diagnosed and treated psychiatrically, and a 1938 draft law would have allowed courts to prescribe mental therapy, not prison. See Chris Waters, "Havelock Ellis, Sigmund Freud, and the State: Discourses of Homosexual Identity in Interwar Britain," in *Sexology in Culture: Labelling Bodies and Desires*, ed. Lucy Bland and Laura Doan (Cambridge: Polity Press, 1998), 173.

24. If psychiatric science in western Europe might have been more inclined, during the 1920s, to reject degeneration theories for psychological ones (from Freud and his disciples), Russian psychiatrists continued to rely heavily on degeneration. A number of factors may explain this longevity: the late reception and development of degeneration theory in prerevolutionary Russia; the politicization of the theory then and after 1917; and the suppression of psychologism, which left a discursive vacuum to be filled. Russian degeneration is discussed in Daniel Beer, *Renovating Russia: The Human Sciences and the Fate of Liberal Modernity, 1880–1930* (Ithaca, NY: Cornell University Press, 2008); on its politicization, see Daniel Pick, *Faces of Degeneration: A European Disorder, c. 1848–c.1918* (Cambridge: Cambridge University Press, 1989), 224–25; Daniel Beer, "The Medicalization of Religious Deviance in the Russian Orthodox Church (1880–1905)," *Kritika: Explorations in Russian and Eurasian History* 5, no. 3 (2004): 451–82; Bershtein, "'Psychopathia sexualis' v Rossii nachala veka"; and Irina Sirotkina, *Diagnosing Literary Genius: A Cultural History of Psychiatry in Russia, 1880–1930* (Baltimore, MD: Johns Hopkins University Press, 2002), 123–24, 126, 135.

25. In the early twentieth century, Britain and Germany lacked formal procedures for registering a change of passport sex in hermaphrodites; French hermaphrodites however could apply to a court, which apparently required a medical opinion. See Michel Foucault, "Introduction," *Herculine Barbin: Being the Recently Discovered Memoirs of a Nineteenth-Century French Hermaphrodite* (New York: Pantheon, 1980), 150–51; and Alice Domurat Dreger, *Hermaphrodites and the Medical Invention of Sex* (Cambridge: Harvard University Press, 1998), 80–88.

26. Soviet sex hormone research in the 1920s produced similar outcomes, Bernstein, *The Dictatorship of Sex*, 41–72.

27. On these points see: David L. Hoffmann, *Stalinist Values: The Cultural Norms of Soviet Modernity, 1917–1941* (Ithaca, NY: Cornell University Press, 2003); H. G. Cocks and Matt Houlbrook, eds., *Palgrave Advances in the Modern History of Sexuality* (Basingstoke, UK: Palgrave, 2005); Lucy Bland and Laura Doan, eds., *Sexology in Culture: Labelling Bodies and Desires* (Cambridge: Polity Press, 1998); Franz X. Eder, Lesley Hall, and Gert Hekma, eds., *Sexual Cultures in Europe: National Histories* (Manchester, UK: Manchester University Press, 1999).

28. Gail W. Lapidus, *Women in Soviet Society: Equality, Development, and Social Change* (Berkeley: University of California Press, 1978); Stites, *The Women's Liberation Movement in Russia*. An influential document collection shaped perceptions: Rudolph Schlesinger, ed., *The Family in the USSR* (London: Routledge and Kegan Paul, 1949).

29. For extensive reading of NEP-era sex-themed fiction, see Carleton, *Sexual Revolution in Bolshevik Russia*.

30. Naiman, *Sex in Public*; Bernstein, *The Dictatorship of Sex*.

31. Bernstein, *The Dictatorship of Sex*.

32. Kiaer and Naiman, eds., *Everyday Life in Early Soviet Russia*, see the editors' introduction, 2.

33. The concept of "biopower" is elaborated in Michel Foucault, *The History of Sexuality*, vol. 1, *An Introduction*, trans. Robert Hurley (London: Penguin, 1978). On Soviet sexological medicine, see e.g., Susan Gross Solomon, "The Demographic Argument in Soviet Debates over the Legalization of Abortion in the 1920's," *Cahiers du Monde russe et soviétique* 33, no. 1 (1992): 59–82; idem, "The Soviet-German Syphilis Expedition to Buriat Mongolia, 1928," *Slavic Review* 52, no. 2 (1993): 204–32; idem, "Innocence and Sexuality in Soviet Medical Discourse," in *Women in Russia and Ukraine*, ed. Rosalind Marsh (Cambridge: Cambridge University Press, 1996), 121–30; Bernstein, "'The Dictatorship of Sex': Science, Glands, and the Medical Construction of Gender Difference in Revolutionary Russia,"; Janet Hyer, "Fertility Control in Soviet Russia: A Case Study in Gender Control and Professionalization" (Ph.D. diss., University of Toronto, 2007); Stephen P. Frank, "Ask the Doctor! Peasants and Medical-Sexual Advice in Riazan Province, 1925–1928," in *The Human Tradition in Modern Russia*, ed. William B. Husband (Wilmington, DE: Scholarly Resources, 2000), 93–108. Dan Healey, "Unruly Identities: Soviet Psychiatry Confronts the 'Female Homosexual' of the 1920s," in *Gender in Russian History and Culture, 1800–1990*, ed. Linda Edmondson (Basingstoke, UK: Palgrave, 2001), 116–38; idem, "Sexual Cultures in Russia," in *The Blackwell Encyclopedia of Sociology*, ed. George Ritzer (Oxford: Blackwell, 2007), 8:4223–27.

34. Healey, *Homosexual Desire in Revolutionary Russia*; Frances L. Bernstein, "Prostitutes and Proletarians: The Soviet Labor Clinic as Revolutionary Laboratory," in *The Human Tradition in Modern Russia*, ed. Husband, 113–28; N. B. Lebina and M. B. Shkarovskii, *Prostitutsiia v Peterburge* (Moscow: Progress-Akademiia, 1994); Elizabeth Waters, "Victim or Villain: Prostitution in Post-revolutionary Russia," in *Women and Society in Russia and the Soviet Union*, ed. Linda Edmondson (Cambridge: Cambridge University Press, 1992), 160–77. On

the ideological dimensions of prostitution, see Elizabeth A. Wood, "Prostitution Unbound: Representations of Sexual and Political Anxieties in Postrevolutionary Russia," in *Sexuality and the Body in Russian Culture*, ed. Jane T. Costlow, Stephanie Sandler, and Judith Vowles (Stanford, CA: Stanford University Press, 1993), 124–37. On infanticide, see Sharon A. Kowalsky, "Making Crime and Sex Soviet: Women, Deviance, and the Development of Criminology in Early Soviet Russia" (Ph.D. diss., University of North Carolina, 2004), chap. 5.

35. For a study of Russian criminal prosecutions for homosexuality before 1917 and after 1934, see Healey, *Homosexual Desire in Revolutionary Russia*. Crime records are used, but without a systematic examination of the practices of Soviet justice, in Lebina and Shkarovskii, *Prostitutsiia v Peterburge*.

36. "Critical histories" is used here to characterize histories of medicine written by "externalist" social or cultural historians who emphasize the influence of cultural and social factors on medicine, doctors, and patients. Such histories can be contrasted with "internalist" histories of medicine, often written by medical professionals and usually emphasizing a narrative of progress to superior knowledge. The distinctions between these two views of medical history are of course not always so clear-cut, and the question of who reads medical histories, and to what purpose, underlies the problem of interpretation in medical-history writing. Journals such as the contemporary Russian-language *Sudebno-meditsinskaia ekspertiza (Forensic Medical Expertise)* episodically touch upon the histories of the discipline, and furnish the critical externalist historian with useful primary material. For a discussion of the distinctions between externalist and internalist histories of science in this context, see Susan G. Solomon, "Reflections on Western Studies of Soviet Science," in *The Social Context of Soviet Science*, ed. L. L. Lubrano and S. G. Solomon (Boulder, CO: Westview Press, 1980), 1–29; an important recent critique of the "internalist-externalist" historiographical scheme is offered by Frank Huisman and John Harley Warner, "Medical Histories," in *Locating Medical History: The Stories and Their Meanings*, ed. F. Huisman and J. H. Warner (Baltimore, MD: Johns Hopkins University Press, 2004), 1–30.

37. Michael Clark and Catherine Crawford, eds., *Legal Medicine in History* (Cambridge: Cambridge University Press, 1994); M. Anne Crowther and Brenda White, *On Soul and Conscience: The Medical Expert and Crime* (Aberdeen: University of Aberdeen Press, 1988); Thomas R. Forbes, *Surgeons at the Bailey: English Forensic Medicine to 1878* (New Haven, CT: Yale University Press, 1985); Janet A. Tighe, "A Question of Responsibility: The Development of American Forensic Psychiatry, 1838–1930" (Ph.D. diss., University of Pennsylvania, 1983); Roger Smith, *Trial by Medicine: Insanity and Responsibility in Victorian Trials* (Edinburgh: Edinburgh University Press, 1981); H. J. Walls, "The Forensic Science Service in Great Britain: A Short History," *Journal of the Forensic Science Society*, no. 16 (1976): 273–78.

38. For a guide to this literature in German-speaking central Europe, see Thomas N. Burg, "Forensic Medicine in the Nineteenth-Century Habsburg Monarchy," University of Minnesota, Minneapolis Centre for Austrian Studies

Working Paper 96-2, http://www.cas.umn.edu/pdf/wp962.pdf (accessed 17 April 2007).

39. Textbooks and encylopedias offer useful summaries of the facts of this history. An important chronicle of the tsarist legacy compiled by 1920s practitioners is in V. Rozhanovskii, "Sudebno-meditsinskaia ekspertiza v dorevoliutsionnoi Rossii i v SSSR," *Sudebno-meditsinskaia ekspertiza*, supplement to no. 6 (1927): 1–105; conference activity in the discipline is detailed in A. M. Gamburg, *Razvitie sudebnomeditsinskoi nauki i ekspertizy (po materialam s"ezdov i soveshchanii)* (Kiev: Gos. Med. Iz-vo USSR, 1962). Useful on forensic psychiatry, despite authorship by perpetrators of anti-dissident psychiatric incarceration is the work of G. V. Morozov, D. R. Lunts, and N. I. Felinskaia, *Osnovnye etapy razvitiia otechestvennoi sudebnoi psikhiatrii* (Moscow: Meditsina, 1976). Morozov, director of the infamous Serbskii Institute of Forensic Psychiatry during the 1970s, and Lunts, a psychiatrist at the institute, are identified as perpetrators in Victor Nekipelov, *Institute of Fools: Notes from the Serbsky* (New York: Farrar Straus Giroux, 1980).

40. Elisa M. Becker, "Judicial Reform and the Role of Medical Expertise in Late Imperial Russian Courts," *Law and History Review* 17, no. 1 (1999): 1–26. Critical histories of the medical profession in prerevolutionary Russia link it closely to the politics of reform, but also note strong impulses later in the period for cooperation with the regime; see Nancy Mandelker Frieden, *Russian Physicians in an Era of Reform and Revolution, 1856–1905* (Princeton, NJ: Princeton University Press, 1981); John F. Hutchinson, *Politics and Public Health in Revolutionary Russia, 1890–1918* (Baltimore, MD: Johns Hopkins University Press, 1990).

41. Kenneth M. Pinnow, "Making Suicide Soviet: Medicine, Moral Statistics, and the Politics of Social Science in Bolshevik Russia, 1920–1930" (Ph.D. diss., Columbia University, 1998); idem, "Counting and Cutting: Forensic Medicine as a Science of Society in Bolshevik Russia, 1920–29," in *Russian Modernity: Politics, Knowledge, Practices*, ed. David L. Hoffmann and Yanni Kotsonis (Basingstoke, UK, and New York: Macmillan Press, 2000), 115–37. Pinnow demonstrates that chief forensic expert Leibovich was a prime mover in studies of suicide, and in propagating a sociological approach to the question, during the NEP era.

42. In selecting cases for this database, I have defined "sex crimes" narrowly, using the 1922 and 1926 RSFSR criminal code articles concerning rape and the sexual abuse of minors and the "sexually immature." The legislation is discussed in chaps. 1, 2 and 3. I have excluded from the sample cases of sexual harassment and transmission of venereal diseases (few turned up in these archives), and also cases of keeping a brothel, a crime targeting pimps. Prostitution itself was not a formal crime, and so prostitutes themselves did not figure in the sex crime records of the 1920s except when bringing charges of rape or sexual abuse. An interdepartmental commission uniting physicians, women's activists, social workers, and police scrutinized prostitution during the 1920s; it deserves further study. See Waters, "Victim or Villain."

43. The crime case database was compiled from archives of these two

regions, located in *Leningradskii oblastnoi gosudarstvennyi arkhiv v Vyborge* (State Archive of Leningrad Province in Vyborg) and *Gosudarstvennyi arkhiv Sverdlovskoi oblasti* (State Archive of Sverdlovsk Province, Ekaterinburg). The individual cases are supplemented by local prosecutors' and criminal investigators' reports and documents from the same archives. Additionally, contemporary Soviet newspaper reports about sex crimes, including some coincidentally in the database, have been used. I am indebted to Natalia Ismailova for her work in collecting the case files in Vyborg, and to Aleksei Kilin of the State University of the Urals, Ekaterinburg, for his work in collecting the case files in Ekaterinburg.

44. The sources here come chiefly from the archives of the RSFSR People's Commissariat of Health, held at the Gosudarstvennyi arkhiv Rossiiskoi Federatsii (State Archive of the Russian Federation, Moscow).

45. Extensive use has been made of the resources at the Gosudarstvennaia Tsentral'naia Nauchnaia Meditsinskaia Biblioteka (Central State Scientific-Medical Library, Moscow). I am indebted to Sergei Ivashkin, who assisted me in collecting materials from this library. Local medical journals were also consulted for both sample regions. Valuable material was consulted on the development of forensic medicine in provincial Russia in the library holdings of Saratov Medical University's Department of Forensic Medicine (Kafedra sudebnoi meditsiny, Saratovskii meditsinskii universitet), and I am extremely grateful to its director, Professor Iurii Alekseevich Nekliudov, for access to this collection. Also consulted were the Saratov provincial archives of state and party. Unfortunately, Saratov's court records of crime for the 1920s were largely destroyed by archivists fearing German occupation during the Great Patriotic War.

46. On the cultural revolution, see Sheila Fitzpatrick, ed., *Cultural Revolution in Russia, 1928–31* (Bloomington: Indiana University Press, 1978).

47. Bernstein, *The Dictatorship of Sex*, 183–92.

48. The Soviet censor, Glavlit, was formally responsible for censoring scientific publications, but this specialized function has not yet been described in detail; there was a decline in the number of scientific publications produced in the later 1930s. See Nikolai Krementsov, *Stalinist Science* (Princeton, NJ: Princeton University Press, 1997), 44. Krementsov describes the increasing difficulties for biomedical laboratory researchers seeking to publish their findings during and after this period, in his work *The Cure: A Story of Cancer and Politics from the Annals of the Cold War* (Chicago, IL: University of Chicago Press, 2002), 18–33.

49. I am grateful to Sergei N. Ivashkin for his assistance at Moscow's Central State Scientific Medical Library, where he retrieved these case histories. The library's subject catalog headings (*"germafroditizm," "interseksual'nost'"*) formed the basis of the search. So as to focus on encounters between Soviet doctors and articulate hermaphrodites occuring during the 1920s and 1930s, a few articles published during this era that discussed prerevolutionary, post-mortem, or infant cases have been excluded. A handful of cases from forensic

medical textbooks of the era have been included. The result is a sample displaying relatively broad geographic spread: from Leningrad to the Urals, and from Baku to Ukraine.

1—Soviet Doctors and Bolshevik Justice

1. N. V. Popov, *Sudebnaia meditsina*, 3rd ed. (Moscow: Medgiz, 1950), 5–25; M. G. Serdiukov, *Sudebnaia ginekologiia i sudebnoe akusherstvo*, 2nd ed. (Moscow: Medgiz, 1964), 7–14; A. P. Gromov, *Kurs lektsii po sudebnoi meditsine* (Moscow: Meditsina, 1970), 12–17.

2. The forensic gynecologist Serdiukov at least mentions midwifery briefly in his exposition of the development of obstetric and gynecological science in early modern Russia, yet he ignores the application of midwifery in Muscovite or imperial jurisprudence; see, Serdiukov, *Sudebnaia ginekologiia*, 7–8.

3. Daniel H. Kaiser, "'He Said, She Said': Rape and Gender Discourse in Early Modern Russia," *Kritika: Explorations in Russian and Eurasian History* 3, no. 2 (2002): 197–216.

4. For Soviet views, see Popov, *Sudebnaia meditsina*, 5–25; Serdiukov, *Sudebnaia ginekologiia*, 7–14; Gromov, *Kurs lektsii po sudebnoi meditsine*, 12–17. A recent excellent survey of the pre-reform era discipline is Elisa Marielle Becker, "Medicine, Law, and the State: The Emergence of Forensic Psychiatry in Imperial Russia" (Ph.D. diss., University of Pennsylvania, 2003), 20–192.

5. Gromov, *Kurs lektsii po sudebnoi meditsine*, 13. One of the first such textbooks was Sergei A. Gromov, *Kratkoe izlozhenie sudebnoi meditsiny* (St. Petersburg: 1832), which dealt extensively with sexual topics, including hermaphroditism, infertility, rape, "unnatural intercourse" (sodomy, masturbation, lesbianism and bestiality), virginity, and pregnancy.

6. On the increasing reliance upon medical evidence in investigations of suicide at this time, see Susan K. Morrissey, *Suicide and the Body Politic in Imperial Russia* (Cambridge: Cambridge University Press, 2006), 77–105, 128–48.

7. Becker, "Medicine, Law, and the State," 24n6, 32–37; on physicians' patterns of employment in late tsarist Russia, see Frieden, *Russian Physicians*, 210–21, 324, 328–37.

8. Girish Bhat, "The Moralization of Guilt in Late Imperial Russian Trial by Jury: The Early Reform Era," *Law and History Review* 15, no. 1 (1997): 77–113. The differences for forensic medicine implied by jury trials are explored in Catherine Crawford, "Legalizing Medicine," in *Legal Medicine in History*, ed. Catherine Crawford and Michael Clark (Cambridge: Cambridge University Press, 1994).

9. Popov, *Sudebnaia meditsina*, 16.

10. On pre-reform privileging of medical expertise, and post-reform consternation at challenges to expert opinions, see Becker, "Medicine, Law, and the State," 115–21, 339–44.

11. Rozhanovskii, "Sudebno-meditsinskaia ekspertiza v dorevoliutsionnoi Rossii i v SSSR," 26.

12. Rozhanovskii, "Sudebno-meditsinskaia ekspertiza," 26; Gromov, *Kurs lektsii po sudebnoi meditsine*, 13–15.

13. Becker, "Medicine, Law, and the State."

14. For the Soviet critique, see Rozhanovskii, "Sudebno-meditsinskaia ekspertiza," 27. The Rein Commission (1912–1914) in fact recommended the establishment of a free-standing health administration with responsibility for forensic medicine, among other medical services, in the last years of the tsarist era. See Hutchinson, *Politics and Public Health in Revolutionary Russia*, 98.

15. On the medical profession's relationship to the tsarist regime, see Frieden, *Russian Physicians*; Julie V. Brown, "The Professionalization of Russian Psychiatry: 1857–1911" (Ph.D. diss., University of Pennsylvania, 1981); Hutchinson, *Politics and Public Health in Revolutionary Russia*.

16. "Glasnyi sud i vrachi eksperty," *Arkhiv sudebnoi meditsiny i obshchestvennoi gigieny* (1867) [no further publication details given], cited in E. F. Bellin, "Ocherk uslovii deiatel'nosti nashei sudebno-meditsinskoi ekspertizy. Prichiny neudovletvoritel'nosti eia i mery k ustraneniiu ikh," *Vestnik obshchestvennoi gigieny, sudebnoi i prakticheskoi meditsiny* no. 2 (1889), kn. 2, sec. 3: 1–24; quote at 4–5.

17. Bellin, "Ocherk uslovii deiatel'nosti nashei sudebno-meditsinskoi ekspertizy," 5. On the "patchwork of non-binding decisions" won in cassation courts in favour of experts' rights, see Becker, "Medicine, Law, and the State," 361–64.

18. Bellin, "Ocherk uslovii deiatel'nosti nashei sudebno-meditsinskoi ekspertizy," 8–10. For an exhaustive summary of critics' views, see A. I. Smirnov, "O nedostatkakh sudebno-meditsinskoi ekspertizy," *Vestnik obshchestvennoi gigieny, sudebnoi i prakticheskoi meditsiny* 15 (1892): kn. 1, sec. 3: 1–23; kn. 2, sec. 3: 33–56; kn. 3, sec. 3: 57–76. For commentators' views expressed at medical conferences, see Gamburg, *Razvitie sudebnomeditsinskoi nauki i ekspertizy*, 29–35. Even doctors in private practice, summoned by the police or courts to furnish medical opinions, were denied payment for their services; see Frieden, *Russian Physicians*, 266.

19. Hutchinson, *Politics and Public Health in Revolutionary Russia*, 95–103, 139–42. The phrase "cleansing hurricane" was used by a leader of Russia's liberal medical professionals, D. N. Zhbankov of the Pirogov Society, to characterize the February 1917 revolution; Hutchinson, *Politics and Public Health in Revolutionary Russia*, 143.

20. Hutchinson, *Politics and Public Health in Revolutionary Russia*, 143–72.

21. Iu. A. Nekliudov, "Iakov L'vovich Leibovich—vidnyi deiatel' otechestvennoi sudebnoi meditsiny," *Sudebno-meditsinskaia ekspertiza*, no. 5 (2003): 48–49; Rozhanovskii, "Sudebno-meditsinskaia ekspertiza v dorevoliutsionnoi Rossii i v SSSR," 43–44, 56.

22. From the Communist Party program devised at the Eighth Party Congress (18–22 March 1919), as quoted in G. D. Petrov, *Ocherki istorii otechestvennoi meditsiny* (Moscow: Gos. iz-vo meditsinskoi literatury, 1962), 10–11. See also Susan Gross Solomon and John F. Hutchinson, "The Problem of

Health Reform in Russia," in *Health and Society in Revolutionary Russia*, ed. Susan Gross Solomon and John F. Hutchinson (Bloomington: Indiana University Press, 1990), xi.

23. "Medical police" entailed a view of health policy subordinate to the requirements of the maintenance of public order, by preventing epidemics and improving sanitation, for example. It had its heyday in eighteenth- and early nineteenth-century enlightened monarchies; see Crowther and White, *On Soul and Conscience*, 8–10; Catherine Crawford, "Medicine and the Law," in *Companion Encylcopedia of the History of Medicine*, ed. W. F. Bynum and R. Porter, 2 vols. (New York and London: Routledge, 1993), 2:1626–27. For the characterization of prerevolutionary Russia's health administration as a "medical police" regime, see Solomon and Hutchinson, "The Problem of Health Reform in Russia," x-xi.

24. Rozhanovskii, "Sudebno-meditsinskaia ekspertiza v dorevoliutsionnoi Rossii i v SSSR," 44–46.

25. Rozhanovskii, "Sudebno-meditsinskaia ekspertiza v dorevoliutsionnoi Rossii i v SSSR," 46–47.

26. Rozhanovskii, "Sudebno-meditsinskaia ekspertiza v dorevoliutsionnoi Rossii i v SSSR," 47–49. For the 1921 decree, "Polozhenie o sudebno-meditsinskikh ekspertakh," *Biulleten' Narodnogo komissariata zdravookhraneniia*, no. 1 (1922): 5–7. The 1921 decree extended doctors' rights of access to case files compiled by people's investigators, and permitted medical experts to make a final statement in trials, on forensic medical issues arising from the case, following summations given by prosecutors and defense.

27. Ia. Leibovich, "Sudebno-meditsinskaia ekspertiza pri NEP'e," *Ezhenedel'nik sovetskoi iustitsii*, no. 2 (1923): 36–38, quoted at 37. Leibovich's career is charted in Nekliudov, "Iakov L'vovich Leibovich."

28. Ia. Leibovich, "Piat' let sudebnoi meditsiny," *Ezhdenedel'nik sovetskoi iustitsii*, no. 34 (1923): 775–77, quoted at 775.

29. Rozhanovskii, "Sudebno-meditsinskaia ekspertiza v dorevoliutsionnoi Rossii i v SSSR," 56–57.

30. This orientation was particularly evident in Leibovich's own work on suicide, as well as his promotion of other forensic specialists' studies of suicide. See Pinnow, "Making Suicide Soviet;" idem, "Counting and Cutting," in *Russian Modernity: Politics, Knowledge, Practices*, ed. Hoffmann and Kotsonis, 115–37.

31. Ia. Leibovich, "Godovoi otchet po sudeb.-meditsinskoi ekspertize v RSFSR za 1925 g.," *Sudebno-meditsinskaia ekspertiza*, no. 5 (1927): 96–128; idem, "Godovoi otchet po sudebno-meditsinskoi ekspertize v RSFSR za 1924 g.," *Sudebno-meditsinskaia ekspertiza*, no. 4 (1926): 104–36.

32. For example, N. V. Popov, "IV-yi Moskovskii gubernskii rasshirennyi sudebno-meditsinskii s"ezd," *Sudebno-meditsinskaia ekspertiza*, no. 1 (1925): 99–115; L.[eibovich?], "Nizhegorodsoe gubernskoe soveshchanie po sudebno-meditsinskoi ekspertize byvsh. 26 marta 1925 g.," *Sudebno-meditsinskaia ekspertiza*, no. 2 (1925): 194–98; "Rasshirennyi nauchnyi s"ezd sudebnykh vrachei i predstavitelei iustitsii v g. Ivanove-Vosnesenske 23–25 dekabria

1927 g.," *Sudebno-meditsinskaia ekspertiza*, no. 9 (1928): 135–64 and no. 10 (1928): 156–66; "XXII [Dvadtsatoe vtoroe] nauchnoe zasedanie Obshchestva meditsinskoi ekspertizy g. Leningrada i oblasti ot 21 maia 1928 g.," *Sudebno-meditsinskaia ekspertiza*, no. 11 (1929): 180–87; see Nekliudov, "Iakov L'vovich Leibovich."

33. Ia. L. Leibovich, *Prakticheskoe rukovodstvo po sudebnoi meditsine*, 2nd ed. (Moscow: Izdanie Narodnogo komissariata iustitsii, 1923) and 3rd ed. (Moscow: Iuridicheskoe izdatel'stvo Narkomiusta RSFSR, 1927); idem, *Sudebnaia ginekologiia. Rukovodstvo dlia vrachei i iuristov* (Khar'kov: Iurdicheskoe iz-vo Narkomiusta USSR, 1928); Iu. Kratter, "Rukovodstvo sudebnoi meditsiny. Dlia vrachei i studentov, ch. 4, Sudebnaia seksologiia. Avtorizovannyi perev. so 2-go nemetsk. izd. pod red. i s dopolneniiami Ia. Leibovicha," *Sudebno-meditsinskaia ekspertiza*, no. 9 (1928): 1–38 and 10 (1928): 67–114.

34. Prescriptions that counselled the suppression and sublimation of sexuality, in party and non-party writing about sex, abounded. See Naiman, *Sex in Public;* Carleton, *Sexual Revolution in Bolshevik Russia;* Bernstein, *The Dictatorship of Sex*.

35. On the health commissariat's drive for sexual education via advice literature and sexual health clinics, see Bernstein, *The Dictatorship of Sex*.

36. See the thematic essays in Cocks and Houlbrook, eds., *Palgrave Advances in the Modern History of Sexuality;* for various national trajectories, see Eder, Hall, and Hekma, eds., *Sexual Cultures in Europe: National Histories*.

37. The radical wing of the European sex reform movement regularly hailed the Soviet example; see Ralf Dose, "The World League for Sexual Reform: Some Possible Approaches," in *Sexual Cultures in Europe: National Histories*, ed. Eder, Hall, and Hekma.

38. Civil War-era Marxist expectations that law would wither away as socialism deepened were replaced with an acceptance of the need for a conventional "bourgeois" legal system under NEP (1921–1928). Nevertheless, Bolshevik law departed from liberal western systems in two significant respects. The first was that Bolsheviks refused to be constrained by the law; they rejected the principle of the rule of law as "bourgeois." Second, in criminal law they introduced the principle of analogy. If an act was not enumerated in Soviet criminal law as an offense, but contradicted revolutionary values, it could be prosecuted by analogy to an existing crime. These departures from liberal legal tradition were most actively applied in the use of extralegal terror and secret police against political opponents. On these points see, e.g., Peter H. Juviler, *Revolutionary Law and Order* (New York: Free Press, 1976), 15–38; Laura Engelstein, "Combined Underdevelopment: Discipline and the Law in Imperial and Soviet Russia," *American Historical Review* 98, no. 2 (1993): 338–53; Peter H. Solomon, Jr., *Soviet Criminal Justice under Stalin* (Cambridge: Cambridge University Press, 1996). The routine functioning of the conventional legal system (prosecutions not ordinarily regarded as "political") could also be subject to extralegal intervention, but the degree to which this took place remains to be studied. Prosecutions by analogy do not appear among the sex crime case samples that are studied in

this book. For examples of the use of the principle of analogy against female prostitutes (as "hooligans") in early 1920s Petrograd, see Lebina and Shkarovskii, eds., *Prostitutsiia v Peterburge,* 169–70.

39. Tsarist jurists who drafted a widely hailed criminal code in 1903 had incorporated emergent ideas of sexual modernity (including a degree of recognition of equality of the sexes, and a medicalized view of sexuality, albeit in implicit terms), but Tsar Nicholas II refused to enact in full the draft. On these issues see Engelstein, *The Keys to Happiness,* 75–84. On how Bolshevik jurists developed the 1922 RSFSR Criminal Code, see Healey, *Homosexual Desire in Revolutionary Russia,* 115–22. This code became the basis for the penal codes of all subsequent union republics when the Soviet Union was formed in 1924; the language and structure of these codes varied little, although republics believed by the Bolsheviks to be "less developed" also had chapters in their codes dealing with "survivals of primitive custom," such as polygamy, bride price, sodomy, and male prostitution. See Healey, *Homosexual Desire in Revolutionary Russia,* 158–62.

40. As the title of the fifth chapter of the code proclaimed; see Healey, *Homosexual Desire in Revolutionary Russia,* 115.

41. "Article 166. Sexual intercourse with persons not having reached sexual maturity is punished by the deprivation of liberty for a term of not less than three years with strict isolation." Leibovich, *Prakticheskoe rukovodstvo po sudebnoi meditsine,* 2nd ed., 165.

42. "Article 167. Sexual intercourse with persons not having reached sexual maturity, accompanied by defloration or the satisfaction of sexual passion in perverted forms is punished by the deprivation of liberty for a term of not less than five years." Leibovich, *Prakticheskoe rukovodstvo po sudebnoi meditsine,* 2nd ed., 165.

43. Russian gynecologists wrote authoritative works on defloration before 1917 that were in use well into the twentieth century: V. Merzheevskii, "Sudebno-meditsinskoe izsledovanie devstvennoi plevy. Material k voprosu o rastlenii," *Arkhiv sudebnoi meditsiny i obshchestvennoi gigieny,* no. 3, sec. 2 (1871): 5–43; idem, *Sudebnaia ginekologiia. Rukovodstvo dlia vrachei i iuristov* (St. Petersburg: B. G. Ianpol'skii, 1878), 77–109; E. F. Bellin, *Sudebnaia meditsina rastleniia. Atlas iz 20 khromolitografirovannykh tablits* (St. Petersburg: Meditsinskii Departament, Minsterstvo vnutrennykh del, 1898); see also Serdiukov, *Sudebnaia ginekologiia.*

44. "Article 168. The corruption of children or minors, accomplished by means of depraved acts in relation to them, is punished by the deprivation of liberty for a term of up to five years." Leibovich, *Prakticheskoe rukovodstvo po sudebnoi meditsine,* 2nd ed., 166. In this code, "children" *(maloletnie)* were defined for the purposes of punishment as up to 14 years of age, and "minors" *(nesovershennoletnie)* were 14 to 18 years old.

45. Engelstein, *The Keys to Happiness,* 75–84. In the 1903 draft code, nonpenetrative sexual acts with minors were to be punished equally when inflicted on boys as well as girls; earlier laws only protected girls in this respect.

46. "Article 169. Rape, i.e., sexual intercourse with the use of physical or psychological force or by means of the use of the helpless condition of the

victimized person, is punished by the deprivation of liberty for a term not less than three years." Leibovich, *Prakticheskoe rukovodstvo po sudebnoi meditsine*, 2nd ed., 166.

47. "Article 169a. The compulsion of a woman to enter into a sexual liaison by a person in relation to whom the woman is materially or professionally dependent is punished by the penalties provided under article 169." Leibovich, *Prakticheskoe rukovodstvo po sudebnoi meditsine*, 2nd ed., 166. For a study of complaints raised via administrative and trade-union channels, see Lisa Granik, "The Trials of the *Proletarka*: Sexual Harassment Claims in the 1920s," in *Reforming Justice in Russia, 1864–1996: Power, Culture, and the Limits of Legal Order*, ed. Peter Solomon, Jr. (Armonk, NY: M. E. Sharpe, 1997), 131–67.

48. In the 1922 Criminal Code, these crimes were described in articles 155 (venereal disease infection) and articles 170 and 171. The present book deals only tangentially with cases under these articles; see the introduction.

49. D. Kurskii and P. Stuchka, "Instruktivnye pis'ma. Direktivnoe pis'mo NKIu i verkhsuda RSFSR po primeneniiu Ugol. Kod. redaktsii 1926 g.," *Sudebnaia praktika RSFSR*, no. 1 (1927): 8–11.

50. Peter H. Solomon, Jr., "Soviet Penal Policy, 1917–1934: A Reinterpretation," *Slavic Review* 39, no. 2 (1980): 195–217. On official class favoritism and disfavor in early Soviet society, see Sheila Fitzpatrick, "Ascribing Class: The Construction of Social Identity in Soviet Russia," *Journal of Modern History*, no. 65 (1993): 745–70; and Golfo Alexopoulos, *Stalin's Outcasts: Aliens, Citizens, and the Soviet State, 1926–1936* (Ithaca, NY: Cornell University Press, 2003).

51. See articles 162 (location of examinations) and 171 (access to case files) of the RSFSR Criminal Procedure Code (1922), quoted in Leibovich, *Prakticheskoe rukovodstvo po sudebnoi meditsine*, 2nd ed., 154.

52. The continued scarcity of dedicated examination rooms for forensic medical functions was a complaint throughout the 1920s. See for example, Rozhanovskii, "Sudebno-meditsinskaia ekspertiza v dorevoliutsionnoi Rossii i v SSSR," 47. Article 191 of the Criminal Procedure Code was equivocal about privacy for examined persons: "The investigator should not be present during the examination of a person of the opposite sex if the subject is examined unclothed, except in those cases when this person does not object to the investigator's presence."

53. See article 275 quoted in Leibovich, *Prakticheskoe rukovodstvo po sudebnoi meditsine*, 2nd ed., 156. The forensic psychiatrist N. P. Brukhanskii, whose work was regarded in the 1930s with suspicion, was clearly given wide access to attend trials and view court records during the 1920s, both as an expert witness and as a researcher-observer. See his *Materialy po seksual'noi psikhopatologii* (Moscow: M. i S. Sabashnikov, 1927). A similar ease of access to court records was accorded in the 1920s to a younger psychiatrist who advanced rapidly during the 1930s: see V. A. Vnukov, "Iz praktiki sudebno-psikhiatricheskikh ekspertiz," *Prestupnik i prestupnost'*, no. 2 (1927): 253–63.

54. For the survey of medical experts, see Rozhanovskii, "Sudebno-meditsinskaia ekspertiza v dorevoliutsionnoi Rossii i v SSSR," 77.

55. In the case of minors, family members or guardians could lodge a complaint. A small proportion of sexual crimes were detected in *flagrante delicto*: of 330 sexual crimes detected by the police during the first half of 1928 in the Urals province, 102 were detected in the act; these formed part of a larger total of 868 sexual crime cases arising in the province during the period. See Gosudarstvennyi arkhiv Sverdlovskoi oblasti (GASO) 854/1/139/7 ob.

56. *Ugolovnyi kodeks, s predisloviem D. I. Kurskogo* (Moscow: Izd. moskovskogo gubernskogo suda, 1924), 625.

57. By definition, such abandoned investigations left very little trace in the local courts' archival records. In Petrograd a complaint of sexual intercourse and supposed defloration (article 167) of a 12-year-old girl was quashed in 1924 after two gynecological examinations confirmed that the victim was still a virgin; see Leningradskii oblastnoi gosudarstvennyi arkhiv v Vyborge (LOGAV), 2205/1/1969 (Lukomskii, 1922–1924). In Sverdlovsk in 1927, a case of sexual intercourse with a 12-year-old girl not supposed to have reached maturity (article 151 [1926]) was dropped after extensive forensic medical investigation uncovered a history of previous sexual partners; GASO 340/2/476 (Vorob'ev, 1926–1927).

58. Liberal-leaning jurists in the early Soviet era criticized the pretrial investigation on the same grounds of secrecy and lack of access for the defense advocate to the case files; see P. I. Liublinskii, *Predvaritel'noe sledstvie* (Moscow: Pravo i Zhizn', 1923). Prosecutors and senior jurists were more likely to criticize the poor quality of the pretrial investigations, which left better-educated justice workers much remedial work before a case could be sent to trial: See comments by one comrade Novosel'skii, a Saratov prosecutor, in Iakovlev, "Raionnoe Soveshchanie sudebno-meditsinskikh ekspertov s predstaviteliami sudebno-sledstvennykh organov, proiskhodivshee v g. Saratove s 6 po 9 sentiabria 1925 goda," *Sudebno-meditsinskaia ekspertiza*, no. 3 (1925): 83–94, at page 86; for the Supreme Court's view, see Predsedatel' UKK Verkhsuda RSFSR Chelyshev, "Doklad UKK o praktike po delam o polovykh prestupleniiakh za vtoruiu polovinu 1926 goda," *Sudebnaia praktika RSFSR*, no. 6 (1927): 4–8.

59. On agit-prop "demonstration trials" (pokazatel'nye protsessy), see Elizabeth Wood, *Performing Justice: Agitation Trials in Early Soviet Russia* (Ithaca, NY: Cornell University Press, 2005); Julie A. Cassiday, *The Enemy on Trial: Early Soviet Courts on Stage and Screen* (DeKalb, IL: Northern Illinois University Press, 2000).

60. On post-reform trials, see V. Merzheevskii, "Perechen' ugolovnykh del, razbiravshikhsia pri zakrytykh dveriakh v s.-peterburgskom okruzhnom sude," *Arkhiv sudebnoi meditsiny i obshchestvennoi gigieny*, no. 3, sec. 2 (1869): 73–86; Petr Zeidler, "Perechen' ugolovnykh del, razbiravshikhsia v s.-peterburgskom okruzhnom sude, pri zakrytykh dveriakh, s uchastiem vrachei-ekspertov," *Arkhiv sudebnoi meditsiny i obshchestvennoi gigieny*, no. 4, sec. 2 (1870): 58–68; idem, "Perechen' ugolovnykh del, razsmatrivavshikhsia v s.-peterburgskom okruzhnom sude, pri zakrytykh dveriakh, s uchastiem vrachei ekspertov," *Arkhiv sudebnoi meditsiny i obshchestvennoi gigieny*, no. 4, sec. 2 (1871): 48–60. Only ten

out of 194 trials in this book's sample were closed—or closed for part of the proceedings.

61. Iakovlev, "Raionnoe Soveshchanie sudebno-meditsinskikh ekspertov s predstaviteliami sudebno-sledstvennykh organov, proiskhodivshee v g. Saratove s 6 po 9 sentiabria 1925 goda," 86. An early Soviet chronicler of forensic medical history noted the adaptability of this teaching method to the forensic investigation, and to forensic training for non-specialist doctors and jurists, Rozhanovskii, "Sudebno-meditsinskaia ekspertiza v dorevoliutsionnoi Rossii i v SSSR," 47, 75–76.

62. GARF A482/25/104/16, 18ob, 103–4.

63. Rozhanovskii, "Sudebno-meditsinskaia ekspertiza v dorevoliutsionnoi Rossii i v SSSR," 75; Gamburg, *Razvitie sudebnomeditsinskoi nauki i ekspertizy*, 38; on the bureau, see E. K. Krasnushkin, G. M. Segal, and Ts. M. Fainberg, eds., *Pravonarusheniia v oblasti seksual'nykh otnoshenii* (Moscow: Izdanie Moszdravotdela, 1927).

64. See Kowalsky, "Making Crime and Sex Soviet," 85–118; Rozhanovskii, "Sudebno-meditsinskaia ekspertiza v dorevoliutsionnoi Rossii i v SSSR," 76; Juviler, *Revolutionary Law and Order*, 30–33.

65. N. V. Popov, "O rabote Moskovskoi Sudebno-Meditsinskoi Ekspertizy," *Moskovskii meditsinskii zhurnal*, no. 7 (1924): 83–89.

66. On Izhevskii's leadership see, e.g., N. I. Izhevskii, "Vtoroi vserossiiskii s"ezd sudebno-meditsinskikh ekspertov v g. Moskve (25 fevralia–3 marta 1926 goda)," *Leningradskii meditsinskii zhurnal*, no. 4 (apr) (1926): 143–51.

67. Sverdlovsk's forensic medical infrastructure was comparatively weak, but it was able to hold a conference of jurists, police, and doctors in July 1926; see Rozhanovskii, "Sudebno-meditsinskaia ekspertiza v dorevoliutsionnoi Rossii i v SSSR," 99–100. On Bazhenov, see his *Spravochnik po sudebnoi meditsine i ekspertize v sviazi s nachal'nymi poniatiiami po anatomii, fiziologii cheloveka, sotsial'noi gigiene, sanitarii i skoroi pomoshchi* (Sverdlovsk: Izdanie 4 shkoly NKVD Administrativno-Militseiskikh rabotnikov, 1929).

68. The establishment of the Central Institute of Forensic Medicine is described in GARF, A482/24/38. Leibovich was demoted and made director of the forensic medical faculty in Tomsk University at some point during the cultural revolution, see GARF A406/12/2789/63 and A406/12/2387. Leibovich served at Tomsk from 1932 to 1936, and later directed the forensic medical faculty at Vinnitsa Medical Institute, 1939–1941. "The fate of Ia. L. Leibovich after the occupation of Vinnitsa by German Fascist forces is unknown," writes Iurii Nekliudov in "Iakov L'vovich Leibovich," 49.

69. For early deliberations, see GARF A482/25/104/16, 18ob, 103–4; A482/25/190/1–12 (1921); A482/25/286/1–8 (1923). For Leningrad courses, see M. D. Mazurenko, Iu. V. Zimina, and I. N. Ivanov, "K 70-letiiu kafedry sudebnoi meditsiny Sankt-Peterburgskoi meditsinskoi akademii poslediplomnogo obrazovaniia," *Sudebno-meditsinskaia ekspertiza*, no. 2 (1995): 47–48; O. Kh. Porksheian and V. K. Belikov, "Fotografiia iz arkhiva kafedry sudebnoi meditsiny Sankt-Peterburgskoi akademii poslediplomnogo obrazovaniia," *Sudebno-*

meditsinskaia ekspertiza, 37, no. 4 (1994): 43–47. See also Gamburg, *Razvitie sudebnomeditsinskoi nauki*, 38.

2— Sexual Maturity and the Threshold of Sexual Citizenship

1. On these points I am indebted to Natalia Gerodetti for access to the manuscript of her now published study, *Modernising Sexualities: Towards a Socio-Historical Understanding of Sexualities in the Swiss Nation* (Bern and Berlin: Peter Lang Verlag, 2005).

2. Helmut Gaupner, "Sexual Consent—The Criminal Law in Europe and Overseas," *Archives of Sexual Behavior* 29, no. 5, 415–61.

3. Engelstein, *The Keys to Happiness*, 75–84.

4. Engelstein, *The Keys to Happiness*, 78.

5. On changes in sex education and concepts of sexual self control, especially after the 1905 Revolution, see Engelstein, *The Keys to Happiness*, 225–36.

6. Engelstein, *The Keys to Happiness*, 83. On U.S. medical discourses of "normal" and "abnormal" sexuality, see Estelle B. Freedman, "'Uncontrolled Desires': The Response to the Sexual Psychopath, 1920–1960," *Passion and Power: Sexuality in History*, ed. Kathy Peiss and Christina Simmons (Philadelphia, PA: Temple University Press, 1989), 199–225; Robertson, *Crimes against Children*.

7. From the verb *rastlevat'*, *rastlit'*, "to deprive of virginity; to corrupt morally." The term *rastlenie* offered opportunities for figurative readings of moral corruption, as discussed later in this chapter.

8. It is not a simple matter to reconstruct from available archival sources what the drafters of Soviet Russia's first criminal code intended with regard to sexual activity. We do know from commentaries in the archives that the Bolsheviks working on a draft criminal code wanted to purge the law of religious and moral language and to secularize penal norms. It is also clear from the modest paperwork relating to the drafting of the section of the code on sex crime that until quite late in the process, the Bolshevik jurist M. Iu. Kozlovskii, tasked with drafting the law, expected little change in this field. His early versions drew heavily on the 1903 Draft Criminal Code. The final radically revised text was the product of a commission led by the Bolshevik activist jurist P. A. Krasikov and the Justice Commissariat's director of prisons and representative to the Cheka (secret police), L. A. Savrasov. See Healey, *Homosexual Desire in Revolutionary Russia*, 115–22.

9. See table 9 in Ia. Leibovich, "Godovoi otchet po sudeb.-meditsinskoi ekspertize v RSFSR za 1925 g.," *Sudebno-meditsinskaia ekspertiza*, no. 5 (1927): 96–128.

10. Ia. Leibovich, *Sudebnaia ginekologiia. Rukovodstvo dlia vrachei i iuristov* (Khar'kov: Iurdicheskoe iz-vo Narkomiusta USSR, 1928), 9–10.

11. Ia. Leibovich, "Polovaia zrelost' v ugolovnom i grazhdanskom zakonodatel'stve," *Voprosy zdravookhraneniia*, no. 14 (1928): 40–44; all quotations in this paragraph at page 40.

12. On tsarist marriage-age norms, see T. A. Bernshtam, *Molodezh' v obriadovoi zhizni russkoi obshchiny XIX–nachala XX v.* (Leningrad: Nauka, 1988), 41–51; for Kurskii's explanations during the 1925–1926 Soviet legislative debates on marriage age, see Schlesinger, ed., *The Family in the USSR*, 110–66.

13. The expectation that the individual body yielded information about the social body informed forensic medical work on suicide too. See Morrissey, *Suicide and the Body Politic in Imperial Russia;* Pinnow, "Making Suicide Soviet."

14. V. M. Tarnovskii, *Polovaia zrelost', eia techenie, otkloneniia i bolezni* (St. Petersburg, M. M. Stasiulevich: 1886).

15. Engelstein, *The Keys to Happiness*, 228.

16. Tarnovskii, *Polovaia zrelost'*, 6–7, 35.

17. Implicitly, in "Great Russia" this "median" as general norm lay behind a 1927 resolution of forensic medical doctors in Ivanovo-Voznesensk, who argued that because 16 was the average age of the onset of sexual maturity "as a rule in the median zone of our republic," therefore the "sexual maturity" standard in the RSFSR criminal code ought to be replaced by an age of consent of 16; see "Rezoliutsii Ivanovo-voznesenskogo rasshirennogo S"ezda sudebnykh vrachei, predstavitelei iustitsii i professorov" in "Rasshirennyi nauchnyi s"ezd sudebnykh vrachei i predstavitelei iustitsii v g. Ivanove-Vosnesenske 23–25 dekabria 1927 g.," *Sudebno-meditsinskaia ekspertiza,* no. 9 (1928): 135–64 and no. 10 (1928): 156–66, quoted at no. 10 (1928): 164–66.

18. See for example the 1898 study of 1,012 women by Pargamin in Belaia Tserkov', and another by Veber in St. Petersburg, both involving comparisons for first menstruation in Russians and Jews, cited in N. V. Viazemskii, *O polovoi zrelosti s pedagogicheskoi tochki zreniia* (St. Petersburg: M. M. Stasiulevich, 1906), 17–18.

19. Viazemskii, *O polovoi zrelosti,* 19.

20. N. Zak, "Materialy k kharakteristike fizicheskago razvitiia detei," *Vestnik obshchestvennoi gigieny, sudebnoi i prakticheskoi meditsiny* (January 1898), sec. 2: 1–34. For a survey of studies of girls that also resisted explanations based on race, while still working within racial terms of reference, see L. Vinogradova-Lukirskaia, "K voprosu ob izsledovanii rosta i vesa uchenits srednikh uchebnykh zavedenii," *Vestnik obshchestvennoi gigieny, sudebnoi i prakticheskoi meditsiny* 21 (1894): kn. 2, sec. 2: 64–94; kn. 3, sec. 2: 186–218.

21. See for example Viazemskii, *O polovoi zrelosti*, 12, 17; E. Ia. Gindes, *Perekhodnyi vozrast* (Baku: Narkompromtorg, 1923), 20; K. N. Krzhishkovskii, *Fiziologiia polovoi zhizni* (Leningrad: Priboi, 1926), 22; Leibovich, *Sudebnaia ginekologiia*, 27.

22. For a summary of nineteenth-century legislation and social patterns of youthful marriage, see Bernshtam, *Molodezh' v obriadovoi zhizni*, 41–51. On the law in the Caucasus, see V. Merzheevskii, *Sudebnaia ginekologiia. Rukovodstvo dlia vrachei i iuristov* (St. Petersburg: B. G. Ianpol'skii, 1878), 1.

23. N. S. Kiselev, "Vliianie rannikh brakov na zhenshchin i rozhdaemykh imi detei," *Vestnik obshchestvennoi gigieny, sudebnoi i prakticheskoi meditsiny* (February 1897), sec. 2: 121–39.

24. Kiselev, "Vliianie rannikh brakov na zhenshchin i rozhdaemykh imi detei," 122–25, 135.

25. For a draft questionnaire on the onset of menstruation in Russian and non-Russian women of the empire, proposed to the Anthropological Society of Moscow, see D. P. Nikol'skii, "Programma dlia sobiraniia svedenii o polovoi zrelosti zhenshchin," *Vestnik obshchestvennoi gigieny, sudebnoi i prakticheskoi meditsiny,* (November 1901): sec.3: 1722–23.

26. Gindes, *Perekhodnyi vozrast,* 18, 20.

27. Gindes, *Perekhodnyi vozrast,* 20. For similar assertions, see L. M. Vasilevskii, *Polovoe zdorov'e* (Moscow: G. F. Mirimanov, 1925), 15.

28. K. N. Krzhishkovskii, *Fiziologiia polovoi zhizni* (Leningrad: Priboi, 1926), 22.

29. Leibovich, *Sudebnaia ginekologiia,* 9, 26. Leibovich cited three studies of first menstruation in the northern capital. Gruzdev's, published in the early 1890s, surveyed 12,000 women in-migrants to St. Petersburg and found an average age of 15¾ years for first menses; Rodzevich's, based on 12,439 cases arrived at an average age of 16 years, while a Soviet study by Belugin in 1924 based on 1,250 maternity hospital records yielded the lowest age, 14¾ years.

30. "*The thousand-year yoke of the woman of the East has made her a premature wife, mother and slave, and turns her prematurely into an old woman!* Without denying the somewhat earlier maturation of southern girls (a modest difference), I absolutely reject tales about 9–10-year-old mature women of the South: they are in fact `children in increased danger', the victims of a fatal delusion and the age-old exploitation of women. The fewer rights women have, the less their sexual maturity is valued; the more women enjoy full civil rights, the more their sexual maturity is held in higher esteem, all other things being equal." Leibovich, "Polovaia zrelost' v ugolovnom i grazhdanskom zakonodatel'stve," 43 (original emphasis).

31. Further examples, see V. A. Riasentsev, "K voprosu ob opredelenii polovoi zrelosti zhenshchin," *Sudebno-meditsinskaia ekspertiza,* no. 7 (1927): 26–29; Saratov Forensic Medical Institute professor M. I. Raiskii's comments in "Rasshirennyi nauchnyi s"ezd sudebnykh vrachei i predstavitelei iustitsii v g. Ivanove-Vosnesenske 23–25 dekabria 1927 g.," no. 9: 161; Bazhenov, *Spravochnik po sudebnoi meditsine,* 60; V. Vladimirskii, "Polovaia zrelost'," in *Bol'shaia meditsinskaia entsiklopediia,* ed. N. A. Semashko (Moscow: OGIZ RSFSR, 1933), 26:298–99.

32. Tarnovskii, *Polovaia zrelost',* 10–12.

33. Tarnovskii, *Polovaia zrelost',* 13–15. On the significance of tempering the will with the disciplines of cold, see Catriona Kelly, "The Education of the Will: Advice Literature, *Zakal,* and Manliness in Early Twentieth-Century Russia," in *Russian Masculinities in History and Culture,* ed. Barbara Evans Clements, Rebecca Friedman, and Dan Healey (Basingstoke, UK: Palgrave Macmillan, 2001), 131–51

34. Tarnovskii, *Polovaia zrelost',* 16–17. Given Tarnovskii's condemnation of seafood and fried poultry, the recommendation of "white meat" likely

indicated a preference for pork, the staple meat of eastern Europe but not considered a "red" meat. For strikingly similar dietary recommendations for the avoidance of premature sexual maturation, from Soviet sex experts in 1933, see Z. Gurevich, "Polovaia zhizn'," in *Bol'shaia meditsinskaia entsiklopediia*, ed. N. A. Semashko (Moscow: OGIZ RSFSR, 1933), 26: 282–98, especially 286; and A. O. Edel'shtein, "Polovoe vospitanie," in the same volume, 299–302, especially 301.

35. It was of no concern whatsoever, for example, to Tarnovskii in his manual on sexual maturity.

36. Viazemskii, for example, on the rural idyll: "Girls of the countryside have none of the factors weighing on their city cousins: none of the mental, moral or intellectual exhaustion; they live constantly in fresh air that forges their entire organism, giving them flourishing health. Their way of life protects them from all manner of nervous stimulants that the life of the city girl, even of the lowest class, abounds with; such stimulants are the source of irritants for upper-class girls that evoke the premature appearance of menstrual flows and threaten so many diverse troubles. The peasant girl's imagination, growing up as she does in the fresh air and living in absolute ignorance of literature, music, the arts, which are so much part of life for girls of the prosperous classes, is absolutely peaceful." Viazemskii, *O polovoi zrelosti*, 20–21.

37. For example, studies of 20,000 women in 1887 conducted by doctors Gorvits and Benzenger, reported in Viazemskii, *O polovoi zrelosti*, 21. These contrasted with studies of thousands of city-dwelling women conducted in St. Petersburg by physicians Gruzdev (in the 1890s) and Rodzevich (no date was given for his study), cited in Leibovich, *Sudebnaia ginekologiia*, 26.

38. Leibovich, *Sudebnaia ginekologiia*, 26; Gurevich, "Polovaia zhizn'," 286. It is striking that many forensic medical authorities said nothing specifically about peasant puberty or trained their sights specifically on town-dwellers, for example N. V. Popov, "Neskol'ko zamechanii po voprosu o vremeni nastupleniia polovoi zrelosti," *Sudebno-meditsinskaia ekspertiza*, no. 7 (1927): 29–33; and Riasentsev, "K voprosu ob opredelenii polovoi zrelosti zhenshchin," 26–29.

39. Gindes, *Perekhodnyi vozrast*, 20; Krzhishkovskii, *Fiziologiia polovoi zhizni*, 24.

40. Tarnovksii, *Polovaia zrelost'*, 10. Tarnovskii's subject in this book was the sexual maturity of young officers, so his comments on the working class were relatively brief.

41. Viazemskii, *O polovoi zrelosti*, 19, 24; see also Tarnovksii, *Polovaia zrelost'*, 25.

42. Viazemskii, *O polovoi zrelosti*, 25.

43. Engelstein, *The Keys to Happiness*, 240.

44. For typical commentary on environmental influences that inspired early sexual awareness and thus activity (which in itself allegedly stimulated maturation), see for example Gindes, *Perekhodnyi vozrast*, 21; and on wet dreams triggered by conversations, books, and plays of louche content, B. N. Khol'tsov, *Funktsional'nye rasstroistva muzhskogo polovogo apparata i funktsional'nye rasstroistva mochevykh organov nervnogo proiskhozhdeniia*

(Leningrad: Prakticheskaia meditsina, 1926), 20–21. Tarnovskii's *zakal* as a device for delaying sexual maturation still figured in the prescriptions of a Leningrad professor: on cold-water sponge baths, bedrooms filled with fresh cold air, getting rid of cozy bedclothes, and the Müller system of vigorous exercises before lights out, see Krzhishkovskii, *Fiziologiia polovoi zhizni*, 24.

45. Soviet sexologists nevertheless did conduct some large surveys in the 1920s specifically on the rural population, most notably Z. A. Gurevitsch and A. J. Woroschbit, "Das Sexualleben der Bauerin in Russland," *Zeitschrift fur Sexualwissenschaft und Sexualpolitik* 18, nos. 1, 2 (1931, 1932): 51–74; 81–110. Moreover, sexological studies of non-Russian populations were often by definition studies of rural agricultural or nomadic populations. See for example S. F. Baronov and T. Ia. Kuz'mina, "Vremia nastupleniia zrelosti i polovaia zhizn' zhenshchin-kazachek," in *Kazaki* (1930), further publication details unknown, as found in the Central State Scientific-Medical Library, Moscow.

46. See comments from Dr. Gorodkov and Dr. M. I. Raiskii of the Saratov Forensic Medical Institute, in "Rasshirennyi nauchnyi s"ezd sudebnykh vrachei i predstavitelei iustitsii v g. Ivanove-Vosnesenske 23–25 dekabria 1927 g.," quoted at no. 9: 158, 162; Riasentsev, "K voprosu ob opredelenii polovoi zrelosti zhenshchin," 26–29, especially 29.

47. Krasnushkin, "K psikhologii i psikhopatlogii polovykh pravonarushenii," in *Pravonarusheniia v oblasti seksual'nykh otnoshenii*, ed. Krasnushkin, Segal, and Fainberg, 20; and B. S. Man'kovskii, "Sovremennaia polovaia prestupnost'," in the same volume, pp. 85, 88.

48. V. S. Piaternev, "K voprosu ob opredelenii polovoi zrelosti zhenshchiny," *Sudebno-meditsinskaia ekspertiza*, no. 11 (1929): 21–26.

49. L. B. Leitman, "K voprosu o polovom sovershennoletii," *Sudebno-meditsinskaia ekspertiza*, no. 9 (1928): 75–78, see esp. 77.

50. "Rasshirennyi nauchnyi s"ezd sudebnykh vrachei i predstavitelei iustitsii v g. Ivanove-Vosnesenske 23–25 dekabria 1927 g.," no. 9, 162.

51. For example, studies of 20,000 women in 1887 conducted by doctors Gorvits and Benzenger, reported in Viazemskii, *O polovoi zrelosti*, 21. These contrasted with studies of thousands of city-dwelling women conducted in St. Petersburg by physicians Gruzdev (in the 1890s) and Rodzevich (no date was given for this study), cited in Leibovich, *Sudebnaia ginekologiia*, 26. Rodzevich's study of 50,000 women, is also mentioned in Nikol'skii, "Programma dlia sobiraniia svedenii o polovoi zrelosti zhenshchin," 1722–23.

52. Viazemskii, *O polovoi zrelosti*, 5; Gindes, *Perekhodnyi vozrast*, 19.

53. Leibovich, *Prakticheskoe rukovodstvo po sudebnoi meditsine*, 2nd ed., 98; for a similar treatment in a handbook for police investigators, see Bazhenov, *Spravochnik po sudebnoi meditsine*, 60.

54. See for example cases of defloration or attempted sexual assault from rural districts in Petrograd province in LOGAV 2205/1/454 (Novokreshchenov, 1922–23), l. 24; 2205/1/464 (Mantunen-Iantunen, 1923), l. 94; and 2205/1/1939 (Veislits, 1924), l. 22.

55. N. V. Popov, "Neskol'ko zamechanii po voprosu o vremeni

nastupleniia polovoi zrelosti," *Sudebno-meditsinskaia ekspertiza,* no. 7 (1927): 29–33, quoted at 30. For strikingly similar definitions of sexual maturity, see Riasentsev, "K voprosu ob opredelenii polovoi zrelosti zhenshchin," 27; "Rasshirennyi nauchnyi s"ezd sudebnykh vrachei i predstavitelei iustitsii v g. Ivanove-Vosnesenske 23–25 dekabria 1927 g.," no. 9: 161 (for comments by professor Raiskii); Leibovich, *Sudebnaia ginekologiia,* 10; Piaternev, "K voprosu ob opredelenii polovoi zrelosti zhenshchiny," 21–26, especially at 22.

56. Popov, "Neskol'ko zamechanii," 31.

57. Popov, "Neskol'ko zamechanii," 31–32.

58. Leibovich, *Sudebnaia ginekologiia,* 36; idem, "Polovaia zrelost' v ugolovnom i grazhdanskom zakonodatel'stve"; Riasentsev, "K voprosu ob opredelenii polovoi zrelosti zhenshchin," 29.

59. As quoted in Leibovich, *Sudebnaia ginekologiia,* 36.

60. For a tsarist view of women's psychosexual maturation—or lack of it!—see Viazemskii, *O polovoi zrelosti,* 20; the Soviet-era Baku pediatrician was evidently schooled before the revolution and had little faith in its messages where the emancipation of women was concerned: "Obviously girls have not got used to the new condition of women's emancipation; [the authorities] have not penetrated her psychology to betray her genetic sexual instincts and even in the present day, regardless of the great achievement of the emancipation of women, she still belongs more to the family than to society. This eternal female psychology will only change gradually with the reform of the family and the establishment of new conditions of socioeconomic life, but will life become better when a woman ceases to be a woman and when one of the sources of the satisfaction of the higher emotions, spiritual elevation, and poetic experiences, disappears from life? No reform will reconstruct woman, for all of physical nature is based on two principles, the male and the female, and these principles will remain in humans." Gindes, *Perekhodnyi vozrast,* 54.

61. Bernstein, *The Dictatorship of Sex;* Vasilevskii, *Polovoe zdorov'e,* 14, 23; Krzhishkovskii, *Fiziologiia polovoi zhizni,* 42; L. Ia. Iakobzon, *Polovaia kholodnost' zhenshchiny* (Leningrad: Prakticheskaia meditsina, 1927), 137.

62. Popov, "Neskol'ko zamechanii," 32. Summarizing the state of the question for forensic gynecologists in 1930, one authority wrote that a woman must have "full consciousness of the significance of a sexual life and of becoming pregnant" as well as functional full development of the organism; being a mother must be harmless for both "soma and psyche" of the young mother. G. G. Genter, "K voprosu o polovoi zrelosti zhenshchiny," *Vrachebnaia gazeta,* no. 12 (1930): 912–17, quoted at 917.

63. Popov was one of the forensic medical authorities who presided over the adoption of these guidelines, which were formulated with the NKVD and justice commissariat officials. The rules distinguished between "the biological meaning" of sexual maturity and the meaning of the term "from the viewpoint of forensic-medical practice." Sexual maturity was defined in a specific appendix as: "a) the ability to give birth and nurse a child; b) the presence of sufficient mental development in general and specifically in relation to the upbringing of

the child; c) ability to lead an independent existence." This appendix warned doctors that first menstruation, or ability to get pregnant, did not in and of themselves constitute "sexual maturity in the forensic-medical sense"; the concept acquired an ideologized social element that reflected the needs of Soviet natalist policies. See "Pravila ambulatornogo sudebno-meditsinskogo akushersko-ginekologicheskogo issledovaniia," GARF 482/25/879/21-28 (1934).

64. Leibovich, *Sudebnaia ginekologiia*, 32–33. A Berlin gynecologist, V. Liepmann, was the source of Leibovich's conception of psychosexual maturity, but the idea of woman as overwhelmingly determined by her sexuality had a long pedigree in European thought. The most compelling statement of the thesis for Leibovich's generation was Otto Weininger's *Sex and Character* (1903); see Chandak Sengoopta, *Otto Weininger: Sex, Science, and Self in Imperial Vienna* (Chicago, IL: University of Chicago Press, 2000); on Weininger's impact in Russia, Engelstein, *The Keys to Happiness*, 299–333.

65. The study was Piaternev, "K voprosu ob opredelenii polovoi zrelosti zhenshchiny."

66. For favorable comments from Dr. A. S. Iavorskii at the conference, "Rasshirennyi nauchnyi s"ezd sudebnykh vrachei i predstavitelei iustitsii v g. Ivanove-Vosnesenske 23–25 dekabria 1927 g.," see no. 9: 160.

67. Leitman, "K voprosu o polovom sovershennoletii."

68. Comments by Dr. L. M. Eidlin, "Rasshirennyi nauchnyi s"ezd sudebnykh vrachei i predstavitelei iustitsii v g. Ivanove-Vosnesenske 23–25 dekabria 1927 g.," no. 9: 159. Eidlin's medical specialization was not stated in this account; he presented a conference paper on shock to this audience in a later session.

69. Comments by *guberniia* judge Nikonov, Dr. A. S. Iavorskii, and professor M. I. Raiskii, "Rasshirennyi nauchnyi s"ezd sudebnykh vrachei i predstavitelei iustitsii v g. Ivanove-Vosnesenske 23–25 dekabria 1927 g.," no. 9: 159, 161.

70. By the late 1920s, Freud's ideas had been interpreted by Soviet authorities as ideologically unsound for their supposed lack of a materialist foundation.

71. Predsedatel' UKK Verkhsuda RSFSR Chelyshev, "Doklad UKK o praktike po delam o polovykh prestupleniiakh za vtoruiu polovinu 1926 goda," 4–8.

72. L. B. Leitman, "Dannye osvidetel'stvovaniia po voprosam, sviazannym s polovym instinktom" (A paper delivered at the Volga Regional Conference of forensic medical experts [Povolzhskoe soveshanie sudebnykh meditsinskikh ekspertov], Saratov, 1925; copy held at Saratov Medical University, Department of Forensic Medicine), 332–53; methods for detecting false claims of defloration or rape are mentioned at 339–40.

73. For this reason most forensic experts argued that an age of protection or consent ought to be substituted for the sexual maturity benchmark. See Popov, "Neskol'ko zamechanii po voprosu o vremeni nastupleniia polovoi zrelosti," 33.

74. Leitman, "Dannye osvidetsl'stvovaniia po voprosam, sviazannym s polovym instinktom," 333–34, 341–42.

75. Leitman's moralizing is more explicit in her suggestions for dealing with claims of rape, which she said must be approached with "great scepticism." "Dannye osvidetsl'stvovaniia po voprosam, sviazannym s polovym instinktom," 339.

76. "Rasshirennyi nauchnyi s"ezd sudebnykh vrachei i predstavitelei iustitsii v g. Ivanove-Vosnesenske 23–25 dekabria 1927 g.," no. 9: 159; for a similar complaint about the exclusive female gendering of the crime of "defloration" from a forensic gynecologist, also note Popov's comments at 160.

77. "Rasshirennyi nauchnyi s"ezd sudebnykh vrachei i predstavitelei iustitsii v g. Ivanove-Vosnesenske 23–25 dekabria 1927 g.," no. 9: 159.

78. One case of sexual assault on a young male occurs in the Sverdlovsk sample; four cases occur in the Petrograd sample.

79. It is striking, for example, that Leibovich's textbook on forensic gynecology contained a chapter on sexual maturity but said nothing about male sexual maturity either in regard to heterosexual or homosexual relations. Leibovich, *Sudebnaia ginekologiia*, chap. 1, "Sexual maturity."

80. Tarnovskii, *Polovaia zrelost'*, 2; Viazemskii, *O polovoi zrelosti*, 5; V. M. Bekhterev, "O polovom ozdorovlenii," *Vestnik znaniia*, no. 9 (1910): 924–37; no. 10 (1910): 1–19, see no. 9, 931; Gindes, *Perekhodnyi vozrast*, 19; Popov, "Neskol'ko zamechanii," 30.

81. For examples of this hydraulic rhetoric, see Tarnovskii, *Polovaia zrelost'*, 3–5, 24–25; Viazemskii, *O polovoi zrelosti*, 6, 8, 10. For Soviet views, see Vasilevskii, *Polovoe zdorov'e*, 10–12, 15 (quoted at 11); Krzhishkovskii, *Fiziologiia polovoi zhizni*, 18–19.

82. Popov, "Neskol'ko zamechanii," 30.

83. Leitman, "K voprosu o polovom sovershennoletii," 77.

84. Bernstein, *The Dictatorship of Sex*, 147–58.

85. Naiman, *Sex in Public*, 191–98.

86. Cases selected for examination are investigations for crimes under articles 166 and 167 (1922 RSFSR Criminal Code) or article 151 (1926 revision); further cases are those under article 153 of the 1926 code, all drawn from the later Sverdlovsk sample. (Article 153 in the 1926 code, on rape, replaced article 169, which said nothing about the sexual maturity standard; however in 1926 the revised concept of rape included as an aggravating circumstance the rape of "persons not having achieved sexual maturity," with a penalty of up to eight years imprisonment.) Twenty-six of the cases are from Petrograd files; 18 are from the files of Sverdlovsk. The number of convictions under these articles of the penal code during the 1920s is difficult to establish for lack of national crime statistics. In Moscow province for the three years 1924–1926, 45 convictions under articles 166/167 were registered, compared to 167 convictions for rape (article 169). Man'kovskii, "Sovremennaia polovaia prestupnost'," 85.

87. Chelyshev, "Doklad UKK o praktike po delam o polovykh prestupleniiakh za vtoruiu polovinu 1926 goda," 5.

88. Chelyshev, "Doklad UKK o praktike po delam o polovykh prestupleniiakh za vtoruiu polovinu 1926 goda," 5; M. Andreev, "Neskol'ko

zamechanii o proizvodstve del po 166–169 st. st. Ugolovnogo Kodeksa," *Ezhenedel'nik sovetskoi iustitsii*, no. 38 (1924): 905–6.

89. A small proportion of sexual crimes was detected in *flagrante delicto*: of 330 sexual crimes detected by beat police during the first half of 1928 in the Urals province, 102 were detected in the act; these formed part of a larger total of 868 sexual crime cases arising in the province during the period. See GASO 854/1/139/7 ob.

90. By definition, such abandoned investigations left very little trace in the local courts' archival records. In Petrograd a complaint of sexual intercourse and defloration (article 167) of a 12-year-old girl was quashed in 1924 after two gynecological examinations confirmed the victim's virginity; LOGAV 2205/1/1969 (Lukomskii, 1922–1924). In Sverdlovsk in 1927, a case of sexual intercourse with a 12-year-old girl not supposed to have reached maturity (article 151 [1926]) was dropped after extensive forensic medical investigation uncovered a history of previous sexual partners; GASO 340/2/476 (Vorob'ev, 1926–1927). Of the 868 sex crime cases investigated in Urals province in the first half of 1928, 142 cases were quashed at this stage "for lack of a crime" and 42 "for other reasons." GASO 854/1/139/7 ob.

91. Cases of this type did not normally call for a forensic investigation of the sexual maturity of the victim. Examples include LOGAV 2205/1/2330 (Petroskii, 1924), in which the victim was a five-year-old girl; and GASO 340/2/403 (Shutov, 1927), victim may have consented but at 10 years of age was deemed not sexually mature and 340/2/1177 (Serebriakov, 1927–1928), victim was 6 years old.

92. I owe this discussion to a similar distinction drawn between child rape and the rape of teenage girls in New York City during the first three decades of the twentieth century explained in Stephen Robertson, "Age of Consent Law and the Making of Modern Childhood in New York City, 1886–1921," *Journal of Social History* 35, no. 4 (2002): 781–98.

93. If no force was evident, then the encounter might still be a crime (as statutory rape) under these articles if the girl had not yet achieved sexual maturity; see for example LOGAV 2205/1/1613 (Tunenin, 1923–1924).

94. Contradictory forensic medical opinions added to the ambiguity in such cases, for example GASO 340/2/172 (Domrachev, 1926–1927) and 340/1/545 (Golubtsov, 1926–1927), discussed later in this chapter.

95. For example, in the case of a sixteen-year-old girl "raped" by her employer [LOGAV 2205/1/1613 (Tunenin, 1923–1924)], the alleged crime was first qualified as rape (article 169) with potential penalties of a minimum three years' imprisonment. Under the presumption that the victim was sexually immature when raped, the crime was requalified under article 166 (intercourse with the sexually immature) and with a similar prison term but under "strict isolation." Had defloration of a sexually immature person been proven (article 167), the penalty would be not less than five years. Developments in this investigation led to an acquittal, discussed below.

Actual sentencing patterns in cases brought to trial showed that rapes were treated relatively mildly (with two-thirds of sentences falling between one and four years' duration in Moscow province in the years 1924 to 1926 and penalties for "sexual maturity" offenses (articles 166 and 167) being more severe (with about 65 percent of sentences being two to six years, while in defloration cases, 23 percent of sentences between six and ten years); Man'kovskii, "Sovremennaia polovaia prestupnost'," 99.

96. Nannies: LOGAV 2205/1/1134, GASO 340/2/111, ibid. 340/2/774; lodgers: LOGAV 2205/1/955, GASO 340/2/172 and 340/2/96. Employers in town: LOGAV 2205/1/1613, for a shop assistant; in the countryside: GASO 340/2/545, for a 13-year-old victim who was both a nanny and required to mow hay for her employer. Teachers: GASO 340/2/1441 for a physics teacher accused of raping a pupil who upon investigation turned out to be an 18-year-old, "sexually mature" woman.

97. GASO 148/1/237 and 340/2/1201. The Bolsheviks deliberately dropped incest *(krovosmeshenie)* from their penal codes during the drafting process of 1920–1922. For M. Iu. Kozlovskii's 1920 draft containing an article prohibiting incest, see GARF A353/4/301/11ob; note also Healey, *Homosexual Desire in Revolutionary Russia*, 305 n. 108.

98. Among sexual assaults on teenagers only one rape by a complete stranger appears: GASO 340/2/26, in which the victim is a deaf-mute girl of 15 or 16 years of age; she was introduced to her assailant by an older teenage girl who sought to find a sexual companion for her male friends. In another case (GASO 340/2/1418), the complainant met the alleged rapist while strolling with a girlfriend in a park on a holiday; they met three young men who invited them to go for a boat ride. Rapes by strangers appear more frequently in the sample when reported on behalf of child-victims under 12 or when the victims were over 18–20 years of age.

99. For a 1922 group rape in a village of Petrograd province, see LOGAV 2205/1/454. The Komsomol rape in Sverdlovsk province is recorded in GASO 340/2/1463.

100. Leitman, "Dannye osvidetel'stvovaniia po voprosam, sviazannym s polovym instinktom," 339–40; Andreev, "Neskol'ko zamechanii o proizvodstve del po 166-169 st. st. Ugolovnogo Kodeksa," 905–6.

101. The Saratov forensic gynecologist Leitman listed a typical series of questions posed by police to medical experts in rape cases: "1. Has sexual intercourse or depraved action taken place in this case? 2. If so, then was it accompanied by loss of virginity? 3. Are there any signs of damage outside the sex organs and is it possible to establish whether they occurred simultaneously with sexual intercourse? 4. Did sexual intercourse take placemany times, repeatedly, or once?"

102. LOGAV 2205/1/1613/69.

103. Attempted crimes could be punished as though they had been completed under articles 13 and 14 of the RSFSR 1922 Criminal Code but the courts had the ability to adjust punishments according to the actual degree of harm to the victim. Many cases of attempted rape were reported by women in

the larger sample of sex crimes from both Petrograd and Sverdlovsk, pointing to a desire to clarify their reputations despite the considerable potential for bad publicity that could result.

104. LOGAV 2205/1/1613/45–47, 69ob.

105. LOGAV 2205/1/1613/19, 20, 21.

106. LOGAV 2205/1/1613/60. Article 13 signalled an attempted crime, to be treated as though accomplished.

107. LOGAV 2205/1/1613/65. The staff gynecologist Vera Aleksandrovna Degtiarova furnished expertise in several cases in the Petrograd sample, but I was unable to trace any evidence of her publications or activity in the discipline. Her name is absent, e.g., in an all-male list of officers and members of the Leningrad Scientific Society of Medical Expertise established in 1925; see "Obzor deiatel'nosti Nauchnogo Obshchestva meditsinskoi ekspertizy gor. Leningrada za 1925 goda," *Sudebno-meditsinskaia ekspertiza*, no. 4 (1926): 161. It would become unusual for the criminal investigator to attend such examinations later in the decade when procedures were clarified. A lay witness was a feature not only in forensic medical examinations of living persons, but more commonly in police searches of residences or personal effects for evidence.

108. LOGAV 2205/1/1613/93.

109. LOGAV 2205/1/1613/100.

110. LOGAV 2205/1/1613/110ob.

111. Among the Petrograd cases with prompting from senior levels to consider the sexual maturity of the victim, see, e.g., LOGAV 2205/1/617, 2205/1/955, and 2205/1/1134.

112. LOGAV 2205/1/955/49.

113. LOGAV 2205/1/955/12, 14. One of the doctors, Petr Pavlovich Aksakov, qualified as a physician in 1903 at Kazan University and as a forensic medical specialist in 1909: GARF A482/30/2/69.

114. In the case file there is no documentation relating to the second examination, which was perhaps removed when the tables turned against the complainant; but the original indictment against Valentina's violator contains this passage: "On the basis of information from an examination of citizen Valentina Sokolova, the forensic-medical expert Dr. Ogievich came to the conclusion that the full development of the breasts allows one to deem Sokolova fully developed in sexual terms over the past year, but that from the other side her still undeveloped labia majora indicate that Sokolova was sexually undeveloped until age 15, or at the very least until age 14." LOGAV 2205/1/955/49. Ogievich's professional data: GARF A482/30/2/79.

115. For a directive to press charges against Sokolova issued by the same court that heard her complaint, see LOGAV 2205/1/955/66.

116. A Petrograd case that preceded the Fidel' investigation by just two months ended with the superior provincial-level court rebuking a local court for confusing the age of majority with sexual maturity in October 1922, just as the new RSFSR Criminal Code was coming into effect. See LOGAV 2205/1/617/78–78ob.

117. GASO 340/2/26/8, 8 ob., 105 ob. The victim was referred to in this examination as a "minor" *(nesovershennoletniaia)* but handwritten corrections convert this to "adult" (i.e., ~~ne~~*sovershennoletniaia*), see 8. The trade union representative was evidently present as a lay witness. On the day before, the victim had been examined by three doctors at Krasnoufimsk Soviet Hospital, but only to determine when she had lost her virginity and to detect other signs of rape; see 2, 2 ob.

118. GASO 340/2/111 (a second medical examination one month after the first appears to found the victim's sexual maturity on her age, 14 years, 1928); GASO 340/2/1441 (a female student's age, 18, is apparently sufficient for local medical officials to designate her "sexually mature," 1929).

119. A 1924 Petrograd case includes a determination of sexual maturity in an 18-year-old woman that appears to turn implicitly on her advanced age as well as explicitly on the fact "that she has been menstruating for more than a year." See LOGAV 2205/1/2399/44.

120. GASO 340/2/1201/4, 17. Solid witness testimony against her father, who had also terrorized Mariia's sister Tasia, and medical evidence about her lost virginity were used by the court to sentence Taigunov to eight years in prison, the maximum available. Revulsion at the incestuous nature of the crime, and the father's use of "perverse" methods of intercourse (as the sitting position he adopted was apparently regarded) were perhaps the unspoken reasons for this unusually stern penalty; GASO 340/2/1201/20, 78.

121. GASO 340/2/545.

122. GASO 340/2/545/11, 11 ob., 55, 55 ob. A Dr. Kriukov, who gave the first opinion on Zhukova, inspected another rape victim, 13 years old, just over two weeks after this examination. By then he may have been better acquainted with the new forensic terminology, but he was still attentive to menstruation as the determinant of sexual maturity, which he said this new victim had not yet reached despite the recent onset of her first periods. In this case he said her "womb was still undeveloped" and "childlike." (He was not among the doctors who wrote the general statement that menstruation was identical to maturity.) See GASO 340/2/213/9, 11.

123. GASO 340/2/545/54, 54 ob., 56, 56 ob., 60, 60 ob.

124. GASO 340/2/545/66.

125. GASO 340/2/545/73.

126. Peretts was a recently qualified staff gynecologist *(ordinator)* in the Sverdlovsk Gynecological Institute. He was already secretary of the local medical society and in the early 1920s a bitter opponent of Soviet policy on abortion. See, e.g., "Deiatel'nost' Ural'skogo meditsinskogo o-va v g. Ekaterinburge v 1922 g.," *Ural'skoe meditsinskoe obozrenie*, nos. 2–3 (1923): 148; V. G. Peretts, "Statistika abortov po Ekaterinburgskomu Povival'no-ginekologicheskomu institutu za 1920–1921 g.g.," *Ural'skoe meditsinskoe obozrenie*, no. 1 (1922): 64–72; idem, "Dva goda deistviia tsirkuliara o dopustimosti iskusstvennogo vykidysha po sotsial'nym pokazaniiam," *Ural'skoe meditsinskoe obozrenie*, nos. 2–3 (1923): 53–61; idem, "Isskustvennyi

vykidysh s obshchestvenno-meditsinskoi tochki zreniia," *Ural'skii vrach,* nos. 4–5 (1922): 126–39. This last article began by quoting the New Testament, John 8.1–11. Peretts wrote in more conformity with Soviet conventions by the time of the cultural revolution, commenting on training for obstetric-gynecology specialists in Sverdlovsk in 1929: idem., "Oshchushchaetsia li v Ural'skoi oblasti nedostatok v akusherakh ginekologakh?" *Ural'skii meditsinskii zhurnal,* no. 9 (1929): 18–20.

127. GASO 340/1/545/93, 94.

128. The questions from the defense advocate were: (1) From what age does sexual maturity usually begin in girls? (2) Does it ever happen that sexual maturity occurs earlier than age 14? (3) What somatic phenomena characterize the onset of sexual maturity in girls? (4) Can one consider the appearance of menstruation in Zhukova Serafima some months before 12 July 1926 [in part] a sign of the onset of her sexual maturity, inasmuch as Golubtsova and Nekrasova, witnesses in the case, confirm that Zhukova had been bleeding? (GASO 340/1/545/95).

129. GASO 340/1/545/96.

130. The peculiarity of Zhukova's irregular first menses (beginning in spring and not resuming until autumn) was perceived as a characteristic of peasant sexual maturation.

131. The case file contains a handwritten copy of a newspaper story dated 20 July 1926—i.e., only a week after Zhukova made her complaint—outlining the crime against her and recalling grievances against Golubtsov relating to financial transactions in his village. The correspondent characterized Golubtsov as a wealthy peasant, used to buying his way out of trouble, alleging that his relatives tried to buy off Zhukova with a promise of fine clothing and a payment of 200 rubles. It is unclear where this story was in fact published. GASO 340/1/545/44, 44 ob., 45.

132. GASO 340/1/545/98, 98 ob., 99.

133. Examples of Degtiarova's determinations of sexual maturity: LOGAV 2205/1/1134/45; LOGAV 2205/1/1613/65; 2205/1/1869/32.

134. GASO 340/2/172/55. Of the victim, Chernoskutova, he wrote that "on the day of examination she had achieved a degree of physical development corresponding to her age of the time (13 to 13½), and had already at that time menstruated twice; yet nevertheless she was only at the very beginning of sexual maturity since she had not yet reached 14 years of age." Bazhenov was commenting in May 1927 on his examination of the girl in March 1926, which was the first of three medical inspections she endured in spring 1926. Bazhenov's opinion, that Chernoskutova was still a virgin, was disproved in two subsequent examinations, including one conducted by V. G. Peretts of Sverdlovsk Gynecological Institute in April 1926 (32, 32 ob.); each examination was for evidence of rape or defloration. None of the medical experts drawn into this case was prompted to comment on Chernoskutova's sexual maturity until a new people's investigator contacted Bazhenov in May 1927. The case was not resolved until October 1927 when a lodger sharing the flat with

Chernoskutova and her guardian (her godmother) was convicted of article 151(2), sexual intercourse with a person not having achieved sexual maturity, and of being an accessory to the crime, respectively (118, 119). For his expert opinion (June 1927) that a girl of 14 was not sexually mature, based on a range of developmental factors including height, weight, breast size, genital size, and pigmentation, and no menstruation as yet, see GASO 340/2/774/22, 22 ob.

135. "Defloration of little girls is a crime [when] committed sexually on a girl under 14 years of age, regardless of whether the act of copulation took place with the consent of the deflowered party, because *sexual maturity*, in our climatic conditions, begins only from age 14." Bazhenov, *Spravochnik po sudebnoi meditsine*, 60.

136. GASO 340/2/206: Bazhenov's expert opinion regarding Klavdiia Gileva, 25, 25 ob.; previous medical expertise and central regional discussion of the case, 3, 9, 16, 18, 20.

137. For another example of prosecutorial prompting to get people's investigators to commission forensic medical opinions on the sexual maturity of the victim in such crimes, see GASO 340/2/358/30, 30 ob. (November 1926).

138. GASO 340/2/476/37.

139. GASO 340/2/476/33. Two boys, 11 years old, testified how they played "getting married" with Mazurina and a girlfriend in a peasant hut while adults were doing fieldwork. The girls cooked food for the boys, fed them, and then lay down with them on mattresses and in a hayloft (13, 13 ob., 14, 14 ob.).

140. No evidence of bruising or resistance was evident by the time her complaint was raised, and without witnesses there was no evidence upon which to base a rape case. In addition to the forensic inspections of Mazurina, four of her partners were examined for their sexual maturity and capacity, a rare example of resort to medical assessment about male sexual maturity. (GASO 340/2/476/45, 45 ob.).

141. Some cases of defloration (article 167 or 151) of girls of 13–15 years that lack any reference at all to the sexual maturity standard by police investigators or medical experts suggest that where a girl was viewed by these officials as physically "developed," the test of whether she was sexually mature was simply not applied. Evidence of repeated intercourse based on medical expertise threw a girl's claims that consent was refused into doubt. Police regarded these girls as immoral and did not direct forensic medical personnel to comment on the girls' sexual maturity. Medical experts did not volunteer such comments either. A 1923 prosecution of a 60-year-old of the defloration of a 15-year-old girl ultimately failed in the Petrograd courts (despite a raft of previous convictions) for this reason, LOGAV 2205/1/536 (Borisov, 1923). For a similar case, this time with a 48-year-old guardian engaging in a lengthy sexual liaison with a 13-year-old foster daughter, see LOGAV 2205/1/414 (Shumovskii, 1921–23).

142. GASO 340/2/257/8: Her sexual immaturity was determined by a district physician in Pervoural'sk Hospital, but the doctor's terse certificate

says nothing about what led to this opinion.

143. GASO 340/2/257/un-numbered sentencing document, page 4.

144. See reference to witness Vetoshkin's statements, GASO 350/2/257/un-numbered indictment document, page 3.

145. Leitman, "Dannye osvidetel'stvovaniia po voprosam, sviazannym s polovym instinktom."

146. She concluded this certificate with the comment that "the girl herself is nervous and upset, and shaken by the misfortune that has fallen to her, to which I attest." LOGAV 2205/1/454/3.

147. LOGAV 2205/1/454/105: the leading defendant said in his testimony that he first heard about the police investigation against him when he met Popova in the village and asked if the rumors that she had gone to the authorities to report the rape were true; she supposedly responded by saying that her aunt had launched the complaint after hearing rumors in the village about the encounter between Popova and the defendant.

148. GASO 340/2/774/2 is the guardian's complaint, upon which the senior investigator has scrawled in the top corner: "Send cit[izen] Maslykova to crim[inal] invest[igation] to establish if she has achieved sexual maturity, and if this is confirmed then refuse to proceed on the basis of art. 11 of the Criminal Procedural Code. Check the precise age of Maslykova using documents. 28 April 1927."

149. "My advice was not taken and you have wasted time on the investigation which you may have had no right to conduct, if Maslykova has reached sexual maturity . . . Surely it is for operatives of the Criminal Investigation [Department] when the woman has reached sexual maturity, to open cases of rape, *in no other way than* following a complaint from the victim, which is lacking in this case." GASO 340/2/775/20, 20 ob. The senior investigator also complained about the operative working on the complaint, one Goshev, "judged by many as among the worst" policemen in Sverdlovsk, the subject of many prior reprimands and possessed of atrocious handwriting.

150. His composite approach to her sexual maturity took in Maslykova's height, weight, breast development and pigmentation, and hair coverage. She had not yet begun to menstruate. He said nothing about any injuries. Bazhenov concluded, "The subject is 14 years old and has not yet achieved sexual maturity at the present time." GASO 340/2/774/22 ob.

151. GASO 340/2/774/29, 29 ob., 31, 31 ob.

152. GASO 340/2/1418/55, 89. Vinegar essence—concentrated acetic acid—was (and is) used in diluted form as a spermicide in Russia and elsewhere. It was also used as a means to suicide by poisoning, and was withdrawn from sale across the country in the late 1930s because of this (email communication from Elena Shulman, Department of History, University of California at Los Angeles, 28 July 2004).

153. GASO 340/2/1418/2. "Citizenness Arzhannikova is 15 years old, her physical development corresponds to this age . . . Hymen is intact, not broken. Arzhannikova is a virgin. Periods have been occurring for three years. She has

achieved sexual maturity." Bazhenov also mentioned her "well-developed" breasts and hair on the pubis. A minor scratch was observed on one leg.

154. GASO 340/2/1418/39: "I do not find any case for a crime, for according to the act of forensic-medical examination Arzhannikova's hymen has not been violated and no indications of the use of force on the victim are apparent . . . The fact that Arzhannikova was in the company of other men all night and up to 2 p.m. the following day diminishes Katugin's guilt." This protest did not prevent the Sverdlovsk Okrug Court from convicting Katugin a month later, and sentencing him to three years in prison, GASO 340/2/1418/55.

155. GASO 340/2/1418/55, 56, 84, 85.

156. GASO 340/2/172/13 ob., 14.

157. GASO 340/2/172/14-14 ob.: "Question [from investigator]: Tell me, Citizen Domrachev, did you yourself try to incline Chernoskutova to have sex with you? Answer: never, I did not try. Question: Tell me, Citizen Domrachev, and what if there had been her consent [to sexual relations]? Answer: I would consider such an action to be a crime."

158. LOGAV 2205/1/362/54, 54 ob.

159. GASO 340/2/257/4: Suspending their 18-month-sentences, the court observed, "but taking into account that Kirsanov Vasilii [and] Kuznetsov Fedor have no previous convictions, committed the given crime only because they knew that Iuliia Rybakova had had sexual intercourse before them [*do ikh*] and not being aware that she was still in a state of not having achieved sexual maturity, the Court therefore finds that they cannot be considered socially dangerous to the public."

160. Two cases from Petrograd reveal defendants claiming "sexual impotence" as part of their denials of guilt; their claims to medical exculpation were deemed unfounded by forensic medical experts. In a 1923 case a 60-year-old man's claim of impotence was supposedly based on his "advanced age," yet a forensic medical commission consisting of a gynecologist, venereologist, and psychiatrist found him robustly healthy: "The subject is 60 years old, with well-developed musculature and correct body structure. No deformities (hernia, etc.) whatsoever in the region of the sex organs. Vision is balanced, reacts well to light and accommodation [sic]. . . Reflexes of the tendons are quick, balanced. Scrotal reflex (cremaster) is normal. No pathological reflexes. The sex organs are well-developed, *testiculi* (testicles) *[iaichki]* are not atrophied. On the mental side no deviations from the norm are observed. On the basis of the above it is concluded that there are no indications to deny the possibility that the subject could have sexual intercourse with women," LOGAV 2205/1/536/27, 60. In another case of 1923–1924, a man of 37 claimed he had been receiving treatment for "sexual impotence" and gonorrhea; he presented a certificate from a doctor to this effect, but Petrograd's forensic medical commission found no evidence of impotence: "Scrotal reflexes are very quick…Sexual organs well developed. Testicles of prominent size. Sexual organ — the same. From the mental side no deviations are observed. [There are] no indications whatsoever of sexual impotence." LOGAV 2205/1/2472/146, 146 ob.

161. These cases are LOGAV 2205/1/419: (a 35-year-old man is accused of pederasty under article 167 with two boys; they are not examined by doctors); LOGAV 2205/1/689 (a 25-year-old music teacher is accused of sexual abuse of pupils, none of whom are examined); LOGAV 2205/1/2235 (a 6-year-old boy submitted to receptive anal intercourse from a 17-year-old youth who paid him 49 kopeks; the younger boy was examined for physical damage but none is found); LOGAV 2205/1/203 (two 19-year-old homeless youths have consensual anal intercourse with a 13-year-old orphan they befriend in October Railway Station; the "victim" is assumed to be a "minor" and incapable of informed consent, and no medical expertise on his sexual maturity is commissioned). In the last two cases, police and courts were most concerned with these boys being seduced into "corruption with . . . money" (LOGAV 2205/1/2235/29 ob.), and the issue of consent was clouded with the implicit threat of male prostitution. The only case observed in the Sverdlovsk sample is GASO 340/2/827: in 1927, a gynecologist visiting Pervoural'sk to give sexual enlightenment lectures invites a 17-year-old youth to his lodgings; the youth accuses the lecturer of trying to masturbate with him. Forensic medical examination revealed no evidence of "masturbation" and no question of sexual maturity was raised. A senior prosecutor dropped the case.

162. LOGAV 2205/1/2399/1 (Koni's participation). At the time of this case, Koni was giving lectures on the law relating to forensic medicine, on medical ethics, and on courtroom procedure at the Petrograd Institute for the Professional Development of Doctors; see M. D. Mazurenko, Iu. V. Zimina, and I. N. Ivanov, "K 70-letiiu kafedry sudebnoi meditsiny Sankt-Peterburgskoi meditsinskoi akademii poslediplomnogo obrazovaniia," *Sudebno-meditsinskaia ekspertiza*, no. 2 (1995): 47–48.

163. LOGAV 2205/1/2399/44.

164. LOGAV 2205/1/2399/1.

165. GASO 340/2/476/33.

166. GASO 340/2/476/18 (24 November 1926).

167. GASO 340/2/476/16 (23 November 1926).

168. Nikolaev's view of the 18-year-olds, expressed on 25 November 1926 after examination for their sexual maturity and "to answer the question, were they capable of the defloration of Mazurina," was that they "have achieved sexual maturity and therefore are entirely capable of a sexual life." GASO 340/2/476/19, 19 ob. The terse judgement also betrayed a focus on sexual functionality, perhaps determined by people's investigator Riabov's questions.

169. GASO 340/2/476/45, 45 ob. The case was dropped on 31 March 1927 by order of a judicial review session of the Urals Provincial Court, Sverdlovsk.

170. See, e.g., two articles about crimes under articles 166 and 167 from the Petrograd local press: E. G[ard], "Khuzhe ubiistva," *Krasnaia gazeta* 249, no. 639 (31.X.24): 3; G. M., "Pedagog-rastlitel'," *Krasnaia gazeta* 163, no. 553 (21.VII.24): 3.

3—Soviet Medicine and Rape as a Crime of Everyday Life

1. See, e.g., Kate Goldberg, "The Taboo of Sexual Violence in Russian Society," *Interface: Bradford Studies in Language, Culture, and Society*, no. 1 (1995): 119–47, claim at 120; also note Susan Brownmiller, *Against Our Will: Men, Women, and Rape* (Harmondsworth, UK: Penguin, 1975), 228.

2. Alexandra Kollontai, "The Social Basis of the Woman Question," in *Selected Writings of Alexandra Kollontai*, trans. Alix Holt (London: Allison & Busby, 1977). Even for a Bolshevik feminist like Kollontai, rape was a dramatic rhetorical flourish rather than a problem to be examined in its own right. "Consider all those gentlemen owning and administering industrial enterprises who force women among their workforce and clerical staff to satisfy their sexual whims, using the threat of dismissal to achieve their ends. Are they not, in their own way, practising `free love'? All those `masters of the house' who rape their servants and throw them out pregnant on to the street, are they not adhering to the formula of `free love'?"

Lenin wrote nothing about rape as such, yet in a 1920 conversation with Clara Zetkin he noted that revolution brought with it "unbridled force" and "suffering" in sexual relations, but again this was a symptom of more important problems. ("The desire and urge to enjoyment easily attain unbridled force at a time when powerful empires are tottering, old forms of rule breaking down, when a whole social world is beginning to disappear.... It is easily comprehensible that the very involved complex of problems brought into existence should occupy the mind of the youth, as well as of women. They suffer particularly under present-day sexual grievances."). Nikolai Bukharin and Evegenii Preobrazhenskii did not refer to rape in their minuscule chapters on sex equality, and communism's view of crime, in their 1919 guide to the new ideology. See Nikolai Bukharin and Evgenii Preobrazhenskii, *The ABC of Communism*, trans. E. and C. Paul (Harmondsworth, UK: Penguin, 1969), 226–29, 271–77.

On rape as revolutionary rhetorical weapon in fiction and polemics, see Eric Naiman, *Sex in Public*, 60–63.

3. The drafter of the first Bolshevik penal code, jurist M. Iu. Kozlovskii, held that "crimes against... female honor" would need little revision from pre-1917 legislation. Healey, *Homosexual Desire in Revolutionary Russia*, 121.

4. Brownmiller, *Against Our Will*, 72; Lynne Attwood, "'She was asking for it': Rape and Domestic Violence against Women," in *Post-Soviet Women: From the Baltic to Central Asia*, ed. Mary Buckley, 99–118 (Cambridge: Cambridge University Press, 1997), 101.

5. Naiman, *Sex in Public*, 250–88. Sexual harassment and confusion about sexual ethics more generally have received attention in the work of Lisa Granik, Frances Bernstein, and Gregory Carleton. The rape by Red Army soldiers of German women in 1945 is another area of recent historical interest, see e.g., Norman Naimark, *The Russians in Germany: A History of the Soviet Zone of Occupation, 1945–1949* (Cambridge: Belknap Press of Harvard University Press, 1995).

6. Naiman, *Sex in Public*, 256, 268, 275, 282, 283. Banditry (article 76 in the 1922 Criminal Code) was described as organized bands conducting armed attacks against Soviet or private institutions or individuals, and was punishable with death, or imprisonment for at least three years. The language of this article indicated theft and murder were the imagined motives for such crimes; in the Chubarov case, prosecutors used the principle of analogy to extend its meaning to include gang rape.

7. On French rape law reform, see Georges Vigarello, *A History of Rape, from the Sixteenth to the Twentieth Centuries*, trans. Jean Birrell (Cambridge: Polity Press, 2001), 211–12.

8. S. P. Mokrinskii and V. Natanson, *Prestupleniia protiv lichnosti. Kommentarii k VI glave* (Khar'kov: Narkomiusta USSR, 1928), 109; S. V. Poznyshev, *Ocherk osnovnykh nachal nauki ugolovnogo prava, 2, Osobennaia chast'*. (Moscow: Iuridicheskoe izdatel'stvo NKIust, 1923), 58; A. Estrin, *Ugolovnoe pravo SSSR i RSFSR* (Moscow: Iuridicheskoe iz-vo NKIu RSFSR, 1927), 60.

9. E. P. Frenkel', *Polovye prestupleniia* (Odessa: Svetoch, 1927), 14, 19.

10. For a discussion of the "blank spot" in the historiography, see Marianna Murav'eva, "Metodologicheskie problemy sovremennoi istoriografii seksual'nogo nasiliia na Zapade i v Rossii," *Gendernye issledovaniia* 13 (2005): 171–89.

11. Complaints about sexual abuse that were examined by Soviet trade unions are discussed in Lisa Granik, "The Trials of the *Proletarka*: Sexual Harassment Claims in the 1920s," in *Reforming Justice in Russia, 1864–1996: Power, Culture, and the Limits of Legal Order*, ed. Peter Solomon, Jr., (Armonk, NY: M. E. Sharpe, 1997).

12. Man'kovskii, "Sovremennaia polovaia prestupnost'," 86.

13. Tsentr dokumentatsii obshchestvennykh organizatsii Sverdlovskoi oblasti (TsDOOSO) 4/7/324/137, 137 ob.

14. Man'kovskii, "Sovremennaia polovaia prestupnost'," 80. Man'kovskii did not present data for the final quarter of 1926.

15. The number of convictions for rape and defloration in 1913 was 1,060 according to A. A. Gertsenzon, "Polovaia prestupnost' v do-revoliutsionnoi Rossii (Statisticheskii ocherk)," in *Pravonarusheniia v oblasti seksual'nykh otnoshenii*, ed. Krasnushkin, Segal, and Fainberg, 109. This figure was a three-fold increase over convictions for the same crimes in 1900.

16. "Doklad Ugolovnoi Kassatsionnoi Kollegii Verkhovnogo Suda RSFSR o rabote za 1926 god," *Sudebnaia praktika RSFSR*, no. 22, 23 (1927): 22: 2–6; 23: 5–9; statistics cited at 23: 10.

17. Predsedatel' UKK Verkhsuda RSFSR Chelyshev, "Doklad UKK o praktike po delam o polovykh prestupleniiakh za vtoruiu polovinu 1926 goda," 4–8, statistics at 6; "Doklad Ugolovnoi Kassatsionnoi Kollegii Verkhovnogo Suda RSFSR o rabote za 1926 god," 23: 11.

18. TsDOOSO, 4/3/272/138, 139. For advice to police and jurists, see also M. Andreev, "Neskol'ko zamechanii o proizvodstve del po 166-169 st. st. Ugolovnogo Kodeksa," *Ezhenedel'nik sovetskoi iustitsii*, no. 38 (1924): 905–6; *Ugolovnyi kodeks, s predisloviem D. I. Kurskogo* (Moscow: Izd. moskovskogo gubernskogo suda, 1924), 625.

19. Gosudarstvennyi arkhiv Sverdlovskoi Oblasti (GASO) 854/1/139/7ob.

20. See, e.g., Gromov, *Kratkoe izlozhenie sudebnoi meditsiny*, 175; Merzheevskii, *Sudebnaia ginekologiia*, 79. Tsarist authorities on detecting the signs of rape naturally did differ in other respects; their moral language belonged to the nineteenth century. Thus, Gromov (174, 181) referred to women's motives for launching rape claims in terms of seeking compensation for "loss of honor" *(beschestie)* and to women's sexual innocence as "moral virginity" *(nravstvennaia devstvennost')*. Merzheevskii expressed the view, widespread among European medical experts, that there was very little evidentiary difference detectable between a vigorous session of consensual sexual intercourse and a rape leaving "insignificant traces of a struggle . . . on body or clothing" (52).

21. Bazhenov, *Spravochnik po sudebnoi meditsine*, 57.

22. Leitman, "Dannye osvidetel'stvovaniia po voprosam, sviazannym s polovym instinktom," 32–53.

23. Gromov, *Kratkoe izlozhenie sudebnoi meditsiny*, 174. Compensation for the "loss of honor" was a common response to rape claims in France into the early nineteenth century, Vigarello, *A History of Rape*.

24. Merzheevskii, *Sudebnaia ginekologiia*, 114.

25. Leibovich, *Prakticheskoe rukovodstvo po sudebnoi meditsine*, 2nd ed., 101.

26. Leibovich, *Sudebnaia ginekologiia*, 71.

27. Leibovich, *Sudebnaia ginekologiia*, 72.

28. Izhevskii, 46, with eight years' service as a military doctor and twelve as a forensic doctor, was directing the city's forensic medical bureau in 1920; at that date, Degtiareva was not yet on the staff, and her career is not possible to trace. For a register of Petrograd forensic medical experts in 1920, see Gosudarstvennyi arkhiv Rossiiskoi Federatsii (GARF), A482/30/2/67-85, Izhevskii's personal data at 74.

29. "Rasshirennyi nauchnyi s"ezd sudebnykh vrachei i predstavitelei iustitsii v g. Ivanove-Vosnesenske 23–25 dekabria 1927 g.," quoted at no. 9: 159. See the discussion of Nikonov's comments in chap. 2.

30. GASO 340/2/855/3ob, Zuev 1926.

31. For examples, from Saratov in the mid-1920s, of the popular resort to forensic medical experts to certify virginity or confirm its loss, and a forensic gynecologist's commentary, see Leitman, "Dannye osvidetel'stvovaniia po voprosam, sviazannym s polovym instinktom," 34–35, 40–41. Leibovich calculated, based on incomplete statistical returns, that Soviet Russia's forensic experts conducted 1,296 examinations for "virginity" in 1924; the total for 1925 was 1,838. See Ia. Leibovich, "Godovoi otchet po sudebno-meditsinskoi ekspertize v RSFSR za 1924 g.," *Sudebno-meditsinskaia ekspertiza*, no. 4 (1926): 136; idem, "Godovoi otchet po sudeb.-meditsinskoi ekspertize v RSFSR za 1925 g.," *Sudebno-meditsinskaia ekspertiza*, no. 5 (1927): 128.

32. Two examples of rape resulting in a victim's loss of virginity and suicide are found in LOGAV 2205/1/1193 Ivanov 1923 (suicide); GASO 340/2/250 Trushnikov, 1927 (attempted suicide).

33. GASO 340/1/149/3, 3ob. Volkov, 1926.

34. LOGAV 2205/1/1620/1v, 12, Domanskii and Loshkanaev 1924.

35. See, e.g., Leitman, "Dannye osvidetel'stvovaniia po voprosam, sviazannym s polovym instinktom," 42–44; Leibovich, *Sudebnaia ginekologiia*, 37. That digital examinations were controversial is evident from prerevolutionary regulations requiring parental or guardian consent if minors were examined for virginity and claims arose blaming doctors for damaging their subjects' hymens. See Bellin, *Sudebnaia meditsina rastleniia. Atlas iz 20 khromolitografirovannykh tablits*, 23.

36. A third expert of uncertain specialism participated in this examination. LOGAV 2205/1/1063/26 (Vasil'ev et al.).

37. Degtiareva testified that a "virgin vagina during insertion of a finger smoothly surrounds it; and entry of a finger is only possible when the opening of the hymen permits the finger. The vagina of a women having repeated intercourse does not present resistance to the entry of two fingers unless there is a special illness—vaginism." LOGAV 2205/1/1063/112 (Vasil'ev et al.).

38. See, e.g., LOGAV 2205/1/1475/74 Golovanov 1922; LOGAV 2205/1/1620/12 Domanskii 1924; LOGAV 2205/1/2287/43 Kulikov 1924. Before the revolution, forensic authority Merzheevskii had proposed insertion of a rubber sphere to establish the degree of damage to the hymen; Bellin had challenged this. In Saratov in the 1920s, Leitman criticized the Merzheevskii sphere, arguing that a "simple glass rod" could be easily sterilized, was safe, easy to obtain, and served the purpose. She also explained techniques of digital examination. See Bellin, *Sudebnaia meditsina rastleniia*, 22–23; Leitman, "Dannye osvidetel'stvovaniia po voprosam, sviazannym s polovym instinktom," 344. In one Petrograd case of suspected child abuse, expert gynecologist Lur'e reported using a goose-quill to examine a 10-year-old girl's hymen. LOGAV 2205/1/1704/18.

39. Bazhenov, *Spravochnik po sudebnoi meditsine*.

40. GASO 340/2/656/3-3ob. Bannikov 1927.

41. See, e.g., GASO 340/1/149/3ob. Volkov 1926; GASO 340/2/855/4 Zuev 1926.

42. LOGAV 2205/1/614/4, 4ob., 29, 29ob. Fortov 1923. The expert, A. A. Matushak of the Petrograd forensic medical service, does not appear in a 1920 register of the city's forensic experts, 1920, GARF A482/30/2/67-85.

43. LOGAV 2205/1/2399/44, 44ob. Abramov 1924.

44. Abramov was tried with an accomplice, also a Putilov metalworker, who as a minor received a suspended sentence. Both workers clearly benefited from the class-based sentencing policies of the early Soviet era that favored lighter penalties for supposedly redeemable friends of the regime.

45. Merzheevskii, *Sudebnaia ginekologiia*, 92; Ivan Smol'skii, *K voprosu o rastlenii v sudebno-meditsinskom otnoshenii* (St. Petersburg: Tip. M. D. Lomkovskii, 1898 [originally published in *Vestnik gigieny, sudebnoi i prakticheskoi meditsiny*, no. 9, September 1898]), 743; Leibovich, *Prakticheskoe rukovodstvo po sudebnoi meditsine*, 2nd ed., 100; Leitman, "Dannye osvidetel'stvovaniia po voprosam, sviazannym s polovym instinktom," 342; Bazhenov, *Spravochnik po sudebnoi meditsine*, 58.

46. The psychiatrists noted "there are signs of physical degeneration (high forehead, third eyelid, etc.); in Pershina's mental sphere no deviations from the norm are observed," LOGAV 2205/1/2287/43 (Kulikov). One of the psychiatrists was Professor L. G. Orshanskii, director of the Lenin Diagnostic Institute of Forensic Neurology and Psychiatry, funded by the Petrograd provincial health department. Orshanskii had had a long prerevolutionary career in the Petersburg psychiatric establishment. He was particularly devoted to the detection of signs of degeneracy in his subjects, yet as a forensic expert he typically pronounced such individuals otherwise fit to answer for themselves. On his career, see Morozov, Lunts, and Felinskaia, *Osnovnye etapy razvitiia otechestvennoi sudebnoi psikhiatrii*, 137–40, and his file in the personnel records of the Diagnostic Institute: Tsentral'nyi gosudarstvennyi arkhiv Sankt-Peterburga (TsGA SPb) 2895/6/42.

47. LOGAV 2205/1/2287/44, 46, 46 ob., 47.

48. *Ugolovnyi kodeks, s predisloviem D. I. Kurskogo*, 624–25.

49. GASO 340/1/149/3ob., 4, 5 Volkov 1926.

50. "Even if the complainant proves that she cried out, or if insignificant traces of a struggle turn up on her body or clothing, this in no way proves the fact of rape (unfortunately prosecutors and judges, ours as well as foreign ones, hold such opinions), since to accept these phenomena as proof of forcible accomplishment of copulation would lead to virtually every innocent girl's first experience of intercourse being designated a rape. Therefore only a morally spoiled girl habituated to sexual relations would agree to this act without any struggle and would endure the introduction of the sex organ into the vagina without sensing any pain. Ask any prostitute (or frequently—a young newlywed wife) about the loss of her innocence and she will tell you about that fact (having no grounds not to tell the truth) in terms that lead straight to the actions foreseen by the 1325th article [*sic*—1253rd or 1532nd were intended, i.e., rape] of the Criminal Code, punishable by the deprivation of the right to property and exile to katorga for four to eight years!" (Merzheevskii, *Sudebnaia ginekologiia*, 115) For Soviet-era observations, see Leitman, "Dannye osvidetsl'stvovaniia po voprosam, sviazannym s polovym instinktom," 334; Leibovich, *Sudebnaia ginekologiia*, 70–72, implies that rape claims from adult women are implausible and a significant degree of bodily injury must be detected to confirm a crime. A leading Stalin-era textbook noted that in ordinary sexual relations women put up resistance "merely 'for show,'" some claimants injured themselves to simulate rape, and conversely, that even a relatively brutal rape might leave few traces of resistance: E. E. Rozenblium, M. G. Serdiukov, and V. M. Smol'ianinov, *Sudebno-meditsinskaia akushersko-ginekologicheskaia ekspertiza* (Moscow: Sovetskoe zakonodatel'stvo, 1935), 38, 42, 43.

51. LOGAV 2205/1/521/3, 15, 16, 16ob. Aleksanichev 1922. For a case of an experienced woman who lacked injuries but rallied witness statements to back her claim, see LOGAV 2205/1/569 Antonov 1923.

52. GASO 340/2/104/4, 4ob., 12 Kozhevnikov, 1927.

53. See e.g., GASO 340/2/995 Topkosov 1927; GASO 340/2/628 Ushakov, 1926.

54. GASO 340/2/223/8 Berdiugin 1927.

55. In the late 1920s, judges still weighed up class distinctions when setting sentences and this motley group of peasants, who garnered considerable support in their village against the verdict, evidently showed no remorse and displayed attributes of primitive ignorance commonly ascribed to the peasantry by Soviet sexologists discussing the crime of rape. See, e.g., G. M. Segal, "K probleme polovoi prestupnosti," in *Pravonarusheniia v oblasti seksual'nykh otnoshenii*, ed. Krasnushkin, Segal, and Fainberg, 22.

56. Saratov's leading expert noted that the stories told by victims whose assault was confirmed by unmistakable signs were usually "simple"; those told by claimants who did not have clear "objective data" (forensic medical corroboration) "display a special, vague character" and required special caution; Leitman, "Dannye osvidetsl'stvovaniia po voprosam, sviazannym s polovym instinktom," 340. For a view from an authoritative textbook that discounted the word of the sexually experienced rape claimant as tainted by "a nervous character" or "hysteria," and noted that fewer women "accustomed to the sexual act" were likely to make claims of rape, see D. P. Kosorotov, *Uchebnik sudebnoi meditsiny* (Moscow and Leningrad: Gosudarstvennoe izdatel'stvo, 1928), 234, 236.

57. Cases involving sexually experienced women who did not display physical injuries but who reported rapes quickly and enlisted witnesses: LOGAV 2205/1/569 Antonov 1923; GASO 340/2/104 Kozhevnikov, 1927. It seems likely that most women caught in these circumstances would not have witnesses to call upon and would not bring forward complaints of rape, reasoning that they would not be believed.

58. LOGAV 2205/1/45 Osipov 1922.

59. Degtiareva's reluctant statement about trauma in the rape of Ol'ga Rubina (LOGAV 2205/1/1063/112 Vasil'ev 1923) indicates her awareness of the psychological dimension of rape; Aksakov had been providing forensic expertise to the courts since 1909 and was undoubtedly as aware of these questions as his junior colleague; see the 1920 Petrograd register of forensic medical experts, GARF A482/30/2/69. In another case file he was described as a venereologist: LOGAV 2205/1/2287/44, Kulikov 1924. The Morozova rape claim was only one aspect of the case against her tormentor, who was also accused of discrediting Soviet power and bribe taking; on these charges he was found guilty: LOGAV 2205/1/45/186, 186ob., 187 Osipov 1922.

60. GASO 340/2/68/2, 17 Budaev 1928.

61. GASO 340/2/68/110 Budaev 1928. The sole reference to the Zhenotdel appears in the sentencing document. The three accused men may have used their links to the Communist Party (one was a full member, one a candidate, and the youngest a Komsomol member) to suppress further inquiry by the Zhenotdel, but this is only conjecture. Normally the party was quick to expel adherents accused of sexual criminality.

62. Initial sentences of six, four, and two years were reduced to two years (for the leader of the gang, Budaev) and one year's "compulsory labor" for each of his two accomplices; GASO 340/2/68/122, 122ob. Budaev 1928.

63. GASO 340/2/77 Ponomarev et al., 1927–28.
64. GASO 340/2/77/47, 47ob. Ponomarev et al., 1927–28.
65. First examination: GASO 340/2/77/3; second GASO 340/2/77/6; third (likely dated 5 October 1927) GASO 340/2/77/22.
66. A district people's investigator, a CID-level policeman, composed the indictment for this case on 21 November 1927; GASO 340/2/77/47, 47ob., 48, 48ob.
67. Ponomarev and two adult accomplices were given eight-year prison terms "with strict isolation." Minor accomplices, ranging in age from 14 to 17, received reduced terms that were suspended as part of an amnesty marking the tenth anniversary of the October Revolution. An appeal to the RSFSR Supreme Court, heard in August 1928, left all sentences in place; GASO 340/2/77/95, 95ob.

4—Doctors of the Mind and Sex Crime

1. See, e.g., Jan Goldstein, *Console and Classify: The French Psychiatric Profession in the Nineteenth Century* (Cambridge: Cambridge University Press, 1987); Andrew Scull, "Psychiatry and Social Control in the Nineteenth and Twentieth Centuries," *History of Psychiatry*, no. 2 (1991): 149–69; idem, *The Most Solitary of Afflictions: Madness and Society in Britain, 1700–1900* (New Haven, CT: Yale University Press, 1993).
2. Frank J. Sulloway, *Freud, Biologist of the Mind: Beyond the Psychoanalytic Legend* (London: Fontana, 1980), 277–319.
3. Harry Oosterhuis, *Stepchildren of Nature: Krafft-Ebing, Psychiatry, and the Making of Sexual Identity* (Chicago, IL: University of Chicago Press, 2000), 77–99; Jeffrey Weeks, *Sexuality and Its Discontents: Meanings, Myths, and Modern Sexualities* (London: Routledge & Kegan Paul, 1985), 67.
4. For statistics, see David Joravsky, *Russian Psychology: A Critical History* (Oxford and Cambridge, MA: Basil Blackwell, 1989), 420. On psychiatrists' turn to private income after 1910, see Sirotkina, *Diagnosing Literary Genius*, 96.
5. Tikhon Ivanovich Iudin, *Ocherki istorii otechestvennoi psikhiatrii* (Moscow: Medgiz, 1951), 358.
6. Brown, "The Professionalization of Russian Psychiatry: 1857–1911," 268–89. Daniel Beer argues that Brown's reading of political discontent among tsarist psychiatrists is overdrawn, and he presents important evidence that fear of revolution stalked psychiatric pronouncements; see Daniel Beer, *Renovating Russia*, 88–92. While accepting that this fear was present among leaders of the discipline after 1905, particularly those engaged in moving psychiatry into the "bourgeois" realm of "minor psychiatry" (discussed later in this chapter), I would suggest that the systemic conflict between state and psychiatrists over the penal role of asylums remained an important day-to-day source of resentment, especially for those psychiatrists who went on to serve the Bolshevik regime.
7. Becker, "Judicial Reform and the Role of Medical Expertise," 1–26.
8. On psychoanalysis, see Etkind, *Eros nevozmozhnogo*, trans. as *Eros of the*

Impossible; Miller, *Freud and the Bolsheviks*. On cultural history, see Sirotkina, *Diagnosing Literary Genius*, 6–10, and the essays in *Madness and the Mad in Russian Culture*, ed. Angela Brintlinger and Ilya Vinitsky (Toronto: University of Toronto Press, 2007).

9. Julie V. Brown, "Revolution and Psychosis: the Mixing of Science and Politics in Russian Psychiatric Medicine, 1905–13," *Russian Review* 46 (1987): 283–302; idem, "Social Influences on Psychiatric Theory and Practice in Late Imperial Russia," in *Health and Society in Revolutionary Russia*, ed. Susan G. Solomon and John Hutchinson (Bloomington and Indianapolis: Indiana University Press, 1990).

10. On translations of Krafft-Ebing, and his Russian analogues, see Bershtein, "'Psychopathia sexualis' v Rossii nachala veka," 414–41; Healey, *Homosexual Desire in Revolutionary Russia*, 81–92.

11. P. V. Petrov, ed., *Trudy pervago s"ezda ofitserov-vospitatelei kadetskikh korpusov (22–31 dekabria 1908 g.)* (St. Petersburg: M. M. Stasiulevich, 1909), 293–380; on the application of sexological methods in education more broadly, see Engelstein, *The Keys to Happiness*, 215–53.

12. Bershtein, "'Psychopathia sexualis' v Rossii nachala veka," 419.

13. Bershtein, "'Psychopathia sexualis' v Rossii nachala veka," 436.

14. See, e.g., psychiatric textbooks, P. I. Kovalevskii, *Sudebnaia psikhiatriia* (St. Petersburg: M. Akinfiev & I. Leont'ev, 1902); V. I. Serbskii, *Sudebnaia psikhopatologiia*, 2nd ed. (Moscow: M. i S. Sabashnikovy, 1900), 85–89; idem, *Rukovodstvo k izucheniiu dushevnykh boleznei* (Moscow, 1906), 64–68; idem, *Psikhiatriia. Rukovodstvo k izucheniiu dushevnykh boleznei* (Moscow: Studencheskaia Meditsinskaia Izdatel'skaia Komissiia, 1912), 71–74, 476–77.

15. On early use of the "psychopathy" diagnosis in 1880s trials, see Becker, "Medicine, Law, and the State," 383 n. 182. In the 1915–1916 investigation of Dmitrii Saval'ev, a peasant, 25, who raped a 17-year-old youth while both were held in a Moscow remand prison, police and three psychiatrists (including T. E. Segalov and L. A. Prozorov, practitioners later in the Soviet penal system) sent the perpetrator for psychiatric examination because he seemed to be insane. Under observation for two months in the Moscow District Hospital for the Mentally Ill, Saval'ev was found to have simulated mental illness. Despite finding signs of physical degeneration, his sexual deviations were characterized in moral, not medical, language: "The moral outlook of the subject presents defects of an enormous degree. He is dreadfully corrupt; this is evident in his manner of behavior and speech." The case against him appears to have been abandoned in the chaos of revolution. Tsentral'nyi gosudarstvennyi istoricheskii arkhiv goroda Moskvy (TsGIAgM), 142/13/116/13, 18, 19–24 ob. (Ob osvidetel'stvovanii lits pr. kr. Dmitriia Nikolaeva Savel'eva).

16. On Russian adaptations of degeneration theory, see Beer, *Renovating Russia*.

17. On the history of the concept of psychopathy, see Henry Werlinder, *Psychopathy, A History of the Concepts: Analysis of the Origin and Development of a Family of Concepts in Psychopathology* (Uppsala: University of Uppsala, 1978);

Robert A. Nye, *Crime, Madness, and Politics in Modern France: The Medical Concept of National Decline* (Princeton, NJ: Princeton University Press, 1984).

18. Serbskii, *Psikhiatriia*, 476–77.

19. Serbskii, *Psikhiatriia*, 616; V. M. Tarnovskii, *Izvrashchenie polovogo chuvstva. Sudebno-psikhiatricheskii ocherk* (St. Petersburg, 1885), 52–53, 104–5.

20. Psychiatrists' enthusiasm for working with the Bolsheviks is discussed in Brown, "The Professionalization of Russian Psychiatry," 395–96; and Sirotkina, *Diagnosing Literary Genius*, 146–49. Note also the conventional late-Soviet account presented by Morozov, Lunts, and Felinskaia in *Osnovnye etapy razvitiia otechestvennoi sudebnoi psikhiatrii*, 129–61.

21. On the founding of the institute, see Iudin, *Ocherki istorii otechestvennoi psikhiatrii*, 372. On Orshanskii's career, see Morozov, Lunts, and Felinskaia, *Osnovnye etapy razvitiia otechestvennoi sudebnoi psikhiatrii*, 137–40; and records of the Diagnostic Institute, TsGA SPb, 2895/6/42 (dates of birth and death not available). On Ostankov, see Iudin, *Ocherki istorii otechestvennoi psikhiatrii*, 130, 243, 419. In 1911, Minister of Education L. A. Kasso expelled hundreds of activist Moscow students; several professors including psychiatrist V. P. Serbskii resigned in protest. Ostankov was offered Serbskii's job in 1912. The "Kasso affair professors" were demonstratively reinstated after the February Revolution in 1917, but Serbskii died almost simultaneously; see Sirotkina, *Diagnosing Literary Genius*, 91. Ostankov lectured at the Petrograd forensic medical course on forensic psychopathology; see M. D. Mazurenko, Iu. V. Zimina, and I. N. Ivanov, "K 70-letiiu kafedry sudebnoi meditsiny Sankt-Peterburgskoi meditsinskoi akademii poslediplomnogo obrazovaniia," *Sudebno-meditsinskaia ekspertiza*, no. 2 (1995): 47–48.

22. On Lents, see Joravsky, *Russian Psychology*, 300; A. K. Lents, *Kriminal'nye psikhopaty (Sotsiopaty)* (Leningrad: Rabochii sud, 1927). On statistics, see "Vesti s mest. Diagnosticheskii Institut Sudebnoi Nevrologii i Psikhiatrii," *Sudebno-meditsinskaia ekspertiza*, no. 2 (1925): 205–6.

23. Iudin, *Ocherki istorii otechestvennoi psikhiatrii*, 372. On Krasnushkin, see V. M. Banshchikov, "Zasluzhennyi deiatel' nauki professor E. K. Krasnushkin (Zhizn' i nauchnaia deiatel'nost'). 1885–1951 gg.," in *Izbrannye trudy*, ed. E. K. Krasnushkin (Moscow: Medgiz, 1960); and Kowalsky, "Making Crime and Sex Soviet," 99–101.

24. Indeed, the "Moscow school" now wrote the history, and defined the new heroes, for Soviet psychiatry. See Julie V. Brown, "Heroes and Non-Heroes: Recurring Themes in the Historiography of Russian-Soviet Psychiatry," in *Discovering the History of Psychiatry*, ed. Mark S. Micale and Roy Porter (New York and Oxford: Oxford University Press, 1994). On Serbskii, see Sirotkina, *Diagnosing Literary Genius*, 24–25, 90–92, 139–40.

25. On Soviet criminology, see Sharon A. Kowalsky, "Making Crime and Sex Soviet"; and Solomon, "Soviet Penal Policy, 1917–1934," 195–217.

26. On Fishman's appointment to lecture at Urals State University, see "Khronika. Na meditsinskom fakul'tete Ural-Universiteta," *Ural'skoe meditsinskoe obozrenie*, no. 2–3 (1923): 150–51. Ekaterinburg had one specialist hospital for

nerve and psychiatric patients, as of 1 December 1920, with 60 beds for nerve patients and 30 for psychiatric cases: I. K. Kurdov, "Sostoianie meditsinkskoi organizatsii v g. Ekaterinburge v 1920 godu," *Ural'skoe meditsinskoe obozrenie,* no. 1 (1922): 73–89. On Segalin, who later did take part in Stalin-era political trials as an expert, see Sirotkina, *Diagnosing Literary Genius,* 164–76; and G. V. Segalin, "Osnovnye zadachi evriko-patologii kak ucheniia o patologii genial'nosti i patologii tvorchestv," *Ural'skii vrach,* nos. 3, 4–5 (1922): 3: 61–67, 4–5: 105–18; idem, *Nervno-psikhicheskaia ustanovka muzykal'no-odarennogo cheloveka* (Sverdlovsk: Izdanie Uraloblrabis, 1927). His name does not appear in any of this book's Sverdlovsk sample of 128 sex crime cases.

27. For a summary of the legislation and procedural rules, see S. N. Ippolitov, *Sbornik zakonopolozhenii o sudebno-meditsinskikh izsledovaniiakh* (St. Petersburg: K. L. Rikker, 1910), 245–50; and see the detailed discussion in Becker, "Judicial Reform and the Role of Medical Expertise." On psychiatrists' ire over the incarceration of the criminally insane in asylums, see Brown, "The Professionalization of Russian Psychiatry," 272.

28. See Leibovich, *Prakticheskoe rukovodstvo po sudebnoi meditsine,* 2nd ed., 150–74; and note the commentary accompanying Soviet legislation in N. P. Brukhanskii, *Sudebnaia psikhiatriia* (Moscow: M. i S. Sabashnikovy, 1928), 355–92; the 1924 list of questions for police to doctors is at 365.

29. Leibovich, *Prakticheskoe rukovodstvo po sudebnoi meditsine,* 3rd ed., 159; Brukhanskii, *Sudebnaia psikhiatriia,* 367–70. How far these rules were applied is unknown. Brukhanskii, citing comments by psychiatrist T. E. Segalov in the above pages, suggested that in Moscow all parties, including experts, attended pretrial sessions and imputability was determined then. Moscow's court records for the 1920s are currently inaccessible and cannot be checked for actual practices.

30. Prof. A. K. Lents (Minsk), "Tasks and plan of contemporary criminal psychiatric expertise," report to Second All-Russian congress of for-med experts, 19–28 Feb 1926. GARF 482/1/596/241–44, quotation at 241.

31. Kowalsky, "Making Crime and Sex Soviet," 95–98, quotation at 97.

32. V. A. Vnukov and A. O. Edel'shtein, "O kharaktere lichnosti pravonarushitelia i mekhanizmakh pravonarushenii v oblasti polovykh otnoshenii," in *Pravonarusheniia v oblasti seksual'nykh otnoshenii, ed. Krasnushkin, Segal, and Fainberg,* 23–76, quotation at 36.

33. Among recent histories that rely heavily on early Soviet psychiatrists' views of the sexually disordered and criminal are Healey, *Homosexual Desire in Revolutionary Russia;* Bernstein, *The Dictatorship of Sex;* Naiman, *Sex in Public.* Kowalsky, "Making Crime and Sex Soviet," 85–101, discusses psychiatrists' bids to gain authority as diagnosticians of crime. Note also Daniel Beer's argument that criminologists exerted substantial influence over Bolshevik conceptions of social deviance; Beer, *Renovating Russia,* 165–204. For a detailed 1920 Health Commissariat decree on "psychiatric observation in places of detention," authorizing wards for mentally disturbed prisoners, and psychiatric commissions to review cases and recommend early release, see

Leibovich, *Prakticheskoe rukovodstvo po sudebnoi meditsine*, 2nd ed., 173–74. This decree replaced one of 1918.

34. Of the 194 sex crime cases, 66 come from Petrograd. Thus, in this unscientific sample, 19 out of 66 (just under 29 percent) of Petrograd cases have some form of psychiatric expertise. By comparison, only 7 percent of the Sverdlovsk cases (9 out of 128) have psychiatric interventions.

35. Psychiatric expertise of victims is discussed later in this chapter. In this sample, one witness was also subjected to psychiatric examination: GASO 340/2/377/22 ob. (Kutkin, 1927).

36. On Russian ideas of masculine self-control, see Kelly, "The Education of the Will."

37. LOGAV 2205/1/1024/25 (Mutovozov, 1923).

38. LOGAV 2205/1/1154/3, 29 (Tyrin, 1922).

39. In a case of sexual touching of a 2½-year-old girl, a rural investigator transferred the accused from Petrograd province's outlying Schlisselburg prison to the city's Diagnostic Institute for psychiatric evaluation; LOGAV 2205//1/429/20, 21 (Potapov, 1922).

40. LOGAV 2205/1/419/2, 23, 24, 29 (Lobanov, 1922); Orshanskii judged that this 35-year-old homeless man living in Nikolaevskii Railway Station, accused of committing "pederasty" with two homeless boys, had a limited personality but was mentally healthy and therefore imputable.

41. LOGAV 2205/1/2214/126, 126 ob (Miats, 1924). Tarle figured in several sex crime cases as a psychiatrist supplying expertise to the Petrograd Forensic Medical Bureau, but further biographical information does not survive.

42. GASO 340/2/995/11, 11ob, 23, 23ob (Topkosov, 1927). Sverdlovsk police gave more elaborate instructions to psychiatrists in the 1927 case against Mikhail Drugov, accused of attempted murder, hooliganism, and illegal distilling. Drugov's violent attack on his wife was witnessed by a neighbor who accused Drugov of sexual perversion. People's investigator Krotov wrote to a colleague: "I designate you to . . . commission expertise from an appropriate doctor-psychiatrist, in order to establish the mental illness, imputability and the duration of his illness, of the prisoner DRUGOV Mikhail Mikhailovich, held at the present time in the Sverdlovsk DPZ while under investigation. One of the characteristic symptoms giving us cause to suspect the abnormality of citzen Drugov is his systematic so-called persecution mania *[mania presledovaniia]*, which results in his attacks on his wife, denunciations to the investigatory organs of all sorts of complaints against various individuals for non-existent crimes, the distribution of counter-revolutionary rumors, etc. You are required to pay attention to these aspects in your investigation. The expertise should be conducted in the briefest possible period and I should receive its results in not less than one week." Despite this urgency, Fishman did not write his opinion until six months had elapsed, as Drugov was held under observation for an extended period; regardless of Fishman's ambivalence about his mental capacity, Drugov was judged imputable and received a two-

year sentence. GASO 340/2/1096/52, 96, 96ob (Drugov, 1927).

43. LOGAV 2205/1/245/75 (Petrov, 1922). Petrov's surviving record from the Diagnostic Institute's archives says little except to give details of his arrival and visitors; TsGA SPb 2895/5/574 (Petrov, Vasilii Andreevich).

44. Healey, *Homosexual Desire in Revolutionary Russia*, 220.

45. From [A. M. Khaletskii], "Glava XXI. Psikhopaticheskie lichnosti," in V. A. Vnukov and Ts. M. Feinberg, *Sudebnaia psikhiatriia. Uchebnik dlia iuridicheskikh vuzov* (Moscow: OGIZ, 1936), 227–53, quotations at 250, 252. A rare leading woman in this profession, Ts. M. Feinberg hinted at patient awareness of psychopathy as a diagnosis in the 1920s in her history of the Serbskii Institute of Forensic Psychiatry (Moscow): *Sudebno-psikhiatricheskaia ekspertiza i opyt raboty instituta sudebnoi psikhiatrii im. prof. Serbskogo za XXV let* (Moscow: Tsent. n.-i. institut sudebnoi psikhiatrii im. prof. Serbskogo MZ SSSR, 1947), 6, 8.

46. Foucault posited this phenomenon in relation to the dialog between psychiatrists and homosexuals about same-sex love that began in the 1870s and 1880s with the work of Richard von Krafft-Ebing. See Foucault, *The History of Sexuality*, vol. 1, *An Introduction*, 100–101. See also Oosterhuis, *Stepchildren of Nature*.

47. LOGAV 2205/1/2214/209-209 ob, 249-249 ob; 250 (Miats, 1924). Miats evidently used his party connections to improve his treatment while his case was investigated. Later, during hospitalization, Miats telephoned the Petrograd provincial health department's deputy director with numerous angry complaints, prompting a visit from a health department official, LOGAV 2205/1/2214/253ob. Sreznevskii's commission examined Miats on the premises of the Pathological-Reflexological Institute. Sreznevskii appears as an expert, for the prosecution, as "private-docent of the Military Medical Academy" in an earlier case file; he served this time alongside Ostankov, not opposing him: LOGAV 2205/1/1395/1g (Mikhailov, 1923).

48. GASO 340/2/214/84, 98 (Shestakov, 1924–1927). The long delay in trying this case was likely the result of waiting for travelling court sessions to reach this region.

49. Shestakov was "illiterate" according to the case file, but the appeal court's decision is explicitly a response to his personal complaint, and does not mention the presence of any advocate or prosecutor intervening in the appeal; moreover, he appears to have conducted his own defense during his retrial: GASO 340/2/214/63-63 ob.; 114–115 ob. (Shestakov, 1924–1927).

50. GASO 340/2/214/63 ob. (Shestakov, 1924–1927).

51. LOGAV 2205/1/1193/148 (Ivanov, 1923), original emphasis.

52. LOGAV 2205/1/1193/144, 145 (Ivanov, 1923). The case file runs out at the acquittal, which is very terse; one may speculate that Ivanov was sent for further observation in the Diagnostic Institute.

53. In another Petrograd case, that of Vladimir Zharnovskii, the suspect's own appeal to the investigator for psychiatric assessment was honored, and he was sent to the Diagnostic Institute for examination by Orshanskii (LOGAV

2205/1/689/48, 71–71 ob. [Zharnovskii, 1922]). During that time, the suspect's mother visited the institute several times to see her son, and probably confirmed aspects of his anamnesis to Orshanskii, e.g., his claim that his father had committed suicide in a mental asylum. See TsGA SPb 2895/5/235 (Zharnovskii's patient file at Diagnostic Institute).

54. LOGAV 2205/1/2472/145, 146-146 ob., 158 ob. (Kivi, 1923).

55. LOGAV 2205/1/1395 (Mikhailov, 1923–1925).

56. LOGAV 2205/1/1395/34, 62–64, 112 ob. (Mikhailov, 1923–1925). Under article 167 (aggravated statutory rape) he received ten years; the 1922 Criminal Code prescribed a minimum sentence of five years for this offense. He also received a simultaneous sentence of five years under article 168 (nonpenetrative sex acts with minors). Charges of conventional rape and of consensual sexual intercourse with a sexually immature person were dropped.

57. The quotations in this paragraph are found in LOGAV 2205/1/1395/118-118 ob. (Mikhailov, 1923–1925).

58. LOGAV 2205/1/1395/135 (Mikhailov, 1923–1925).

59. On another bid for exculpation on psychiatric grounds (chronic alcoholism), see LOGAV 2205/1/1704/64-64 ob. (Moniakov, 1924). In Sverdlovsk, a violent offender who was subjected to examination by psychiatrist Fishman argued that his wife (who testified against him) should be seen by Fishman as well: GASO 340/2/1096/134-134 ob. (Drugov, 1927).

60. See, e.g., Engelstein, The *Keys to Happiness*, 359–420; Jeffrey Brooks, *When Russia Learned to Read: Literacy and Popular Literature, 1861–1917* (Princeton, NJ: Princeton University Press, 1985); Louise McReynolds, *Russia at Play: Leisure Activities at the End of the Tsarist Era* (Ithaca, NY: Cornell University Press, 2003).

61. For an early Soviet psychiatrist's dreams of therapy in the prison setting, see E. K. Krasnushkin, "Chto takoe prestupnik?" *Prestupnik i prestupnost'*, sbornik 1 (1926): 6–33, especially 6.

62. GASO 340/2/820 (Kotkov, 1927).

63. GASO 340/2/820/49 (Kotkov, 1927).

64. In a very similar case, which resulted in two trials (1925–1927) of the defendant, a conviction was secured, in large part because medical expertise was obtained quickly, and two examinations of the mental condition of the 16-year-old victim confirmed her "delayed development" in mental capacity. The victim's father made the original complaint, and psychiatric experts, by confirming that the victim was not capable of understanding the nature of the crime, effectively deemed his complaint admissible. GASO 340/2/258/129-130 ob. (Dolganov, 1925). For yet another long-delayed referral for psychiatric assessment of the victim in a rural rape case, this time securing a conviction based on witness evidence, see GASO 340/2/228 (Antipin, 1926).

65. LOGAV 2205/1/1024 (Mutovozov, 1923).

66. LOGAV 2205/1/1024/25 (Mutovozov, 1923). Deafness and blindness were viewed as signs of degeneration, and the disabled were held to be both vulnerable to sexual abuse and likely to engage in sexual deviation themselves.

A year after this case, the People's Commissariat of Justice issued guidelines for the conduct of psychiatric expertise; among the recommended questions for police to put to doctors was a reference to deafness as indicative of unfavourable heredity; see Brukhanskii, *Sudebnaia psikhiatriia*, 366. Prosecutors discussed the association in a conference with forensic specialists: "Rasshirennyi nauchnyi s"ezd sudebnykh vrachei i predstavitelei iustitsii v g. Ivanove-Vosnesenske 23–25 dekabria 1927 g." See intervention by Fedorchukov in no. 9, p. 145. See also Vnukov i Edel'shtein, "O kharaktere lichnosti pravonarushitelia i mekhanizmakh pravonarushenii v oblasti polovykh otnoshenii," 23–76, especially 47–48.

67. LOGAV 2205/1/1024/33–33 ob. (Mutovozov, 1923). Shumkov was perhaps G. E. Shumkov, the author of a 1905 report on the organization of military psychiatric services during the Russo-Japanese War. see Iudin, *Ocherki istorii otechestvennoi psikhiatrii*, 361, and Morozov, Lunts, and Felinskaia, *Osnovy etapy razvitiia otechestvennoi sudebnoi psikhiatrii*, 334.

68. LOGAV 2205/1/2287/43 (Kulikov, 1924). The psychological impact of sexual assault on the victim is another, less frequently noted, area that psychiatrists were asked to comment upon. For one rural case from Petrograd province, in which police asked specifically for a medical expert to comment on this aspect, see LOGAV 2205/1/2235/25 (Boronin, 1924).

69. GASO 340/2/995/23, 23 ob., 10, 48 ob. (Topkosov, 1927). His comrades received varying sentences: the gang leader Topkosov, an adult with a previous conviction for theft, a relatively hefty four years; two minor accomplices, Lodochnikov and Antipin, one year six months each. Topkosov appealed the sentences on behalf of all three, and the RSFSR Supreme Court decreed their release, just three months after the trial, in recognition of their worker status and youth, in connection with the (evidently, on-going) amnesty for the tenth anniversary of the October Revolution: GASO 340/2/995/61. Prison crowding led to frequent amnesties during the 1920s, including this one.

70. Zvedeninov's evidence as a "bystander," i.e., a witness, was also valued in this case since the victim, a sexually experienced woman, and other forms of evidence were not available; see the discussion of rape evidence in chap. 3. Another Sverdlovsk case features a psychiatric assessment of a feebleminded witness, the brother who witnessed his sister's rape: GASO 340/2/377 (Kutkin, 1927). Despite the subject's reputation as "slow-witted" *(maloumnyi)*—in his sister's words—he was deemed capable of describing the events of the crime reliably, first by a village medical station physician and then by an Irbit city doctor.

71. The quotations in this paragraph are from LOGAV 2205/1/2472/247–247 ob., 260-260 ob., 299-299 ob. (Kivi, 1923).

72. LOGAV 2205/1/245/65, 66 (Petrov, 1922); Latin phrase in original. A hand-written instruction, from a justice official, on Orshanskii's cover note accompanying the expert opinion, directs that Petrov remain at the Diagnostic Institute.

73. LOGAV 2205/1/1193/148, 149, 150 (Ivanov, 1923).

74. LOGAV 2205/1/2214 (Miats, 1924). The sentencing and indictment documents in this file lack page numbers.

75. E. G[ard], "Delo Miatsa," *Krasnaia gazeta* 201, no. 591 (5 September

1924): 3; pretrial assessment: LOGAV 2205/1/2214/126-126 ob. (Miats, 1924).

76. According to the newspaper account, Miats proclaimed, "My father perished on the barricades in 1905 and I vowed then to avenge him! . . . And I was true to my oath!" The account says he ascribed his illness to exhaustion and said he would "rework" himself to correct it. In characteristic fashion he said he would suffer in prison, but he swore that "if inside there I hear the guns of counterrevolution roaring, I will break through the prison walls, tear up the prison bars and go there, to the streets, to fight for Soviet power!" E. G[ard], "Delo Miatsa," *Krasnaia gazeta* 203, no. 593 (8 September 1924): 3. The court's sentence said "he is in need of compulsory medical treatment for a nerve (not a mental) *[ot nervnoi /ne dushevnoi/]* illness." LOGAV 2205/1/2214 (Miats, 1924), unnumbered sentencing document.

77. The court cited a joint instruction of the Justice and Internal Affairs Commissariats of 19 November 1924, which set out the basis for early release on incurable and grave medical grounds. Miats satisfied the criteria under point "a"—"an organic disease of the central nervous system." The same point cited "severe forms of neurosis, psychoneurosis and psychopathies" as grounds for early release. See Brukhanskii, *Sudebnaia psikhiatriia*, 387–88.

78. All material in this paragraph comes from LOGAV 2205/1/492/20, 21, 62, 68 (Potapov, 1922).

79. LOGAV 2205/1/1704/64-64 ob. (Moniakov, 1924).

80. The defendant, 52-year-old Il'ia Moniakov, was said to "have applied to join the ranks of the VKP(b) [Communist Party] after the death of comrade Lenin." Married, with no previous convictions, he had village schooling and was a painter working for a tram depot. He obtained "personal amnesty" *(chastnaia amnestiia)* after petitioning the All-Russian Central Executive Committee of the Soviets (VTsIK), and the decree releasing him was signed by Avel' Safronovich Enukidze, Secretary of the Presidium of VTsIK: LOGAV 2205/1/1704/79 (Moniakov, 1924).

81. LOGAV 2205/1/1802/52ob-53, 54, 71 (Eshoi, 1924). Isolation and loss of prisoners' rights were incremental measures available to the courts when they wished to emphasize the severity of the crime.

82. From the preliminary assessment of Mutovozov: "Regarding psyche: *clear consciousness, complete orientation, does not express hallucinatory ideas. Clearly expressed emotive coloration, answers questions with detail and circumstances.* Says that he comes from a family with a poor neuropsychiatric condition: father, mother and nearest relatives use alcohol intensively. There is mental illness on the collateral lines of the family. Masturbates from childhood to the present. *Has had sexual intercourse with women but did not curtail his masturbation even when living with his wife. Experienced sexual satisfaction (erection and emission of semen) exposing his sex organs in the presence of children.* At the present time [sic] two girls were visiting him (one 16 years old, the other 14) and he undressed them, 'looked at them,' experienced strong sexual arousal at that time, ending with emission of semen. He paid the girls 5 million rubles for this. *He made no attempts to rape them, nor did he engage in pederasty."* Compare this with Tarle's testimony in court: "Does not deny the fact of undressing the girls, does not deny that he touched their

sex organs. He admits the immorality of his acts. Memory intact. No inclination to fits of temporary insanity observed. [He suffers from] neurosis in the form of hysteria, developed on the soil of his alcoholic-degenerated family background; as result his degeneration expresses itself in sexual deviations in the form of onanism, depraved [*liubostrastnye*] acts upon children, etc., however indications of mental illness are not present and he is imputable." LOGAV 2205/1/1024/2, 34-34 ob., 90-91 (Mutovozov, 1923). The emphasis, handwritten underlining of the preliminary assessment, suggests the people's investigator receiving the report selected these passages—descriptions of Mutovozov's mental capacity and his sexual psychology—as useful evidence.

83. LOGAV, 2205/1/1024/33 ob. (Mutovozov, 1923).

84. LOGAV 2205/1/1154/51–52 (Tyrin, 1922). On the Tauride Gardens before 1917, see Healey, *Homosexual Desire in Revolutionary Russia*, 32, 279 n55.

85. LOGAV 2205/1/1154/29–29 ob. (Tyrin, 1922).

86. See LOGAV 2205/1/419/24 (Lobanov, 1922), in which Orshanskii describes Lobanov as having "a marked attraction for persons of the same sex" and "suffers from sexual perversion in the form of pederasty, but he is *mentally healthy*." (Original emphasis.) Citing his "perversion," the court sentenced Lobanov to two years imprisonment. Note also Orshanskii's expertise in LOGAV 2205/1/689 (Zharnovskii, 1922), discussed in Dan Healey, "Early Soviet Forensic Psychiatric Approaches to Sex Crime, 1917–1934," in *Madness and the Mad in Russian Culture*, ed. Brintlinger and Vinitsky, 150–68.

87. Kowalsky, "Making Crime and Sex Soviet."

88. For example, Healey, *Homosexual Desire in Revolutionary Russia*; Bernstein, *The Dictatorship of Sex*; Naiman, *Sex in Public*.

89. See Orshanskii, "Analiz psikhologicheskii i psikhopatologicheskii," in *Polovye prestupleniia*, ed. A. A. Zhizhilenko and L. G. Orshanskii (Leningrad: Rabochii sud, 1927), 41–90; and the essays by Krasnushkin, Edel'shtein, and Vnukov in *Pravonarusheniia v oblasti seksual'nykh otnoshenii*, ed. Krasnushkin, Segal, and Fainberg; and note the prominent work by another Moscow psychiatrist, N. P. Brukhanskii, *Materialy po seksual'noi psikhopatologii* (Moscow: M. i S. Sabashnikov, 1927).

90. Psychiatrists' bids for control over wider categories of criminals were a feature of the profession's emergence in the late nineteenth century; see Becker, "Judicial Reform and the Role of Medical Expertise," 23.

91. On psychiatrists' claims, see Sirotkina, *Diagnosing Literary Genius*.

92. On the concept of "speaking Bolshevik" as a "little tactic of the habitat" used by the resourceful ordinary Soviet citizen, from which I draw this analogy, see Stephen Kotkin, *Magnetic Mountain: Stalinism as a Civilization* (Berkeley and Los Angeles: University of California Press, 1995). For a lucid perspective on the process of discourse adoption, see Ian Hacking, "Making up People," in *Forms of Desire: Sexual Orientation and the Social Constructionist Controversy*, ed. Edward Stein (New York: Garland, 1990).

93. Bershtein, "'Psychopathia sexualis' v Rossii nachala veka."

94. These findings support the general conclusion made by Beer in his study of the "human sciences" and degeneration theory as they were transformed under the Bolsheviks. See Beer, *Renovating Russia*.

5—Bodies in Search of a Sex

1. I use the term hermaphrodite to refer to persons of mixed or ambiguous physical sex in history. The term preferred by contemporary subjects of this type is "intersexual," and I reserve this term for references to contemporary persons and their concerns.

2. Anne Fausto-Sterling, *Sexing the Body: Gender Politics and the Construction of Sexuality* (New York: Basic Books, 2000), 32–36; idem, "The Five Sexes: Why Male and Female Are Not Enough," *The Sciences* 33 (March/April 1993): 20–24; Ruth Gilbert, *Early Modern Hermaphrodites: Sex and Other Stories* (Basingstoke, UK, and New York: Palgrave, 2002), 41–50. One can speculate that another group of hermaphrodites, those who successfully "passed" during their entire lives as members of one or the other sex, also existed but by definition have left no historical record.

3. Other cultures have found various devices to integrate hermaphrodites and individuals who do not conform to patterns of sexual dimorphism. See Gilbert Herdt, ed., *Third Sex, Third Gender: Beyond Sexual Dimorphism in Culture and History* (New York: Zone Books, 1996).

4. These arguments are derived from Ornella Moscucci, "Hermaphroditism and Sex Difference: The Construction of Gender in Victorian England," *Science and Sensibility: Gender and Scientific Enquiry, 1780–1945*, ed. Marina Benjamin, 174–99 (Oxford: Basil Blackwell, 1991).

5. Foucault, "Introduction," *Herculine Barbin*, and *The History of Sexuality*, vol. 1, *An Introduction*.

6. By the end of the nineteenth century, European doctors found that the vast majority of persons of ambiguous sex were pseudohermaphrodites; "true" hermaphrodites, possessing one ovary and one teste, were extremely rare. Dreger, *Hermaphrodites*, 139–66. Dreger finds that French doctors were more inclined to require legal gender swaps in cases of "error of sex" than British ones.

7. For the suicide of an early patient diagnosed in this fashion, see Foucault, *Herculine Barbin*.

8. In Britain the Liverpool physician William Blair Bell first questioned the worth of gonadal diagnosis in 1915; in the U.S., Hugh Hampton Young conducted holistic assessments of gender on hermaphrodite patients from the mid-1920s. See Fausto-Sterling, *Sexing the Body*, 40–44.

9. The most thorough examination of the period in U.S. medicine is Alison Redick, "American History XY: The Medical Treatment of Intersex, 1916–1955" (Ph.D. diss, New York University, 2004). Redick designates her period the "Era of Idiosyncrasy." Neither Fausto-Sterling nor Dreger seriously examines the 1910s to the 1950s, when diagnostic approaches to the hermaphrodite were in flux.

10. Dreger, *Hermaphrodites*, 157–66. On the rise of cosmetic surgery as a means of "passing" as a culturally desirable kind of person, see Sander L. Gilman, *Making the Body Beautiful: A Cultural History of Aesthetic Surgery* (Princeton, NJ: Princeton University Press, 1999). Gilman does not question the notion that surgery for hermaphrodites is "reconstructive," 275.

11. Fausto-Sterling, *Sexing the Body*, 45–114; see also Dreger, *Hermaphrodites*, 167–201. Both scholars acknowledge the influence of the U.S. intersexual rights movement, emerging in the 1990s from the first American generation of hermaphrodites "corrected" by modern medicine. This movement argues against many features of the "correction of sex" in intersexed infants, and points out the long-term damage caused by medical overconfidence and failure to disclose to patients and parents the nature of interventions applied in such cases. A distinctive view of this history that attempts to reconstruct the reasoning of U.S. medical practitioners is in Redick, "American History XY."

12. I distinguish here between treatments of the hermaphrodite as actually existing individual, which has had little attention, and hermaphroditism as a cultural idea, which had some currency in the Silver Age. On Nikolai Berdiaev's rejection of physical "hermaphroditism" as a caricature of "[t]he holy, mystical idea of androgyny," see Eric Naiman, *Sex in Public*, 41. On Vasilii Rozanov's anti-liberal thought and his frequent resort to metaphors of sterility (if not hermaphroditism), see Laura Engelstein, *The Keys to Happiness*, 299–333.

13. "Russian [legislation] is absolutely silent on this subject," in A. E. Ianovskii, "Germafrodity (s iuridich. tochki zreniia)," *Entsiklopedicheskii slovar'*, ed. F. A. Brokgauz and I. A. Efron (St. Petersburg: I. A. Efron, 1893), 8A:536. For the text of a People's Commissariat of Internal Affairs 1926 circular on how to alter the passport sex of hermaphrodites, see Leibovich, *Sudebnaia ginekologiia*, 126.

14. I. V. Bertenson, "Novyi primer tak nazyvaemago germafroditizma i voobshche o dvusnastnosti v sudebno-meditsinskom otnoshenii," *Arkhiv sudebnoi meditsiny i obshchestvennoi gigieny*, sec. 2 (March 1865): 75–87.

15. A. I. Struzhenskii, "Sluchai muzhskogo germafroditizma," *Vestnik obshchestvennoi gigieny, sudebnoi i prakticheskoi meditsiny* (October 1898), sec. 2: 754–55.

16. For a range of cases, and a discussion of the medico-legal difficulties they threw up for Russian doctors, see A. P. Garin, "Sluchai gipospadii, kak predmeta sudebno-meditsinskago issledovaniia i voprosy o 'pole' pri nepravil'nom obrazovanii polovykh organov voobshche," *Vestnik obshchestvennoi gigieny, sudebnoi i prakticheskoi meditsiny* 29 (1896), kn. 2, sec. 3: 49–65.

17. See, e.g., a review of cases published by doctors Gamrekelov, Fedorov, Milovidov, and Bykhovskii discussed in Franz L. von Neugebauer, *Hermaphroditismus beim Menschen* (Leipzig: Dr. W. Klinkhardt, 1908).

18. E. F. Bellin, *Sluchai zatrudnitel'nago opredeleniia pola i grazhdanskikh prav. Muzhchina ili zhenshchina?* (Khar'kov: Tip. Zil'berberg, 1898).

19. Engelstein, *The Keys to Happiness*, 210–11, 228–29, 296–98.

20. This discussion of Neugebauer's career is based on Dreger, *Hermaphrodites*, 61–63, 79–80.

21. Neugebauer, *Hermaphroditismus beim Menschen*.

22. "Medical police" entailed a view of public health subordinate to the requirements of central administration, and had its heyday in eighteenth- and early nineteenth-century enlightened monarchies. In tsarist Russia, public health was in the remit of the Ministry of Internal Affairs. See Solomon and Hutchinson, "The Problem of Health Reform in Russia," x-xi.

23. Doctors serving the tsarist police had a related but distinct role in identifying members of the outlawed "Skoptsy" or Castrates' sect, a late eighteenth-century offshoot of the Russian Orthodox Church that practiced self-castration in men and youths, and genital mutilation in women. See Laura Engelstein, *Castration and the Heavenly Kingdom: A Russian Folktale* (Ithaca, NY: Cornell University Press, 1999).

24. The legislation did not however mention hermaphroditism specifically, referring only to "inability to copulate." See Merzheevskii, *Sudebnaia ginekologiia*, 20–30.

25. For a description of the procedures of *"brakovka"* or rejection on medical grounds during recruitment, see, e.g., D. T. Andreev, "Materialy po voinskomu prisutstvuiu Krasninskago uezda Smolenskoi gub. s 1874 g. po 1895 g.," *Vestnik obshchestvennoi gigieny, sudebnoi i prakticheskoi meditsiny*, (May 1899), sec. 2: 553–71 and (October 1899), sec. 2 (1899): 1282–92. The number of draftees rejected as being of doubtful manhood was apparently very small. Hermaphrodites would have fallen under an article prescribing rejection for having "deformities of the sex organ," and only a tiny number of these are recorded in medical reviews of the recruitment process. For one case of hypospadia (a condition in which the urethra does not emerge from the tip of the penis, but elsewhere) see Dr. Nikitin, "Svedeniia o rekrutakh," *Sbornik sochinenii po sudebnoi meditsine, sudebnoi psikhiatrii, meditsinskoi politsii, k obshchestvennoi gigiene, epidemiologii, meditsinskoi geografii i meditsinskoi statistike* 3, pt. 2 (1872): 22–24.

26. See, e.g., Bertenson, "Novyi primer," 82–83; and for a sarcastic critique of provincial police and doctors for suspicion of a bearded hermaphrodite (living as a woman) as a credible prostitute, Mikhailov, "Sluchai germafroditizma," *Arkhiv sudebnoi meditsiny i obshchestvennoi gigieny* 1, sec. 5 (1870): 15–16.

27. "Germafroditizm po deistvuiushchemu zakonodatel'stvu," *Vestnik obshchestvennoi gigieny, sudebnoi i prakticheskoi meditsiny* (January 1913): 119–21.

28. On these research agendas in Central Europe, see Chandak Sengoopta, "Glandular Politics: Experimental Biology, Clinical Medicine, and Homosexual Emancipation in Fin-de-Siècle Central Europe," *Isis*, no. 89 (1998): 445–73. For the early Soviet dimension, see Bernstein, "'The Dictatorship of Sex': Science, Glands and the Medical Construction of Gender Difference in Revolutionary Russia," 138–60; and Naiman, *Sex in Public*, 143–47, 290–91.

29. Healey, *Homosexual Desire in Revolutionary Russia*, 126–51.

30. Robert A. Nye, "Sex Difference and Male Homosexuality in French Medical Discourse, 1830–1930," *Bulletin of the History of Medicine* 63 (1989): 32–51; Dreger, *Hermaphrodites*, 119–21.

31. On the "spectre of homosexuality" as a fear generated by

hermaphrodites, see Fausto-Sterling, "The Five Sexes," 23.

32. On Leibovich's attempts to give forensic medicine a distinctly social orientation, and his activities in charting suicide, see Kenneth M. Pinnow, "Counting and Cutting," in *Russian Modernity: Politics, Knowledge, Practices*, ed. Hoffmann and Kotsonis, 115–37.

33. GARF 482/30/2/86 (Petrograd), 123 (Saratov). In each city, the numbers recorded included "determinations of age, sex and physical development," and might not thus contain any sex determinations as such.

34. Fifteen of these took place in Moscow; in the previous year, 31 such cases were recorded for Russia with 10 in Moscow, where medical expertise was concentrated. See Ia. Leibovich, "Godovoi otchet po sudeb.-meditsinskoi ekspertize v RSFSR za 1925 g.," *Sudebno-meditsinskaia ekspertiza*, no. 5 (1927): 96–128.

35. GARF 482/30/6/45 (Saratov), 145 (Leningrad), 151 ob. (Moscow). These were explicitly designated "determinations of sex." No figures for Sverdlovsk appear in these archival reports.

36. Leibovich, *Sudebnaia ginekologiia*, 116–32.

37. S. Braude, "Nedorazvitie liudi: muzhchina ili zhenshchina? Dostizheniia sovremennoi khirurgii" *Vecherniaia Moskva*, no. 302, 12 December 1926, p. 2. I am indebted to Nikolia Krementsov for bringing this article to my attention, and for supplying background information on Golianitskii. The patients are so briefly described in this short newspaper item that I have not included them in the database of hermaphrodite medical case histories constructed for this chapter.

38. Yet textbooks did mention the passport sex change rules as one option; for example, Rozenblium, Serdiukov, and Smol'ianinov, *Sudebno-meditsinskaia akushersko-ginekologicheskaia ekspertiza*, 203; Popov, *Sudebnaia meditsina*, 343.

39. A textbook reflecting the legislative reforms of the Khrushchev era states that hermaphrodites and "transvestites" should apply with a forensic medical opinion to a court (and not registry offices) for changes to passport sex. See Serdiukov, *Sudebnaia ginekologiia i sudebnoe akusherstvo*, 36–37, 44, 47–49.

40. The decree was "Postanovlenie Soveta Ministrov SSSR ot 28/VIII 1974 g., no. 677, punkt 9." See I. V. Golubeva, *Germafroditizm (Klinika, diagnostika, lechenie)* (Moscow: Meditsina, 1980), 105–6.

41. The database of case histories is discussed in the introduction, and the articles from which these cases are drawn are listed separately in the bibliography.

42. As in other jurisdictions, Russian tsarist and Soviet doctors seldom saw the infant hermaphrodite as an acute medical emergency. The perception changed in the middle of the twentieth century when U.S. psychologist John Money shifted the focus of medical attention from teenage and adult intersex patients to infants, with his protocols for medical intervention to assign sex in the first 18 months of life. These protocols—adopted by many medical establishments globally—are now under attack from intersex patients, the first generation of infants thus treated. See Redick, "American History XY."

43. In focusing on medical practices, I adopt an approach similar to that

found in Geertje Mak, "Doubting Sex from Within: A Praxiographic Approach to a Late Nineteenth-Century Case of Hermaphroditism," *Gender and History* 18, no. 2 (2006): 332–56.

44. Krementsov, *Stalinist Science*. On the cultural revolution, Fitzpatrick, ed., *Cultural Revolution in Russia, 1928–31*.

45. Christopher M. Davis, "Economics of Soviet Public Health, 1928–1932: Development Strategy, Resource Constraints, and Health Plans," in *Health and Society in Revolutionary Russia*, ed. Solomon and Hutchinson, 146–72.

46. Bernstein, *The Dictatorship of Sex*, 183–92.

47. A rare collaborative article between a Soviet practitioner and a French physician began in this fashion. See V. V. Bobin and Henri Neuville, "K voprosu ob istinnom germafroditizme," *Trudy Krymskogo meditsinskogo instituta* 1 (1935): 3–18. Bobin and Neuville examined a case from the 1920s in which the patient had died; Bobin sent a preserved tissue sample to Neuville for examination in Paris, where he was deputy director of the Laboratory of Comparative Anatomy at France's National Museum of Natural History, and their resulting article was published with a French abstract. A lively medical "trade" in specimens and wax castings and other artefacts for the study of hermaphroditism developed in the nineteenth century, Dreger, *Hermaphrodites*, 67–68. Soviet scientists were often prevented by Stalinist xenophobia from exchanging research objects with foreigners, see Krementsov, *The Cure*.

48. Compare a blatantly politicized passage on homosexuality's association with aristocrats and fascism in Germany in Rozenblium, Serdiukov, and Smol'ianinov, *Sudebno-meditsinskaia akushersko-ginekologicheskaia ekspertiza*, 46, with a passage contrasting "conservative" and "modern" approaches to treating hermaphrodites cited later in this chapter.

49. That medical case histories of the hermaphrodite were an "entertaining" genre for this specialist readership is asserted by Dreger in *Hermaphrodites*, 59–60.

50. See, e.g., Elizabeth Waters, "The Modernization of Russian Motherhood, 1917–1937," *Soviet Studies* 44, no. 1 (1992): 123–35. Of course, cases in which the intersexed individual was untroubled by the condition constitute a group not represented in this sample.

51. V. L. Beder, "K voprosu ob interseksual'nosti (Sluchai semeinogo germafroditizma u 3-kh brat'ev)," *Sovremennaia psikhonevrologiia* 11, no. 12 (1930): 430–46.

52. I am indebted to Geertje Mak, who first directed my attention to these problems of social adjustment. See also Mak, "Doubting Sex from Within."

53. M. M. Tarabukhin, "Sluchai lozhnogo zhenskogo germafroditizma," *Akusherstvo i ginekologiia* 4 (1938): 109.

54. I. A. Matusis and A. N. Pavlov, "K voprosu o germafroditizme," *Odesskii meditsinskii zhurnal* 2 (1928): 107–12.

55. A. I. Ataev, "K voprosu o germafroditizme," *Zhurnal teoreticheskoi i prakticheskoi meditsiny* (Azerbaidzhanskii gos. universitet) 4, no. 2 (1930): 147–50.

56. Getman-Sycheva, "Sluchai germafroditizma," *Vrachebnaia gazeta* 11 (1930): 857–60.

57. Bernstein, *The Dictatorship of Sex*, 73–99. Evidence of the anti-pleasure ethos in sexual enlightenment in a provincial newspaper is examined in Frank, "Ask the Doctor!" in *The Human Tradition in Modern Russia*, ed. Husband. The idea of heterosexual desire as humanity's "default setting" under ideal conditions (whether some form of technocratic capitalism, or socialism) is a constant of twentieth-century Russian thinking. See Dan Healey, "What Can We Learn from the History of Homosexuality in Russia?" *History Compass*, 1, no. 1 (2003), DOI: 10.1111/1478-0542.047.

58. L. A. Krivskii, "K voprosu o germafroditizme," *Trudy gosudarstvennogo instituta meditsinskikh znanii (Leningrad)* 1 (1927): 112–31.

59. I. I. Shirokogorov and R. A. Dykhno-Leibzon, "Iavliaetsia li polovaia zheleza u zhenshchin organom, opredeliaiushchim pol? Dva sluchaia muzhskikh polovykh zhelez u zhenshchin—pseudohermaphroditismus masculinus," *Zhurnal teoreticheskoi i prakticheskoi meditsiny* 4, no. 1 (1930): 399–420.

60. On the "old paternalistic tradition of lying to the patient for the patient's own good" in Soviet medical practice, see Richard De George, "Biomedical Ethics," *Science and the Soviet Social Order*, ed. Loren R. Graham (Cambridge: Harvard University Press, 1990), 210. For a general late Soviet view, see A. N. Orlov, "'Sviataia' lozh' vo blago, vo spasen'e," in *Kraevaia nauchno-prakticheskaia konferentsiia sudebnykh medikov Krasnoiarskogo kraia. Tezisy dokladov 13–14 fevral'ia 1987 goda* (Krasnoiarsk: Krasnoiarskii kraevoi otdel zdravookhraneniia, 1987), 44–49. On the use of such lies when treating hermaphroditism, see Golubeva, *Germafroditizm*, 106.

61. For another Turkish intersexual living as a woman, whose modesty and cultural background led to her refusal to submit to all the examinations the physician wished to make, see N. A. Uimanov, "Sluchai pseudohermaphroditismus completus," *Zhurnal teoreticheskoi i prakticheskoi meditsiny* 3, no. 3–4 (1928): 232–27.

62. Paula A. Michaels, *Curative Powers: Medicine and Empire in Stalin's Central Asia* (Pittsburgh, PA: University of Pittsburgh Press, 2003).

63. Before the Nuremburg Code on permissible medical experiments (1947), western medicine seldom made clear distinctions between "innovative therapy" and experimentation on humans when no therapeutic benefit was foreseen. That Weimar German doctors were bound by ethical standards limiting their conduct in these fields was fiercely contested at the Nuremburg doctors' trial, and judges there heard disturbing "evidence of widespread, ethically suspect medical research" not only in Germany. See Michael A. Grodin, "Historical Origins of the Nuremburg Code," *Medicine, Ethics, and the Third Reich: Historical and Contemporary Issues*, ed. John Michalczyk (Kansas City: Sheed & Ward, 1994), 169–94, quoted at 192. Krementsov mentions Grigorii Roskin's experimentation on incurable Moscow cancer patients in 1939, but whether they gave informed consent is not clear. See Krementsov, *The Cure*, 31–32.

64. Ia. L. Leibovich, "Homo generis neutrius," *Klinicheskaia meditsina* 3–4, nos. 7–8 (1922): 33–34.

65. See the case of "Efrem Ignat'ev" in I. F. Kozlov, "Sluchai zhenskogo

lozhnogo germafroditizma," *Kazanskii meditsinskii zhurnal* 17, no .2 (1921): 224–32.

66. Franz Neugebauer, "Quarante-quatre erreurs de sexe révélées par l'opération. Soixante-douze opérations chirurgicales d'urgence, de complaisance ou de complicité pratiquées chez des pseudo-hermaphrodites et personnes de sexe douteux," *Revue de gynécologie et de chirurgie abdominale*, 4 (1900): 457–518; Dreger, *Hermaphrodites*, 115–16. For a French doctor's refusal of a patient's demand for an operation *de complicité* in the 1890s, see Mak, "Doubting Sex from Within," 350–51.

67. Rozenblium, Serdiukov, and Smol'ianinov, *Sudebno-meditsinskaia akushersko-ginekologicheskaia ekspertiza*, 210.

68. Bobin and Neuville, "K voprosu ob istinnom germafroditizme." For a later report of successful urethroplasty in a 22-year-old hermaphrodite (a teacher living as a man), from a Kazan' surgical clinic, see V. A. Gusynin, "Ob uretroplastike v plane khirurgicheskogo ispravleniia pola pri germafroditizme," *Khirurgiia* 12 (1938): 109–14. This patient had undergone preliminary reconstructive surgery as a 12-year-old but abandoned that course of treatment; he was described as having a "bitter awareness of the deformity of his sex organs and his inability to have a sex life. Sexual feeling awoke in him with great power, but he is ashamed of this feeling because of his physical defect" (110). In four operations between March and November 1937, an artificial urethra was constructed using pedicle flap techniques (employing a tissue-flap from the thigh, which remained, connected "to the mother-soil" of the thigh, until a later procedure; these techniques were applied, after 1945, in the first American and British female-to-male transsexual surgeries. A photograph of the patient's phallus in the act of urination demonstrated the surgeon's art, 113.

69. M. A. Daniakhii, "Materialy k izucheniiu polovykh anomalii u cheloveka," *Akusherstvo i ginekologiia* 4 (1938): 104–8.

70. See, e.g., Gusynin, "Ob uretroplastike," 109.

71. Getman-Sycheva, "Sluchai germafroditizma," 859.

72. Z. A. Andreeva, "K voprosu o germafroditizme u cheloveka," *Zhurnal akusherstva i zhenskikh boleznei* 39, no. 6 (1928): 715–28.

73. On Young, see Redick, "American History XY," 12–13, 85–146; Fausto-Sterling, *Sexing the Body*, 42–44.

74. Redick says of Young's often inconsistent approach: "Factors that influenced a sex assignment included, in order of significance: gonads, libido, the feasibility of surgery, the desires of the parents, the personality or 'psychological sex' of the subject, and finally, the desires of the subject him or herself." See "American History XY," 87.

75. Andreeva, "K voprosu o germafroditizme u cheloveka," 715.

76. On Russian women who adopted male personas in war and peacetime, see Healey, *Homosexual Desire in Revolutionary Russia*, 63–69.

77. Although Perm' University was only founded after the 1917 Revolution, the Urals region had a long tradition of gynecological medicine, focused in Ekaterinburg (later named Sverdlovsk), and the region had rich

bibliographic resources. See A. M. Novikov and I. K. Kurdov, "Kratkii ocherk deiatel'nosti Ural'skogo Meditsinskogo Obshchestva v g. Ekaterinburge za 31 god ego sushchestvovaniia (1890–1921 g.g.)," *Ural'skoe meditsinskoe obozrenie* 1 (1922): 90–94. Sexological studies were well developed in Perm' by the late 1920s. See, e.g., N. K. Nakariakov, "Uchenie o seksual'nom gormone v svete noveishikh nauchnykh dannykh," *Ural'skii meditsinskii zhurnal* 6 (1929): 43–52, and other articles in this journal.

78. See Nelly Oudshoorn, *Beyond the Natural Body: An Archaeology of Sex Hormones* (London and New York: Routledge, 1994).

79. Andreeva, "K voprosu o germafroditizme u cheloveka," 726.

80. Andreeva, "K voprosu o germafroditizme u cheloveka," 725–26.

81. Fausto-Sterling, *Sexing the Body*, 56–63.

82. Andreeva, "K voprosu o germafroditizme u cheloveka," 727.

83. Andreeva, "K voprosu o germafroditizme u cheloveka," 727.

84. Healey, *Homosexual Desire in Revolutionary Russia*, 150.

85. The attempts at hermaphrodite "reconstruction" undertaken by Moscow Professor Golianitskii in the mid-1920s, for example, did require a change of passport sex. Yet even Golianitskii reportedly said that in deciding what sex to assign to his patients, he considered the hermaphrodite's "desires and self-definition" to be decisive. See Braude, "Nedorazvitie liudi: muzhchina ili zhenshchina? Dostizheniia sovremennoi khirurgii." It is possible that Golianitskii's operations were more experimental and crude than this newspaper report suggested. Two years later, according to psychiatrist P. B. Gannushkin, speaking in a closed-door discussion in the People's Commissariat of Health, the Moscow city health department investigated a doctor, perhaps Golianitskii, who "changed sex [in patients] and made women of men, and vice versa, by means of rather primitive operations. We had to review a huge quantity of case histories in which one and the same person figured as Konstantin and as Ekaterina, etc. . . . We found a way out of the problem in the following manner: we wrote that it was a rare case in which psychopathic patients fell into the hands of a doctor-psychopath. I don't know whether this was correct, but it eased the problem"; GARF A482/25/478/86–86ob.

Conclusion—Reflections on the Fate of a Sexual Revolution

1. Frances Bernstein draws useful distinctions between Soviet sexual enlightenment and the international sex reform movement—a movement that hailed Soviet sexual values as progressive. See *The Dictatorship of Sex*, 99, 132, and passim. On the sex reform movement, see Dose, "The World League for Sexual Reform," in *Sexual Cultures in Europe*, ed. Eder, Hall, and Hekma.

2. Matthew Waites, *The Age of Consent: Young People, Sexuality, and Citizenship* (Basingstoke, UK: Palgrave Macmillan, 2005), 32–39; David T. Evans, "Sexual Citizenship," in *The Blackwell Encyclopedia of Sociology*, ed. George Ritzer (Oxford: Blackwell, 2007), 4205–9.

3. Fitzpatrick, "Ascribing Class," 745–70; Alexopoulos, *Stalin's Outcasts*;

idem, "Soviet Citizenship, More or Less: Rights, Emotions, and States of Civic Belonging," *Kritika: Explorations in Russian and Eurasian History* 7, no. 3 (2005): 487–528. On national identity formation and ascription, see Terry Martin, *The Affirmative Action Empire: Nations and Nationalism in the Soviet Union, 1923–1939* (Ithaca, NY: Cornell University Press, 2001).

4. For the struggle against Muslim marriage practices, see Douglas Northrop, *Veiled Empire: Gender & Power in Stalinist Central Asia* (Ithaca, NY: Cornell University Press, 2004). Varying assessments of the meaning and danger of homosexuality also illustrate the Bolsheviks' calibration of the sexual revolution to match perceptions about a given society's place on the pathway to modernity, Healey, *Homosexual Desire in Revolutionary Russia*, 153–62.

5. Homosexuals in tsarist and Soviet Russia also looked to medicine to explain their condition. See Healey, *Homosexual Desire in Revolutionary Russia*, 69–72, 84, 104–5.

6. Hoffmann, *Stalinist Values*, 88–117.

7. Hoffmann, *Stalinist Values*, 96. For the prerevolutionary roots of transformative medicine, see Daniel Beer, "Blueprints for Change: The Human Sciences and the Coercive Transformation of Deviants in Russia, 1890–1930," *Osiris* 22 (2007): 26–47.

8. Naiman, *Sex in Public*.

9. Bernstein, *The Dictatorship of Sex*, 189.

10. Bernstein, *The Dictatorship of Sex*, 190–91.

11. The conference was held in Brno, Czechoslovakia, instead. See Bernstein, *The Dictatorship of Sex*, 27–28; Dose, "The World League for Sexual Reform," in *Sexual Cultures in Europe*, ed. Eder, Hall, and Hekma, 247. According to local press reports before the event, a Soviet delegate, Kiev professor Pasche-Oserski who had attended previous WLSR congresses, was expected to attend, but later reports do not mention him. See "K mezinárodnímu kongresu Svìtové ligy pro sexuální reformu v Brnì," *Moravské noviny*, 12 August 1932, 3, and subsequent reports in the same newspaper, 20–26 September 1932. WLSR activities were arrested by the rise of fascism, but Dose shows that affiliated national organizations managed a quiet revival after 1945.

12. Hoffmann, *Stalinist Values*, 98–99; Healey, *Homosexual Desire in Revolutionary Russia*, 196–97.

13. Iu. A. Nekliudov, "Iakov L'vovich Leibovich—vidnyi deiatel' otechestvennoi sudebnoi meditsiny," *Sudebno-meditsinskaia ekspertiza*, no. 5 (2003): 48–49; On Smol'ianinov, see Marina Sorokina, "People and Procedures: Toward a History of the Investigation of Nazi Crimes in the USSR," *Kritika: Explorations in Russian and Eurasian History* 6, no. 4 (2005).

14. Central Institute established, see GARF A482/24/301/1–4 ob. (Dokladnye zapiski o rabote i dalneishikh zadachakh Gos. NII sudebnoi meditsny). By 1931 Leibovich was directing a faculty of forensic medicine in Tomsk. See GARF A406/12/2798/63 (Narodnyi komissariat roboche-krest'iaskoi inspektsii RSFSR, Gruppa zdravookhraneniia. Delo o razrabotke zaiavleniia vrachei Moskovskoi oblastnoi sudebno-meditsinskoi ekspertizy o neudovletvorite'noi sostoianii

delo sudebno-meditsinskoi ekspertizy. Ianvar' 1931 g.–iiul' 1932 g.). For Smolianinov's activities summarised, see GARF A482/24/1254/11 (Stennogr. Soveshchanii nachal'nikov Upravelenii i otdelov NKZ RSFSR "O rabote n.i.i. sudebnoi psikhiatrii ot 15.IV.1939). Popov reports on efforts by police to take control of forensic services, GARF A482/24/301.

15. The 1934 Rules are found at GARF A482/25/879/22-29 (Delo po rassmotreniiu i dorabotke proekta pravil ambulatornogo sudebno-med. akush.-ginekologicheskogo issledovanii, 11.IV.1934-21.VI.1934). For a list of medical personnel who contributed to the rules, see GARF A482/25/879/30.

16. GARF A482/25/879/25, 27ob.

17. Some examples: chapter by Soviet gynaecologist E. M. Shvartsman and appended to V. Shtekkel', *Ginekologiia*, trans. E. Bogaevskaia et al. (Moscow-Leningrad: Gosudarstvennoe izdatel'stvo biologicheskoi i meditsinskoi literatury, 1936), 632; A. M. Furmanov, "Istochniki i proiavleniia seksual'nosti v detskom i podrostkovom vozraste," *Vrachebnoe delo*, no. 10 (1934): 673–78. One authority extolled "the careful transferral of sexual desire to the realm of labor and cultural interests, including the tasks of sexual education rationally in the system of general labor education" as a means of deferring sexual life until marriage. See D. Gorfin, "Polovaia zhizn'," in *Bol'shaia sovetskaia entsiklopediia* (Moscow: OGIZ RSFSR, 1940), 46: 163–69, quoted at 162. Note also A. O. Edel'shtein, "Polovoe vospitanie," in *Bol'shaia meditsinskaia entsiklopediia*, ed. N. A. Semashko (Moscow: OGIZ RSFSR, 1933), 46: 299–302.

18. GARF A482/25/879/23ob, 24, 27.

19. GARF A482/25/879/24, 24ob, 25.

20. The rules discussed the signs of anal intercourse in boys, men, and women, a reflection of Stalin's recriminalization of sodomy in March 1934. See GARF A482/25/879/24, 24ob.; and Healey, *Homosexual Desire in Revolutionary Russia*, 193–94.

21. GARF A482/25/879/24.

22. The RSFSR People's Commissar of Justice discussed the inadmissibility of alcoholism as a mitigating defense in a 1936 speech: Nikolai Krylenko, "Ob izmeneniiakh i dopolneniiakh kodeksov RSFSR," *Sovetskaia iustitsiia* 15, no. 7 (1936): 1–5.

23. For one example, see Healey, *Homosexual Desire in Revolutionary Russia*, 213–14.

24. Only in 1968 would a specific set of rules for medical expertise on men's "sexual conditions" be issued: Minsterstvo zdravookhraneniia SSSR, *Pravila sudebno-medtisinskoi ekspertizy polovykh sostoianii muzhchin* (Moscow: Minzdrav SSSR, 1968).

25. Healey, *Homosexual Desire in Revolutionary Russia*, 200.

BIBLIOGRAPHY

Primary Sources

Archives

State Archive of the Russian Federation (GARF): f. A482, People's Commissariat of Public Health; f. A406, People's Commissariat of Worker-Peasant Inspection

State Archive of Leningrad Province in Vyborg (LOGAV): f. 2205, Leningrad courts, 1922–1924

Central State Archive of St. Petersburg (TsGA SPb): f. 2895, Leningrad Provincial Health Department (Gubzdravotdel)

State Archive of Sverdlovsk Province, Ekaterinburg (GASO): f. 854, Sverdlovsk provincial police administration, 1920–1940; f. 138, Ekaterinburg provincial court, 1921–1924; f. 148, Sverdlovsk provincial court, 1922–1937; f. 340, Sverdlovsk district court, 1925–1930

Centre for Documentation of Social Organizations of Sverdlovsk Province, Ekaterinburg (TsDOOSO): f. 4, Reports [to Communist Party] on operation of courts, procuracy

Published Essays and Books

Andreev, D. T. "Materialy po voinskomu prisutstviiu Krasninskago uezda Smolenskoi gub. s 1874 g. po 1895 g." *Vestnik obshchestvennoi gigieny, sudebnoi i prakticheskoi meditsiny* sec. 2 (1899): May, 553–71; October, 1282–92.

Andreev, M. "Neskol'ko zamechanii o proizvodstve del po 166–169 st. st. Ugolovnogo Kodeksa." *Ezhenedel'nik sovetskoi iustitsii*, no. 38 (1924): 905–6.

Bazhenov, N. K. *Spravochnik po sudebnoi meditsine i ekspertize v sviazi s nachal'nymi poniatiiami po anatomii, fiziologii cheloveka, sotsial'noi gigiene, sanitarii i skoroi pomoshchi*. Sverdlovsk: Izdanie 4 shkoly NKVD Administrativno-Militseiskikh rabotnikov, 1929.

Bekhterev, V. M. "O polovom ozdorovlenii." *Vestnik znaniia*, nos. 9–10 (1910): 9: 924–37; 10: 1–19.

Bellin, E. F. "Ocherk uslovii deiatel'nosti nashei sudebno-meditsinskoi ekspertizy; prichiny neudovletvoritel'nosti eia i mery k ustraneniiu ikh." *Vestnik obshchestvennoi gigieny, sudebnoi i prakticheskoi meditsiny*, no. 2, kn. 2, sec. 3 (1889): 1–24.

———. "Sluchai lozhnago muzhskago germafroditizma." *Trudy Khar'kovskogo meditsinskogo obshchestva*, vyp. 2 (1893): 332–35.

———. *Sluchai zatrudnitel'nago opredeleniia pola i grazhdanskikh prav. Muzhchina ili zhenshchina?* Khar'kov: Tip. Zil'berberg, 1898.

———. *Sudebnaia meditsina rastleniia. Atlas iz 20 khromolitografirovannykh tablits*. St. Petersburg: Meditsinskii Departament, Ministerstvo vnutrennykh del, 1898.

Bertenson, I. V. "Novyi primer tak nazyvaemago germafroditizma i voobshche o dvusnastnosti v sudebno-meditsinskom otnoshenii." *Arkhiv sudebnoi meditsiny i obshchestvennoi gigieny*, Marc sec. 2 (March 1865): 75–87.

Braude, S. "Nedorazvitie liudi: muzhchina ili zhenshchina? Dostizheniia sovremennoi khirurgii" *Vecherniaia Moskva*, no. 302, 12 December 1926.

Brukhanskii, N. P. "Antisotsial'nye dushevno-bol'nye i psikhopaty." In *2-e Vserossiiskoe soveshchanie po voprosam psikhiatrii i nevrologii*, edited by Anon., 42–44. Moscow, 1924.

———. "Vvedenie v kriminal'nuiu psikhpatologiiu." *Sudebno-meditsinskaia ekspertiza*, no. 1 (1925): 39–98.

———. "Psikhiatricheskaia ekspertiza v sviazi s voprosami zakonodatel'stva." *Moskovskii meditsinskii zhurnal*, no. 3 (1926): 47–50.

———. *Materialy po seksual'noi psikhopatologii*. Moscow: M. i S. Sabashnikovy, 1927.

———. *Ocherki po sotsial'noi psikhopatologii*. Moscow: M. i S. Sabashnikovy, 1928.

———. *Sudebnaia psikhiatriia*. Moscow: M. i S. Sabashnikovy, 1928.

———. "Proekt redaktsii stat'i vzamen st. st. 151, 152, 153 UK RSFSR, red. 1926 g." In *Trudy psikhiatricheskoi kliniki (Gedeonovka)*. Vyp. 1. Edited by R. I. Belkin. Smolensk: Smolenskii gos. universitet, 1930.

Bukharin, Nikolai, and Evgenii Preobrazhenskii. *The ABC of Communism*. Translated by E. and C. Paul. Harmondsworth, UK: Penguin, 1969.

Chelyshev, [M. I.]. Predsedatel' UKK Verkhsuda RSFSR. "Doklad UKK o praktike po delam o polovykh prestupleniiakh za vtoruiu polovinu 1926 goda." *Sudebnaia praktika RSFSR*, no. 6 (1927): 4–8.

"Deiatel'nost' Ural'skogo meditsinskogo o-va v g. Ekaterinburge v 1922 g." *Ural'skoe meditsinskoe obozrenie*, nos. 2–3 (1923): 148.

"Doklad Ugolovnoi Kassatsionnoi Kollegii Verkhovnogo Suda RSFSR o rabote za 1926 god." *Sudebnaia praktika RSFSR*, no. 22, 23 (1927): 22: 2–6; 23: 5–9.

"XXII [Dvadtsat' vtoroe] nauchnoe zasedanie Obshchestva meditsinskoi ekspertizy g. Leningrada i oblasti ot 21 maia 1928 g." *Sudebno-meditsinskaia ekspertiza*, no. 11 (1929): 180–87.

Edel'shtein, A. O. "Polovoe vospitanie." In *Bol'shaia meditsinskaia entsiklopediia*, edited by N. A. Semashko, vol. 26: 299–302. Moscow: OGIZ RSFSR, 1933.

Estrin, A. *Ugolovnoe pravo SSSR i RSFSR*. Moscow: Iuridicheskoe iz-vo NKIu RSFSR, 1927.

Feinberg, Ts. M. *Sudebno-psikhiatricheskaia ekspertiza i opyt raboty instituta sudebnoi psikhiatrii im. prof. Serbskogo za XXV let*. Moscow: Tsent. n.-i. institut sudebnoi psikhiatrii im. prof. Serbskogo MZ SSSR, 1947.

Frenkel', E. P. *Polovye prestupleniia*. Odessa: Svetoch, 1927.
G[ard], E. "Khuzhe ubiistva." *Krasnaia gazeta* 249, no. 639 (31.X.24): 3.
———. "Delo Miatsa." *Krasnaia gazeta* 199, no. 589 (3.IX.24): 3; 200, no. 590 (4.IX.24): 3; 201, no. 591 (5.IX.24): 3; 203, no. 593 (8.IX.24): 3.
Garin, A. P. "Sluchai gipospadii, kak predmeta sudebno-meditsinskago issledovaniia i voprosy o `pole' pri nepravil'nom obrazovanii polovykh organov voobshche." *Vestnik obshchestvennoi gigieny, sudebnoi i prakticheskoi meditsiny*, no. 29, kn. 2, sec. 3 (1896): 49–65.
Genter, G. G. "K voprosu o polovoi zrelosti zhenshchiny." *Vrachebnaia gazeta*, no. 12 (1930): 912–17.
"Germafroditizm po deistvuiushchemu zakonodatel'stvu." *Vestnik obshchestvennoi gigieny, sudebnoi i prakticheskoi meditsiny* (January 1913): 119–21.
Gertsenzon, A. A. "Polovaia prestupnost' v do-revoliutsionnoi Rossii (Statisticheskii ocherk)." In *Pravonarusheniia v oblasti seksual'nykh otnoshenii*, ed E. K. Krasnushkin, G. M. Segal, and Ts. M. Fainberg. Moscow: Izdanie Moszdravotdela, 1927.
Gindes, E. Ia. *Perekhodnyi vozrast*. Baku: Narkompromtorg, 1923.
Golubeva, I. V. *Germafroditizm (Klinika, diagnostika, lechenie)*. Moscow: Meditsina, 1980.
Gromov, A. P. *Kurs lektsii po sudebnoi meditsine*. Moscow: Meditsina, 1970.
Gromov, Sergei A. *Kratkoe izlozhenie sudebnoi meditsiny*. St. Petersburg, 1832.
Gurevich, Z. "Polovaia zhizn'." In *Bol'shaia meditsinskaia entsiklopediia*, edited by N. A. Semashko, 26: 282–98. Moscow: OGIZ RSFSR, 1933.
———. "Polovoi vopros." In *Bol'shaia meditsinskaia entsiklopediia*, edited by N. A. Semashko, 26: 302–17. Moscow: OGIZ RSFSR, 1933.
Gurevitsch [Gurevich], Z. A., and A. J. Woroschbit. "Das Sexualleben der Bauerin in Russland." *Zeitschrift für Sexualwissenschaft und Sexualpolitik* 18, nos. 1, 2 (1931–1932): 51–74, 81–110.
Iakobzon, L. Ia. *Polovaia kholodnost' zhenshchiny*. Leningrad: Prakticheskaia meditsina, 1927.
Iakovlev. "Raionnoe Soveshchanie sudebno-meditsinskikh ekspertov s predstaviteliami sudebno-sledstvennykh organov, proiskhodivshee v g. Saratove s 6 po 9 sentiabria 1925 goda." *Sudebno-meditsinskaia ekspertiza*, no. 3 (1925): 83–94.
Ianovskii, A. E. "Germafrodity (s iuridich. tochki zreniia)." In *Entsiklopedicheskii slovar'*, edited by F. A. Brokgauz and I. A. Efron, 8A:536. St. Petersburg: I. A. Efron, 1893.
Ippolitov, S. N. "Kratkii ocherk deiatel'nosti meditsinskogo soveta po sudebno-meditsinskoi chasti 1804–1904 gody." *Vestnik obshchestvennoi gigieny, sudebnoi i prakticheskoi meditsiny* (April 1907): 548–71.
———. *Sbornik zakonopolozhenii o sudebno-meditsinskikh issledovaniia*. St. Petersburg: K. L. Rikker, 1910.
Izhevskii, N. I. "Vtoroi vserossiiskii s"ezd sudebno-meditsinskikh ekspertov v g. Moskve (25 fevralia–3 marta 1926 goda)." *Leningradskii meditsinskii zhurnal*, no. 4 (April 1926): 143–51.

Khol'tsov, B. N. *Funktsional'nye rasstroistva muzhskogo polovogo apparata i funktsional'nye rasstroistva mochevykh organov nervnogo proiskhozhdeniia.* Leningrad: Prakticheskaia meditsina, 1926.
"Khronika. Na meditsinskom fakul'tete Ural-Universiteta." *Ural'skoe meditsinskoe obozrenie,* no. 2–3 (1923): 150–51.
Kiselev, N. S. "Vliianie rannikh brakov na zhenshchin i rozhdaemykh imi detei." *Vestnik obshchestvennoi gigieny, sudebnoi i prakticheskoi meditsiny,* sec. 2 (February 1897): 121–39.
Kollontai, Alexandra. *Love of Worker Bees.* Translated by Cathy Porter. London: Virago, 1977.
———. *Selected Writings of Alexandra Kollontai.* Translated by Alix Holt. London: Allison & Busby, 1977.
Kosorotov, D. P. *Uchebnik sudebnoi meditsiny.* Moscow and Leningrad: Gosudarstvennoe izdatel'stvo, 1928.
Kovalevskii, P. I. *Sudebnaia psikhiatriia.* St. Petersburg: M. Akinfiev & I. Leont'ev, 1902.
Krasnushkin, E. K. "Chto takoe prestupnik?" *Prestupnik i prestupnost'.* Sbornik 1 (1926): 6–33.
———, G. M. Segal, and Ts. M. Fainberg, eds. *Pravonarusheniia v oblasti seksual'nykh otnoshenii.* Moscow: Izdanie Moszdravotdela, 1927.
Kratter, Iu. "Rukovodstvo sudebnoi meditsiny. Dlia vrachei i studentov. Ch. IV. Sudebnaia seksologiia. Avtorizovannyi perev. so 2-go nemetsk. izd. pod red. i s dopolneniiami Ia. Leibovicha (Prilozhenie)." *Sudebno-meditsinskaia ekspertiza,* nos. 9, 10, [11?] (1928): 9: 1–38; 10: 39–67; 11: 68–114.
Krzhishkovskii, K. N. *Fiziologiia polovoi zhizni.* Leningrad: Priboi, 1926.
Kurdov, I. K. "Sostoianie meditsinskoi organizatsii v g. Ekaterinburge v 1920 godu." *Ural'skoe meditsinskoe obozrenie,* no. 1 (1922): 73–89.
Kurskii, D., and P. Stuchka. "Instruktivnye pis'ma. Direktivnoe pis'mo NKIu i verkhsuda RSFSR po primeneniiu Ugol. Kod. redaktsii 1926 g." *Sudebnaia praktika RSFSR,* no. 1 (1927): 8–11.
L. "Nizhegorodskoe gubernskoe soveshchanie po sudebno-meditsinskoi ekspertize byvsh. 26 marta 1925 g." *Sudebno-meditsinskaia ekspertiza,* no. 2 (1925): 194–98.
Leibovich, Ia. "Tri goda sudebnoi meditsiny." *Ezhenedel'nik sovetskoi iustitsii,* no. 7 (1922): 7–8.
———. "Sudebno-meditsinskaia ekspertiza pri NEP'e." *Ezhenedel'nik sovetskoi iustitsii,* no. 2 (1923): 36–38.
———. "Piat' let sudebnoi meditsiny." *Ezhdenedel'nik sovetskoi iustitsii,* no. 34 (1923): 775–77.
———. *Prakticheskoe rukovodstvo po sudebnoi meditsine.* 2nd ed. Moscow: Izdanie Narodnogo komissariata iustitsii, 1923.
———. "O popravkakh i dopolneniiakh v deistvuiushchii Ugolovnyi Kodeks, predlozhennykh Narkomzdravom." *Sudebno-meditsinskaia ekspertiza,* no. 1 (1925): 24–28.
———. "Tezisy po dokladu d-ra Ia. L. Leibovicha. Itogi Deiatel'nosti sud.-med.-ekspertizy za sem' let i blizhaishie zadachi." A paper delivered at the 2nd

All-Russian Conference of Forensic Medical Experts, Moscow, 1926; copy held in GARF A-482/1/596/209–10, 1926.

———. "Godovoi otchet po sudebno-meditsinskoi ekspertize v RSFSR za 1924 g." *Sudebno-meditsinskaia ekspertiza*, no. 4 (1926): 104–36.

———. "Godovoi otchet po sudeb.-meditsinskoi ekspertize v RSFSR za 1925 g." *Sudebno-meditsinskaia ekspertiza*, no. 5 (1927): 96–128.

———. *Prakticheskoe rukovodstvo po sudebnoi meditsine*. 3rd ed. Moscow: Iuridicheskoe izdatel'stvo Narkomiusta RSFSR, 1927.

———. "Polovaia zrelost' v ugolovnom i grazhdanskom zakonodatel'stve." *Voprosy zdravookhraneniia*, no. 14 (1928): 40–44.

———. "Stat'i Ugolovnogo Kodeksa 1926 g., kasaiushchiesia sudebno-meditsinskoi ekspertizy." *Problemy prestupnosti*, no. 3 (1928): 164–72.

———. *Sudebnaia ginekologiia. Rukovodstvo dlia vrachei i iuristov*. Khar'kov: Iurdicheskoe iz-vo Narkomiusta USSR, 1928.

Leitman, L. B. "Dannye osvidetel'stvovaniia po voprosam, sviazannym s polovym instinktom." A paper delivered at the Volga Regional Conference of forensic-medical experts (Povolzhskoe soveshanie sudebnykh meditsinskikh ekspertov). Saratov, 1925.

———. "K voprosu o polovom sovershennoletii." *Sudebno-meditsinskaia ekspertiza*, no. 9 (1928): 75–78.

Lents, A. K. *Kriminal'nye psikhopaty (Sotsiopaty)*. Leningrad: Rabochii sud, 1927.

Liublinskii, P. I. *Predvaritel'noe sledstvie*. Moscow: Pravo i Zhizn', 1923.

———. *Prestupleniia v oblasti polovykh otnoshenii*. Moscow-Leningrad: Iz-vo L. D. Frenkel', 1925.

———. "Polovye posiagatel'stva protiv detei (Po dannym Leningrada)." *Problemy prestupnosti*, no. 1 (1926): 91–122.

M., G. "Pedagog-rastlitel'." *Krasnaia gazeta* 163, no. 553 21.VII.24): 3.

Man'kovskii, B. S. "Sovremennaia polovaia prestupnost'." In *Pravonarusheniia v oblasti seksual'nykh otnoshenii*, edited by E. K. Krasnushkin, G. M. Segal, and Ts. M. Fainberg. Moscow: Mosdravotdel, 1927.

Merzheevskii, V. O. "Perechen' ugolovnykh del, razbiravshikhsia pri zakrytykh dveriakh v s.-peterburgskom okruzhnom sude." *Arkhiv sudebnoi meditsiny i obshchestvennoi gigieny*, no. 3, sec. 2 (1869): 73–86.

———. "Sudebno-meditsinskoe izsledovanie devstvennoi plevy. Material k voprosu o rastlenii." *Arkhiv sudebnoi meditsiny i obshchestvennoi gigieny*, no. 3, sec. 2 (1871): 5–43.

———. "Obvinenie v iznasilovanii 18-ti-letnei devushki." *Sbornik sochinenii po sudebnoi meditsine, sudebnoi psikhiatrii, meditsinskoi politsii, k obshchestvennoi gigiene, epidemiologii, meditsinskoi geografii i meditsinskoi statistike* 2, pt. 1 (1872): 10–22.

———. *Sudebnaia ginekologiia. Rukovodstvo dlia vrachei i iuristov*. St. Petersburg: B. G. Ianpol'skii, 1878.

Mokrinskii, S. P., and V. Natanson. *Prestupleniia protiv lichnosti. Kommentarii k VI glave*. Khar'kov: Narkomiusta USSR, 1928.

Nakariakov, N. K. "Uchenie o seksual'nom gormone v svete noveishikh nauchnykh dannykh." *Ural'skii meditsinskii zhurnal*, no. 6 (1926): 43–52.
Neugebauer, Franz L. von. *Hermaphroditismus beim Menschen*. Leipzig: Dr. W. Klinkhardt, 1908.
Nikitin, Dr. "Svedeniia o rekrutakh." *Sbornik sochinenii po sudebnoi meditsine, sudebnoi psikhiatrii, meditsinskoi politsii, k obshchestvennoi gigiene, epidemiologii, meditsinskoi geografii i meditsinskoi statistike* 3, pt. 2 (1872): 22–24.
Nikol'skii, D. P. "Programma dlia sobiraniia svedenii o polovoi zrelosti zhenshchin." *Vestnik obshchestvennoi gigieny, sudebnoi i prakticheskoi meditsiny* sec. 3 (November 1901): 1722–23.
Novikov, A. M., and I. K. Kurdov. "Kratkii ocherk deiatel'nosti Ural'skogo Meditsinskogo Obshchestva v g. Ekaterinburge. Za 31 god ego sushchestvovaniia (1890–1921 g.g.)." *Ural'skoe meditsinskoe obozrenie*, no. 1 (1922): 90–94.
"Obzor deiatel'nosti Nauchnogo Obshchestva meditsinskoi ekspertizy gor. Leningrada za 1925 goda." *Sudebno-meditsinskaia ekspertiza*, no. 4 (1926): 161.
Orshanskii, L. G. "Analiz psikhologicheskii i psikhopatologicheskii." In *Polovye prestupleniia*, edited by A. A. Zhizhilenko and L. G. Orshanskii, 41–90. Leningrad: Rabochii sud, 1927.
Peretts, V. G. "Iskusstvennyi vykidysh s obshchestvenno-meditsinskoi tochki zreniia." *Ural'skii vrach*, no. 4–5 (1922): 126–39.
———. "Statistika abortov po Ekaterinburgskomu Povival'noginekologicheskomu institutu za 1920–1921 g.g." *Ural'skoe meditsinskoe obozrenie*, no. 1 (1922): 64–72.
———. "Dva goda deistviia tsirkuliara o dopustimosti iskusstvennogo vykidysha po sotsial'nym pokazaniiam." *Ural'skoe meditsinskoe obozrenie*, no. 2–3 (1923): 53–61.
———. "Oshchushchaetsia li v Ural'skoi oblasti nedostatok v akusherakh ginekologakh?" *Ural'skii meditsinskii zhurnal*, no. 9 (1929): 18–20.
Petrov, P. V., ed. *Trudy pervago s"ezda ofitserov-vospitatelei kadetskikh korpusov (22–31 dekabria 1908 g.)*. St. Petersburg: M. M. Stasiulevich, 1909.
Piaternev, V. S. "K voprosu ob opredelenii polovoi zrelosti zhenshchiny." *Sudebno-meditsinskaia ekspertiza*, no. 11 (1929): 21–26.
Popov, N. V. "O rabote Moskovskoi Sudebno-Meditsinskoi Ekspertizy." *Moskovskii meditsinskii zhurnal*, no. 7 (1924): 83–89.
———. "IV-yi [Chetvertyi] Moskovskii gubernskii rasshirennyi sudebno-meditsinskii s"ezd." *Sudebno-meditsinskaia ekspertiza*, no. 1 (1925): 99–115.
———. "Neskol'ko zamechanii po voprosu o vremeni nastupleniia polovoi zrelosti." *Sudebno-meditsinskaia ekspertiza*, no. 7 (1927): 29–33.
———. *Sudebnaia meditsina*. 3rd ed. Moscow: Medgiz, 1950.
Poznyshev, S. V. *Ocherk osnovnykh nachal nauki ugolovnogo prava*. Pt. 2. *Osobennaia chast'*. Moscow: Iuridicheskoe izdatel'stvo NKIust, 1923.
"Rasshirennyi nauchnyi s"ezd sudebnykh vrachei i predstavitelei iustitsii v g. Ivanove-Vosnesenske 23–25 dekabria 1927 g." *Sudebno-meditsinskaia ekspertiza*, nos. 9, 10 (1928): 9: 135–64; 10: 156–66.

Riasentsev, V. A. "K voprosu ob opredelenii polovoi zrelosti zhenshchin." *Sudebno-meditsinskaia ekspertiza*, no. 7 (1927): 26–29.
Rozenblium, E. E., M. G. Serdiukov, and V. M. Smol'ianinov. *Sudebno-meditsinskaia akushersko-ginekologicheskaia ekspertiza*. Moscow: Sovetskoe zakonodatel'stvo, 1935.
Rozhanovskii, V. "Sudebno-meditsinskaia ekspertiza v dorevoliutsionnoi Rossii i v SSSR." *Sudebno-meditsinskaia ekspertiza*, no. 6 (1927): 1–105.
Schlesinger, Rudolph, ed. *The Family in the USSR*. London: Routledge and Kegan Paul, 1949.
Segal, G. M. "K probleme polovoi prestupnosti." In *Pravonarusheniia v oblasti seksual'nykh otnoshenii*, edited by E. K. Krasnushkin, G. M. Segal, and Ts. M. Fainberg. Moscow: Izdanie Moszdravotdela, 1927.
Segalin, G. V. "Osnovnye zadachi evriko-patologii kak ucheniia o patologii genial'nosti i patologii tvorchestv." *Ural'skii vrach*, nos. 3, 4–5 (1922): 3: 61–67; 4–5: 105–18.
———. *Nervno-psikhicheskaia ustanovka muzykal'no-odarennogo cheloveka*. Sverdlovsk: Izdanie Uraloblrabiz, 1927.
———. "K patogenezu leningradskikh uchenykh i deiatelei iskusstv." *Klinicheskii arkhiv genial'nosti i odarennosti*, no. 3 (1928): 3–21.
Serbskii, V. I. *Sudebnaia psikhopatologiia*. 2nd ed. Moscow: M. i S. Sabashnikovy, 1900.
———. *Rukovodstvo k izucheniiu dushevnykh boleznei*. Moscow, 1906.
———. *Psikhiatriia. Rukovodstvo k izucheniiu dushevnykh boleznei*. Moscow: Studencheskaia Meditsinskaia Izdatel'skaia Komissiia, 1912.
Serdiukov, M. G. *Sudebnaia ginekologiia i sudebnoe akusherstvo*. 2nd ed. Moscow: Medgiz, 1964.
Smirnov, A. I. "O nedostatkakh sudebno-meditsinskoi ekspertizy." *Vestnik obshchestvennoi gigieny, sudebnoi i prakticheskoi meditsiny* 15 (1892): kn. 1, sec. 3: 1–23; kn. 2, sec. 3: 33–56; kn. 3, sec. 3: 57–76.
Smol'skii, Ivan. *K voprosu o rastlenii v sudebno-meditsinskom otnoshenii*. St. Petersburg: Tip. M. D. Lomkovskii, 1898.
Struzhenskii, A. I. "Sluchai muzhskogo germafroditizma." *Vestnik obshchestvennoi gigieny, sudebnoi i prakticheskoi meditsiny* sec. 2 (October 1898): 754–55.
Tarnovskii, V. M. *Polovaia zrelost', eia techenie, otkloneniia i bolezni*. St. Petersburg: M. M. Stasiulevich, 1886.
Tolstoi, Lev N[ikolaevich]. "Kreitserova sonata." In *Povesti i rasskazy*, 273–336. Moscow: Sovremennik, 1987.
Ugolovnyi kodeks, s predisloviem D. I. Kurskogo. Moscow: Izd. moskovskogo gubernskogo suda, 1924.
Vasilevskii, L. M. *Polovoe zdorov'e*. Moscow: G. F. Mirimanov, 1925.
"Vesti s mest. Diagnosticheskii Institut Sudebnoi Nevrologii i Psikhiatrii." *Sudebno-meditsinskaia ekspertiza*, no. 2 (1925): 205–6.
Viazemskii, N. V. *O polovoi zrelosti s pedagogicheskoi tochki zreniia*. St. Petersburg: M. M. Stasiulevich, 1906.
Vinogradova-Lukirskaia, L. "K voprosu ob izsledovanii rosta i vesa uchenits srednikh uchebnykh zavedenii." *Vestnik obshchestvennoi gigieny, sudebnoi i prakticheskoi*

meditsiny 21 (1894): kn. 2, sec. 2: 64–94; kn. 3, sec. 2: 186–218.
Vladimirskii, V. "Polovaia zrelost'." In *Bol'shaia meditsinskaia entsiklopediia*, edited by N. A. Semashko, 26: 298–99. Moscow: OGIZ RSFSR, 1933.
Vnukov, V. A. "Iz praktiki sudebno-psikhiatricheskikh ekspertiz." *Prestupnik i prestupnost'*, no. 2 (1927): 253–63.
———. *Problema izucheniia lichnosti prestupnika v svete marksistskoi kriminologii*. Khar'kov: Iuridicheskoe izdatel'stvo NKIu USSR, 1930.
———, and A. Brusilovskii. *Psikhologiia i psikhopatologiia svidetel'skikh pokazanii maloletnikh i nesovershennoletnikh*. Kiev [?]: Iurid. izd. NKIu USSR, 1929.
———, and A. O. Edel'shtein. "O kharaktere lichnosti pravonarushitelia i mekhanizmakh pravnoarushenii v oblasti polovykh otnoshenii." In *Pravonarusheniia v oblasti seksual'nykh otnoshenii*, edited by E. K. Krasnushkin, G. M. Segal, and Ts. M. Fainberg, 23–76. Moscow: Izdanie Moszdravotdela, 1927.
———, and Ts. M. Feinberg. *Sudebnaia psikhiatriia. Uchebnik dlia iuridicheskikh vuzov*. Moscow: OGIZ, 1936.
Zak, N. "Materialy k kharakteristike fizicheskago razvitiia detei." *Vestnik obshchestvennoi gigieny, sudebnoi i prakticheskoi meditsiny* sec. 2 (January 1898): 1–34.
Zeidler, Petr. "Perechen' ugolovnykh del, razbiravshikhsia v s.-peterburgskom okruzhnom sude, pri zakrytykh dveriakh, s uchastiem vrachei-ekspertov." *Arkhiv sudebnoi meditsiny i obshchestvennoi gigieny*, no. 4, sec. 2 (1870): 58–68, and no. 4, sec. 2 (1871): 48–60.
Zetkin, Klara. *Reminiscences of Lenin*. New York: International Publishers, 1934.

Published Case Histories of Hermaphrodites, Used in Database

Andreeva, Z. A. "K voprosu o germafroditizme u cheloveka." *Zhurnal akusherstva i zhenskikh boleznei* 39, no. 6 (1928): 715–28.
Ataev, A. I. "K voprosu o germafroditizme." *Zhurnal teoreticheskoi i prakticheskoi meditsiny (Azerbaidzhanskii gos. universitet)* 4, no. 2 (1930): 147–50.
Bagdasarov, G. A., and I. F. Shishov. "O germafroditizme." *Urologiia* 8, no. 4 (1931): 136–39.
Beder, V. L. "K voprosu ob interseksual'nosti (Sluchai semeinogo germafroditizma u 3-kh brat'ev)." *Sovremennaia psikhonevrologiia* 11, no. 12 (1930): 430–46.
Bobin, V. V., and Henri Neuville. "K voprosu ob istinnom germafroditizme." *Trudy Krymskogo meditsinskogo instituta*, no. 1 (1935): 3–18.
Daniakhii, M. A. "Materialy k izucheniiu polovykh anomalii u cheloveka." *Akusherstvo i ginekologiia*, no. 4 (1938): 104–8.
Fedorovich, D. P. "O lozhnom germafroditizme." *Problemy endokrinologii*, no. 5 (1936): 56–60.
Getman-Sycheva. "Sluchai germafroditizma." *Vrachebnaia gazeta*, no. 11 (1930): 857–60.
Gusynin, V. A. "Ob uretroplastike v plane khirurgicheskogo ispravleniia pola pri germafroditizme." *Khirurgiia*, no. 12 (1938): 109–14.

Ioffe, T. M. "K voprosu o muzhskom naruzhnom psevdogermafroditizme." In *Sbornik trudov gosp. akushersko-ginekologicheskoi kliniki Khar'kovskogo meditsinskogo instituta*, edited. Khar'kovskii meditsinskii institut. Khar'kov, 1936.

Irger, Iu. M. "K kazuistike lozhnogo zhenskogo germafroditizma." *Kazanskii meditsinskii zhurnal*, no. 10 (1936): 1262–64.

Komeshko, K. K. "O germafroditizme." *Zapadno-oblastnoi kompleksnyi nauchno-issledovatel'nyi institut klinicheskii sbornik (Smolensk)*, no. 2 (1934): 62–74.

Kozlov, I. F. "Sluchai zhenskogo lozhnogo germafroditizma." *Kazanskii meditsinskii zhurnal* 17, no. 2 (1921): 224–32.

Krasnushkin, E. K., and N. G. Kholzakova. "Dva sluchaia zhenshchin ubiits-gomoseksualistok." *Prestupnik i prestupnost'*, sbornik 1 (1926): 105–20.

Krasovitov, K. P. "Sluchai istinnogo germafroditizma." *Kubanskii nauchno-meditsinskii vestnik*, no. 5–8 (1921): 205–12.

Krivskii, L. A. "K voprosu o germafroditizme." *Trudy gosudarstvennogo instituta meditsinskikh znanii (Leningrad)*, no. 1 (1927): 112–31.

Leibovich, Ia. L. "Homo generis neutrius." *Klinicheskaia meditsina* 3–4, no. 7–8 (1922): 33–34.

Matusis, I. A., and A. N. Pavlov. "K voprosu o germafroditizme." *Odesskii meditsinskii zhurnal*, no. 2 (1928): 107–12.

Morgulis, B. O. "K voprosu o germafroditizme." *Klinicheskaia meditsina* 8, no. 10 (1930): 531–35.

Rodd, N. P. "Sluchai pseudohermaphroditismus masculinus externus." In *Deti doshkol'nogo vozrasta*. Khar'kov, 1929.

Rozental', T. K. "K voprosu o konstitutsional'nom gipogenitalizme." *Nauchnaia meditsina*, no. 3 (1919): 325–31.

Shirokogorov, I. I., and R. A. Dykhno-Leibzon. "Iavliaetsia li polovaia zheleza u zhenshchin organom, opredeliaiushchim pol? Dva sluchaia muzhskikh polovykh zhelez u zhenshchin—pseudohermaphroditismus masculinus." *Zhurnal teoreticheskoi i prakticheskoi meditsiny* 4, no. 1 (1930): 399–420.

Smorodintsev, A. A. "K kazuistike germafroditizma." *Zhurnal akusherstva i zhenskikh boleznei* 40, no. 1 (1929): 122.

Tarabukhin, M. M. "Sluchai lozhnogo zhenskogo germafroditizma." *Akusherstvo i ginekologiia*, no. 4 (1938): 109.

Topchan, A. B. "Sluchai germafroditizma." *Urologiia* 10, no. 1 (1933): 41–44.

Tsimkhes, I. L. "Sluchai istinnogo gipoplasticheskogo germafroditizma (hermaphroditismus verus hypoplasticus)." *Kazanskii meditsinskii zhurnal*, no. 1 (1923): 61–68.

Uimanov, N. A. "Sluchai pseudohermaphroditismus completus." *Zhurnal teoreticheskoi i prakticheskoi meditsiny* 3, no. 3–4 (1928): 232–27.

Secondary Sources

Abelove, Henry. "Freud, Male Homosexuality, and the Americans." In *The Lesbian and Gay Studies Reader*, edited by H. Abelove, M. A. Barale, and D. Halperin. New York and London: Routledge, 1993.

Alexopoulos, Golfo. *Stalin's Outcasts: Aliens, Citizens, and the Soviet State, 1926–1936*. Ithaca, NY: Cornell University Press, 2003.

———. "Soviet Citizenship, More or Less: Rights, Emotions, and States of Civic Belonging." *Kritika: Explorations in Russian and Eurasian History* 7, no. 3 (2005): 487–528.

Attwood, Lynne. "'She was asking for it': Rape and Domestic Violence against Women." In *Post-Soviet Women: From the Baltic to Central Asia*, edited by Mary Buckley, 99–118. Cambridge: Cambridge University Press, 1997.

Banshchikov, V. M. "Zasluzhennyi deiatel' nauki professor E. K. Krasnushkin (Zhizn' i nauchnaia deiatel'nost'), 1885–1951 gg." In *Izbrannye trudy*, edited by E. K. Krasnushkin. Moscow: Medgiz, 1960.

Becker, Elisa M. "Judicial Reform and the Role of Medical Expertise in Late Imperial Russian Courts." *Law and History Review* 17, no. 1 (1999): 1–26.

———. "Medicine, Law, and the State: The Emergence of Forensic Psychiatry in Imperial Russia." Ph.D. diss., University of Pennsylvania, 2003.

Beer, Daniel. "The Medicalization of Religious Deviance in the Russian Orthodox Church (1880–1905)." *Kritika: Explorations in Russian and Eurasian History* 5, no. 3 (2004): 451–82.

———. "Blueprints for Change: The Human Sciences and the Coercive Transformation of Deviants in Russia, 1890–1930." *Osiris* 22 (2007): 26–47.

———. *Renovating Russia: The Human Sciences and the Fate of Liberal Modernity, 1880–1930*. Ithaca, NY: Cornell University Press, 2008.

Bernshtam, T. A. *Molodezh' v obriadovoi zhizni russkoi obshchiny XIX–nachala XX v.* Leningrad: Nauka, 1988.

Bernstein, Frances L. "'The Dictatorship of Sex': Science, Glands, and the Medical Construction of Gender Difference in Revolutionary Russia." In *Russian Modernity: Politics, Knowledge, Practices*, edited by David L. Hoffmann and Yanni Kotsonis, 138–60. Basingstoke, UK, and New York: Macmillan Press, 2000.

———. "Prostitutes and Proletarians: The Soviet Labor Clinic as Revolutionary Laboratory." In *The Human Tradition in Modern Russia*, edited by William B. Husband. Wilmington, DE: Scholarly Resources, 2000.

———. *The Dictatorship of Sex: Lifestyle Advice for the Soviet Masses*. DeKalb: Northern Illinois University Press, 2007.

Bershtein, Evgenii. "'Psychopathia sexualis' v Rossii nachala veka. Politika i zhanr." In *Eros i pornografiia v russkoi kul'ture/Eros and Pornography in Russian Culture*, edited by M. Levitt and A. Toporkov, 414–41. Moscow: Ladomir, 1999.

Bhat, Girish. "The Moralization of Guilt in Late Imperial Russian Trial by Jury: The Early Reform Era." *Law and History Review* 15, no. 1 (1997): 77–113.

Bland, Lucy, and Laura Doan, eds. *Sexology in Culture: Labelling Bodies and Desires*. Cambridge: Polity Press, 1998.

Brintlinger, Angela, and Ilya Vinitsky, eds. *Madness and the Mad in Russian Culture*. Toronto: University of Toronto Press, 2007

Brooks, Jeffrey. *When Russia Learned to Read: Literacy and Popular Literature, 1861–1917*. Princeton, NJ: Princeton University Press, 1985.
Brown, Julie V. "The Professionalization of Russian Psychiatry: 1857–1911." Ph.D. diss., University of Pennsylvania, 1981.
———. "Revolution and Psychosis: The Mixing of Science and Politics in Russian Psychiatric Medicine, 1905-1913." *Russian Review* 46 (1987): 283–302.
———. "Social Influences on Psychiatric Theory and Practice in Late Imperial Russia." In *Health and Society in Revolutionary Russia*, edited by Susan G. Solomon and John Hutchinson. Bloomington: Indiana University Press, 1990.
———. "Heroes and Non-Heroes: Recurring Themes in the Historiography of Russian-Soviet Psychiatry." In *Discovering the History of Psychiatry*, edited by Mark S. Micale and Roy Porter. New York and Oxford: Oxford University Press, 1994.
Brownmiller, Susan. *Against Our Will: Men, Women, and Rape*. Harmondsworth, UK: Penguin, 1975.
Carleton, Gregory. *Sexual Revolution in Bolshevik Russia*. Pittsburgh, PA: University of Pittsburgh Press, 2005.
Cassiday, Julie A. *The Enemy on Trial: Early Soviet Courts on Stage and Screen*. DeKalb: Northern Illinois University Press, 2000.
Clark, Michael, and Catherine Crawford, eds. *Legal Medicine in History*. Cambridge: Cambridge University Press, 1994.
Clements, Barbara E. *Bolshevik Feminist: The Life of Aleksandra Kollontai*. Bloomington: Indiana University Press, 1979.
Cocks, H. G., and Matt Houlbrook, eds. *Palgrave Advances in the Modern History of Sexuality*. Basingstoke, UK: Palgrave, 2005.
Crawford, Catherine. "Medicine and the Law." In *Companion Encyclopedia of the History of Medicine*, edited by W. F. Bynum and R. Porter. 2 vols. New York and London: Routledge, 1993.
Crowther, M. Anne, and Brenda White. *On Soul and Conscience: The Medical Expert and Crime*. Aberdeen: University of Aberdeen Press, 1988.
Davis, Christopher M. "Economics of Soviet Public Health, 1928–1932: Development Strategy, Resource Constraints, and Health Plans." In *Health and Society in Revolutionary Russia*, edited by Susan Gross Solomon and John F. Hutchinson, 146–72. Bloomington: Indiana University Press, 1990.
De George, Richard. "Biomedical Ethics." In *Science and the Soviet Social Order*, edited by Loren R. Graham. Cambridge: Harvard University Press, 1990.
Dreger, Alice Domurat. *Hermaphrodites and the Medical Invention of Sex*. Cambridge: Harvard University Press, 1998.
Eder, Franz X., Lesley Hall, and Gert Hekma, eds. *Sexual Cultures in Europe: National Histories*. Manchester: Manchester University Press, 1999.
Engelstein, Laura. *The Keys to Happiness: Sex and the Search for Modernity in Fin-de-Siècle Russia*. Ithaca, NY: Cornell University Press, 1992.
———. "Combined Underdevelopment: Discipline and the Law in Imperial and Soviet Russia." *American Historical Review* 98, no. 2 (1993): 338–53.

———. *Castration and the Heavenly Kingdom: A Russian Folktale*. Ithaca, NY: Cornell University Press, 1999.
Etkind, Aleksandr. *Eros nevozmozhnogo. Istoriia psikhoanaliza v Rossii*. Saint Petersburg: Meduza, 1993.
Fausto-Sterling, Anne. "The Five Sexes: Why Male and Female Are Not Enough." *The Sciences*, no. 33 (March/April 1993): 20–24.
———. *Sexing the Body: Gender Politics and the Construction of Sexuality*. New York: Basic Books, 2000.
Fitzpatrick, Sheila. "Ascribing Class: The Construction of Social Identity in Soviet Russia." *Journal of Modern History* 65, no. 4 (1993): 745-70.
Forbes, Thomas R. *Surgeons at the Bailey: English Forensic Medicine to 1878*. New Haven, CT: Yale University Press, 1985.
Foucault, Michel. *The History of Sexuality. Vol. 1. An Introduction*. Translated by Robert Hurley. London: Penguin, 1978.
———. *Herculine Barbin: Being the Recently Discovered Memoirs of a Nineteenth-Century French Hermaphrodite*. New York: Pantheon, 1980.
Frank, Stephen P. "Ask the Doctor! Peasants and Medical-Sexual Advice in Riazan Province, 1925–1928." In *The Human Tradition in Modern Russia*, edited by William B. Husband, 93–108. Wilmington, DE: Scholarly Resources, 2000.
Freedman, Estelle B. "'Uncontrolled Desires': The Response to the Sexual Psychopath, 1920–1960." In *Passion and Power: Sexuality in History*, edited by Kathy Peiss and Christina Simmons, 199–225. Philadelphia, PA: Temple University Press, 1989.
Frieden, Nancy Mandelker. *Russian Physicians in an Era of Reform and Revolution, 1856–1905*. Princeton, NJ: Princeton University Press, 1981.
Gamburg, A. M. *Razvitie sudebnomeditsinskoi nauki i ekspertizy (po materialam s"ezdov i soveshchanii)*. Kiev: Gos. Med. Iz-vo USSR, 1962.
Gaupner, Helmut. "Sexual Consent—The Criminal Law in Europe and Overseas." *Archives of Sexual Behavior* 29, no. 5 (2000): 415-61.
Gerodetti, Natalia. *Modernising Sexualities: Towards a Socio-Historical Understanding of Sexualities in the Swiss Nation*. Bern and Berlin: Peter Lang Verlag, 2005.
Gilbert, Ruth. *Early Modern Hermaphrodites: Sex and Other Stories*. Basingstoke, UK, and New York: Palgrave, 2002.
Gilman, Sander L. *Making the Body Beautiful: A Cultural History of Aesthetic Surgery*. Princeton, NJ: Princeton University Press, 1999.
Goldberg, Kate. "The Taboo of Sexual Violence in Russian Society." *Interface: Bradford Studies in Language, Culture, and Society*, no. 1 (1995): 119–47.
Goldman, Wendy Z. *Women, the State, and Revolution: Soviet Family Policy and Social Life*. Cambridge: Cambridge University Press, 1993.
Goldstein, Jan. *Console and Classify: The French Psychiatric Profession in the Nineteenth Century*. Cambridge: Cambridge University Press, 1987.
Granik, Lisa. "The Trials of the *Proletarka*: Sexual Harassment Claims in the 1920s." In *Reforming Justice in Russia, 1864–1996: Power, Culture, and the*

Limits of Legal Order, edited by Peter Solomon, Jr., 131–67. Armonk, NY: M. E. Sharpe, 1997.

Grodin, Michael A. "Historical Origins of the Nuremburg Code." In *Medicine, Ethics, and the Third Reich: Historical and Contemporary Issues,* edited by John J. Michalczyk. Kansas City, MO: Sheed & Ward, 1994.

Healey, Dan. *Homosexual Desire in Revolutionary Russia: The Regulation of Sexual and Gender Dissent.* Chicago, IL: University of Chicago Press, 2001.

———. "Unruly Identities: Soviet Psychiatry Confronts the 'Female Homosexual' of the 1920s." In *Gender in Russian History and Culture, 1800–1990,* edited by Linda Edmondson. Basingstoke, UK, and New York: Palgrave, 2001.

———. "Sexual Cultures in Russia." In *The Blackwell Encyclopedia of Sociology,* edited by George Ritzer, vol. 8. Oxford: Blackwell, 2007.

Herdt, Gilbert, ed. *Third Sex, Third Gender: Beyond Sexual Dimorphism in Culture and History.* New York: Zone Books, 1996.

Hoffmann, David L. *Stalinist Values: The Cultural Norms of Soviet Modernity, 1917–1941.* Ithaca, NY: Cornell University Press, 2003.

Hutchinson, John F. *Politics and Public Health in Revolutionary Russia, 1890–1918.* Baltimore, MD: Johns Hopkins University Press, 1990.

Hyer, Janet. "Fertility Control in Soviet Russia: A Case Study in Gender Control and Professionalization." Ph.D. diss, University of Toronto, 2007.

Iudin, Tikhon Ivanovich. *Ocherki istorii otechestvennoi psikhiatrii.* Moscow: Medgiz, 1951.

Joravsky, David. *Russian Psychology: A Critical History.* Oxford: Basil Blackwell, 1989.

Juviler, Peter H. *Revolutionary Law and Order.* New York: Free Press, 1976.

Kaiser, Daniel H. "'He Said, She Said': Rape and Gender Discourse in Early Modern Russia." *Kritika: Explorations in Russian and Eurasian History* 3, no. 2 (2002): 197–216.

Kelly, Catriona. "The Education of the Will: Advice Literature, *Zakal,* and Manliness in Early Twentieth-Century Russia." In *Russian Masculinities in History and Culture,* edited by Barbara Evans Clements, Rebecca Friedman, and Dan Healey, 131–51. Basingstoke, UK: Palgrave Macmillan, 2001.

Kiaer, Christina, and Eric Naiman, eds. *Everyday Life in Early Soviet Russia: Taking the Revolution Inside.* Bloomington: Indiana University Press, 2006.

Kotkin, Stephen. *Magnetic Mountain: Stalinism as a Civilization.* Berkeley and Los Angeles: University of California Press, 1995.

Kowalsky, Sharon A. "Making Crime and Sex Soviet: Women, Deviance, and the Development of Criminology in Early Soviet Russia." Ph.D. diss., University of North Carolina, 2004.

Krementsov, Nikolai. *Stalinist Science.* Princeton, NJ: Princeton University Press, 1997.

———. *The Cure: A Story of Cancer and Politics from the Annals of the Cold War.* Chicago: University of Chicago Press, 2002.

Lapidus, Gail W. *Women in Soviet Society: Equality, Development, and Social Change.* Berkeley: University of California Press, 1978.

Lebina, Nataliia B. *Entsiklopediia banal'nostei. Sovetskaia posvednevnost'. Kontury, simvoly, znaki*. St. Petersburg: Dmitrii Bulavin, 2006.
——, and M. B. Shkarovskii. *Prostitutsiia v Peterburge*. Moscow: Progress-Akademiia, 1994.
Levin, Eve. *Sex and Society in the World of the Orthodox Slavs, 900–1700*. Ithaca, NY: Cornell University Press, 1989.
Levitt, M., and A. Toporkov, eds. *Eros i pornografiia v russkoi kul'ture/Eros and Pornography in Russian Culture*. Moscow: Ladomir, 1999.
Mak, Geertje. "Doubting Sex from Within: A Praxiographic Approach to a Late Nineteenth-Century Case of Hermaphroditism." *Gender and History* 18, no. 2 (2006): 332–56.
Matich, Olga. *Erotic Utopia: The Decadent Imagination in Russia's Fin-de-siècle*. Madison: University of Wisconsin Press, 2005.
Mazurenko, M. D., Iu. V. Zimina, and I. N. Ivanov. "K 70-letiiu kafedry sudebnoi meditsiny Sankt-Peterburgskoi meditsinskoi akademii poslediplomnogo obrazovaniia." *Sudebno-meditsinskaia ekspertiza*, no. 2 (1995): 47–48.
McReynolds, Louise. *Russia at Play: Leisure Activities at the End of the Tsarist Era*. Ithaca, NY: Cornell University Press, 2003.
Miller, Martin. *Freud and the Bolsheviks: Psychoanalysis in Imperial Russia and the Soviet Union*. New Haven, CT: Yale University Press, 1998.
Møller, Peter Ulf. *Postlude to the Kreutzer Sonata: Tolstoi and the Debate on Sexual Morality in Russian Literature in the 1890s*. Leiden and New York: E. J. Brill, 1988.
Morozov, G. V., D. R. Lunts, and N. I. Felinskaia. *Osnovnye etapy razvitiia otechestvennoi sudebnoi psikhiatrii*. Moscow: Meditsina, 1976.
Morrissey, Susan K. *Suicide and the Body Politic in Imperial Russia*. Cambridge: Cambridge University Press, 2006.
Moscucci, Ornella. "Hermaphroditism and Sex Difference: The Construction of Gender in Victorian England." In *Science and Sensibility: Gender and Scientific Enquiry, 1780–1945*, edited by Marina Benjamin. Oxford: Basil Blackwell, 1991.
Murav'eva, Marianna. "Metodologicheskie problemy sovremennoi istoriografii seksual'nogo nasiliia na Zapade i v Rossii," *Gendernye issledovaniia* 13 (2005): 171–89.
Naiman, Eric. *Sex in Public: The Incarnation of Early Soviet Ideology*. Princeton, NJ: Princeton University Press, 1997.
Naimark, Norman M. *The Russians in Germany: A History of the Soviet Zone of Occupation, 1945-1949*. Cambridge: Belknap Press of Harvard University Press, 1995.
Nekipelov, Victor. *Institute of Fools: Notes from the Serbsky*. New York: Farrar Straus Giroux, 1980.
Nekliudov, Iu. A. "Iakov L'vovich Leibovich—vidnyi deiatel' otechestvennoi sudebnoi meditsiny." *Sudebno-meditsinskaia ekspertiza* 5 (2003): 48–49.
Northrop, Douglas. *Veiled Empire: Gender and Power in Stalinist Central Asia*. Ithaca, NY: Cornell University Press, 2004.

Nye, Robert A. *Crime, Madness, and Politics in Modern France: The Medical Concept of National Decline.* Princeton, NJ: Princeton University Press, 1984.

———. "Sex Difference and Male Homosexuality in French Medical Discourse, 1830–1930." *Bulletin of the History of Medicine,* no. 63 (1989): 32–51.

Oosterhuis, Harry. *Stepchildren of Nature: Krafft-Ebing, Psychiatry, and the Making of Sexual Identity.* Chicago, IL: University of Chicago Press, 2000.

Petrov, G. D. *Ocherki istorii otechestvennoi meditsiny.* Moscow: Gos. iz-vo meditsinskoi literatury, 1962.

Pick, Daniel. *Faces of Degeneration: A European Disorder, c. 1848–c.1918.* Cambridge: Cambridge University Press, 1989.

Pinnow, Kenneth M. "Making Suicide Soviet: Medicine, Moral Statistics, and the Politics of Social Science in Bolshevik Russia, 1920–1930." Ph.D. diss., Columbia University, 1998.

———. "Counting and Cutting: Forensic Medicine as a Science of Society in Bolshevik Russia, 1920–29." In *Russian Modernity: Politics, Knowledge, Practices,* edited by David L. Hoffmann and Yanni Kotsonis, 115-37. Basingstoke, UK, and New York: Macmillan Press, 2000.

Porksheian, O. Kh., and V. K. Belikov. "Fotografiia iz arkhiva kafedry sudebnoi meditsiny Sankt-Peterburgskoi akademii poslediplomnogo obrazovaniia." *Sudebno-meditsinskaia ekspertiza* 37, no. 4 (1994): 43–47.

Redick, Alison. "American History XY: The Medical Treatment of Intersex, 1916–1955." Ph.D. diss, New York University, 2004.

Robertson, Stephen. "Signs, Marks, and Private Parts: Doctors, Legal Discourses, and Evidence of Rape in the United States, 1823–1930." *Journal of the History of Sexuality* 8, no. 3 (1998): 345-88.

———. "Separating the Men from the Boys: Masculinity, Psychosexual Development, and Sex Crime in the United States, 1930s–1960s." *Journal of the History of Medicine and Allied Sciences* 56 (2001): 3–36.

———. "Age of Consent Law and the Making of Modern Childhood in New York City, 1886–1921." *Journal of Social History* 35, no. 4 (2002): 781–98.

———. *Crimes against Children: Sexual Violence and Legal Culture in New York City, 1880–1960.* Chapel Hill: University of North Carolina Press, 2005.

Scull, Andrew. "Psychiatry and Social Control in the Nineteenth and Twentieth Centuries." *History of Psychiatry,* no. 2 (1991): 149–69.

———. *The Most Solitary of Afflictions: Madness and Society in Britain, 1700–1900.* New Haven, CT: Yale University Press, 1993.

Sengoopta, Chandak. "Glandular Politics: Experimental Biology, Clinical Medicine, and Homosexual Emancipation in Fin-de-Siècle Central Europe." *Isis,* no. 89 (1998): 445-73.

Sirotkina, Irina. *Diagnosing Literary Genius: A Cultural History of Psychiatry in Russia, 1880–1930.* Baltimore, MD: Johns Hopkins University Press, 2002.

Smith, Roger. *Trial by Medicine: Insanity and Responsibility in Victorian Trials.* Edinburgh: Edinburgh University Press, 1981.

Solomon, Peter H., Jr. "Soviet Penal Policy, 1917–1934: A Reinterpretation." *Slavic Review* 39, no. 2 (1980): 195-217.

———. *Soviet Criminal Justice under Stalin*. Cambridge: Cambridge University Press, 1996.
Solomon, Susan Gross. "Reflections on Western Studies of Soviet Science." In *The Social Context of Soviet Science*, edited by L. L. Lubrano and S. G. Solomon. Boulder CO: Westview Press, 1980.
———. "The Demographic Argument in Soviet Debates over the Legalization of Abortion in the 1920's." *Cahiers du Monde russe et soviétique* 33, no. 1 (1992): 59–82.
———. "The Soviet-German Syphilis Expedition to Buriat Mongolia, 1928." *Slavic Review* 52, no. 2 (1993): 204–32.
———. "The Expert and the State in Russian Public Health: Continuities and Changes across the Revolutionary Divide." In *The History of Public Health and the Modern State*, edited by Dorothy Porter, 183–223. Amsterdam: Editions Rodopi B. V., 1994.
———. "Innocence and Sexuality in Soviet Medical Discourse." In *Women in Russia and Ukraine*, edited by Rosalind Marsh, 121–30. Cambridge: Cambridge University Press, 1996.
———, and John Hutchinson, eds. *Health and Society in Revolutionary Russia*. Bloomington: Indiana University Press, 1990.
Stites, Richard. *The Women's Liberation Movement in Russia: Feminism, Nihilism, and Bolshevism, 1860–1930*. Princeton, NJ: Princeton University Press, 1978.
Sulloway, Frank J. *Freud, Biologist of the Mind: Beyond the Psychoanalytic Legend*. London: Fontana, 1980.
Tighe, Janet A. "'Be It Ever So Little': Reforming the Insanity Defense in the Progressive Era." *Bulletin of the History of Medicine* 57 (1983): 397–411.
———. "A Question of Responsibility: The Development of American Forensic Psychiatry, 1838–1930." Ph.D. diss., University of Pennsylvania, 1983.
———. "The Legal Art of Psychiatric Diagnosis: Searching for Reliability." In *Framing Disease: Studies in Cultural History*, edited by Charles E. Rosenberg and Janet Golden, 206–26. New Brunswick, NJ: Rutgers University Press, 1992.
Vigarello, Georges. *A History of Rape, from the Sixteenth to the Twentieth Centuries*. Translated by Jean Birrell. Cambridge: Polity Press, 2001.
Walls, H. J. "The Forensic Science Service in Great Britain: A Short History." *Journal of the Forensic Science Society*, no. 16 (1976): 273–78.
Waters, Chris. "Havelock Ellis, Sigmund Freud, and the State: Discourses of Homosexual Identity in Interwar Britain." In *Sexology in Culture: Labelling Bodies and Desires*, edited by Lucy Bland and Laura Doan, 165–80. Cambridge: Polity Press, 1998.
Waters, Elizabeth. "The Modernisation of Russian Motherhood, 1917–1937." *Soviet Studies* 44, no. 1 (1992): 123–35.
———. "Victim or Villain: Prostitution in Post-revolutionary Russia." In *Women and Society in Russia and the Soviet Union*, edited by Linda Edmondson, 160–77. Cambridge: Cambridge University Press, 1992.
Weeks, Jeffrey. *Sexuality and Its Discontents: Meanings, Myths, and Modern Sexualities*. London: Routledge & Kegan Paul, 1985.

Werlinder, Henry. *Psychopathy: A History of the Concepts. Analysis of the Origin and Development of a Family of Concepts in Psychopathology*. Uppsala: University of Uppsala, 1978.
Wood, Elizabeth A. "Prostitution Unbound: Representations of Sexual and Political Anxieties in Postrevolutionary Russia." In *Sexuality and the Body in Russian Culture,* edited by Jane T. Costlow, Stephanie Sandler, and Judith Vowles, 124–31. Stanford, CA: Stanford University Press, 1993.
———. *The Baba and The Comrade: Gender and Politics in Revolutionary Russia*. Bloomington: Indiana University Press, 1997.
———. *Performing Justice: Agitation Trials in Early Soviet Russia*. Ithaca, NY: Cornell University Press, 2005.

INDEX

age of consent, 10, 15, 29, 38–42, 50, 82, 160, 164–65, 189n17
age, minimum, for marriage, 41, 44–46, 53, 56, 165, 168

Bazhenov, N. K., 34, 72–73, 76–77, 90, 94, 115, 200n134, 202n150, 202n153,
Bebel, A., 4
Becker, Elisa Marielle, 20
Bellin, E. F., 21–22, 138, 208n38
Bernstein, Frances, 6, 7, 13, 166, 214n33, 228n1
Bershtein, Evgenii, 107, 132
Bolsheviks. *See* Communist Party

censorship, 5, 8, 12, 15, 106, 143, 179n48
change of sex, in passport, 11, 137, 141–42, 156, 157, 170, 175n25, 222n13, 224n38, 228n85
Chernyshevskii, N. G., 4
Communist Party (*see also* Komsomol, Zhenotdel), 6, 12, 22–23, 27, 33, 41–42, 83–84, 85, 100, 111, 116, 125–26, 127, 128–29, 131, 147, 159, 160, 166, 168, 219n80
compulsory therapy, 11, 28, 110, 116, 120, 125, 219n76
criminal responsibility (*vmeniaemost'*), 109–12, 119, 122–26, 127–28, 132, 215n42, 219n82
criminology, 34–35, 85, 109, 111, 113, 130, 214n33

degeneration, 11, 74, 96, 107, 121–22, 123, 124, 128, 132, 163, 175n24, 209n46, 212n15, 217n66, 220n82
Degtiarova, V. A., 66–67, 69, 72, 79, 160, 198n107, 200n133
desire, 8, 9, 15, 37, 43, 54–55, 103, 107, 108, 132–33, 151, 158, 162–63, 168, 205n2, 226n57, 230n17; female, 6, 10, 15, 49–50, 51–56, 60, 89, 97, 168; hermaphrodite, 134, 145, 147, 150, 151, 153, 227n74, 228n85; male, 37, 44, 50, 53, 60, 113, 126–29
determination of sex, 11, 140
Dostoevskii, F. M., 20, 106

Engels, F., 4
Engelstein, Laura, 42, 138
expertise: collective (in panels), 14, 79, 89–90, 92–96, 108, 109, 114, 116, 119, 121–22, 128, 130–31, 141, 160–61, 203n160; courtroom, 9, 19–22, 31–33, 36, 67, 112, 123–24, 126–27, 131, 132, 160–61, 163, 204n162, 219n82

Fishman (a Sverdlovsk psychiatrist), 109, 115, 117, 123, 130, 213n26, 215n42, 217n59
forensic gynecology, 20, 23, 26, 29, 30, 50–52, 54, 66–67, 69–73, 79, 87–89, 92, 94–96, 150, 153, 154, 156, 160, 163, 167, 180n2, 184n43, 193n62, 194n64, 195n79, 197n101, 198n107, 199n126,

250 INDEX

200n126, 203n160, 204n161, 207n31, 208n38
forensic medicine (*see also* expertise; forensic gynecology, forensic psychiatry) 4, 8–9, 17–36, 87–89, 108, 140–41, 161, 167, 181n14, 187n68, 224n32; historiography of, 13–14, 18; institutions of, 20, 22–24, 33–36, 49, 52, 54, 56–57, 108–9, 110, 115, 118, 124, 126, 128, 132, 167, 187n68, 229n14; laws governing, 19–20, 28–31, 37–42, 60–65, 66, 85–87, 108–12, 137–41, 159–60, 162; training in, 19, 20, 33–36, 167, 204n162
forensic psychiatry (*see also* psychiatry), 7, 11, 13, 23, 28, 29–30, 34–35, 54, 60, 90, 96, 104–33, 158, 160–61, 162, 167, 170, 175n23, 185n53, 209n46, 211n15, 213n21, 214n29, 214n33, 216n45, 216n43, 217n64, 217n66, 219n82
Freud, Sigmund, 6, 55, 104–5, 175n24; Freudianism and psychoanalysis, 7–8, 10, 53, 55, 103, 105, 106, 153, 163, 174n17, 194n70

Golianitskii, I. A., 140, 228n85
gynecology. *See* forensic gynecology

Health, People's Commissariat of, 9, 11, 21, 22–24, 25–27, 31, 33–36, 39–40, 41, 108, 110, 130, 139, 159, 161, 166, 167, 228n85
hermaphrodites, hermaphroditism, 8, 11–12, 15, 133, 134–58, 162, 163–64, 166, 170, 175n25, 180n5, 222n12, 223n25, 224n42, 228n85
historiography, 12–14, 18, 20, 83–84, 105–6, 130, 134–37, 177n36
Hoffmann, David, 166
homosexuality, 3, 13, 38, 105, 107, 135, 138, 139, 140, 144, 150, 152, 153, 156, 163, 167, 225n48, 229n4; same-sex "crimes," 78, 114, 128–29, 130, 204n161
hormones, sex, 6–7, 59, 136, 139,
143, 150–51, 152–55, 156–57, 163
Internal Affairs, People's Commissariat of, 23, 34, 39, 141, 167, 219n77
Internal Affairs, Ministry of, 9, 19–22, 44, 139, 223n22
intersex. *See* hermaphrodites, hermaphroditism
Izhevskii, N. I., 34, 35, 89, 92, 93, 131, 161, 207n28

justice, Soviet: advocates, for the defense, 32–33, 35, 70–71, 79, 80, 115, 116, 124, 131–32, 186n58, 200n128, 216n49; courts, 8, 9, 14, 24, 26, 27, 30, 31, 32–33, 36, 37, 57, 60, 65, 67, 69, 71–73, 75, 76, 78, 79, 84, 86–87, 89–90, 95–102, 103, 108–11, 112, 115–19, 121, 123–33, 141, 159, 160–61, 185n53, 197n103, 198n116, 203n154, 203n159, 214n29, 216n48, 218n69, 224n39; judges, 19, 28, 30–31, 33, 55, 57–58, 87, 90, 94, 97, 100, 110, 116, 123, 124, 131, 169, 210n55; pretrial investigation, 20, 31–32, 87, 110, 124, 125, 130, 186n58, 214n29; prosecutors (*prokurory*), 11, 16, 26, 31–33, 36, 40, 50, 51, 52, 61–62, 64, 65, 66–68, 69–70, 72, 73–74, 76–77, 78, 79, 84, 87, 97–98, 99–100, 101, 110, 115, 116–17, 120–22, 123, 124, 125, 128, 131, 159–61, 170, 186n58, 201n137, 206n6; sentencing policy and practice (*see also* compulsory therapy, criminal responsibility), 29, 30, 33, 39, 63, 72, 74, 76–77, 78–79, 84, 86–87, 92, 96, 98–102, 110, 116, 117, 119–20, 122, 123, 125–26, 127, 128, 129, 131, 196n95, 208n44, 210n55, 218n69, 219n76
justice, tsarist, 3, 18, 19–22, 86, 88, 105, 107, 108, 110, 209n50

Kaiser, Daniel, 18
Kollontai, Aleksandra, 6–8, 60, 174n18, 205n2

Komsomol (Young Communist League), 49, 53, 64, 79, 84, 86, 90–91, 210n61
Koni, A. F., 35, 79–80, 161, 204n162
Kowalsky, Sharon, 111, 130
Krafft-Ebing, Richard von, 105, 106–7, 216n46
Krasnushkin, E. K., 109, 130

Leibovich, L. Ia., 9–11, 23, 25–27, 33–35, 40–41, 45–46, 50, 52, 71, 80, 81, 88, 90, 140, 149, 160, 167, 178n41, 187n68, 194n64, 195n79, 207n31, 209n50, 224n32, 229n14
Lenin, V. I., 3, 5, 8, 23, 108, 124, 166, 174, 205, 219
Lents, A. K., 108–9, 111, 118, 124
Loviagin, N. I., 22, 25

midwives and midwifery, 18, 32, 67, 69, 75, 90, 91, 94, 117, 165, 180n2
Minakov, P. A., 34, 35
Moscow, 19, 23, 34, 35, 43, 45, 50, 85, 108, 109, 115, 130, 131, 140, 153, 167, 212n15, 213n24, 213n29, 224n34, 228n85; Bureau for the Study of the Personality of the Criminal and Criminality, 34; Institute of Forensic Psychiatry ("Serbskii Institute"), 109, 167, 178n39, 216n45; State Institute for the Study of Criminality and the Criminal, 34
Muscovy, 18, 137

Naiman, Eric, 5, 13, 83, 166, 174n18, 214n33
non-responsibility *(nevmeniaemost')*. *See* criminal responsibility

Okinchits, L., 67
Orshanskii, L. G., 34, 108, 114, 115, 122, 124, 126, 130, 131, 161, 209n46, 215n40, 216n53, 218n72, 220n86
Osipov, V. P., 119
Ostankov, P. A., 35, 108, 114, 116, 119, 122, 125, 213n21, 216n47

Peretts, V. G., 71–72, 199n126, 200n134
Petrograd (St. Petersburg, Leningrad), 14, 16, 23, 34, 35, 44, 45, 61, 64, 65–69, 72, 75, 78, 79, 80, 83–84, 89, 92–96, 97, 99–100, 108, 112–18, 120–23, 125, 126–31, 132, 137, 140, 148, 153, 160–61, 162, 165, 169, 190n29, 198n107, 203n160, 207n28, 209n46, 216n47; Diagnostic Institute of Forensic Neurology and Psychiatry, 81, 109, 114, 115, 118, 124, 126, 128, 132, 209n46, 215n39, 216n43, 216n53; Forensic Medical Bureau *(Otedelenie sudebno-meditsinskoi ekspertizy Petrogubzdravotdela)*, 34, 65, 66, 68, 89, 92, 95, 118, 160, 207n28, 215n41; Military-Medical Academy, 35, 75, 95, 119, 148; State Institute for the Professional Development of Doctors, 35, 204n162
police *(militsiia)*, 9, 11, 16, 17, 19–21, 23, 24, 26, 27, 30, 31–32, 34, 37, 39–41, 50, 51, 52, 55–56, 57, 58, 60–62, 64–65, 68–69, 72–73, 75–76, 77, 78, 80–81, 84, 85, 87, 89, 90–103, 105–6, 108–10, 113–15, 118, 120–21, 123, 126, 128–30, 159–61, 167, 169, 170, 178n42, 186n55, 187n67, 196n89, 197n101, 201n141, 202n149, 215n42, 217n66; Criminal Investigation Department *(ugolovnyi rozysk)*, 16, 31–32, 60–62, 92, 95, 96, 102, 202n149, 211n66
Pinnow, Kenneth, 14, 178n41
Popov, N. V., 50–52, 59, 167–68, 193n63, 229n14
prostitution, 13, 30, 78, 123, 128–29, 138, 139, 178 n42, 204 n161
psychiatry *(see also* forensic psychiatry), 140, 150, 175n24, 211n6, 216n46

rape, 8, 10–11, 14, 18, 29–32, 37, 55–56, 57, 61–65, 66–67, 69–79, 83–103, 111, 113, 115, 116–17, 118–19, 121–22, 125, 140, 160, 161, 163, 165, 168–69, 171, 175n22, 178n42, 180n5, 184n46, 196n92, 196n95, 197n98, 197n101, 197n103, 202n149, 205n2, 207n20, 209n50, 210n56, 217n70; Chubarov Alley group rape case (1926), 64, 83–84, 206n6
Rein, G. E., 22

Saratov, 14, 33, 35, 49, 51, 53, 56–57, 59, 74, 77, 87, 91, 109, 140, 146, 165, 179n45, 186n58, 207n31, 208n38, 210n56; Forensic Medical Institute, 49, 52, 54, 56–57
Segalin, G. V., 109, 130, 213n26
Semashko, N. A., 22, 23
Serbskii, V. P., 108, 109, 213n21
sex reformers, international, 12, 159, 164, 167, 228n1, 229n11
sexual citizenship (*see also* sexual revolution), 10, 37–42, 50, 58, 60, 62, 69, 81–82, 159, 164–65, 169, 170
sexual enlightenment, Soviet, 6, 7, 13, 59, 163, 164, 166, 167, 168, 204n161, 226n57, 228n1
sexual maturity (*polovaia zrelost'*) (*see also* sexual citizenship), 7, 10, 29, 32, 37–82, 84, 86, 89, 90, 95, 102, 103, 134, 160, 162, 164–65, 168, 170, 190n30, 193n63, 195n79, 195n86, 196n95, 200n128, 200n134, 201n141, 202n149
sexual psychopathy, 11, 105, 107–8, 112, 113, 119–20, 122, 124, 125, 126–29, 131–32, 162–63, 165, 170
sexual revolution (*see also* sexual citizenship), 4–16, 27, 37, 39, 57, 60, 84, 90, 97, 102–3, 137, 140, 142, 152–53, 156, 159,
164–65, 166–67, 169, 171, 229n4; periodization of, 15, 166–67, 171
Shumkov, G. E., 122, 127–29, 218n67
Smol'ianinov, V. M., 167
Sreznevskii, V. V., 116, 118, 119, 123–24, 125, 216n47
suicide, 14, 19, 26, 63, 65, 76, 86, 91, 117, 140, 178n41, 180n6, 182n30, 189n13, 202n152, 207n32, 217n53, 221n7, 224n32
surgery, 11, 136, 139, 140, 143, 144, 148–49, 149–57, 170, 222n10, 227n68, 227n74
Sverdlovsk (Ekaterinburg), 14, 15, 16, 34, 35, 42, 61, 64, 69–73, 74, 75–77, 78, 81, 85, 87, 89–94, 98, 99–100, 109, 112, 114–17, 120–21, 122–23, 130, 161, 187n67, 199n126, 200n134, 204n161, 213n26, 215n34, 215n42, 227n77

Tarle (a Petrograd psychiatrist), 114, 116, 122, 125, 128, 215n41, 219n82
Tarnovskii, V. M., 42–43, 46–48
therapy, compulsory. *See* compulsory therapy
Tolstoi, L. N., 5, 106
Triumfov, A. V., 126–27

virginity, 10, 51–58, 68–69, 70, 74, 75, 80, 81, 84, 90–97, 99–102, 117, 160, 162, 168–69, 171, 181n5, 188n7, 197n101, 207n20, 207n31, 208n35

Young, H. H., 153, 157–58, 221n8, 227n74

Zetkin, Clara, 8, 205n2
Zhenotdel (Communist Party women's department), 85, 100, 147, 210n61

www.ingramcontent.com/pod-product-compliance
Lightning Source LLC
Chambersburg PA
CBHW032212230426
43672CB00011B/2532